Microsoft® SQL Server® 2014

QUERY TUNING & OPTIMIZATION

About the Author

Benjamin Nevarez is a SQL Server MVP and independent consultant based in Los Angeles, California, who specializes in SQL Server query tuning and optimization. He is the author of *Inside the SQL Server Query Optimizer* and has contributed to other SQL Server books, including *SQL Server 2012 Internals*. With more than 20 years of experience in relational databases, Benjamin has also been a speaker at many SQL Server conferences, including the PASS Summit, SQL Server Connections, and SQLBits. Benjamin's blog can be found at www.benjaminnevarez .com, and he can also be reached by e-mail at admin@benjaminnevarez.com and on Twitter at @BenjaminNevarez.

About the Technical Editor

Dave Ballantyne works as a SQL Server data architect for Win Technologies, part of the BetWay group, and lives near London, England. He is a regular speaker at UK and European events and user groups, and currently is supporting the London SQL community by organizing the "SQL Supper" user group. He takes a keen interest in all things SQL and data related and is never happier than when picking apart a poorly executing query. He has also created an open sourced add-in for SQL Server data tools (SSDT) called "TSQL Smells," which detects and reports on "suspect" code within a project. It can be found at http://tsqlsmellsssdt.codeplex.com. Outside of work, he is a husband, father of three, and an exasperated archer.

Microsoft® SQL Server® 2014

QUERY TUNING & OPTIMIZATION

Benjamin Nevarez

New York   Chicago   San Francisco
Athens   London   Madrid
Mexico City   Milan   New Delhi
Singapore   Sydney   Toronto

Cataloging-in-Publication Data is on file with the Library of Congress

McGraw-Hill Education books are available at special quantity discounts to use as premiums and sales promotions, or for use in corporate training programs. To contact a representative, please visit the Contact Us pages at www.mhprofessional.com.

Microsoft® SQL Server® 2014 Query Tuning & Optimization

4 5 6 7 8 9 QVS/QVS 21 20 19 18 17

ISBN   978-0-07-182942-7
MHID   0-07-182942-3

Sponsoring Editor Wendy Rinaldi	**Proofreader** Lisa McCoy	**Art Director, Cover** Jeff Weeks
Editorial Supervisor Janet Walden	**Indexer** Karin Arrigoni	**Cover Designer** Jeff Weeks
Project Manager Harleen Chopra, Cenveo® Publisher Services	**Production Supervisor** Jean Bodeaux	
Technical Editor Dave Ballantyne	**Composition** Cenveo Publisher Services	
Copy Editor Bart Reed	**Illustration** Cenveo Publisher Services	

Information has been obtained by McGraw-Hill Education from sources believed to be reliable. However, because of the possibility of human or mechanical error by our sources, McGraw-Hill Education, or others, McGraw-Hill Education does not guarantee the accuracy, adequacy, or completeness of any information and is not responsible for any errors or omissions or the results obtained from the use of such information.

This book is dedicated to my parents, Guadalupe Chavez and Humberto Nevarez.

Contents at a Glance

Contents

Acknowledgments

A number of people contributed to making this book a reality. First, I would like to thank everyone on the McGraw-Hill Education team with whom I worked directly or indirectly on this book: Wendy Rinaldi, Harleen Chopra, Bart Reed, and Janet Walden—and especially to Wendy for coordinating the entire project while trying to keep me on schedule. A very special thank-you has to go out to my technical editor, Dave Ballantyne. His amazing feedback was critical to improving the quality of the chapters of the book.

In addition to Dave and the McGraw-Hill Education team, there is a host of other people who have indirectly influenced the book through their work covering SQL Server query tuning and optimization topics: Kalen Delaney, Cesar Galindo-Legaria, Craig Freedman, Conor Cunningham, Ken Henderson, Lubor Kollar, Eric Hanson, Goetz Graefe, and others. Thanks go out as well to the bloggers in the SQL Server community from whom I also learned a lot. The long list of names would be impossible to include here.

Finally, on the personal side, I would like to thank my family: my wife, Rocio, and my three Boy Scout sons, Diego, Benjamin, and David. Thank you all for your unconditional support and patience every time I need to work on another SQL Server book.

Introduction

This book covers query tuning and optimization in SQL Server and gives you the tools and knowledge necessary to get peak performance from your queries and applications. We mostly relate query optimization with the work performed by the query optimizer in which an efficient execution plan is produced, although sometimes we may not be happy with its query execution performance and may try to improve it by performing additional changes—or what we call "query tuning." However, it is important to understand that the results we originally get from the query processor will greatly depend on all the information we feed it—for example, our database design, the defined indexes, and even some configuration settings. There are many ways in which we can impact the work performed by the query processor, which is why it is extremely important to understand how we can help this SQL Server component to do a superior job. Providing quality information to the query processor will most likely result in high-quality execution plans, which will also improve the performance of your databases. Finally, no query processor is perfect, and it is important to understand the reasons why sometimes we may not, in fact, get a good execution plan or good query performance and to know what possible solutions are available.

Who Should Read This Book

This book is intended to be read by any SQL Server professional: database developers, database administrators, data architects—basically anybody who submits more than just trivial queries to SQL Server. I expect that you have some experience with SQL Server and familiarity with the SQL language.

What This Book Covers

This book covers how to get the best performance from your queries and use this knowledge to create high-performing applications. It shows how a better understanding of what the SQL Server query processor does behind the scenes can help both database administrators and developers to write better queries and to provide the query processor with the information it needs to produce efficient execution plans. In the same way, this book shows how you can use your newfound knowledge of the query processor's inner workings and SQL Server tools to troubleshoot cases when your queries are not performing as expected.

Chapter 1 starts with an overview of the architecture of the SQL Server relational database engine and then continues by looking in great detail at how to use execution plans, the primary tool we'll use to interact with the SQL Server query processor.

Chapter 2 is a continuation of Chapter 1 and provides you with additional tuning tools and techniques, such as SQL trace, extended events, and DMVs, to find out how your queries are using system resources or to root out performance-related problems. The chapter ends with an introduction to the data collector, a feature introduced with SQL Server 2008.

Chapters 3 and 4 go deep into the internals of the query optimizer and the query processor operators. Chapter 3 explains how the query optimizer works and shows why this knowledge can give you a great background to troubleshoot, optimize, and better tune your queries. In Chapter 4, you learn about the most used query operators employed in the execution plans created by the query optimizer.

After two chapters about the architecture and internals of the query processor, Chapter 5 puts your feet back on the ground by covering indexes. Indexing is one of the most important techniques used in query tuning and optimization, and one that can dramatically improve the performance of your queries and databases.

Statistics is another essential topic required for query tuning and optimization and troubleshooting. Statistics are used by the query optimizer to make decisions toward finding an efficient execution plan, and this information is also available to you so you can use it to troubleshoot cardinality estimation problems. Statistics are covered in Chapter 6.

In-Memory OLTP, better known as Hekaton, is without a doubt the most important technology introduced with SQL Server 2014, and Chapter 7 covers how this new component can help you to develop high-performance applications. Hekaton is, in fact, a new database engine whose main features include tables and indexes optimized for main memory data access, stored procedures compiled to native code, and the elimination of locks and latches.

Query optimization is a relatively expensive operation, so if plans can be cached and reused, this optimization cost can be avoided. How plan caching works and why it is extremely important for the performance of your queries and SQL Server in general are covered in Chapter 8.

Chapter 9 is an introduction to data warehouses and explains how the SQL Server query optimizer can identify fact and dimension tables and can optimize star join queries. The chapter also covers columnstore indexes, a feature introduced with SQL Server 2012 that is based in columnar storage and new batch processing algorithms that can improve the performance of star join queries by several orders of magnitude.

The last chapter of the book discusses the challenges the SQL Server processor still faces today after more than four decades of query optimization research. Recommendations and workarounds for complex queries for which the query optimizer may not be able to provide efficient plans are provided. Finally, hints, which must be used with caution and only as a last resort when no other option is available, are introduced as a way to take explicit control over the execution plan for a given query.

Chapter 1

An Introduction to Query Tuning and Optimization

In This Chapter

- ▶ Architecture
- ▶ Execution Plans
- ▶ SET STATISTICS TIME / IO
- ▶ Summary

We all have been there: suddenly you get a phone call notifying you of an application outage and asking you to urgently join a conference bridge. After joining the call, you are told that the application is so slow that the company is not able to conduct business; it is losing money and potentially customers too. And usually nobody on the call is able to provide any additional information that can help you find out what the problem is. So, what you should do? Where do you start? And after troubleshooting and fixing the issue, how do you avoid these problems in the future?

Although an outage can be created for several different reasons, including a hardware failure and an operating system problem, as a database professional, you should be able to proactively tune and optimize your databases and be ready to quickly troubleshoot any problem that eventually may occur. This book provides you with the knowledge and tools required to do just that. By focusing on SQL Server performance, and more specifically on query tuning and optimization, this book can help you, first, to avoid these performance problems by optimizing your databases and, second, to quickly troubleshoot and fix them if they happen to appear.

One of the best ways to learn how to improve the performance of your databases is not only to work with the technology, but to understand how the technology works, what it can do for you, how to get the most benefit out of it, and even what its limitations are. The most important SQL Server component impacting the performance of your queries is the SQL Server query processor, which includes the query optimizer and the execution engine. With a perfect query optimizer, you could just submit any query and you would get a perfect execution plan every time. And with a perfect execution engine, each of your queries would run in just a matter of milliseconds. But the reality is that query optimization is a very complex problem, and no query optimizer can find the best plan all the time, at least in a reasonable amount of time. For complex queries, there are so many possible execution plans a query optimizer would need to analyze. And even supposing that a query optimizer could analyze all the possible solutions, the next challenge would be to decide which plan to choose. Which one is the most efficient? Choosing the best plan would require estimating the cost of each solution, which again is a very complicated task.

Don't get me wrong: the SQL Server query optimizer does an amazing job and gives you a good execution plan almost all the time. But you still need to understand which information you need to provide to the query optimizer so it can do a good job, which may include providing the right indexes and adequate statistics, as well as defining the required constraints and a good database design. SQL Server even provides you with tools to help you in some of these areas, including the Database Engine Tuning Advisor (DTA) and the auto-create and auto-update statistics features. But there is still more you can do to improve the performance of your databases, especially when you are building high-performance applications. Finally, you need to understand the cases where the query optimizer may not give you a good execution plan and what to do in those cases.

So in order for you to better understand this technology, this chapter starts with an overview of how the SQL Server query processor works and introduces the concepts covered in more detail in the rest of the book. I explain the purpose of both the query optimizer and the execution engine and how they may interact with the plan cache to reuse plans as much as possible. Later, I show you how to work with execution plans, which are the primary tool we'll use to interact with the query processor.

Architecture

At the core of the SQL Server database engine are two major components: the storage engine and the relational engine, also called the query processor. The storage engine is responsible for reading data between the disk and memory in a manner that optimizes concurrency while maintaining data integrity. The query processor, as the name suggests, accepts all queries submitted to SQL Server, devises a plan for their optimal execution, and then executes the plan and delivers the required results.

Queries are submitted to SQL Server using the SQL language (or T-SQL, the Microsoft SQL Server extension to SQL). Because SQL is a high-level declarative language, it only defines what data to get from the database, not the steps required to retrieve that data or any of the algorithms for processing the request. Thus, for each query it receives, the first job of the query processor is to devise a plan, as quickly as possible, that describes the best possible way (or, at the very least, an efficient way) to execute said query. Its second job is to execute the query according to that plan. Each of these tasks is delegated to a separate component within the query processor; the query optimizer devises the plan and then passes it along to the execution engine, which will actually execute the plan and get the results from the database.

The SQL Server query optimizer is a cost-based optimizer. It analyzes a number of candidate execution plans for a given query, estimates the cost of each of these plans, and selects the plan with the lowest cost of the choices considered. Indeed, given that the query optimizer cannot consider every possible plan for every query, it actually has to find a balance between the optimization time and the quality of the selected plan.

Therefore, it is the SQL Server component that has the biggest impact on the performance of your databases. After all, selecting the right or wrong execution plan could mean the difference between a query execution time of milliseconds and one of minutes, or even hours. Naturally, a better understanding of how the query optimizer works can help both database administrators and developers to write better queries and to provide the query optimizer with the information it needs to produce efficient execution plans. This book will demonstrate how you can use your newfound knowledge of the query optimizer's inner workings; in addition, it will give you the knowledge and tools to troubleshoot the cases when the query optimizer is not giving you a good plan.

In order to arrive at what it believes to be the best plan for executing a query, the query processor performs a number of different steps; the entire query-processing process is shown in Figure 1-1.

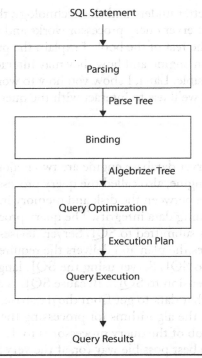

Figure 1-1   *The query-processing process*

We'll look at this whole process in much more detail in Chapter 3, but I'll just run through the steps briefly now:

1. **Parsing and binding**   The query is parsed and bound. Assuming the query is valid, the output of this phase is a logical tree, with each node in the tree representing a logical operation that the query must perform, such as reading a particular table or performing an inner join.

2. **Query optimization**   The logical tree is then used to run the query optimization process, which roughly consists of the following two steps:

    ▶ **Generation of possible execution plans**   Using the logical tree, the query optimizer devises a number of possible ways to execute the query (that is, a number of possible execution plans). An execution plan is, in essence, a set of physical operations (such as an Index Seek or a Nested Loops Join) that can be performed to produce the required result, as described by the logical tree

    ▶ **Cost assessment of each plan**   Although the query optimizer does not generate every possible execution plan, it assesses the resource and time cost of each plan it does generate; the plan that the query optimizer deems to have the lowest cost of those it has assessed is selected and then passed along to the execution engine.

3. **Query execution and plan caching**   The query is executed by the execution engine according to the selected plan; the plan may be stored in memory in the plan cache.

Parsing and Binding

Parsing and binding are the first operations performed when a query is submitted to a SQL Server instance. Parsing makes sure that the T-SQL query has a valid syntax, and it translates the SQL query into an initial tree representation: specifically, a tree of logical operators representing the high-level steps required to execute the query in question. Initially, these logical operators will be closely related to the original syntax of the query and will include such logical operations as "get data from the Customer table," "get data from the Contact table," "perform an inner join," and so on. Different tree representations of the query will be used throughout the optimization process, and this logical tree will receive different names until it is finally used to initialize the Memo structure during the optimization process.

Binding is mostly concerned with name resolution. During the binding operation, SQL Server makes sure that all the object names do exist, and it associates every table and column name on the parse tree with its corresponding object in the system catalog. The output of this second process is called an *algebrizer tree*, which is then sent to the query optimizer.

Query Optimization

The next step is the optimization process, which is basically the generation of candidate execution plans and the selection of the best of these plans according to their cost. As has already been mentioned, the SQL Server query optimizer uses a cost-estimation model to estimate the cost of each of the candidate plans.

Query optimization could be also seen as the process of mapping the logical query operations expressed in the original tree representation to physical operations, which can be carried out by the execution engine. So, it's actually the functionality of the execution engine that is being implemented in the execution plans being created by the query optimizer; that is, the execution engine implements a certain number of different algorithms, and it is from these algorithms that the query optimizer must choose when formulating its execution plans. It does this by translating the original logical operations into the physical operations that the execution engine is capable of performing. Execution plans show both the logical and physical operations for each operator. Some logical operations, such as sorts, translate to the same physical operation, whereas other logical operations map to several possible physical operations. For example, a logical join can be mapped to a Nested Loops Join, Merge Join, or Hash Join physical operator. However, this is not a one-to-one operator matching and follows a more complicated process, which will be explained in more detail in Chapter 3.

Thus, the end product of the query optimization process is an execution plan: a tree consisting of a number of physical operators, which contain the algorithms to be performed by the execution engine in order to obtain the desired results from the database.

Generating Candidate Execution Plans

As stated, the basic purpose of the query optimizer is to find an efficient execution plan for your query. Even for relatively simple queries, there may be a large number of different ways to access the data to produce the same end result. As such, the query optimizer has to select the best possible plan from what may be a very large number of candidate execution plans, and making a wise choice is important because the time taken to return the results to the user can vary wildly, depending on which plan is selected.

The job of the query optimizer is to create and assess as many candidate execution plans as possible, within certain criteria, in order to find a good enough plan, which may be, but it is not necessarily, the optimal plan. We define the search space for a given query as the set of all possible execution plans for that query, in which any possible plan in this search space returns the same results. Theoretically, in order to find the optimum execution plan for a query, a cost-based query optimizer should generate all possible execution plans that exist in that search space and correctly estimate the cost of each plan. However, some complex queries may have thousands, or even millions, of possible execution plans, and although the SQL Server query optimizer can typically consider a large number of candidate execution plans, it cannot perform an exhaustive search of all the possible plans for every query. If it did, the time taken to assess all of the plans would be unacceptably long and could start to have a major impact on the overall query execution time.

The query optimizer must strike a balance between optimization time and plan quality. For example, if the query optimizer spends one second finding a good enough plan that executes in one minute, then it doesn't make sense to try to find the perfect or most optimal plan if this is going to take five minutes of optimization time, plus the execution time. So SQL Server does not do an exhaustive search, but instead tries to find a suitably efficient plan as quickly as possible. As the query optimizer is working within a time constraint, there's a chance that the plan selected may be the optimal plan, but it is also likely that it may just be something close to the optimal plan.

In order to explore the search space, the query optimizer uses transformation rules and heuristics. The generation of candidate execution plans is performed inside the query optimizer using transformation rules, and the use of heuristics limits the number of choices considered in order to keep the optimization time reasonable. The set of alternative plans considered by the query optimizer is referred to as the plan space, and these plans are stored in memory during the optimization process in a component called the Memo. Transformation rules, heuristics, and the Memo structure will be discussed in more detail in Chapter 3.

Assessing the Cost of Each Plan

Searching or enumerating candidate plans is just one part of the optimization process. The query optimizer still needs to estimate the cost of these plans and select the least expensive one. To estimate the cost of a plan, it estimates the cost of each physical operator in that plan, using costing formulas that consider the use of resources such as I/O, CPU, and memory. This cost estimation depends mostly on both the algorithm used by the physical operator and the estimated number of records that will need to be processed. This estimate of the number of records is known as the *cardinality estimation*.

To help with this cardinality estimation, SQL Server uses and maintains statistics, which contain information describing the distribution of values in one or more columns of a table. Once the cost for each operator is estimated using estimations of cardinality and resource demands, the query optimizer will add up all of these costs to estimate the cost for the entire plan. Rather than go into more detail here, I will cover statistics in more detail in Chapter 6.

Query Execution and Plan Caching

Once the query is optimized, the resulting plan is used by the execution engine to retrieve the desired data. The generated execution plan may be stored in memory in the plan cache so it can be reused if the same query is executed again. SQL Server has a pool of memory that is used to store both data pages and execution plans. Most of this memory is used to store database pages, and it is called the *buffer pool*. A portion of this memory contains the execution plans for queries that were optimized by the query optimizer and is referred to as the *plan cache* (and was previously known as the *procedure cache*). The percentage of memory allocated to the plan cache or the buffer pool varies dynamically, depending on the state of the system.

Before optimizing a query, SQL Server first checks the plan cache to see if an execution plan exists for the batch. Query optimization is a relatively expensive operation, so if a valid plan is available in the plan cache, the optimization process can be skipped and the associated cost of this step, in terms of optimization time, CPU resources, and so on, can be avoided. If a plan for the batch is not found, the batch is compiled to generate an execution plan for all queries in the stored procedure, the trigger, or the dynamic SQL batch. Query optimization begins by loading all the interesting statistics. Then the query optimizer validates if the statistics are outdated. For any outdated statistics, when using the statistics default options, it will update the statistics and will proceed with the optimization.

After a plan is found in the plan cache or a new one is created, the plan is validated for schema and data statistics changes. Schema changes are verified for plan correctness. Statistics are also verified: the query optimizer checks for new applicable statistics or outdated statistics. If the plan is not valid for any of these reasons, it is discarded and the batch or individual query is compiled again. Such compilations are known as *recompilations*. This process is summarized in Figure 1-2.

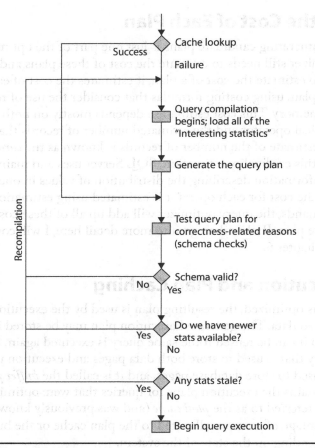

Figure 1-2   *Compilation and recompilation process*

Plans may also be removed from the plan cache when SQL Server is under memory pressure or when certain statements are executed. Changing some configuration options (for example, max degree of parallelism) will clear the entire plan cache. Alternatively, some statements, such as altering a database with certain ALTER DATABASE options, will clear all the plans associated with that particular database.

However, it is also worth noting that reusing an existing plan may not always be the best solution for a given query, and some problems may appear. For example, depending on the data distribution within a table, the optimal execution plan for a query may differ greatly depending on the parameters being used. More details about these problems and the plan cache in general are covered in Chapter 8.

Execution Plans

Now that we have a foundation in the query processor and how it works its magic, it's time to consider how we can interact with it. Primarily, we'll interact with the query processor through execution plans, which as I mentioned earlier are ultimately trees consisting of a number of physical operators that, in turn, contain the algorithms to produce the required results from the database. Given that I will make extensive use of execution plans throughout the book, in this section, I'll show you how to display and read them.

You can request either an actual or an estimated execution plan for a given query, and either of these two types can be displayed as a graphic, text, or XML plan. Any of these three formats shows the same execution plan—the only difference is how they are displayed and the level of detail of information they contain.

When an estimated plan is requested, the query is not executed; the plan displayed is simply the plan that SQL Server would most probably use if the query were executed (bearing in mind that a recompile, which we'll discuss later, may generate a different plan at execution time). However, when an actual plan is requested, the query needs to be executed, and the plan is then displayed along with the query results. Nevertheless, using an estimated plan has several benefits, including displaying a plan for a long-running query for inspection without actually running the query, or displaying a plan for update operations without changing the database.

Graphical Plans

You can display graphical plans in SQL Server Management Studio by clicking the Display Estimated Execution Plan button or the Include Actual Execution Plan button from the SQL Editor toolbar. Clicking Display Estimated Execution Plan will show the plan immediately, without executing the query, whereas, to request an actual execution plan, you need to click Include Actual Execution Plan and then execute the query and click the Execution plan tab.

As an example, copy the following query to the Management Studio Query Editor, select the AdventureWorks2012 database, click the Include Actual Execution Plan button, and execute the query:

```
SELECT DISTINCT(City) FROM Person.Address
```

Then select the Execution Plan tab in the results pane. This displays the plan shown in Figure 1-3.

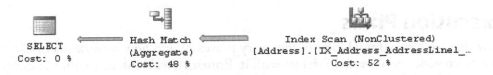

SELECT
Cost: 0 %

Hash Match
(Aggregate)
Cost: 48 %

Index Scan (NonClustered)
[Address].[IX_Address_AddressLine1_...
Cost: 52 %

Figure 1-3   *Graphical execution plan*

NOTE

This book contains a large number of sample SQL queries, all of which are based on the AdventureWorks2012 database, although Chapter 9 additionally uses the AdventureWorksDW2012 database. All code has been tested on SQL Server 2014 RTM. Note that these sample databases are not included in your SQL Server installation by default, but can be downloaded from the CodePlex website. You need to download the family of sample databases for SQL Server 2012. (No sample databases for SQL Server 2014 existed at the time this book was written.) During installation, you may choose to install all the databases or, at least, AdventureWorks2012 and AdventureWorksDW2012.

Each node in the tree structure is represented as an icon that specifies a logical and physical operator, such as the Index Scan and the Hash Aggregate operators, shown in Figure 1-3. The first icon is a language element called the *Result operator*, which represents the SELECT statement and is usually the root element in the plan.

Operators implement a basic function or operation of the execution engine; for example, a logical join operation could be implemented by any of three different physical join operators: Nested Loops Join, Merge Join, or Hash Join. Obviously, many more operators are implemented in the execution engine, and you can see the entire list at http://msdn.microsoft.com/en-us/library/ms191158(v=sql.110).aspx. Logical and physical operators' icons are displayed in blue, except for cursor operators, which are yellow, and language elements are displayed in green:

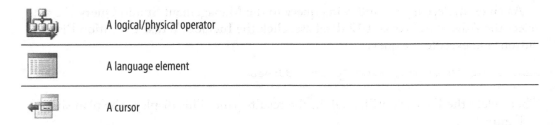

	A logical/physical operator
	A language element
	A cursor

The query optimizer builds an execution plan, choosing from these operators, which may read records from the database, like the Index Scan operator shown in the previous plan; or they may read records from another operator, like the Hash Aggregate, which reads records from the Index Scan operator.

Each node is related to a parent node, connected with arrowheads, where data flows from a child operator to a parent operator and the arrow width is proportional to the number of rows. After the operator performs some function on the records it has read, the results are output to its parent. You can hover the mouse pointer over an arrow to get more information about that data flow, displayed as a tooltip. For example, if you hover the mouse pointer over the arrow between the Index Scan and Hash Aggregate operators, shown in Figure 1-3, you get the data flow information between these operators, as shown in Figure 1-4.

By looking at the actual number of rows, you can see that the Index Scan operator is reading 19,614 rows from the database and sending them to the Hash Aggregate operator. The Hash Aggregate operator is, in turn, performing some operation on this data and sending 575 records to its parent, which you can also see by placing the mouse pointer over the arrow between the Hash Aggregate and the SELECT icon.

Basically, in this plan, the Index Scan operator is reading all 19,614 rows from an index, and the Hash Aggregate is processing these rows to obtain the list of distinct cities, of which there are 575, which will be displayed in the Results window in Management Studio. Notice also how you can see the estimated number of rows, which is the query optimizer's cardinality estimation for this operator, as well as the actual number of rows. Comparing the actual and the estimated number of rows can help you detect cardinality estimation errors, which can affect the quality of your execution plans, as will be discussed in Chapter 6.

To perform their job, physical operators implement at least the following three methods:

- ▶ **Open()**   Causes an operator to be initialized, and may include setting up any required data structures

- ▶ **GetRow()**   Requests a row from the operator

- ▶ **Close()**   Performs some cleanup operations and shuts down the operator once it has performed its role

An operator requests rows from other operators by calling their GetRow() method, which also means that execution in a plan starts from left to right. Because GetRow()

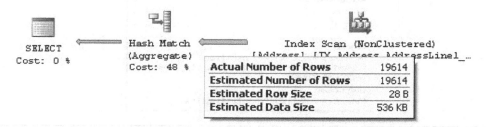

Figure 1-4   *Data flow between the Index Scan and Hash Aggregate operators*

produces just one row at a time, the actual number of rows displayed in the execution plan is also the number of times the method was called on a specific operator, and an additional call to GetRow() is used by the operator to indicate the end of the result set. In the previous example, the Hash Aggregate operator calls the Open() method once, GetRow() 19,615 times, and Close() once on the Index Scan operator.

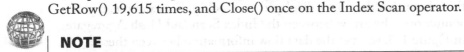

NOTE

For now, I will be explaining the traditional query-processing mode in which operators process only one row at a time. This processing mode has been used in all versions of SQL Server since SQL Server 7.0. Later in Chapter 9, I will touch on the new batch-processing mode, introduced with SQL Server 2012, which is used by operators related to columnstore indexes.

In addition to learning more about the data flow, you can also hover the mouse pointer over an operator to get more information about it. For example, Figure 1-5 shows information about the Index Scan operator; notice that it includes, among other things, a description of the operator and data on estimated costing information, such as the estimated I/O, CPU, operator, and subtree costs.

Index Scan (NonClustered)	
Scan a nonclustered index, entirely or only a range.	
Physical Operation	Index Scan
Logical Operation	Index Scan
Actual Execution Mode	Row
Estimated Execution Mode	Row
Storage	RowStore
Actual Number of Rows	19614
Actual Number of Batches	0
Estimated I/O Cost	0.158681
Estimated Operator Cost	0.180413 (52%)
Estimated Subtree Cost	0.180413
Estimated CPU Cost	0.0217324
Estimated Number of Executions	1
Number of Executions	1
Estimated Number of Rows	19614
Estimated Row Size	28 B
Actual Rebinds	0
Actual Rewinds	0
Ordered	False
Node ID	1
Object	
[AdventureWorks2012].[Person].[Address].[IX_Address_AddressLine1_AddressLine2_City_StateProvinceID_PostalCode]	
Output List	
[AdventureWorks2012].[Person].[Address].City	

Figure 1-5   *Tooltip for the Index Scan operator*

Some of these properties are explained in Table 1-1; others will be explained later in the book.

NOTE

It is worth mentioning that the cost is just internal cost units that are not meant to be interpreted in other units such as seconds or milliseconds.

You can also see the relative cost of each operator in the plan as a percentage of the overall plan, as shown in Figure 1-3. For example, the cost of the Index Scan is 52 percent of the cost of the entire plan. Additional information from an operator or the entire query can be obtained by using the Properties window. So, for example, choosing the SELECT icon and selecting the Properties window from the View menu (or pressing F4) will show some properties for the entire query, as shown in Figure 1-6.

Table 1-2 lists most of the properties shown in Figure 1-6. Other optional properties may appear, depending on the query (for example, Parameter List or Warnings).

Property	Description
Physical Operation	Physical implementation algorithm for the node.
Logical Operation	Relational algebraic operator this node represents.
Actual Number of Rows	Actual number of rows produced by the operator.
Estimated I/O Cost	Estimated I/O cost for the operation. Not all operators incur an I/O cost.
Estimated Operator Cost	The query optimizer–estimated cost for executing this operation. This is the estimated I/O and CPU cost. It also includes the cost of operation as a percentage of the total cost of the query displayed in parentheses.
Estimated Subtree Cost	Estimated cumulative cost for executing this operation and all operations preceding it in the same subtree.
Estimated CPU Cost	Estimated CPU cost for the operation.
Estimated Number of Executions	Estimated number of times this operator will be executed while running the current query.
Number of Executions	Number of times this operator was executed after running the query.
Estimated Number of Rows	Estimated number of rows produced by the operator (cardinality estimate).
Estimated Row Size	Estimated average size of the row being passed through this operator.

Table 1-1   *Operator Properties*

Property	Description
Cached plan size	Plan cache memory in kilobytes used by this query plan.
CompileCPU	CPU time in milliseconds used to compile this query.
CompileMemory	Memory in kilobytes used to compile this query.
CompileTime	Elapsed time in milliseconds used to compile this query.
Degree of Parallelism	Number of threads that can be used to execute the query should the query processor pick a parallel plan.
Memory Grant	Amount of memory in kilobytes granted to run this query.
MemoryGrantInfo	Memory grant estimate as well as actual runtime memory grant information.
Optimization Level	Level of optimization used to compile this query. Shown as StatementOptmLevel on the XML plan. It will be explained in more detail later in this section.
OptimizerHardwareDependentProperties	Hardware-dependent properties that affect cost estimate (and hence, query plan choice), as seen by the query optimizer.
QueryHash	Binary hash value calculated on the query and used to identify queries with similar logic.
QueryPlanHash	Binary hash value calculated on the query execution plan and used to identify similar query execution plans.
Reason For Early Termination Of Statement Optimization	Shown as StatementOptmEarlyAbortReason on the XML plan. It will be explained in more detail later in this section.
RetrievedFromCache	Indicates if plan was retrieved from cache.
Set Options	Status of the set options that affect query cost. Shown as StatementSetOptions on the XML plan. These SET options are ANSI_NULLS, ANSI_PADDING, ANSI_WARNINGS, ARITHABORT, CONCAT_NULL_YIELDS_NULL, NUMERIC_ROUNDABORT, and QUOTED_IDENTIFIER.
Statement	Text of the SQL statement.

Table 1-2 *Query Properties*

Finally, SQL Server Management Studio provides a zooming feature you can use to navigate through large graphical plans that may not fit on the screen. You can access this tool by clicking the plus sign button located at the bottom-right corner of the Execution Plan tab. An example is shown in Figure 1-7. In addition, SQL Sentry Plan Explorer is a popular tool you can use to work with execution plans. You can download it for free at the SQL Sentry website at http://sqlsentry.net/plan-explorer.

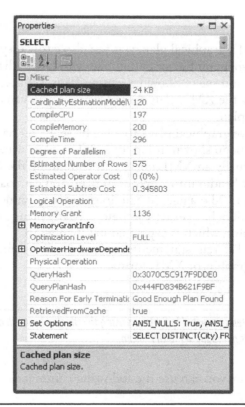

Figure 1-6 *Properties window for the query*

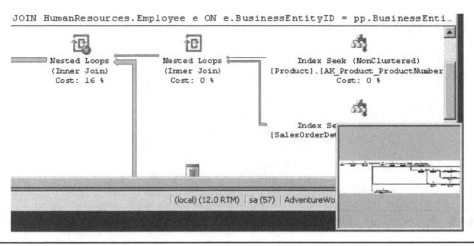

Figure 1-7 *Execution plans zooming feature*

XML

Once you have displayed a graphical plan, you can also easily display it in XML format. Simply right-click anywhere on the execution plan window to display a pop-up menu, as shown in Figure 1-8, and select Show Execution Plan XML…. This will open the XML editor and display the XML plan. As you can see, you can easily switch between a graphical and an XML plan.

If needed, you can save graphical plans to a file by selecting Save Execution Plan As… from the pop-up menu shown in Figure 1-8. The plan, usually saved with an .sqlplan extension, is actually an XML document containing the XML plan, but can be read by Management Studio into a graphical plan. You can load this file again by selecting File and Open in Management Studio in order to immediately display it as a graphical plan, which will behave exactly as before. XML plans can also be used with the USEPLAN query hint, which is explained in Chapter 10.

Table 1-3 shows the different statements you can use to obtain an estimated or actual execution plan in text, graphic, or XML format.

NOTE

When you run any of the statements listed in Table 1-3 using the ON clause, it will apply to all subsequent statements until the option is manually set to OFF again.

To show an XML plan, you can use the following commands:

```
SET SHOWPLAN_XML ON
GO
SELECT DISTINCT(City) FROM Person.Address
GO
SET SHOWPLAN_XML OFF
```

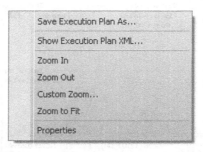

Figure 1-8 *Pop-up menu on the execution plan window*

	Estimated Execution Plan	**Actual Execution Plan**
Text Plan	SET SHOWPLAN_TEXT SET SHOWPLAN_ALL	SET STATISTICS PROFILE
Graphic Plan	Management Studio	Management Studio
XML Plan	SET SHOWPLAN_XML	SET STATISTICS XML

Table 1-3   *Statements for Displaying Query Plans*

This will display a single-row, single-column (titled "Microsoft SQL Server 2005 XML Showplan") result set containing the XML data that starts with the following:

```
<ShowPlanXML xmlns="http://schemas.microsoft.com/sqlserver/2004 ...
```

Clicking the link will show you a graphical plan, and you can then display the XML plan using the same procedure as explained earlier.

You can browse the basic structure of an XML plan via the following exercise. A very simple query will create the basic XML structure, but in this example I show you a query that can provide two additional parts: the missing indexes and parameter list elements. Run the following query and request an XML plan:

```
SELECT * FROM Sales.SalesOrderDetail
WHERE OrderQty = 1
```

Collapse <MissingIndexes>, <RelOp>, and <ParameterList> by clicking the minus sign (-) on the left so you can easily see the entire structure. You should see something similar to Figure 1-9.

```
<?xml version="1.0" encoding="utf-16"?>
<ShowPlanXML xmlns:xsi="http://www.w3.org/2001/XMLSchema-instance" xmlns:xsd="http://www.w3.org/2001/XMLSchema"
  <BatchSequence>
    <Batch>
      <Statements>
        <StmtSimple StatementCompId="1" StatementEstRows="68089" StatementId="1" StatementOptmLevel="FULL" Cardi
          <StatementSetOptions ANSI_NULLS="true" ANSI_PADDING="true" ANSI_WARNINGS="true" ARITHABORT="true" CONC
          <QueryPlan DegreeOfParallelism="1" CachedPlanSize="32" CompileTime="863" CompileCPU="862" CompileMemor
            <MissingIndexes>...</MissingIndexes>
            <MemoryGrantInfo SerialRequiredMemory="0" SerialDesiredMemory="0" />
            <OptimizerHardwareDependentProperties EstimatedAvailableMemoryGrant="101808" EstimatedPagesCached="2
            <RelOp AvgRowSize="112" EstimateCPU="0.0582322" EstimateIO="0" EstimateRebinds="0" EstimateRewinds="
            <ParameterList>...</ParameterList>
          </QueryPlan>
        </StmtSimple>
      </Statements>
    </Batch>
  </BatchSequence>
</ShowPlanXML>
```

Figure 1-9   *XML execution plan*

As you can see, the main components of the XML plan are the <StmtSimple>, <StatementSetOptions>, and <QueryPlan> elements. These three elements include several attributes, some of which were already explained when we discussed the graphical plan. In addition, the <QueryPlan> element also includes other elements such as <MissingIndexes>, <MemoryGrantInfo>, <OptimizerHardwareDependentProperties>, <RelOp>, <ParameterList>, and others not shown in Figure 1-9, such as <Warnings>, which will be also discussed later in this section. <StmtSimple> shows the following for this example:

```
<StmtSimple StatementCompId="1" StatementEstRows="68089" StatementId="1"
StatementOptmLevel="FULL" CardinalityEstimationModelVersion="70"
StatementSubTreeCost="1.13478" StatementText="SELECT * FROM
[Sales].[SalesOrderDetail] WHERE [OrderQty]=@1" StatementType="SELECT"
QueryHash="0x42CFD97ABC9592DD" QueryPlanHash="0xC5F6C30459CD7C41"
RetrievedFromCache="false">
```

<QueryPlan> shows this:

```
<QueryPlan DegreeOfParallelism="1" CachedPlanSize="32" CompileTime="3"
CompileCPU="3" CompileMemory="264">
```

As mentioned, the attributes of these and other elements were already explained when we discussed the graphical plan. Others will be explained later in this section or in other sections of the book.

Text Plans

As you can see in Table 1-3, there are two commands to get estimated text plans: SET SHOWPLAN_TEXT and SET SHOWPLAN_ALL. Both statements show the estimated execution plan, but SET SHOWPLAN_ALL shows some additional information, including the estimated number of rows, estimated CPU cost, estimated I/O cost, and estimated operator cost. However, recent versions of Books Online, including that of SQL Server 2014, indicate that all text versions of execution plans will be deprecated in a future version of SQL Server and, therefore, recommend using the XML versions instead.

You can use the following code to display a text execution plan:

```
SET SHOWPLAN_TEXT ON
GO
SELECT DISTINCT(City) FROM Person.Address
GO
SET SHOWPLAN_TEXT OFF
GO
```

This code will actually display two result sets, the first one returning the text of the T-SQL statement. In the second result set, you see the following text plan (edited to fit the page), which shows the same Hash Aggregate and Index Scan operators displayed earlier in Figure 1-3:

```
|--Hash Match(Aggregate, HASH:([Person].[Address].[City]), RESIDUAL …
|--Index Scan(OBJECT:([AdventureWorks].[Person].[Address]. [IX_Address …
```

SET SHOWPLAN_ALL and SET STATISTICS PROFILE can provide more detailed information than SET SHOWPLAN_TEXT. Also, as shown in Table 1-3, you can use SET SHOWPLAN_ALL to get an estimated plan only and SET STATISTICS PROFILE to actually execute the query. Run the following example:

```
SET SHOWPLAN_ALL ON
GO
SELECT DISTINCT(City) FROM Person.Address
GO
SET SHOWPLAN_ALL OFF
GO
```

The output is shown in Figure 1-10.

Because SET STATISTICS PROFILE actually executes the query, it provides an easy way to look for cardinality estimation problems because you can easily visually compare multiple operators at a time, which could be complicated to do on a graphical or XML plan. Now run the following code:

```
SET STATISTICS PROFILE ON
GO
SELECT * FROM Sales.SalesOrderDetail
WHERE OrderQty * UnitPrice > 25000
GO
SET STATISTICS PROFILE OFF
GO
```

The output is shown in Figure 1-11.

Note that the column EstimateRows was manually moved in Management Studio to be next to the column Rows so you can easily compare the actual against the estimated number of rows. For this particular example, you can see a big difference in cardinality estimation on the Filter operator of 36,395.1 estimated versus five actual rows.

	StmtText	StmtId	NodeId	Parent	PhysicalOp	LogicalOp
1	SELECT DISTINCT(City) FROM Person.Address	1	1	0	NULL	NULL
2	|--Hash Match(Aggregate, HASH:([AdventureWorks...	1	2	1	Hash Match	Aggregate
3	|--Index Scan(OBJECT:([AdventureWorks2012].[...	1	3	2	Index Scan	Index Scan

Figure 1-10 *SET SHOWPLAN_ALL output*

	Rows	EstimateRows	Executes	StmtText
1	5	36395.1	1	SELECT * FROM [Sales].[SalesOrderDetail] WHERE [OrderQty]*[UnitPrice]>@1
2	5	36395.1	1	|--Filter(WHERE:([Expr1003]>($25000.0000)))
3	0	121317	0	|--Compute Scalar(DEFINE:([AdventureWorks2012].[Sales].[SalesOrderDetail].[Li...
4	0	121317	0	|--Compute Scalar(DEFINE:([AdventureWorks2012].[Sales].[SalesOrderDetail]....
5	121317	121317	1	|--Clustered Index Scan(OBJECT:([AdventureWorks2012].[Sales].[SalesOr...

Figure 1-11 *SET STATISTICS PROFILE output*

Additional Plan Properties

One interesting way to learn about the components of an execution plan, including ones of future versions of SQL Server, is to look at the showplan schema. XML plans comply with a published XSD schema, and you can see the current and older versions of this showplan schema at http://schemas.microsoft.com/sqlserver/2004/07/showplan/, which you can also find at the beginning of each XML execution plan. Currently, accessing that location on a web browser will show you links to access the showplan schemas for SQL Server 2014 RTM as "Current version," SQL Server 2012 RTM, SQL Server 2008 RTM, SQL Server 2005 SP2, and SQL Server 2005 RTM.

Covering all the elements and attributes of an execution plan would take a lot of pages; instead, I cover some of the most interesting ones here. Operators used in execution plans will be covered in more detail in Chapter 4. Let's start with the StatementOptmLevel, StatementOptmEarlyAbortReason, and CardinalityEstimationModelVersion attributes of the <StmtSimple> element.

Although these attributes refer to concepts that will be explained in more detail later in the book, it's worth an introduction here. StatementOptmLevel is the query optimization level, which can be either TRIVIAL or FULL. The optimization process may be expensive to initialize and run for very simple queries that don't require any cost estimation, so to avoid this expensive operation for these simple queries, SQL Server uses the trivial plan optimization. If a query does not apply for a trivial optimization, a full optimization will have to be performed. For example, in SQL Server 2014, the following query will produce a trivial plan:

```
SELECT * FROM Sales.SalesOrderHeader
WHERE SalesOrderID = 43666
```

You can use the undocumented (and therefore unsupported) trace flag 8757 to test the behavior if you want to disable the trivial plan optimization.

```
SELECT * FROM Sales.SalesOrderHeader
WHERE SalesOrderID = 43666
OPTION (QUERYTRACEON 8757)
```

The QUERYTRACEON query hint is used to apply a trace flag at the query level. After running the previous query, SQL Server will run a full optimization, which you can verify with StatementOptmLevel as FULL in the resulting plan. You should note that although the QUERYTRACEON query hint is widely known, currently, it is only supported in a limited number of scenarios. At the time of this writing, the QUERYTRACEON query hint is only supported when using the trace flags documented in the article found at http://support.microsoft.com/kb/2801413.

NOTE

This book shows many undocumented and unsupported features. This is so you can use them in a test environment for troubleshooting purposes or to learn the technology, but they are not meant to be used in a production environment and are not supported by Microsoft. I will identify when a statement or trace flag is undocumented and unsupported.

On the other hand, the StatementOptmEarlyAbortReason, or "Reason For Early Termination Of Statement Optimization," attribute can have the values GoodEnoughPlanFound, TimeOut, and MemoryLimitExceeded and only appears when the query optimizer prematurely terminates a query optimization (in older versions of SQL Server, you had to use undocumented trace flag 8675 to see this information). Because the purpose of the query optimizer is to produce a good enough plan as quickly as possible, the query optimizer calculates two values depending on the query at the beginning of the optimization process. The first of these values is the cost of a good enough plan according to the query, and the second one is the maximum time to spend on the query optimization. During the optimization process, if a plan with a cost lower than the calculated cost threshold is found, the optimization process stops, and the found plan will be returned with the GoodEnoughPlanFound value. If, on the other hand, the optimization process is taking longer than the calculated maximum time threshold, optimization will also stop and the query optimizer will return the best plan found so far, with StatementOptmEarlyAbortReason containing the TimeOut value. The GoodEnoughPlanFound and TimeOut values do not mean that there is a problem, and in all three cases, including MemoryLimitExceeded, the plan produced will be correct. However, in the case of MemoryLimitExceeded, the plan may not be optimal. In this latter case, you may need to simplify your query or increase the available memory in your system. These and other details of the query optimization process are covered in Chapter 3.

For example, even when the following query joins four tables and requires a Sort, it still has an early termination and returns "Good Enough Plan Found":

```
SELECT pm.ProductModelID, pm.Name, Description, pl.CultureID,
cl.Name AS Language
FROM Production.ProductModel AS pm
    JOIN Production.ProductModelProductDescriptionCulture AS pl
```

```
        ON pm.ProductModelID = pl.ProductModelID
    JOIN Production.Culture AS cl
        ON cl.CultureID = pl.CultureID
    JOIN Production.ProductDescription AS pd
        ON pd.ProductDescriptionID = pl.ProductDescriptionID
ORDER BY pm.ProductModelID
```

The CardinalityEstimationModelVersion attribute refers to the version of the cardinality estimation model used by the query optimizer. SQL Server 2014 introduces a new cardinality estimator, but you still have the choice of using the old one by changing the database compatibility level or using trace flags 2312 and 9481. More details about both cardinality estimation models will be covered in Chapter 6.

The NonParallelPlanReason optional attribute of the QueryPlan element, which was introduced with SQL Server 2012, contains a description of why a parallel plan may not be chosen for the optimized query. Although the list of possible values is not documented, the following are popular and easy to obtain:

```
SELECT * FROM Sales.SalesOrderHeader
WHERE SalesOrderID = 43666
OPTION (MAXDOP 1)
```

Because we are using MAXDOP 1, it will show this:

```
NonParallelPlanReason="MaxDOPSetToOne"
```

Using the function

```
SELECT CustomerID,('AW' + dbo.ufnLeadingZeros(CustomerID))
    AS GenerateAccountNumber
FROM Sales.Customer
ORDER BY CustomerID;
```

would generate the following:

```
NonParallelPlanReason="CouldNotGenerateValidParallelPlan"
```

If trying to run

```
SELECT * FROM Sales.SalesOrderHeader
WHERE SalesOrderID = 43666
OPTION (MAXDOP 8)
```

on a system with only one CPU, you will get this:

```
<QueryPlan NonParallelPlanReason="EstimatedDOPIsOne"
```

Finally, also introduced with SQL Server 2012, the showplan XSD schema has the OptimizerHardwareDependentProperties element, which provides hardware-dependent properties that can affect the query plan choice, with the following documented attributes:

▶ **EstimatedAvailableMemoryGrant**   An estimate of what amount of memory (KB) will be available for this query at execution time to request a memory grant from

▶ **EstimatedPagesCached**   An estimate of how many pages of data will remain cached in the buffer pool if the query needs to read it again

▶ **EstimatedAvailableDegreeOfParallelism**   An estimate of the number of CPUs that can be used to execute the query should the query optimizer pick a parallel plan

For example, the query

```
SELECT DISTINCT(CustomerID)
FROM Sales.SalesOrderHeader
```

will show this:

```
<OptimizerHardwareDependentProperties
EstimatedAvailableMemoryGrant="101808"
EstimatedPagesCached="8877" EstimatedAvailableDegreeOfParallelism="2" />
```

Warnings on Execution Plans

Execution plans can also show warning messages. Plans containing these warnings should be carefully reviewed because this can cause the query optimizer to choose a less efficient query plan. Before SQL Server 2012, only the ColumnsWithNoStatistics and NoJoinPredicate were available. The SQL Server 2012 showplan schema added six more iterator- or query-specific warnings:

▶ SpillToTempDb

▶ Wait

▶ PlanAffectingConvert

▶ SpatialGuess

▶ UnmatchedIndexes

▶ FullUpdateForOnlineIndexBuild

Let's examine some of them in this section.

ColumnsWithNoStatistics

This warning means that the query optimizer tried to use statistics but none were available. As explained earlier in this chapter, the query optimizer relies on statistics to produce an optimal plan. Perform the following statements to simulate this warning.

Run the following statement to drop the existing statistics for the VacationHours column, if available:

```
DROP STATISTICS HumanResources.Employee._WA_Sys_0000000C_49C3F6B7
```

Next, temporarily disable automatic creation of statistics at the database level:

```
ALTER DATABASE AdventureWorks2012 SET AUTO_CREATE_STATISTICS OFF
```

Then run this query:

```
SELECT * FROM HumanResources.Employee
WHERE VacationHours = 48
```

You will get the plan shown in Figure 1-12.

Notice the warning (the symbol with an exclamation mark) on the Clustered Index Scan operator. If you look at its properties you will see "Columns With No Statistics: [AdventureWorks2012].[HumanResources].[Employee].VacationHours."

Do not forget to reenable the automatic creation of statistics by running the following command. There is no need to create the statistics object dropped previously because it can be created automatically if needed.

```
ALTER DATABASE AdventureWorks2012 SET AUTO_CREATE_STATISTICS ON
```

NoJoinPredicate

A possible problem while using the old-style ANSI SQL-89 join syntax is accidentally missing the join predicate and getting a NoJoinPredicate warning. Let's suppose you intend to run the following query but forgot to include the WHERE clause:

```
SELECT * FROM Sales.SalesOrderHeader soh, Sales.SalesOrderDetail sod
WHERE soh.SalesOrderID = sod.SalesOrderID
```

The first indication of a problem could be that the query takes way too long to execute, even for small tables. Later, you will see that the query also returns a huge result set.

Figure 1-12 *Plan showing a ColumnsWithNoStatistics warning*

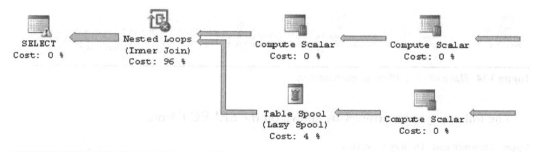

Figure 1-13 *Plan with a NoJoinPredicate warning*

Sometimes, a way to troubleshoot a long-running query is to just stop its execution and request an estimated plan instead. If you don't include the join predicate (in the WHERE clause), you get the plan shown in Figure 1-13.

This time, you can see the warning on the Nested Loops Join as "No Join Predicate" with a different symbol. Notice that you cannot accidentally miss a join predicate if you use the ANSI SQL-92 join syntax because you get an error instead, which is why this syntax is recommended. For example, missing the join predicate in the following query will return an incorrect syntax error:

```
SELECT * FROM Sales.SalesOrderHeader soh JOIN Sales.SalesOrderDetail sod
-- ON soh.SalesOrderID = sod.SalesOrderID
```

NOTE

You can still get, if needed, a join whose result set includes one row for each possible pairing of rows from the two tables, also called a Cartesian product, by using the CROSS JOIN syntax.

PlanAffectingConvert

This warning shows that type conversions were performed that may impact the performance of the resulting execution plan. Run the following example, which declares a variable as nvarchar and then uses it in a query to compare against a varchar column, CreditCardApprovalCode:

```
DECLARE @code nvarchar(15)
SET @code = '95555Vi4081'
SELECT * FROM Sales.SalesOrderHeader
WHERE CreditCardApprovalCode = @code
```

The query returns the plan shown in Figure 1-14.

Figure 1-14 *Plan with a PlanAffectingConvert warning*

The following two warnings are shown on the SELECT icon:

```
Type conversion in expression
(CONVERT_IMPLICIT(nvarchar(15),[AdventureWorks2012].[Sales].[SalesOrderHeader].
[CreditCardApprovalCode],0)) may affect "CardinalityEstimate" in query plan
choice,
Type conversion in expression
(CONVERT_IMPLICIT(nvarchar(15),[AdventureWorks2012].[Sales].[SalesOrderHeader].
[CreditCardApprovalCode],0)=[@code]) may affect "SeekPlan" in query plan choice
```

Obviously, the recommendation is to use similar data types on comparison operations.

SpillToTempDb

This warning shows than an operation didn't have enough memory and had to spill data to disk during execution, which can be a performance problem because of the extra I/O overhead. To simulate this problem, run the following example:

```
SELECT * FROM Sales.SalesOrderDetail
ORDER BY UnitPrice
```

This is a very simple query, and depending on the memory available on your system, you may not get the warning in your test environment, so you may need to try with a larger table instead. The plan shown in Figure 1-15 is generated.

The warning is shown this time on the Sort operator, which includes the message "Operator used tempdb to spill data during execution with spill level 1." The XML plan also shows this:

```
<SpillToTempDb SpillLevel="1" />
```

Figure 1-15 *Plan with SpillToTempDb warning*

UnmatchedIndexes

Finally, the UnmatchedIndexes element can show that the query optimizer was not able to match a filtered index for a particular query (for example, when it is not able to see the value of a parameter). Suppose you create the following filtered index:

```
CREATE INDEX IX_Color ON Production.Product(Name, ProductNumber)
WHERE Color = 'White'
```

Then you run the following query:

```
DECLARE @color nvarchar(15)
SET @color = 'White'
SELECT Name, ProductNumber FROM Production.Product
WHERE Color = @color
```

The IX_Color index is not used at all, and you will get a warning on the plan, as shown in Figure 1-16.

You will be able to see the following on the XML plan (or by looking at the UnmatchedIndexes property of the SELECT operator properties window):

```
<UnmatchedIndexes>
  <Parameterization>
    <Object Database="[AdventureWorks2012]" Schema="[Production]"
      Table="[Product]" Index="[IX_Color]" />
  </Parameterization>
</UnmatchedIndexes>
<Warnings UnmatchedIndexes="true" />
```

However, the following query will use the index:

```
SELECT Name, ProductNumber FROM Production.Product
WHERE Color = 'White'
```

Filtered indexes and the UnmatchedIndexes element will be covered in detail in Chapter 5. For now, remove the index we just created:

```
DROP INDEX Production.Product.IX_Color
```

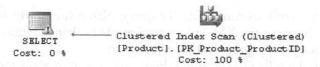

Figure 1-16 *Plan with a UnmatchedIndexes warning*

NOTE

Many exercises in this book will require you to perform changes in the AdventureWorks2012 database. Although the database is reverted back to its original state, you may also consider refreshing a copy of the database after a number of changes or tests.

Getting Plans from a Trace or the Plan Cache

So far we have been testing getting execution plans by directly using the query code in Management Studio. However, getting a plan this way may not always be possible in your environment, and sometimes, you may need to capture, perhaps for troubleshooting purposes, the execution plan from other locations (for example, the plan cache or a current execution). In these cases, you may need to obtain an execution plan from a trace, for example, using SQL trace or extended events, or the plan cache using the sys.dm_exec_query_plan dynamic management function (DMF) or perhaps using some collected data, as in the case of the SQL Server Data Collector. Let's take a look at some of these sources.

sys.dm_exec_query_plan DMF

As mentioned earlier, when a query is optimized, its execution plan may be kept in the plan cache, and the sys.dm_exec_query_plan DMF can be used to return such cached plans, as well as any plan that is currently executing. However, when a plan is removed from the cache, it will no longer be available and the query_plan column of the returned table will be null.

For example, the following query shows the execution plans for all the queries currently running in the system. The sys.dm_exec_requests dynamic management view (DMV), which returns information about each request currently executing, is used to obtain the plan_handle value, which is needed to find the execution plan using the sys.dm_exec_query_plan DMF. A plan_handle is a hash value that represents a specific execution plan, and it is guaranteed to be unique in the system.

```
SELECT * FROM sys.dm_exec_requests
CROSS APPLY
sys.dm_exec_query_plan(plan_handle)
```

The output will be a result set containing the query_plan column, which shows links similar to the one shown in the XML plans section. As explained before, clicking the link shows you requested the graphical execution plan.

In the same way, the following example shows the execution plans for all cached query plans. The sys.dm_exec_query_stats DMV contains one row per query statement within the cached plan and, again, provides the plan_handle value needed by the sys.dm_exec_query_plan DMF.

```
SELECT * FROM sys.dm_exec_query_stats
CROSS APPLY
sys.dm_exec_query_plan(plan_handle)
```

Now suppose you want to find the 10 most expensive queries by CPU usage. You can run the following query to get this information, which will return the average CPU time in microseconds per execution:

```
SELECT TOP 10 total_worker_time/execution_count AS avg_cpu_time,
plan_handle, query_plan
FROM sys.dm_exec_query_stats
CROSS APPLY sys.dm_exec_query_plan(plan_handle)
ORDER BY avg_cpu_time DESC
```

SQL Trace/Profiler

You can also use SQL Trace and/or Profiler to capture execution plans of queries currently executing. You can use the Performance event category in Profiler, which includes the following events:

- ▶ Performance Statistics
- ▶ Showplan All
- ▶ Showplan All For Query Compile
- ▶ Showplan Statistics Profile
- ▶ Showplan Text
- ▶ Showplan Text (Unencoded)
- ▶ Showplan XML
- ▶ Showplan XML For Query Compile
- ▶ Showplan XML Statistics Profile

To trace any of these events, run Profiler, connect to your SQL Server instance, click Events Selection, expand the Performance event category, and select any of the required events. You can select all the columns or only a subset of the columns, specify a column filter, and so on. Click Run to start the trace. Figure 1-17 shows an example of a trace with the Showplan XML event.

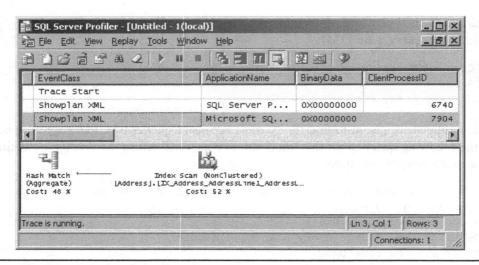

Figure 1-17 *Trace in Profiler showing the Showplan XML event*

You can optionally create a server trace using a script, and even use Profiler as a scripting tool. In order to do that, define the events for your trace, run and stop the trace, and select File | Export | Script Trace Definition | For SQL Server 2005 – 2014…. This will produce the code to run a server trace, which will only be required to specify a filename to capture the trace. Part of the generated code is shown next.

```
/****************************************************/
/* Created by: SQL Server 2014 Profiler          */
/* Date: 12/18/2013  08:37:22 AM          */
/****************************************************/
-- Create a Queue
declare @rc int
declare @TraceID int
declare @maxfilesize bigint
set @maxfilesize = 5

-- Please replace the text InsertFileNameHere, with an appropriate
-- filename prefixed by a path, e.g., c:\MyFolder\MyTrace. The .trc extension
-- will be appended to the filename automatically. If you are writing from
-- remote server to local drive, please use UNC path and make sure server has
-- write access to your network share
```

```
exec @rc = sp_trace_create @TraceID output, 0, N'InsertFileNameHere', @maxfilesize,
NULL
if (@rc != 0) goto error

-- Client side File and Table cannot be scripted

-- Set the events
declare @on bit
set @on = 1
exec sp_trace_setevent @TraceID, 10, 1, @on
exec sp_trace_setevent @TraceID, 10, 9, @on
exec sp_trace_setevent @TraceID, 10, 2, @on
exec sp_trace_setevent @TraceID, 10, 66, @on
exec sp_trace_setevent @TraceID, 10, 10, @on
exec sp_trace_setevent @TraceID, 10, 3, @on
exec sp_trace_setevent @TraceID, 10, 4, @on
exec sp_trace_setevent @TraceID, 10, 6, @on
exec sp_trace_setevent @TraceID, 10, 7, @on
exec sp_trace_setevent @TraceID, 10, 8, @on
exec sp_trace_setevent @TraceID, 10, 11, @on
exec sp_trace_setevent @TraceID, 10, 12, @on
exec sp_trace_setevent @TraceID, 10, 13, @on
```

NOTE

As of SQL Server 2008, all non-XML events mentioned earlier, such as Showplan All, Showplan Text, and so on, are deprecated. Microsoft recommends using the XML events instead. SQL Trace has also been deprecated as of SQL Server 2012. Instead, Microsoft recommends using extended events.

For more details about using Profiler and SQL Trace, refer to SQL Server Books Online.

Extended Events

You can also use extended events to capture execution plans. Although in general, Microsoft recommends using extended events over SQL Trace, as mentioned earlier, the events to capture execution plans are expensive to collect on the current releases of SQL Server. The documentation shows the following warning for all three extended events available to capture execution plans: "Using this event can have a significant performance overhead so it should only be used when troubleshooting or monitoring specific problems for brief periods of time."

You can create and start an extended events session by using CREATE EVENT SESSION and ALTER EVENT SESSION. You can also use the new graphic user interface introduced in SQL Server 2012. Here are the events related to execution plans:

▶ **query_post_compilation_showplan** Occurs after a SQL statement is compiled. This event returns an XML representation of the estimated query plan that is generated when the query is compiled.

▶ **query_post_execution_showplan** Occurs after a SQL statement is executed. This event returns an XML representation of the actual query plan.

▶ **query_pre_execution_showplan** Occurs after a SQL statement is compiled. This event returns an XML representation of the estimated query plan that is generated when the query is optimized.

For example, let's suppose you want to start a session to trace the query_post_execution_showplan event. You could use the following code to create the extended event session:

```
CREATE EVENT SESSION [test] ON SERVER
ADD EVENT sqlserver.query_post_execution_showplan(
    ACTION(sqlserver.plan_handle)
    WHERE ([sqlserver].[database_name]=N'AdventureWorks2012'))
ADD TARGET package0.ring_buffer
WITH (STARTUP_STATE=OFF)
GO
```

More details about extended events will be covered in Chapter 2. In the meantime, you can notice that the ADD EVENT argument shows the event name (in this case, query_post_execution_showplan), ACTION refers to global fields you want to capture in the event session (in this case, plan_handle), and WHERE is used to apply a filter to limit the data you want to capture. The predicate [sqlserver].[database_name]=N'AdventureWorks2012' indicates that we want to capture events for the AdventureWorks2012 database only. TARGET is the event consumer, and we can use it to collect the data for analysis. In this case, we are using the ring buffer target. Finally, STARTUP_STATE is one of the extended event options, and it is used to specify whether or not this event session is automatically started when SQL Server starts.

After the event session is created, you can start it using the ALTER EVENT SESSION statement, as in the following example:

```
ALTER EVENT SESSION [test]
ON SERVER
STATE=START
```

You can use the Watch Live Data feature, introduced with SQL Server 2012, to view the data captured by the event session. In order to do that, expand the Management folder in Object Explorer | Extended Events | Sessions, right-click the extended event session, and select Watch Live Data. Figure 1-18 shows how an example of an execution plan is captured.

You can also run the following code to see this data:

```
SELECT
    event_data.value('(event/@name)[1]', 'varchar(50)') AS event_name,
    event_data.value('(event/action[@name="plan_handle"]/value)[1]',
        'varchar(max)') as plan_handle,
    event_data.query('event/data[@name="showplan_xml"]/value/*') as showplan_xml,
    event_data.value('(event/action[@name="sql_text"]/value)[1]',
        'varchar(max)') AS sql_text
FROM(   SELECT evnt.query('.') AS event_data
    FROM
    (   SELECT CAST(target_data AS xml) AS target_data
        FROM sys.dm_xe_sessions AS s
        JOIN sys.dm_xe_session_targets AS t
            ON s.address = t.event_session_address
        WHERE s.name = 'test'
            AND t.target_name = 'ring_buffer'
    ) AS data
    CROSS APPLY target_data.nodes('RingBufferTarget/event') AS xevent(evnt)
) AS xevent(event_data)
```

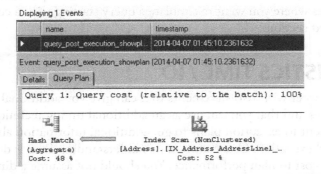

Figure 1-18 *Watch Live Data feature*

After you finish your test, you need to stop and delete the event session. Run the following statements:

```
ALTER EVENT SESSION [test]
ON SERVER
STATE=STOP
GO
DROP EVENT SESSION [test] ON SERVER
```

Finally, some other SQL Server tools can allow you to see plans, including the Data Collector. The Data Collector was introduced with SQL Server 2008 and will be covered in Chapter 2.

Removing Plans from the Plan Cache

You can use a few different commands to remove plans from the plan cache. These commands, covered in more detail in Chapter 8, can be useful during your testing and should not be executed in a production environment, unless the requested effect is desired. The DBCC FREEPROCCACHE statement can be used to remove all the entries from the plan cache. It can also accept a plan handle or a SQL handle to remove only specific plans, or a Resource Governor pool name to remove all the cache entries associated with it. The DBCC FREESYSTEMCACHE statement can be used to remove all the elements from the plan cache or only the elements associated with a Resource Governor pool name. DBCC FLUSHPROCINDB can be used to remove all the cached plans for a particular database.

Finally, although not related to the plan cache, the DBCC DROPCLEANBUFFERS statement can be used to remove all the buffers from the buffer pool. You can use this statement in cases where you want to simulate a query starting with a cold cache, as we will do in the next section.

SET STATISTICS TIME / IO

We close this chapter with two statements that can give you additional information about your queries and that you can use as an additional tuning technique. These can be a great complement to execution plans to get additional information about your queries' optimization and execution. One common misunderstanding I see is developers trying to compare plan cost to plan performance. You should not assume a direct correlation between a query-estimated cost and its actual runtime performance. Cost is an internal unit used by the query optimizer and should not be used to compare plan performance; SET STATISTICS TIME and SET STATISTICS IO can be used instead. This section explains both statements.

You can use SET STATISTICS TIME to see the number of milliseconds required to parse, compile, and execute each statement. For example, run

```
SET STATISTICS TIME ON
```

and then run the following query:

```
SELECT DISTINCT(CustomerID)
FROM Sales.SalesOrderHeader
```

To see the output, you will have to look at the Messages tab of the edit window, which will show an output similar to the following:

```
SQL Server parse and compile time:
   CPU time = 16 ms, elapsed time = 226 ms.

 SQL Server Execution Times:
   CPU time = 16 ms,  elapsed time = 148 ms.
```

"Parse and compile" refers to the time SQL Server takes to optimize the SQL statement, as explained earlier. SET STATISTICS TIME will continue to be enabled for any subsequently executed queries. You can disable it like so:

```
SET STATISTICS TIME OFF
```

As mentioned previously, parse and compile information can also be seen on the execution plan, as in the following:

```
<QueryPlan DegreeOfParallelism="1" CachedPlanSize="16" CompileTime="226"
CompileCPU="9" CompileMemory="232">
```

Obviously, if you only need the execution time of each query, you can see this information in the Management Studio Query Editor.

SET STATISTICS IO displays the amount of disk activity generated by a query. To enable it, run the following statement:

```
SET STATISTICS IO ON
```

Run this next statement to clean all the buffers from the buffer pool to make sure that no pages for this table are loaded in memory:

```
DBCC DROPCLEANBUFFERS
```

Then run the following query:

```
SELECT * FROM Sales.SalesOrderDetail
WHERE ProductID = 870
```

It will show an output similar to the following:

```
Table 'SalesOrderDetail'. Scan count 1, logical reads 1246, physical reads 3,
read-ahead reads 1277, lob logical reads 0, lob physical reads 0,
lob read-ahead reads 0.
```

Here are the definitions of these items, which all use 8K pages:

▶ **Logical reads**   Number of pages read from the buffer pool.

▶ **Physical reads**   Number of pages read from disk.

▶ **Read-ahead reads**   Read-ahead is a performance optimization mechanism that anticipates the needed data pages and reads them from disk. It can read up to 64 contiguous pages from one data file.

▶ **Lob logical reads**   Number of large object (LOB) pages read from the buffer pool.

▶ **Lob physical reads**   Number of large object (LOB) pages read from disk.

▶ **Lob read-ahead reads**   Number of large object (LOB) pages read from disk using the read-ahead mechanism, as explained earlier.

Now, if you run the same query again, you will no longer get physical and read-ahead reads, and you will get an output similar to this:

```
Table 'SalesOrderDetail'. Scan count 1, logical reads 1246, physical reads 0,
read-ahead reads 0, lob logical reads 0, lob physical reads 0,
lob read-ahead reads 0.
```

"Scan count" is defined as the number of seeks or scans started after reaching the leaf level (that is, the bottom level of an index). The only case when scan count will return 0 is when you're seeking for only one value on a unique index, like in the following example:

```
SELECT * FROM Sales.SalesOrderHeader
WHERE SalesOrderID = 51119
```

If you try the following query, in which SalesOrderID is defined in a nonunique index and can return more than one record, you can see that scan count now returns 1:

```
SELECT * FROM Sales.SalesOrderDetail
WHERE SalesOrderID = 51119
```

Finally, in the following example, scan count is 4 because SQL Server has to perform four seeks:

```
SELECT * FROM Sales.SalesOrderHeader
WHERE SalesOrderID IN (51119, 43664, 63371, 75119)
```

Summary

In this chapter, I showed you how a better understanding of what the query processor does behind the scenes can help both database administrators and developers write better queries and provide the query optimizer with the information it needs to produce efficient execution plans. In the same way, I showed you how you can use your newfound knowledge of the query processor inner workings and SQL Server tools to troubleshoot the cases when your queries are not performing as expected. Based on this, the basics of the query optimizer, the execution engine, and the plan cache were explained, and these SQL Server components will be covered in greater detail in later chapters.

Because we will be using execution plans throughout the entire book, I also introduced you to how to read them, their more important properties, and how to obtain them from sources such as the plan cache and a server trace. This section should have given you enough background to follow along through the rest of the book. Query operators were also introduced but will be covered in a lot more detail in Chapter 4 and other sections of the book.

In the next chapter, I provide you with additional tuning tools and techniques such as using SQL Trace, extended events, and DMVs to find out which queries are consuming the most resources or to find out some other performance-related problems.

Chapter 2

Troubleshooting Queries

In This Chapter

In Chapter 1, I introduced you to reading execution plans as the primary tool we'll use to interact with the SQL Server query processor. I also showed you the SET STATISTICS TIME and SET STATISTICS IO statements, which can provide you with additional performance information about your queries. In this chapter we continue where we left off in Chapter 1. I will show you additional tuning tools and techniques you can use to find out how much server resources your queries are using and how to find the most expensive queries on your system.

Dynamic management views (DMVs) were introduced with SQL Server 2005 as a great tool to diagnose problems, tune performance, and monitor the health of a server instance. Many DMVs are available, and the first section in this chapter focuses on sys.dm_exec_requests, sys.dm_exec_sessions, and sys.dm_exec_query_stats, which you can use to find out the server resources, such as CPU and I/O, used by queries running on the system. Many more DMVs will be introduced in other chapters of the book, including later in this chapter when I cover extended events.

Although SQL Trace has been deprecated as of SQL Server 2012, it's still widely used and will be available in some of the next versions of SQL Server. SQL Trace is usually related to SQL Server Profiler because using this tool is the easiest way to define and run a trace, and it is also the tool of choice for scripting and creating a server trace, which is used in some scenarios where running Profiler directly may be expensive. In this chapter, I'll cover some of the trace events we would be more interested in when tracing query execution for performance problems.

Following on the same concept as SQL Trace, in the next section, I will introduce extended events. All the basic concepts and definitions are explained first, including events, predicates, actions, targets, and sessions, and then we will create some sessions to obtain performance information about your queries. Because most SQL Server professionals are already familiar with SQL Trace or Profiler, I also include a section to show you how you can map the old trace events to the new extended events events.

Finally, the Data Collector, a feature introduced with SQL Server 2008, will be shown as a tool that can help you to proactively collect performance data that can be used to troubleshoot performance problems when they occur.

DMVs and DMFs

In this section I'll show you several dynamic management views (DMVs) and dynamic management functions (DMFs) that can help you to find out the amount of server resources used by your queries and to find the most expensive queries in your SQL Server instance.

sys.dm_exec_requests and sys.dm_exec_sessions

The sys.dm_exec_requests DMV can be used to display the requests currently executing on SQL Server, whereas sys.dm_exec_sessions shows the authenticated sessions on the instance. Although these DMVs include many columns, in this section, we will focus on the ones related to resource usage and query performance. You can look at the definitions of the other columns on Books Online.

Both DMVs share several columns, which are defined next:

Column	Definition
cpu_time	CPU time in milliseconds used by this request or by the requests in this session
total_elapsed_time	Total time elapsed in milliseconds since the request arrived or the session was established
reads	Number of reads performed by this request or by the requests in this session
writes	Number of writes performed by this request or by the requests in this session
logical_reads	Number of logical reads that have been performed by the request or by the requests in this session
row_count	Number of rows that have been returned to the client by this request

Basically, sys.dm_exec_requests will show the resources used by a specific request currently executing, whereas sys.dm_exec_sessions will show the accumulated resources of all the requests completed by a session. To understand how these two DMVs collect resources' usage information, we can run the following exercise, using a query that takes at least a few seconds. Open a new query in Management Studio and get its session ID (for example, using SELECT @@SPID), but make sure you don't run anything yet on it because the resource usage will be accumulated on the sys.dm_exec_sessions DMV. Copy and be ready to run the following code on that window:

```
DBCC FREEPROCCACHE
DBCC DROPCLEANBUFFERS
GO
SELECT * FROM Production.Product p1 CROSS JOIN
Production.Product p2
```

Copy the following code to a second window, replacing session_id with the value you obtained in the first window:

```
SELECT cpu_time, reads, total_elapsed_time, logical_reads, row_count
FROM sys.dm_exec_requests
WHERE session_id = 56
GO
SELECT cpu_time, reads, total_elapsed_time, logical_reads, row_count
FROM sys.dm_exec_sessions
WHERE session_id = 56
```

Run the query on the first session and at the same time run the code on the second session several times to see the resources used. The next output shows a sample execution while the query is still running and has not completed yet. Notice that the sys.dm_exec_requests DMV shows the partially used resources and that sys.dm_exec_ sessions shows no used resources yet. Most likely, you will not see the same results for sys.dm_exec_requests.

cpu_time	reads	total_elapsed_time	logical_reads	row_count
468	62	4767	5868	1

cpu_time	reads	total_elapsed_time	logical_reads	row_count
0	0	5	0	1

After the query completes, the original request no longer exists and sys.dm_exec_ sessions now records the resources used by the first query:

cpu_time	reads	total_elapsed_time	logical_reads	row_count

cpu_time	reads	total_elapsed_time	logical_reads	row_count
671	62	6996	8192	254016

If you run the query on the first session again, sys.dm_exec_sessions will accumulate the resources used by both executions, so the values of the results will be slightly more than twice their previous values, as shown next:

cpu_time	reads	total_elapsed_time	logical_reads	row_count

cpu_time	reads	total_elapsed_time	logical_reads	row_count
1295	124	14062	16384	254016

Keep in mind that CPU time and duration may vary slightly during different executions and most likely you will get different values as well. Reads is 8,192 for this execution, and we see the accumulated value 16,384 for two executions. In addition, the sys.dm_exec_requests DMV only shows information of currently executing queries, so you may not see this particular data if a query completes before you are able to query it.

In summary, sys.dm_exec_requests and sys.dm_exec_sessions are useful to inspect the resources currently used by a request or the accumulation of resources used by requests on a session since creation.

sys.dm_exec_query_stats

If you ever worked with any version of SQL Server older than SQL Server 2005, you may remember how difficult it was to find out the most expensive queries in your instance. Performing that kind of analysis would usually require running a server trace in your instance for a period of time and then analyzing the collected data, usually in the size of gigabytes, using third-party tools or your own created methods (a very time-consuming process). Not to mention the fact that running such a trace could also affect the performance of a system, which most likely is having a performance problem already.

DMVs were introduced with SQL Server 2005 and are a great help to diagnose problems, tune performance, and monitor the health of a server instance. In particular, sys.dm_exec_query_stats provides a rich amount of information not available before in SQL Server regarding aggregated performance statistics for cached query plans. This information helps to avoid the need to run a trace, as mentioned earlier, in most of the cases. This view returns a row for each statement available in the plan cache, and SQL Server 2008 added enhancements such as the query hash and plan hash values, which will be explained soon.

Let's take a quick look at understanding how sys.dm_exec_query_stats works and the information it provides. Create the following stored procedure with three simple queries:

```
CREATE PROC test
AS
SELECT * FROM Sales.SalesOrderDetail WHERE SalesOrderID = 60677
SELECT * FROM Person.Address WHERE AddressID = 21
SELECT * FROM HumanResources.Employee WHERE BusinessEntityID = 229
```

Run the following code to clean the plan cache (so it is easier to inspect), remove all the clean buffers from the buffer pool, execute the created test stored procedure, and inspect the plan cache. Note that the code uses the sys.dm_exec_sql_text DMF, which requires a sql_handle or plan_handle value and returns the text of the SQL batch.

```
DBCC FREEPROCCACHE
DBCC DROPCLEANBUFFERS
GO
EXEC test
GO
SELECT * FROM sys.dm_exec_query_stats
CROSS APPLY sys.dm_exec_sql_text(sql_handle)
WHERE objectid = OBJECT_ID('dbo.test')
```

Examine the output. Because the number of columns is too large to show in this book, only some of the columns are shown next:

statement_ start_offset	statement_ end_offset	execution_ count	total_ worker_ time	last_ worker_ time	min_ worker_ time	max_ worker_ time	Text
44	168	1	532	532	532	532	CREATE PROC test AS ...
174	270	1	622	622	622	622	CREATE PROC test AS ...
276	406	1	667	667	667	667	CREATE PROC test AS ...

As you can see by looking at the query text, all three queries were compiled as part of the same batch, which we can also verify by validating they have the same plan_handle and the same sql_handle. The statement_start_offset and statement_end_offset can be used to identify the particular queries in the batch, a process that will be explained later in this section. You can also see in this output the number of times the query was executed and several columns showing the CPU time used by each query, as total_worker_time, last_worker_time, min_worker_time, and max_worker_time. Should the query be executed more than once, the statistics would show the accumulated CPU time on total_worker_time. Not shown in the previous output are additional performance statistics for physical reads, logical writes, logical reads, CLR time, and elapsed time. Table 2-1 shows the list of columns, including performance statistics and their documented description.

Keep in mind that this view only shows statistics for completed query executions. You can look at sys.dm_exec_requests, as explained earlier, for information about queries

Column	Description
total_worker_time	Total amount of CPU time, reported in microseconds (but only accurate to milliseconds), that was consumed by executions of this plan since it was compiled.
last_worker_time	CPU time, reported in microseconds (but only accurate to milliseconds), that was consumed the last time the plan was executed.
min_worker_time	Minimum CPU time, reported in microseconds (but only accurate to milliseconds), that this plan has ever consumed during a single execution.

Table 2-1   *sys.dm_exec_query_stats Performance Statistics Columns*

Column	Description
max_worker_time	Maximum CPU time, reported in microseconds (but only accurate to milliseconds), that this plan has ever consumed during a single execution.
total_physical_reads	Total number of physical reads performed by executions of this plan since it was compiled.
last_physical_reads	Number of physical reads performed the last time the plan was executed.
min_physical_reads	Minimum number of physical reads that this plan has ever performed during a single execution.
max_physical_reads	Maximum number of physical reads that this plan has ever performed during a single execution.
total_logical_writes	Total number of logical writes performed by executions of this plan since it was compiled.
last_logical_writes	Number of logical writes performed the last time the plan was executed.
min_logical_writes	Minimum number of logical writes that this plan has ever performed during a single execution.
max_logical_writes	Maximum number of logical writes that this plan has ever performed during a single execution.
total_logical_reads	Total number of logical reads performed by executions of this plan since it was compiled.
last_logical_reads	Number of logical reads performed the last time the plan was executed.
min_logical_reads	Minimum number of logical reads that this plan has ever performed during a single execution.
max_logical_reads	Maximum number of logical reads that this plan has ever performed during a single execution.
total_clr_time	Time, reported in microseconds (but only accurate to milliseconds), consumed inside Microsoft .NET Framework common language runtime (CLR) objects by executions of this plan since it was compiled. The CLR objects can be stored procedures, functions, triggers, types, and aggregates.
last_clr_time	Time, reported in microseconds (but only accurate to milliseconds), consumed by execution inside .NET Framework CLR objects during the last execution of this plan. The CLR objects can be stored procedures, functions, triggers, types, and aggregates.
min_clr_time	Minimum time, reported in microseconds (but only accurate to milliseconds), that this plan has ever consumed inside .NET Framework CLR objects during a single execution. The CLR objects can be stored procedures, functions, triggers, types, and aggregates.
max_clr_time	Maximum time, reported in microseconds (but only accurate to milliseconds), that this plan has ever consumed inside the .NET Framework CLR during a single execution. The CLR objects can be stored procedures, functions, triggers, types, and aggregates.
total_elapsed_time	Total elapsed time, reported in microseconds (but only accurate to milliseconds), for completed executions of this plan.
last_elapsed_time	Elapsed time, reported in microseconds (but only accurate to milliseconds), for the most recently completed execution of this plan.
min_elapsed_time	Minimum elapsed time, reported in microseconds (but only accurate to milliseconds), for any completed execution of this plan.
max_elapsed_time	Maximum elapsed time, reported in microseconds (but only accurate to milliseconds), for any completed execution of this plan.

Table 2-1 *sys.dm_exec_query_stats Performance Statistics Columns* (Continued)

currently executing. Finally, as explained in Chapter 1, certain types of execution plans may never be cached, and some cached plans may also be removed from the plan cache for several reasons, including internal or external memory pressure on the plan cache. Information for these plans will not be available on sys.dm_exec_query_stats.

Let's now take a look at the statement_start_offset and statement_end_offset values.

Understanding statement_start_offset and statement_end_offset

As you can see from the previous output of sys.dm_exec_query_stats, the sql_handle, the plan_handle, and the text column showing the code for the stored procedure are exactly the same in all three records. The same plan and query are used for the entire batch. So how do we identify each of the SQL statements, for example, supposing that only one of them is really expensive? We have to use the statement_start_offset and statement_end_offset columns. statement_start_offset is defined as the starting position of the query that the row describes within the text of its batch, whereas statement_end_offset is the ending position of the query that the row describes within the text of its batch. Both statement_start_offset and statement_end_offset are indicated in bytes, starting with 0, and a value of −1 indicates the end of the batch.

We can easily extend our previous query to inspect the plan cache to use statement_start_offset and statement_end_offset and get something like the following code:

```
DBCC FREEPROCCACHE
DBCC DROPCLEANBUFFERS
GO
EXEC test
GO
SELECT SUBSTRING(text, (statement_start_offset/2) + 1,
((CASE statement_end_offset
WHEN -1
    THEN DATALENGTH(text)
ELSE
    statement_end_offset
END
    - statement_start_offset)/2) + 1) AS statement_text, *
FROM sys.dm_exec_query_stats
CROSS APPLY sys.dm_exec_sql_text(sql_handle)
WHERE objectid = OBJECT_ID('dbo.test')
```

This would produce output similar to the following (only a few columns are shown):

statement_text	statement_start_offset	statement_end_offset
SELECT * FROM Sales.SalesOrderDetail WHERE SalesOrderID = 60677	44	168
SELECT * FROM Person.Address WHERE AddressID = 21	174	270
SELECT * FROM HumanResources.Employee WHERE BusinessEntityID = 229	276	406

Basically, the query makes use of the SUBSTRING function as well as statement_start_offset and statement_end_offset values, to obtain the text of the query within the batch. Division by 2 is required because the text data is stored as Unicode.

To test the concept for a particular query, you can replace the values for statement_start_offset and statement_end_offset directly for the first statement (44 and 168, respectively) and provide the sql_handle or plan_handle, as shown next, to get the first statement returned:

```
SELECT SUBSTRING(text, 44 / 2 + 1, (168 - 44) / 2 + 1) FROM sys.dm_exec_
sql_text(0x03000500996DB224E0B27201B7A10000010000000000000000000000000
00000000000000000000000000000)
```

sql_handle and plan_handle

The sql_handle value is a hash value that refers to the batch or stored procedure the query is part of and can be used in the sys.dm_exec_sql_text DMF to retrieve the text of the query, as demonstrated previously. Using the example before

```
SELECT * from sys.dm_exec_sql_text(0x03000500996DB224E0B27201B
7A10000010000000000000000000000000000000000000000000000000000)
```

we would get the following in return:

dbid	objectid	number	encrypted	text
5	615673241	1	0	CREATE PROC test AS SELECT * FROM ...

The sql_handle hash is guaranteed to be unique for every batch in the system. The text of the batch is stored in the SQL Manager Cache or SQLMGR, which you can inspect by running the following query:

```
SELECT * FROM sys.dm_os_memory_objects
WHERE type = 'MEMOBJ_SQLMGR'
```

Because a sql_handle has a 1:N relationship with a plan_handle (that is, there can be more than one generated executed plan for a particular query), the text of the batch will remain on the SQLMGR cache store until the last of the generated plans is evicted from the plan cache.

The plan_handle value is a hash value that refers to the execution plan the query is part of and can be used in the sys.dm_exec_query_plan DMF to retrieve such an execution plan. It is guaranteed to be unique for every batch in the system and will remain the same even if one or more statements in the batch are recompiled. Here is an example:

```
SELECT * FROM sys.dm_exec_query_plan(0x05000500996DB224B0C9B
8F80100000001000000000000000000000000000000000000000000000000)
```

Running the code will return the following output, and clicking the query_plan link will display the requested graphical execution plan:

dbid	objectid	number	encrypted	query_plan
5	615673241	1	0	<ShowPlanXML xmlns="http://schemas.microsoft.com/ sqlserver/2004/07/showplan" ...

Cached execution plans are stored in the SQLCP and OBJCP cache stores: object plans, including stored procedures, triggers, and functions, are stored in the OBJCP cache stores, whereas plans for ad hoc, autoparameterized, and prepared queries are stored in the SQLCP cache store.

query_hash and plan_hash

Although sys.dm_exec_query_stats was a great resource, providing performance statistics for cached query plans when it was introduced in SQL Server 2005, one of its limitations was that it was not easy to aggregate the information for the same query when this query was not parameterized. The query_hash and plan_hash columns, introduced with SQL Server 2008, provide a solution to this problem. To understand the problem, let's look at an example of the behavior of sys.dm_exec_query_stats when a query is autoparameterized:

```
DBCC FREEPROCCACHE
DBCC DROPCLEANBUFFERS
GO
SELECT * FROM Person.Address
WHERE AddressID = 12
GO
SELECT * FROM Person.Address
WHERE AddressID = 37
GO
SELECT * FROM sys.dm_exec_query_stats
```

Because in this case AddressID is part of a unique index, the predicate AddressID = 12 would always return a maximum of one record, so it is safe for the query optimizer to autoparameterize the query and use the same plan. Here is the output:

sql_handle	execution_ count	query_ hash	query_ plan_hash
0x020000002D83010497EDC81695B0146B2F0000B7 B2D28D190000000000000000000000000000000000000000	2	0x10E4AFA 44470632D	0x1C9E602 B6F826BBC

In this case, we have only one plan, reused for the second execution, as shown in the execution_count value. Therefore, we can also see that plan reuse is another benefit of parameterized queries. However, we can see a different behavior with the following query:

```
DBCC FREEPROCCACHE
DBCC DROPCLEANBUFFERS
GO
SELECT * FROM Person.Address
WHERE StateProvinceID = 79
GO
SELECT * FROM Person.Address
WHERE StateProvinceID = 59
GO
SELECT * FROM sys.dm_exec_query_stats
```

Because a filter with an equality comparison on StateProvinceID could return zero, one, or more values, it is not considered safe for SQL Server to autoparameterize the query; in fact, both executions return different execution plans. Here is the output:

sql_handle	query_hash	query_plan_hash
0x020000000E311524E986FAF37BD4D922A18E2A758EFF1 A230000000000000000000000000000000000000000000	0x1891A5D AEB303AE2	0x03D4D190 651B0551
0x02000000EBFDF423379C4875CCC482ACD143308C504C7 2F100000000000000000000000000000000000000000000	0x1891A5D AEB303AE2	0xAE5E89B 0A490F3C9

As you can see, the sql_handle, the plan_handle (not shown), and the query_plan_hash have different values because the generated plans are actually different. However, the query_hash is the same because it is the same query, only with a different parameter. Supposing that this was the most expensive query in the system and there are multiple executions with different parameters, it would be very difficult to find out that all those execution plans actually do belong to the same query. This is where query_hash can help. You can use query_hash to aggregate performance statistics of similar queries that are not explicitly or implicitly parameterized. Both query_hash and plan_hash are available on the sys.dm_exec_query_stats and sys.dm_exec_requests DMVs.

The query_hash value is calculated from the tree of logical operators created after parsing just before query optimization. This logical tree is used as the input to the query optimizer. Because of this, two or more queries do not need to have exactly the same text to produce the same query_hash value, as parameters, comments, and some other minor differences are not considered. And, as shown in the first example, two queries with the same query_hash value can have different execution plans (that is, different query_plan_hash values). On the other hand, the query_plan_hash is calculated from the tree of physical operators that makes up an execution plan. Basically, if two plans are the same, although very minor differences are not considered, they will produce the same plan hash value as well.

Finally, a limitation of the hashing algorithms is that they can cause collisions, but the probability of this happening is extremely low. This basically means that two similar queries may produce different query_hash values or that two different queries may produce the same query_hash value, but again, the probability of this happening is extremely low and it should not be a concern.

Finding Expensive Queries

Let's now apply some of the concepts explained in this section and use the sys.dm_exec_query_stats DMV to find the most expensive queries in your system. A typical query to find the most expensive queries on the plan cache based on CPU is shown next. Note that the query is grouping on the query_hash value to aggregate similar queries, regardless of whether or not they are parameterized.

```
SELECT TOP 20 query_stats.query_hash,
    SUM(query_stats.total_worker_time) / SUM(query_stats.execution_count)
        AS avg_cpu_time,
    MIN(query_stats.statement_text) AS statement_text
FROM
    (SELECT qs.*,
    SUBSTRING(st.text, (qs.statement_start_offset/2) + 1,
```

```
    ((CASE statement_end_offset
        WHEN -1 THEN DATALENGTH(ST.text)
        ELSE qs.statement_end_offset END
            - qs.statement_start_offset)/2) + 1) AS statement_text
    FROM sys.dm_exec_query_stats qs
    CROSS APPLY sys.dm_exec_sql_text(qs.sql_handle) AS st) AS query_stats
GROUP BY query_stats.query_hash
ORDER BY avg_cpu_time DESC
```

You may also notice that each returned row represents a query in a batch (for example, a batch with five queries would have five records on the sys.dm_exec_query_stats DMV, as explained earlier). We could trim the previous query into something like the following query to focus at the batch and plan level instead. Notice that there is no need to use the statement_start_offset and statement_end_offset columns to separate the particular queries and that this time we are grouping on the query_plan_hash value.

```
SELECT TOP 20 query_plan_hash,
    SUM(total_worker_time) / SUM(execution_count) AS avg_cpu_time,
    MIN(plan_handle) AS plan_handle, MIN(text) AS query_text
FROM sys.dm_exec_query_stats qs
    CROSS APPLY sys.dm_exec_sql_text(qs.plan_handle) AS st
GROUP BY query_plan_hash
ORDER BY avg_cpu_time DESC
```

These examples are based on CPU time (worker time). Therefore, in the same way, you can update these queries to look for other resources listed on sys.dm_exec_query_stats, such as physical reads, logical writes, logical reads, CLR time, and elapsed time.

Finally, we could also apply the same concept to find the most expensive queries currently executing, based on the sys.dm_exec_requests, like in the following query:

```
SELECT TOP 20 SUBSTRING(st.text, (er.statement_start_offset/2) + 1,
    ((CASE statement_end_offset
WHEN -1
    THEN DATALENGTH(st.text)
ELSE
    er.statement_end_offset
END
- er.statement_start_offset)/2) + 1) AS statement_text
, *
FROM sys.dm_exec_requests er
CROSS APPLY sys.dm_exec_sql_text(er.sql_handle) st
ORDER BY total_elapsed_time DESC
```

SQL Trace

SQL Trace is a SQL Server feature you can use to troubleshoot performance issues. It has been available for several versions of SQL Server, so it is well known by database developers and administrators. However, as noted in Chapter 1, SQL Trace has been deprecated as of SQL Server 2012, and Microsoft recommends using extended events instead.

Although you can trace dozens of events using SQL Trace, in this section, I focus on the ones you can use to measure query resources usage. Because running a trace can take some resources itself, usually, you would want to run it only when you are troubleshooting a query problem, instead of running it all the time. Here are the main trace events we are concerned with regarding query resources usage:

Stored Procedures	RPC:Completed	Occurs when a remote procedure call has been completed.
	SP:Completed	Indicates when the stored procedure has completed.
	SP:StmtCompleted	Indicates that a SQL statement within a stored procedure has completed.
T-SQL	SQL:BatchCompleted	Occurs when a SQL batch has completed.
	SQL:StmtCompleted	Occurs when the SQL statement has completed.

Figure 2-1 shows an example of such a trace configuration on SQL Server Profiler. Usually you would want to use Profiler to run the trace probably for a very short time. If you need to run the trace for, say, hours or a few days, a server trace may be a better choice because it uses fewer resources. Chapter 1 showed how you can use Profiler to script and run a server trace.

Now let's see how it works. Run Profiler and select the previous five events. Run the trace and then execute the following ad hoc query in Management Studio:

```
SELECT * FROM Sales.SalesOrderDetail WHERE SalesOrderID = 60677
```

This query execution will trigger the following events:

▶ SQL:StmtCompleted. SELECT * FROM Sales.SalesOrderDetail WHERE SalesOrderID = 60677

▶ SQL:BatchCompleted. SELECT * FROM Sales.SalesOrderDetail WHERE SalesOrderID = 60677

You could look for ApplicationName as "Microsoft SQL Server Management Studio – Query" in case you see more events. You may also consider filtering by SPID using Profiler's filtering capabilities.

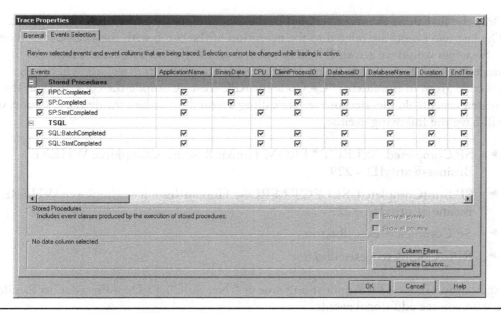

Figure 2-1 *Trace configuration using SQL Server Profiler*

If, on the other hand, we create and execute the same query as part of a simple stored procedure, such as

```
CREATE PROC test
AS
SELECT * FROM HumanResources.Employee WHERE BusinessEntityID = 229
```

and run it, as in

```
EXEC test
```

we would hit the following events:

► SP:StmtCompleted. SELECT * FROM HumanResources.Employee WHERE BusinessEntityID = 229

► SP:Completed. SELECT * FROM HumanResources.Employee WHERE BusinessEntityID = 229

► SP:Completed. EXEC test

► SQL:StmtCompleted. EXEC test

► SQL:BatchCompleted. EXEC test

Only the first three events are related to the execution of the stored procedure per se. The last two events are related to the execution of the batch with the EXEC statement.

So when would we see an RPC:Completed event? For this, we need a remote procedure call (for example, using a .NET application). For this test, we will use the C# code given in the sidebar "C# Code for RPC Test." Compile the code and run the created executable file. Because we are calling a stored procedure inside the C# code, we will have the following events:

▶ SP:Completed. SELECT * FROM HumanResources.Employee WHERE BusinessEntityID = 229

▶ SP:StmtCompleted. SELECT * FROM HumanResources.Employee WHERE BusinessEntityID = 229

▶ SP:Completed. exec dbo.test

▶ RPC:Completed. exec dbo.test

Again, you can look for ApplicationName as ".Net SqlClient Data Provider" in Profiler in case you see additional events.

C# Code for RPC Test

Although looking at .NET code is outside the scope of this book, you can use the following code for the test:

```csharp
using System;
using System.Data;
using System.Data.SqlClient;

class Test
{
    static void Main()
    {
        SqlConnection cnn = null;
        SqlDataReader reader = null;

        try
        {
            cnn = new SqlConnection("Data Source=(local);
                Initial Catalog=AdventureWorks2012;Integrated Security=SSPI");
            SqlCommand cmd = new SqlCommand();
            cmd.Connection = cnn;
            cmd.CommandText = "dbo.test";
```

```
        cmd.CommandType = CommandType.StoredProcedure;
        cnn.Open();
        reader = cmd.ExecuteReader();
        while (reader.Read())
        {
            Console.WriteLine(reader[0]);
        }
        return;
    }
    catch (Exception e)
    {
        throw e;
    }
    finally
    {
        if (cnn != null)
        {
            if (cnn.State != ConnectionState.Closed)
                cnn.Close();
        }
    }
  }
}
```

To compile the C# code, run the following in a command prompt window:

```
csc test.cs
```

You don't need Visual Studio installed, just the Microsoft .NET Framework, which is required to install SQL Server, so it will already be available on your system. You may need to find the CSC executable, though, if it is not included on the system PATH, although it is usually inside the C:\Windows\Microsoft.NET directory. You may also need to edit the used connection string, which assumes you are connecting to a default instance of SQL Server using Windows authentication.

Extended Events

I briefly introduced extended events in Chapter 1 in order to show you how to capture execution plans, and in this section, I provide more information about this feature introduced with SQL Server 2008. There is another important reason for this: as of SQL Server 2012, SQL Trace has been deprecated, making extended events the tool of choice to provide debugging and diagnostic capabilities in SQL Server. Although explaining extended events in full detail is beyond the scope of this book, this section gives you enough background to get started using this feature to troubleshoot your queries.

I introduce the basic concepts of extended events here, including events, predicates, actions, targets, and sessions. Although I mainly use code for the examples in this book, I think it is worth showing you the new extended events graphical user interface too, which is useful if you are new to this technology and can also help you script the definition of extended events sessions in pretty much the same way we use Profiler to script a server trace. The extended events graphical user interface was introduced in SQL Server 2012.

One of my favorite things to do with SQL Trace—and now with extended events— is to use it to learn how several SQL Server tools work. You can run a trace against your instance and run any one of the tools to capture all the T-SQL statements sent from the tool to the database engine. Interestingly, the extended events graphical user interface is not an exception, and you can use SQL Trace or extended events to see how it works. When you start the tool, it first loads all the required extended events information, and by tracing it you can see where the information is coming from. Obviously, you don't have to worry about this for now because I will show you some of the extended events DMVs next.

Extended events are designed to have a low impact on the server performance. They correspond to well-known points in the SQL Server code, so when a specific task is executing, SQL Server will perform a quick check to find out if there are any sessions configured to listen to this event. If no sessions are active, the event will not fire and the SQL Server task will continue with no overhead. If, on the other hand, there are active sessions that have the event enabled, SQL Server will collect the required data associated with the event. Then it will validate the predicate, if any, defined for the session. If the predicate evaluates to false, the task will continue with minimal overhead. If the predicate evaluates to true, the actions defined on the session will be executed. Finally, all the event data is collected by the defined targets for later analysis.

You can use the following statement to find out the list of events available on the current version of SQL Server. You can create an extended events session by selecting one or more of the following events:

```
SELECT name, description
FROM sys.dm_xe_objects
WHERE object_type = 'event' AND
(capabilities & 1 = 0 OR capabilities IS NULL)
ORDER BY name
```

Note that 870 events are returned with SQL Server 2014, including sp_statement_completed, sql_batch_completed, and sql_statement_completed, which we will discuss later.

Each event has a set of columns that you can display by using the sys.dm_xe_object_ columns DMV, as in the following code:

```
SELECT o.name, c.name as column_name, c.description
FROM sys.dm_xe_objects o
JOIN sys.dm_xe_object_columns c
ON o.name = c.object_name
WHERE object_type = 'event' AND
c.column_type <> 'readonly' AND
(o.capabilities & 1 = 0 OR o.capabilities IS NULL)
ORDER BY o.name, c.name
```

An *action* is a programmatic response to an event and provides the capability to execute additional code. Although you can use actions to perform operations such as capturing a stack dump or inserting a debugger break in SQL Server, most likely, they will be used to capture global fields that are common to all the events, such as plan_ handle and database_name. Actions are also executed synchronously. You can run the following code to find the entire list of available actions:

```
SELECT name, description
FROM sys.dm_xe_objects
WHERE object_type = 'action' AND
(capabilities & 1 = 0 OR capabilities IS NULL)
ORDER BY name
```

Predicates are used to limit the data you want to capture, and you can filter against event data columns or against any of the global state data returned by the following query:

```
SELECT name, description
FROM sys.dm_xe_objects
WHERE object_type = 'pred_source' AND
(capabilities & 1 = 0 OR capabilities IS NULL)
ORDER BY name
```

The query returns 44 values, including database_id, session_id, and query_hash. Predicates are Boolean expressions that evaluate to either true or false, and they also support short circuiting, in which an entire expression will evaluate to false as soon as any of its predicates evaluates to false.

Finally, you can use *targets* to specify how you want to collect the data for analysis; for example, you can store event data in a file or keep it in the ring buffer (a ring buffer is a data structure that briefly holds event data in memory in a circular way). These targets are named event_file and ring_buffer, respectively. Targets can consume event data both synchronously and asynchronously, and any target can consume any event. You can list the six available targets by running the following query:

```
SELECT name, description
FROM sys.dm_xe_objects
WHERE object_type = 'target' AND
(capabilities & 1 = 0 OR capabilities IS NULL)
ORDER BY name
```

I cover how to use all these concepts to create event sessions later in this chapter, but first I show you how to find the names of events you may be already familiar with when using SQL Trace.

Mapping SQL Trace Events to Extended Events

You are probably already familiar with some SQL Trace events or you even have traces already configured in your environment. You can use the sys.trace_xe_event_map extended events system table to help you map SQL Trace event classes to extended events events. sys.trace_xe_event_map contains one row for each extended events event that is mapped to a SQL Trace event class. To see how it works, run the following query:

```
SELECT te.trace_event_id, name, package_name, xe_event_name
FROM sys.trace_events te
JOIN sys.trace_xe_event_map txe ON te.trace_event_id = txe.trace_event_id
WHERE te.trace_event_id IS NOT NULL
ORDER BY name
```

The query returns 138 records, some of which are shown next.

trace_event_id	name	package_name	xe_event_name
196	Assembly Load	sqlserver	assembly_load
16	Attention	sqlserver	attention
14	Audit Login	sqlserver	login
15	Audit Logout	sqlserver	logout
18	Audit Server Starts And Stops	sqlserver	server_start_stop
58	Auto Stats	sqlserver	auto_stats
193	Background Job Error	sqlserver	background_job_error
212	Bitmap Warning	sqlserver	bitmap_disabled_warning
137	Blocked Process Report	sqlserver	blocked_process_report

In addition, you can use the sys.trace_xe_event_map system table in combination with the sys.fn_trace_geteventinfo function to map the events configured on an existing trace to extended events. The sys.fn_trace_geteventinfo function returns information about a trace currently running and requires its trace ID. To test it, run your trace (explained previously) and run the following statement to get its trace ID. trace_id 1 is usually the default trace, and you may easily identify your trace by looking at the path column on the output, where NULL is shown if you are running a Profiler trace.

```
SELECT * FROM sys.traces
```

Once you get the trace ID, you can run the following code, in this case, using a trace_id value of 2 (used by the sys.fn_trace_geteventinfo function):

```
SELECT te.trace_event_id, name, package_name, xe_event_name
FROM sys.trace_events te
JOIN sys.trace_xe_event_map txe ON te.trace_event_id = txe.trace_event_id
WHERE te.trace_event_id IN (
SELECT DISTINCT(eventid) FROM sys.fn_trace_geteventinfo(2))
ORDER BY name
```

If we run the trace we created previously in the SQL Trace section, we would get the following output:

trace_event_id	name	package_name	xe_event_name
10	RPC:Completed	sqlserver	rpc_completed
43	SP:Completed	sqlserver	module_end
45	SP:StmtCompleted	sqlserver	sp_statement_completed
12	SQL:BatchCompleted	sqlserver	sql_batch_completed
41	SQL:StmtCompleted	sqlserver	sql_statement_completed

As you can see, the event names of our selected SQL Trace events are very similar to their extended events counterparts, except for SP:Completed, whose extended events name is module_end. Here are the definitions of these events:

rpc_completed	Occurs when a remote procedure call has been completed
module_end	Indicates when the stored procedure has completed
sp_statement_completed	Indicates that a SQL statement within a stored procedure has completed
sql_batch_completed	Occurs when a SQL batch has completed
sql_statement_completed	Occurs when the SQL statement has completed

NOTE

SQL Server 2014 comes with several extended events templates. One of them, called Query Detail Sampling, collects detailed statement and error information and includes the five listed events plus error_reported. It also has some predefined actions and predicates, and it uses the ring_buffer target to collect its data. Its predefined predicated filters collect only 20 percent of the active sessions on the server at any given time, so perhaps that is something you may decide to change.

Creating a Session

At this moment, we have enough information to create an extended events session. Extended events include different DDL commands to work with sessions such as CREATE EVENT SESSION, ALTER EVENT SESSION, and DROP EVENT SESSION. But first I will show you how to create a session using the extended events graphical user interface, which you can use to easily create and manage extended events sessions as well as to script the generated CREATE EVENT code. To start, in Management Studio, expand the Management and Extended Event nodes and right-click Sessions.

NOTE

By expanding the Sessions node, you could see two extended events sessions defined by default: AlwaysOn_health and system_health. system_health is started by default every time SQL Server starts, and it is used to collect several predefined events to troubleshoot performance issues. AlwaysOn_health, which is off by default, is a session designed to provide monitoring for Availability Groups, a feature introduced with SQL Server 2012. You can see the events, actions, predicates, targets, and configurations defined for these sessions by looking at their properties or scripting them. To script an extended events session in Management Studio, right-click the session and select both Script Session As and CREATE To.

You should see the New Session Wizard and the New Session dialog. In this section, I briefly introduce the New Session dialog. Once you select it, you should see the screen shown in Figure 2-2, with four different pages: General, Events, Data Storage, and Advanced.

Give the name "Test" to the session and click the Events page in the selection area on the left.

The Events page allows you to select the events for your session. Because this page might have a lot of information, you may want to maximize this window. Searching for events in the event library is allowed; for example, because four of the five events we are looking for contain the word "completed," you could just type this word to search for them, as shown in Figure 2-3.

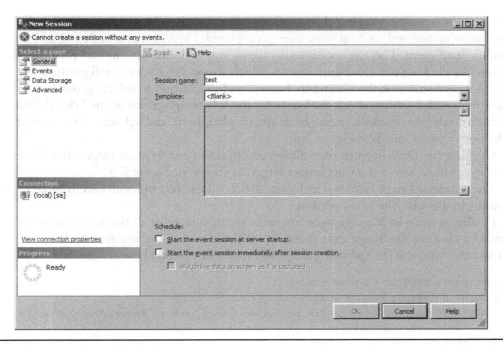

Figure 2-2 *General page of the New Session dialog*

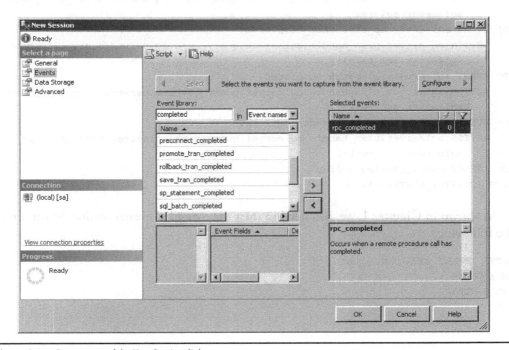

Figure 2-3 *Events page of the New Session dialog*

Click the > button to select the events rpc_completed, sp_statement_completed, sql_batch_completed, and sql_statement_completed. Do a similar search and add the module_end event. The Events page also allows you to define actions and predicates (filters) by clicking the Configure button, which shows the Event Configuration Options section. Click the Configure button, and in addition to selecting our five chosen extended events, check the boxes for the following actions in the Global Fields (Actions) tab: plan_handle, query_hash, query_plan_hash, and sql_text. Your current selections should look like Figure 2-4.

Clicking the Data Storage page allows you to select one or more targets to collect your event data. Select the ring_buffer target, as shown in Figure 2-5.

The Advanced page is shown in Figure 2-6. It allows you to specify additional options to use with the event session.

Finally, as usual in Management Studio, you can also script all the selections you've made by clicking the Script icon at the top of the New Session window. To follow up on our example, use the following script to create our extended events session:

```
CREATE EVENT SESSION test ON SERVER
ADD EVENT sqlserver.module_end(
    ACTION(sqlserver.plan_handle,sqlserver.query_hash,sqlserver.query_plan_hash,
        sqlserver.sql_text)),
ADD EVENT sqlserver.rpc_completed(
    ACTION(sqlserver.plan_handle,sqlserver.query_hash,sqlserver.query_plan_hash,
        sqlserver.sql_text)),
ADD EVENT sqlserver.sp_statement_completed(
    ACTION(sqlserver.plan_handle,sqlserver.query_hash,sqlserver.query_plan_hash,
        sqlserver.sql_text)),
ADD EVENT sqlserver.sql_batch_completed(
    ACTION(sqlserver.plan_handle,sqlserver.query_hash,sqlserver.query_plan_hash,
        sqlserver.sql_text)),
ADD EVENT sqlserver.sql_statement_completed(
    ACTION(sqlserver.plan_handle,sqlserver.query_hash,sqlserver.query_plan_hash,
        sqlserver.sql_text))
ADD TARGET package0.ring_buffer
WITH (STARTUP_STATE=OFF)
```

As shown in Chapter 1, we also need to start the extended events session by running the following:

```
ALTER EVENT SESSION [test]
ON SERVER
STATE=START
```

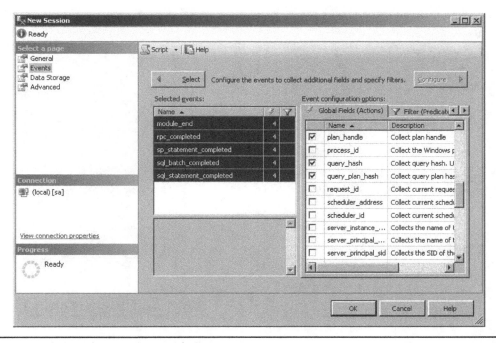

Figure 2-4   *Event configuration options on the Events page*

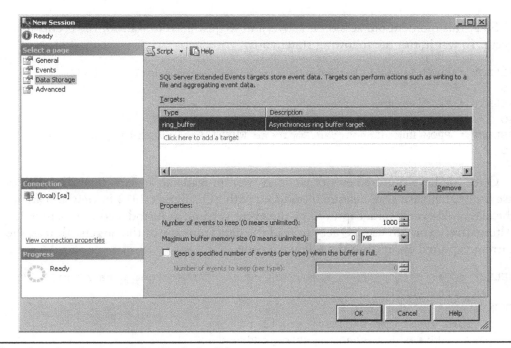

Figure 2-5   *Data Storage page of the New Session dialog*

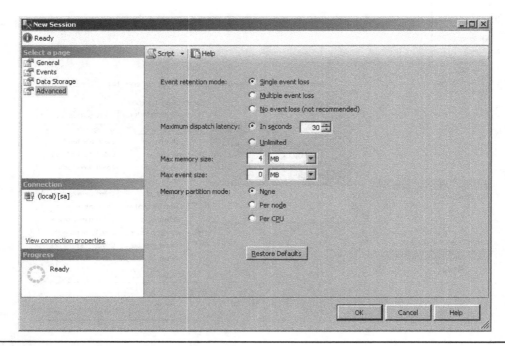

Figure 2-6 *Advanced page of the New Session dialog*

So at this moment our session is active, and we just need to wait for the events to occur. To test it, run the following statements:

```
SELECT * FROM Sales.SalesOrderDetail WHERE SalesOrderID = 60677
GO
SELECT * FROM Person.Address WHERE AddressID = 21
GO
SELECT * FROM HumanResources.Employee WHERE BusinessEntityID = 229
GO
```

Once you have captured events, you may want to read and analyze their data. You can use the Watch Live Data feature introduced with SQL Server 2012 to view and analyze the extended events data captured by the event session, as introduced in Chapter 1. Alternatively, you can use XQuery to read the data from any of the targets. To read the current captured events, run the following code:

```
SELECT name, target_name, execution_count, CAST(target_data AS xml)
    AS target_data
FROM sys.dm_xe_sessions s
     JOIN sys.dm_xe_session_targets t
   ON s.address = t.event_session_address
WHERE s.name = 'test'
```

This shows an output similar to the following:

name	target_name	execution_count	target_data
test	ring_buffer	68	<RingBufferTarget truncated="1" processingTime="267"...

You can open the link to see the captured data in XML format. Because the XML file would be too large to show in this book, only a small sample of the first event captured, showing cpu_time, duration, physical_reads, and logical_reads and writes, is included here:

```
<RingBufferTarget truncated="0" processingTime="0"
totalEventsProcessed="12"
  eventCount="12" droppedCount="0" memoryUsed="5810">
  <event name="sql_batch_completed" package="sqlserver"
    timestamp="2013-05-04T20:08:42.240Z">
    <data name="cpu_time">
      <type name="uint64" package="package0" />
      <value>0</value>
    </data>
    <data name="duration">
      <type name="uint64" package="package0" />
      <value>1731</value>
    </data>
    <data name="physical_reads">
      <type name="uint64" package="package0" />
      <value>0</value>
    </data>
    <data name="logical_reads">
      <type name="uint64" package="package0" />
      <value>4</value>
    </data>
    <data name="writes">
      <type name="uint64" package="package0" />
      <value>0</value>
    </data>
```

However, because reading XML directly is not much fun, we can use XQuery to extract the data from the XML document and get a query like this:

```
SELECT
    event_data.value('(event/@name)[1]', 'varchar(50)') AS event_name,
    event_data.value('(event/action[@name="query_hash"]/value)[1]',
        'varchar(max)') AS query_hash,
    event_data.value('(event/data[@name="cpu_time"]/value)[1]', 'int')
        AS cpu_time,
```

```
        event_data.value('(event/data[@name="duration"]/value)[1]', 'int')
            AS duration,
        event_data.value('(event/data[@name="logical_reads"]/value)[1]', 'int')
            AS logical_reads,
        event_data.value('(event/data[@name="physical_reads"]/value)[1]', 'int')
            AS physical_reads,
        event_data.value('(event/data[@name="writes"]/value)[1]', 'int') AS writes,
        event_data.value('(event/data[@name="statement"]/value)[1]', 'varchar(max)')
            AS statement
FROM(SELECT evnt.query('.') AS event_data
        FROM
        (SELECT CAST(target_data AS xml) AS target_data
            FROM sys.dm_xe_sessions s
            JOIN sys.dm_xe_session_targets t
                ON s.address = t.event_session_address
            WHERE s.name = 'test'
                AND t.target_name = 'ring_buffer'
        ) AS data
        CROSS APPLY target_data.nodes('RingBufferTarget/event') AS xevent(evnt)
    ) AS xevent(event_data)
```

This will show an output similar to the following:

event_name	cpu_time	duration	logical_reads	physical_reads	writes	statement
sql_statement_completed	0	42522	3	24	0	SELECT * FROM Sales.SalesOrderDetail WHERE SalesOrderID = 60677
sql_batch_completed	0	80265	13	48	0	NULL
sql_statement_completed	0	23970	2	16	0	SELECT * FROM Person.Address WHERE AddressID = 21
sql_batch_completed	0	53971	4	24	0	NULL
sql_statement_completed	0	29976	2	16	0	SELECT * FROM HumanResources.Employee WHERE BusinessEntityID = 229
sql_batch_completed	0	64189	20	31	0	NULL

However, using that query, you get all the data for each event, and sometimes you may want to aggregate the data. For example, sorting the data to look for the greatest CPU consumers may not be enough. As you will also see in other areas of this book, sometimes a performance problem may be caused by some query that, even if it does not show up on the top 10 consumers, or even the top 100, it is executed so many times that its aggregated CPU usage can make it one of the top CPU consumers. You can update the previous query to aggregate this data directly, or you can change it to save the info to a temporary table (for example, using SELECT ... INTO) and then group by query_hash and optionally sort as needed, as shown next:

```
SELECT query_hash, SUM(cpu_time) AS cpu_time, SUM(duration) AS duration,
    SUM(logical_reads) AS logical_reads, SUM(physical_reads) AS physical_reads,
    SUM(writes) AS writes, MAX(statement) AS statement
FROM #eventdata
GROUP BY query_hash
```

Again, as I mentioned in Chapter 1, after you finish your test, you need to stop and delete the event session. Run the following statements:

```
ALTER EVENT SESSION [test]
ON SERVER
STATE=STOP
GO
DROP EVENT SESSION [test] ON SERVER
```

You could also use the file target when collecting large amounts of data or running the session for a long time. The following example is exactly the same as before, but using the file target (note the file definition on the C:\Data folder):

```
CREATE EVENT SESSION test ON SERVER
ADD EVENT sqlserver.module_end(
    ACTION(sqlserver.plan_handle,sqlserver.query_hash,sqlserver.query_plan_hash,
        sqlserver.sql_text)),
ADD EVENT sqlserver.rpc_completed(
    ACTION(sqlserver.plan_handle,sqlserver.query_hash,sqlserver.query_plan_hash,
        sqlserver.sql_text)),
ADD EVENT sqlserver.sp_statement_completed(
    ACTION(sqlserver.plan_handle,sqlserver.query_hash,sqlserver.query_plan_hash,
        sqlserver.sql_text)),
ADD EVENT sqlserver.sql_batch_completed(
    ACTION(sqlserver.plan_handle,sqlserver.query_hash,sqlserver.query_plan_hash,
        sqlserver.sql_text)),
ADD EVENT sqlserver.sql_statement_completed(
    ACTION(sqlserver.plan_handle,sqlserver.query_hash,sqlserver.query_plan_hash,
        sqlserver.sql_text))
ADD TARGET package0.event_file(SET filename=N'C:\Data\test.xel')
WITH (STARTUP_STATE=OFF)
```

After starting the session and capturing some events, you can query its data by using the following query and the sys.fn_xe_file_target_read_file function:

```sql
SELECT
    event_data.value('(event/@name)[1]', 'varchar(50)') AS event_name,
    event_data.value('(event/action[@name="query_hash"]/value)[1]',
        'varchar(max)') AS query_hash,
    event_data.value('(event/data[@name="cpu_time"]/value)[1]', 'int')
        AS cpu_time,
    event_data.value('(event/data[@name="duration"]/value)[1]', 'int')
        AS duration,
    event_data.value('(event/data[@name="logical_reads"]/value)[1]', 'int')
        AS logical_reads,
    event_data.value('(event/data[@name="physical_reads"]/value)[1]', 'int')
        AS physical_reads,
    event_data.value('(event/data[@name="writes"]/value)[1]', 'int') AS writes,
    event_data.value('(event/data[@name="statement"]/value)[1]', 'varchar(max)')
        AS statement
FROM
    (
        SELECT CAST(event_data AS xml)
        FROM sys.fn_xe_file_target_read_file
        (
        'C:\Data\test*.xel',
        NULL,
        NULL,
        NULL
        )
    ) AS xevent(event_data)
```

If you inspect the C:\Data folder, you will find a file with a name similar to test_0_130133932321310000.xel. SQL Server adds "_0_" plus an integer representing the number of milliseconds since January 1, 1600, to the specified filename. You can inspect the contents of a particular file by providing the assigned filename or by using a wildcard (such as the asterisk shown in the code) to inspect all the available files. For more details on using the file target, see the SQL Server documentation. Again, don't forget to stop and drop your session when you finish testing.

Finally, I use extended events to show how you can obtain the waits for a specific query, something that was not even possible before extended events. You have to use the wait_info event and select any of the many available fields (such as username or query_hash) or selected actions to apply a filter (or predicate) to it. In this example, I use the session_id. Make sure to replace the session_id as required if you are testing this code.

```
CREATE EVENT SESSION [test] ON SERVER
ADD EVENT sqlos.wait_info(
    WHERE ([sqlserver].[session_id]=(61)))
ADD TARGET package0.ring_buffer
WITH (STARTUP_STATE=OFF)
GO
```

Start the event:

```
ALTER EVENT SESSION [test]
ON SERVER
STATE=START
```

Run some transactions, but notice that they need to be executed in the session ID you specified (and they need to create waits). For example, run the following query:

```
SELECT * FROM Production.Product p1 CROSS JOIN
Production.Product p2
```

Then you can read the captured data:

```
SELECT
    event_data.value('(event/@name)[1]', 'varchar(50)') AS event_name,
    event_data.value('(event/data[@name="wait_type"]/text)[1]', 'varchar(40)')
        AS wait_type,
    event_data.value('(event/data[@name="duration"]/value)[1]', 'int')
        AS duration,
    event_data.value('(event/data[@name="opcode"]/text)[1]', 'varchar(40)')
        AS opcode,
    event_data.value('(event/data[@name="signal_duration"]/value)[1]', 'int')
        AS signal_duration
FROM(SELECT evnt.query('.') AS event_data
        FROM
        (SELECT CAST(target_data AS xml) AS target_data
            FROM sys.dm_xe_sessions s
            JOIN sys.dm_xe_session_targets t
                ON s.address = t.event_session_address
            WHERE s.name = 'test'
                AND t.target_name = 'ring_buffer'
        ) AS data
        CROSS APPLY target_data.nodes('RingBufferTarget/event') AS xevent(evnt)
    ) AS xevent(event_data)
```

Here is the output I get on my system:

event_name	wait_type	wait_type	opcode	signal_duration
wait_info	NETWORK_IO	0	Begin	0
wait_info	NETWORK_IO	0	End	0
wait_info	NETWORK_IO	0	Begin	0
wait_info	NETWORK_IO	0	End	0

Again, this is another example where aggregating the captured data would be beneficial. Finally, don't forget to stop and drop your event session, as indicated previously.

Data Collector

There may be cases when a performance problem occurs and there is little or no information available to troubleshoot it. For example, you may receive a notification that CPU percentage usage was 100 percent for a few minutes, thus slowing down your application, but by the time you connected to the system to troubleshoot, the problem was already gone. Many times, a specific problem is difficult to reproduce, and the only choice is to enable a trace or some other collection of data and wait until the problem happens again. This is where proactively collecting performance data is extremely important, and the Data Collector, a feature introduced with SQL Server 2008, can help you to do just that. The Data Collector allows you to collect performance data, which you can use immediately after a performance problem occurs. You only need to know the time the problem occurred and start looking at the collected data around that period.

Explaining the Data Collector would take an entire chapter, if not an entire book. Therefore, this section is aimed at showing you how to get started. You can get more details about the Data Collector on Books Online or by reading the Microsoft white paper "Using Management Data Warehouse for Performance Monitoring" by Ken Lassesen.

Configuration

The Data Collector is not enabled by default after you install SQL Server. To configure it, you need to follow a two-step process. To configure the first part, expand the Management folder in Management Studio, right-click the Data Collection node, and select Tasks, followed by Configure Management Data Warehouse. This will run the Configure Management Data Warehouse Wizard. Click Next on the Welcome screen. This will take you to the Configure Management Data Warehouse Storage screen, which is shown in Figure 2-7. This screen allows you to select the database you will use to collect data. Optionally, you can create a new database by selecting the New button.

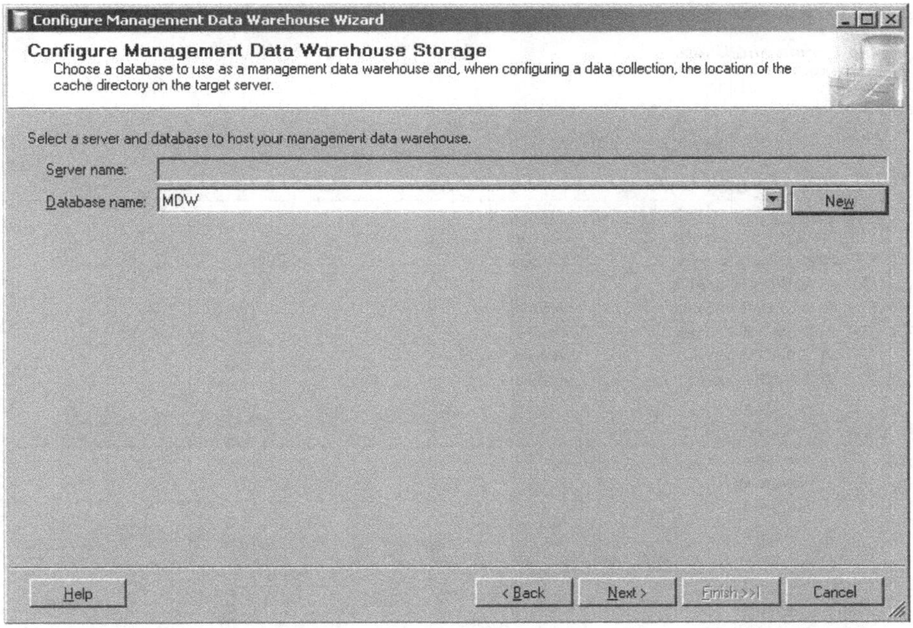

Figure 2-7 *Configure Management Data Warehouse Storage screen*

Select an existing database, or create a new one, and then click Next. The following screen, Map Logins and Users, shown in Figure 2-8, allows you to map logins and users to management data warehouse roles.

Click Next. The Complete the Wizard screen is shown next (see Figure 2-9).

At the Complete the Wizard screen, click Finish. You will then see the Configure Data Collection Wizard Progress screen. Make sure all the steps shown are executed successfully and then click the Close button. This step configured the management data warehouse database and, among other objects, it will create a collection of tables, some of which we will query directly later in this section.

To configure the second step, right-click Data Collection again and select Tasks, followed by Configure Data Collection. This will run the Configure Data Collection Wizard. Click Next. You should see Setup Data Collection Sets, as shown in Figure 2-10.

This is where you select the database to be used as the management data warehouse, which is the database you configured in step 1. You can also configure the cache directory, which is used to collect the data before it is uploaded to the management data warehouse.

Unlike previous versions, in SQL Server 2014 you need to select the Data Collector sets that you want to enable, which in our case requires selecting the System Data Collection Sets. The second collection set, called Transaction Performance Collection Sets, is used by the Hekaton AMR (Analysis, Migration, and Reporting) tool and will be covered in detail in Chapter 7. Click Next and then Finish at the Complete the Wizard screen.

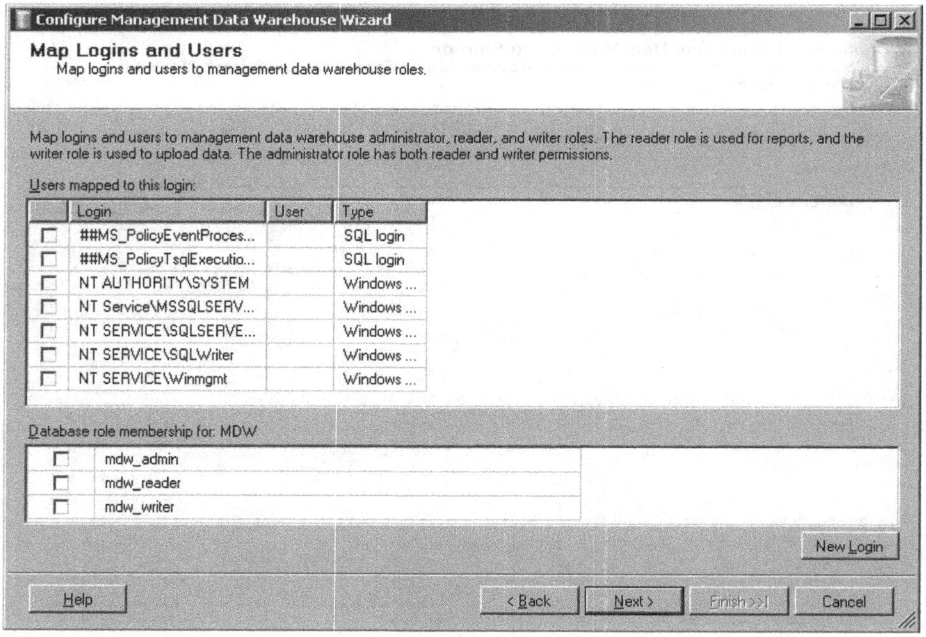

Figure 2-8 *Map Logins and Users screen*

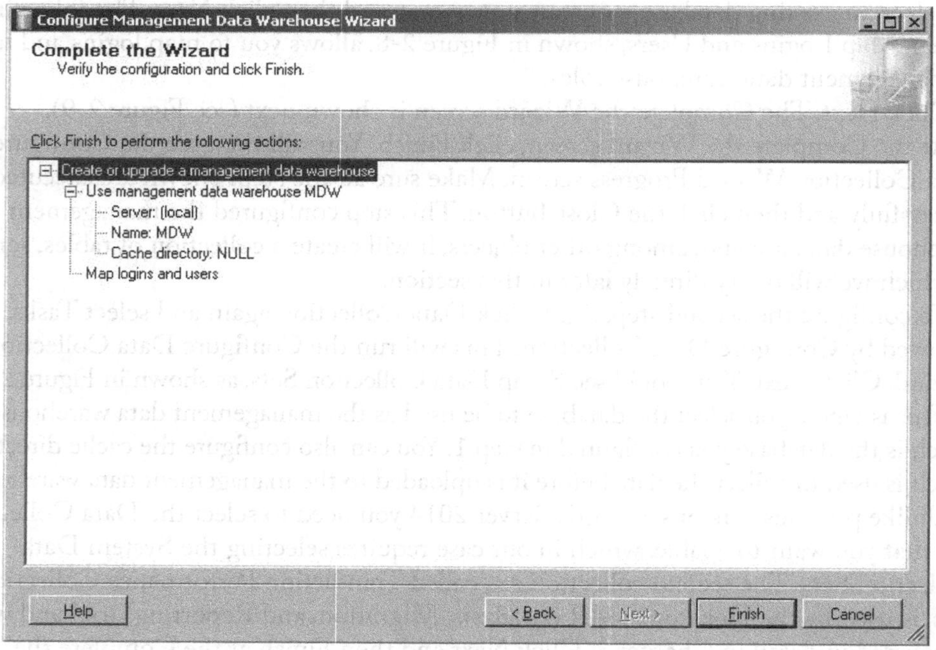

Figure 2-9 *Complete the Wizard screen*

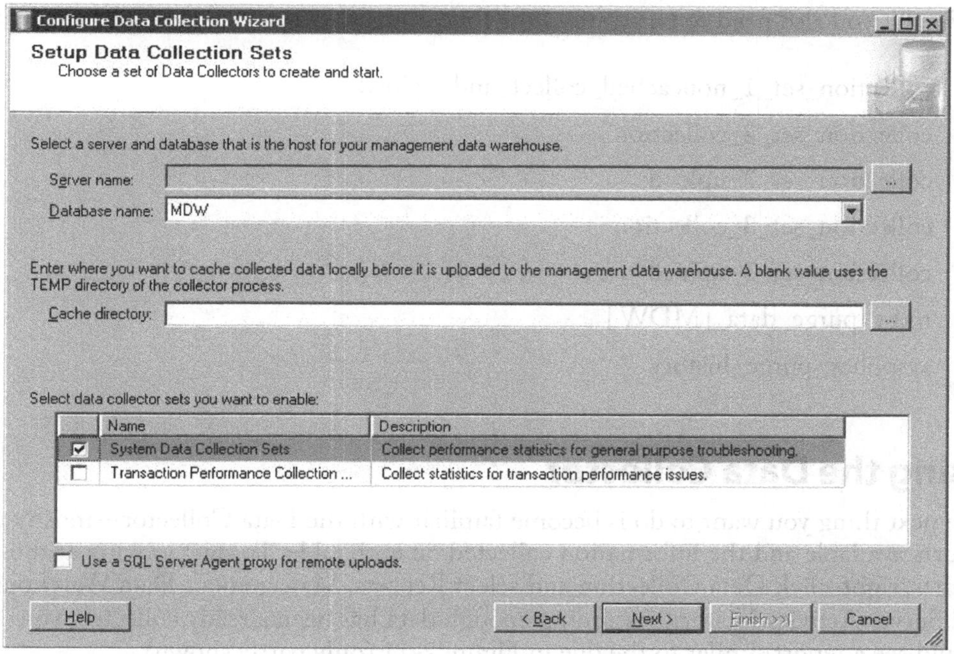

Figure 2-10 *Setup Data Collection Sets screen*

After you finish the Data Collector configuration, among other items, you can see the three enabled system data collection sets: Disk Usage, Query Statistics, and Server Activity. The Utility Information collection set is disabled by default, and it will not be covered in this book. Here is the data collected by the System Data Collection Sets:

Disk Usage	Collects data about disk and log usage for all the databases installed on the SQL Server instance
Query Statistics	Collects query statistics, individual query text, query plans, and specific queries
Server Activity	Collects resource usage statistics and performance data from the server and the SQL Server instance

In addition, it is strongly recommended that you also install the optional Query Hash Statistics collection set, which you can download from http://blogs.msdn.com/b/bartd/archive/2010/11/03/query-hash-statistics-a-query-cost-analysis-tool-now-available-for-download.aspx. The Query Hash Statistics collection set, which unfortunately is not included as part of SQL Server 2014, is based on the query_hash and plan_hash values, as explained earlier in this chapter. It collects historical query and query plan fingerprint statistics, allowing you to easily see the true cumulative cost of the queries in each of your databases. After you install the Query Hash Statistics collection set, you will need to disable the Query Statistics collection set because they collect the same information.

Finally, you also need to be aware of the following SQL Server Agent jobs created:

► collection_set_1_noncached_collect_and_upload

► collection_set_2_collection

► collection_set_2_upload

► collection_set_3_collection

► collection_set_3_upload

► mdw_purge_data_[MDW]

► syspolicy_purge_history

Using the Data Collector

The next thing you want to do is become familiar with the Data Collector—mostly the reports available and the information collected on each table. To start looking at the reports, right-click Data Collection and select Reports, Management Data Warehouse, and Server Activity History. Assuming enough data has been already collected, you should see a report similar to the one in Figure 2-11 (only partly shown).

Clicking the SQL Server section of the % CPU graph will take you to the Query Statistics History report. You can also reach this report by right-clicking Data Collection and then selecting Reports, Management Data Warehouse, and Query Statistics History. In both cases, you end up with the report in Figure 2-12 (only partly shown).

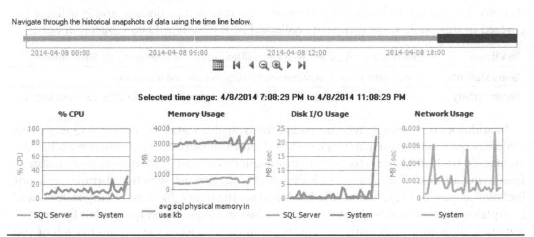

Figure 2-11 *Server Activity History report*

Navigate through the historical snapshots of data using the time line below.

2014-04-08 00:00   2014-04-08 06:00   2014-04-08 12:00   2014-04-08 18:00

Selected time range: 4/8/2014 7:08:29 PM to 4/8/2014 11:08:29 PM

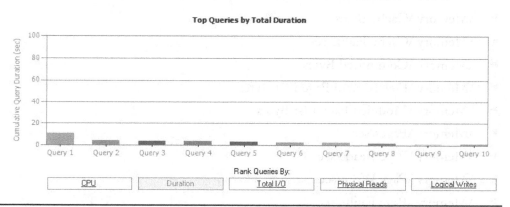

Figure 2-12 *Query Statistics History report*

Running the Query Statistics History report will show you the top 10 most expensive queries ranked by CPU usage, but you also have the choice of selecting the most expensive queries by duration, total I/O, physical reads, and logical writes. The Data Collector includes other reports, and as you saw already, some reports include links to navigate to other reports for more detailed information.

Querying the Data Collector Tables

More advanced users will want to query the Data Collector tables directly to create their own reports or look deeper into the collected data. Creation of custom collection sets is also possible and may be required when you need to capture data that the default installation is not collecting. Having custom collection sets would again require you to create your own queries and reports.

For example, the Data Collector collects multiple performance counters, which you can see by looking at the properties of the Server Activity collection set. To do this, expand both the Data Collection and System Data Collection sets, right-click the Server Activity collection set, and select Properties. In the Data Collection Set

Properties window, select Server Activity – Performance Counters in the Collection Items list box and look at the Input Parameters window. Here is a small sample of these performance counters:

- ► \Memory \% Committed Bytes In Use
- ► \Memory \Available Bytes
- ► \Memory \Cache Bytes
- ► \Memory \Cache Faults/sec
- ► \Memory \Committed Bytes
- ► \Memory \Free & Zero Page List Bytes
- ► \Memory \Modified Page List Bytes
- ► \Memory \Pages/sec
- ► \Memory \Page Reads/sec
- ► \Memory \Page Write/sec
- ► \Memory \Page Faults/sec
- ► \Memory \Pool Nonpaged Bytes
- ► \Memory \Pool Paged Bytes

You can also see a very detailed definition of the performance counters collected in your instance by looking at the snapshots.performance_counter_instances table. Performance counters' data is then stored in the snapshots.performance_counter_values table. One of the most used performance counters by database administrators is '\Processor(_Total)\% Processor Time', which allows you to collect the processor percentage usage. We could use the following query to get the collected data:

```
SELECT sii.instance_name, collection_time, [path] AS counter_name,
       formatted_value AS counter_value_percent
FROM snapshots.performance_counter_values pcv
JOIN snapshots.performance_counter_instances pci
     ON pcv.performance_counter_instance_id = pci.performance_counter_id
JOIN core.snapshots_internal si ON pcv.snapshot_id = si.snapshot_id
JOIN core.source_info_internal sii ON sii.source_id = si.source_id
WHERE pci.[path] = '\Processor(_Total)\% Processor Time'
ORDER BY pcv.collection_time desc
```

An output similar to this will be shown:

collection_time	counter_name	counter_value_percent
2013-05-12 17:14:34.0000000 -07:00	\Processor(_Total)\% Processor Time	19.156125208
2013-05-12 17:13:34.0000000 -07:00	\Processor(_Total)\% Processor Time	18.674633138
2013-05-12 17:12:34.0000000 -07:00	\Processor(_Total)\% Processor Time	18.695325723
2013-05-12 17:11:33.0000000 -07:00	\Processor(_Total)\% Processor Time	17.121825074
2013-05-12 17:10:33.0000000 -07:00	\Processor(_Total)\% Processor Time	21.20307118
2013-05-12 17:09:33.0000000 -07:00	\Processor(_Total)\% Processor Time	22.30240009
2013-05-12 17:08:33.0000000 -07:00	\Processor(_Total)\% Processor Time	21.74221733
2013-05-12 17:07:33.0000000 -07:00	\Processor(_Total)\% Processor Time	21.22852141

There are some other interesting tables, at least from the point of view of query data collection, you may need to query directly. The Query Statistics collection set uses queries defined on the QueryActivityCollect.dtsx and QueryActivityUpload.dtsx SSIS packages, and the collected data is loaded into the snapshots.query_stats, snapshots.notable_query_text, and snapshots.notable_query_plan tables. These tables collect query statistics, query text, and query plans, respectively. If you installed the Query Hash Statistics collection set, the packages QueryHashStatsPlanCollect and QueryHashStatsPlanUpload will be used instead. Another interesting table is snapshots.active_sessions_and_requests, which collects information about SQL Server sessions and requests.

Summary

This chapter has provided you with several tuning techniques you can use to find out how your queries are using system resources such as disk and CPU. I first explained some essential dynamic management views (DMVs) and functions (DMFs) very useful for tracking expensive queries. Two features introduced with SQL Server 2008, extended events and the Data Collector, were explained as well, along with how they can help to capture events and performance data. I also discussed SQL Trace, a feature that has been around in all the SQL Server versions as far as I can remember.

So now that we have the background on how to find the expensive queries in SQL Server, what's next? Our final purpose is to do something to improve the performance of the query, so in order to achieve that, I will cover different approaches in the coming chapters: Is just a better index needed? Maybe your query is sensitive to different parameters, or maybe the query optimizer is not giving you a good execution plan because a used feature does not have good support for statistics. We will cover these and many other issues in the following chapters.

So once we have found the query that may be causing the problem, we still need to troubleshoot what the problem is and find a solution to it. Many times, we would be able to troubleshoot what the problem is just by inspecting all the rich information available in the query execution plan. In order to do that, we need to go deeper into how the query optimizer works and what different operators it provides. I cover those topics in detail in the following two chapters.

Chapter 3

The Query Optimizer

In This Chapter

I n this chapter, I cover how the query optimizer works and introduce the steps it performs in the background, which we don't see. This covers everything, from the time a query is submitted to SQL Server until an execution plan is generated and is ready to be executed. This includes steps such as parsing, binding, simplification, trivial plan optimization, and full optimization. Important components that are part of the query optimizer architecture, such as transformation rules and the Memo structure, are also introduced.

The purpose of the query optimizer is to provide an optimum execution plan, or at least a good enough execution plan; in order to do so, it generates many possible alternatives through the use of transformation rules. These alternative plans are stored for the duration of the optimization process in a structure called the Memo. Unfortunately, a drawback of cost-based optimization is the cost of optimization itself. Given that finding the optimum plan for some queries would take an unacceptably long optimization time, some heuristics are used to limit the number of alternative plans considered instead of using the entire search space—remember that the goal is to find a good enough plan as quickly as possible. Heuristics help the query optimizer to cope with the combinatorial explosion that occurs in the search space as queries get progressively more complex. However, the use of transformation rules and heuristics does not necessarily reduce the cost of the available alternatives, so the cost of each candidate plan is also determined, and the best alternative is chosen based on those costs.

Overview

The query optimization and execution process were introduced in Chapter 1, and will be explained in more detail throughout this chapter. However, before we get started, I'll very briefly describe the inner workings of the query optimization process, which extends both before and after the query optimizer itself. The diagram in Figure 3-1 shows the major phases of the query processing, and each phase will be explained in more detail in the remaining sections of this chapter.

Parsing and binding are the first operations performed when a query is submitted to a SQL Server instance. They produce a tree representation of the query, which is then sent to the query optimizer to perform the optimization process. At the beginning of this optimization process, this logical tree will be simplified, and the query optimizer will check whether the query qualifies for a trivial plan. If it does, a trivial execution plan is returned and the optimization process immediately ends. The parsing, binding, simplification, and trivial plan processes do not depend on the contents of the database (such as the data itself), but only on the database schema and query definition. Because of this, these processes also don't use statistics, cost estimation, or cost-based decisions, all of which are only employed during the full optimization process.

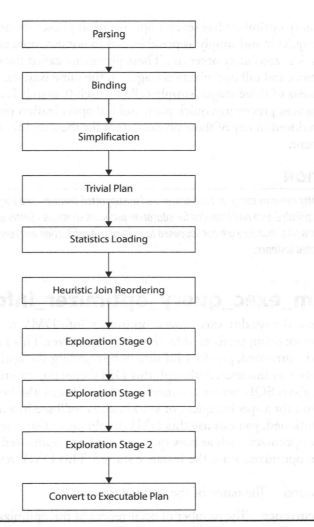

Figure 3-1   *The query-processing process*

If the query does not qualify for a trivial plan, the query optimizer will run the full optimization process, which is executed in up to three stages, and a plan may be produced at the end of any of these stages. In addition, to consider all of the information gathered in the previous phases, such as the query definition and database schema, the full optimization process will use statistics and cost estimation and then select the best execution plan (within the available time) based solely on that plan's cost.

The query optimizer has several optimization phases designed to try to optimize queries as quickly and simply as possible, and to not use more expensive and sophisticated options unless absolutely necessary. These phases are called the simplification, trivial plan optimization, and full optimization stages. In the same way, the full optimization phase itself consists of three stages, simply called search 0, search 1, and search 2 (also called the transaction processing, quick plan, and full optimization phases, respectively). Plans can be produced in any of these phases except for the simplification one, which I'll discuss in a moment.

CAUTION

This chapter contains many undocumented and unsupported features, and they are clearly identified as such. They are included here and intended for education purposes so you can better understand how the query optimizer works, and they are not supposed to be used in a production environment. Use them carefully on your own isolated instance.

sys.dm_exec_query_optimizer_info

You can use the sys.dm_exec_query_optimizer_info DMV to gain additional insight into the work being performed by the query optimizer. This DMV, which is only partially documented, provides information regarding the optimizations performed on the SQL Server instance. Although this DMV contains cumulative statistics recorded since the given SQL Server instance was started, it can also be used to get optimization information for a specific query or workload, as we'll see in a moment.

As mentioned, you can use this DMV to obtain statistics regarding the operation of the query optimizer, such as how queries have been optimized and how many of them have been optimized since the instance started. This DMV returns three columns:

▶ **Counter**   The name of the optimizer event

▶ **Occurrence**   The number of occurrences of the optimization event for this counter

▶ **Value**   The average value per event occurrence

Thirty-eight counters were defined for SQL Server 2005, and a new one, called merge stmt, was added in SQL Server 2008, giving a total of 39, which still continues through SQL Server 2014. To view the statistics for all the query optimizations since the SQL Server instance was started, we can just run the following:

```
SELECT * FROM sys.dm_exec_query_optimizer_info
```

Here is the partial output of one production instance:

counter	occurrence	value
optimizations	691473	1
elapsed time	691465	0.007806012
final cost	691465	1.398120739
trivial plan	29476	1
tasks	661989	332.5988816
no plan	0	NULL
search 0	26724	1
search 0 time	31420	0.01646922
search 0 tasks	31420	1198.811617

The output shows that there have been 691,473 optimizations since the instance was started, that the average elapsed time for each optimization was 0.0078 seconds, and that the average estimated cost of each optimization, in internal cost units, was about 1.398. This particular example shows optimizations of inexpensive queries typical of an OLTP system.

Although the sys.dm_exec_query_optimizer_info DMV was completely documented in the original version of SQL Server 2005 Books Online, more recent versions omit descriptions of nearly half (18 out of 39) of the counters, and instead label them as "Internal only." Therefore, in Table 3-1, I include the current Books Online documentation plus descriptions of the 18 undocumented counters, according to their original documentation, which is still valid for SQL Server 2014. The added descriptions are shown in italics.

The counters can be used in several ways to show important insight about the optimizations being performed in your instance. For example, the next query displays the percentage of optimizations in the instance that include hints. This information could be useful to show how extensive the use of hints in your application is, which in turn can show that your code may be less flexible than anticipated and may require additional maintenance. Hints are explained in detail in Chapter 10.

```
SELECT (SELECT occurrence FROM sys.dm_exec_query_optimizer_info WHERE counter =
    'hints' ) * 100.0 / ( SELECT occurrence FROM sys.dm_exec_query_optimizer_info
    WHERE counter = 'optimizations' )
```

Counter	Occurrence	Value
optimizations	Total number of optimizations.	Not applicable.
elapsed time	Total number of optimizations.	Average elapsed time per optimization of an individual statement (query), in seconds.
final cost	Total number of optimizations.	Average estimated cost for an optimized plan, in internal cost units.
trivial plan	*Total number of trivial plans (used as final plan).*	*Not applicable.*
tasks	*Number of optimizations that applied tasks (exploration, implementation, property derivation).*	*Average number of tasks executed.*
no plan	*Number of optimizations for which no plan was found after a full optimization run, and where no other errors were issued during query compilation.*	*Not applicable.*
search 0	*Total number of final plans found in search 0 phase.*	*Not applicable.*
search 0 time	*Number of optimizations that entered search 0.*	*Average time spent in search 0, in seconds.*
search 0 tasks	*Number of optimizations that entered search 0.*	*Average number of tasks run in search 0.*
search 1	*Total number of final plans found in search 1 phase.*	*Not applicable.*
search 1 time	*Number of optimizations that entered search 1.*	*Average time spent in search 1, in seconds.*
search 1 tasks	*Number of optimizations that entered search 1.*	*Average number of tasks run in search 1.*
search 2	*Total number of final plans found in search 2 phase.*	*Not applicable.*
search 2 time	*Total number of final plans found in search 2 phase.*	*Average time spent in search 2.*
search 2 tasks	*Number of optimizations that entered search 2.*	*Average number of tasks run in search 2.*
gain stage 0 to stage 1	*Number of times search 1 was run after search 0.*	*Average gain from stage 0 to stage 1 as (MinimumPlanCost(search 0) − MinimumPlanCost(search 1)) / MinimumPlanCost(search 0).*

Table 3-1   *sys.dm_exec_query_optimizer_info DMV with Undocumented Counters*

Counter	Occurrence	Value
gain stage 1 to stage 2	*Number of times search 2 was run after search 1.*	*Average gain from stage 1 to stage 2 as (MinimumPlanCost(search 1) − MinimumPlanCost(search 2)) / MinimumPlanCost(search 1).*
timeout	*Number of optimizations for which internal timeout occurred.*	*Not applicable.*
memory limit exceeded	*Number of optimizations for which an internal memory limit was exceeded.*	*Not applicable.*
insert stmt	Number of optimizations that are for INSERT statements.	Not applicable.
delete stmt	Number of optimizations that are for DELETE statements.	Not applicable.
update stmt	Number of optimizations that are for UPDATE statements.	Not applicable.
merge stmt	Number of optimizations that are for MERGE statements.	Not applicable.
contains subquery	Number of optimizations for a query that contains at least one subquery.	Not applicable.
unnest failed	*Number of times where subquery unnesting could not remove the subquery.*	*Not applicable.*
tables	Total number of optimizations.	Average number of tables referenced per query optimized.
hints	Number of times some hint was specified. Hints counted include JOIN, GROUP, UNION, and FORCE ORDER query hints; FORCE PLAN set option; and join hints.	Not applicable.
order hint	Number of times a force order hint was specified.	Not applicable.
join hint	Number of times the join algorithm was forced by a join hint.	Not applicable.
view reference	Number of times a view has been referenced in a query.	Not applicable.
remote query	Number of optimizations where the query referenced at least one remote data source, such as a table with a four-part name or an OPENROWSET result.	Not applicable.

Table 3-1   *sys.dm_exec_query_optimizer_info DMV with Undocumented Counters* (Continued)

Counter	Occurrence	Value
maximum DOP	Total number of optimizations.	Average effective MAXDOP value for an optimized plan. By default, effective MAXDOP is determined by the max degree of parallelism server configuration option, and may be overridden for a specific query by the value of the MAXDOP query hint.
maximum recursion level	Number of optimizations in which a MAXRECURSION level greater than 0 has been specified with the query hint.	Average MAXRECURSION level in optimizations where a maximum recursion level is specified with the query hint.
indexed views loaded	*Number of queries for which one or more indexed views were loaded for consideration for matching.*	*Average number of views loaded.*
indexed views matched	Number of optimizations where one or more indexed views have been matched.	Average number of views matched.
indexed views used	Number of optimizations where one or more indexed views are used in the output plan after being matched.	Average number of views used.
indexed views updated	Number of optimizations of a DML statement that produce a plan that maintains one or more indexed views.	Average number of views maintained.
dynamic cursor request	Number of optimizations in which a dynamic cursor request has been specified.	Not applicable.
fast forward cursor request	Number of optimizations in which a fast-forward cursor request has been specified.	Not applicable.

Table 3-1   *sys.dm_exec_query_optimizer_info DMV with Undocumented Counters (Continued)*

As mentioned previously, you can use this DMV in two different ways: you can use it to get information regarding the history of accumulated optimizations on the system since the instance was started, or you can use it to get optimization information for a particular query or a workload. In order to capture data on the latter, you need to take two snapshots of the DMV—one before optimizing your query and another one after the query has been optimized—and manually find the difference between them. Unfortunately, there is no way to initialize the values of this DMV.

You have several issues to consider when capturing this information. First, you need to eliminate the effects of system-generated queries and queries executed by other users that may be running at the same time as your sample query. Try to isolate the query or workload on your own instance, and make sure that the number of optimizations reported is the same as the number of optimizations you are requesting by checking the "optimizations" counter. If the former is greater, the data probably includes some of those queries submitted by the system or other users. Of course, it's also possible that your own query against the sys.dm_exec_query_optimizer_info DMV may count as an optimization.

Second, you need to make sure that a query optimization is actually taking place. For example, if you run the same query more than once, SQL Server may simply use an existing plan from the plan cache, without performing any query optimization. You can force an optimization by using the RECOMPILE hint (as shown later), using sp_recompile, or by manually removing the plan from the plan cache. For instance, starting with SQL Server 2008, the DBCC FREEPROCCACHE statement can be used to remove a specific plan, all the plans related to a specific resource pool, or the entire plan cache. Although at this point you most likely are working on a test environment, it is worth warning you not to run commands to clear the plan cache of a production environment.

With all of this in mind, the script shown in Listing 3-1 will display the optimization information for a specific query, while avoiding all of the aforementioned issues. The script is based on an original idea by Lubor Kollar from the SQL Server team at Microsoft, and has a section to include the query about which you want to get optimization information.

Listing 3-1   *sys.dm_exec_query_optimizer_info Code*

```
-- optimize these queries now
-- so they do not skew the collected results
GO
SELECT *
INTO after_query_optimizer_info
FROM sys.dm_exec_query_optimizer_info
GO
SELECT *
INTO before_query_optimizer_info
FROM sys.dm_exec_query_optimizer_info
GO
DROP TABLE before_query_optimizer_info
DROP TABLE after_query_optimizer_info
GO
-- real execution starts
GO
SELECT *
INTO before_query_optimizer_info
FROM sys.dm_exec_query_optimizer_info
GO
-- insert your query here
SELECT *
FROM Person.Address
-- keep this to force a new optimization
OPTION (RECOMPILE)
```

```
GO
SELECT *
INTO after_query_optimizer_info
FROM sys.dm_exec_query_optimizer_info
GO
SELECT a.counter,
(a.occurrence - b.occurrence) AS occurrence,
(a.occurrence * a.value - b.occurrence *
b.value) AS value
FROM before_query_optimizer_info b
JOIN after_query_optimizer_info a
ON b.counter = a.counter
WHERE b.occurrence <> a.occurrence
DROP TABLE before_query_optimizer_info
DROP TABLE after_query_optimizer_info
```

Note that some queries are listed twice in the code. The purpose of this is to optimize them the first time they are executed so that their plan can be available in the plan cache for all the executions after that. In this way, we aim as far as possible to isolate the optimization information from the queries we are trying to analyze. Care must be taken that both queries are exactly the same, including case, comments, and so on, and separated in their own batch for the GO statements.

If you run this script against the AdventureWorks2012 database, the output (after you have scrolled past the address data) should look like what's shown next. Note that the times shown obviously may be different from the ones you get in your system, for both this and other examples in this chapter. The output indicates, among other things, that there was one optimization, referencing one table, with a cost of 0.278931474.

counter	occurrence	value
elapsed time	1	0
final cost	1	0.278931474
maximum DOP	1	0
optimizations	1	1
tables	1	1
trivial plan	1	1

Certainly, for this simple query, we could find the same information in some other places, such as in an execution plan. However, as I will show later in this chapter, this DMV can provide optimization information that is not available anywhere else. I will be using this DMV later in this chapter, and you should come to see why it is very useful in providing additional insight into the work being performed by the query optimizer.

Parsing and Binding

Parsing and binding are the first operations that SQL Server executes when you submit a query to a database; they are performed by a component called the Algebrizer. Parsing first makes sure that the T-SQL query has a valid syntax and then uses the query information to build a tree of relational operators. By that, I mean the parser translates the SQL query into an algebra tree representation of logical operators, which is called a *parse tree*. Parsing only checks for valid T-SQL syntax, not for valid table or column names, which are verified in the next phase: binding.

Parsing is similar to the parse functionality available in Management Studio (by clicking the Parse button on the default toolbar) or the SET PARSEONLY statement. For example, the following query will successfully parse on the AdventureWorks2012 database, even when the listed columns and table do not exist in said database:

```
SELECT lname, fname FROM authors
```

However, if you incorrectly write the SELECT or FROM keyword, SQL Server will return an error message complaining about the incorrect syntax.

Once the parse tree has been constructed, the Algebrizer performs the binding operation, which is mostly concerned with name resolution. During this operation, the Algebrizer makes sure that all of the objects named in the query do actually exist, confirms that the requested operations between them are valid, and verifies that the objects are visible (that is, have the appropriate security) to the user running the query. It also associates every table and column name on the parse tree with their corresponding object in the system catalog. Name resolution for views includes the process of view substitution, where a view reference is expanded to include the view definition—for example, to directly include the tables used in the view. The output of the binding operation, which is called an *algebrizer tree,* is then sent to the query optimizer for (as you'll have guessed) optimization.

Originally, this tree will be represented as a series of logical operations that are closely related to the original syntax of the query. These include such logical operations as "get data from the Customer table," "get data from the Contact table," "perform an inner join," and so on. Different tree representations of the query will be used throughout the optimization process, and this logical tree will receive different names until it is finally used to initialize the Memo structure, as we'll discuss later.

There is no documented information about these logical trees in SQL Server, but interestingly, the following query returns the names used by those trees:

```
SELECT * FROM sys.dm_xe_map_values WHERE name = 'query_optimizer_tree_id'
```

The query returns the following output:

map_key	map_value
0	CONVERTED_TREE
1	INPUT_TREE
2	SIMPLIFIED_TREE
3	JOIN_COLLAPSED_TREE
4	TREE_BEFORE_PROJECT_NORM
5	TREE_AFTER_PROJECT_NORM
6	OUTPUT_TREE
7	TREE_COPIED_OUT

I will look at some of these logical trees later in this chapter.

For example, the following query will have the tree representation shown in Figure 3-2:

```
SELECT c.CustomerID, COUNT(*)
FROM Sales.Customer c JOIN Sales.SalesOrderHeader s
ON c.CustomerID = s.CustomerID
WHERE c.TerritoryID = 4
GROUP BY c.CustomerID
```

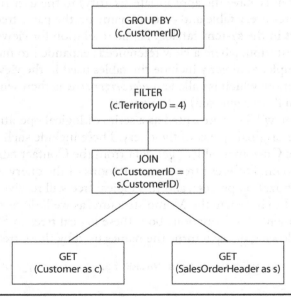

Figure 3-2 *Query tree representation*

There are also several undocumented trace flags that can allow you to see these different logical trees. For example, you can use the following query with the undocumented trace flag 8605. But first enable trace flag 3604, as shown next:

```
DBCC TRACEON(3604)
```

Trace flag 3604 allows you to redirect the trace output to the client executing the command, in this case, SQL Server Management Studio. You will be able to see its output on the query's Messages tab.

```
SELECT ProductID, name FROM Production.Product
WHERE ProductID = 877
OPTION (RECOMPILE, QUERYTRACEON 8605)
```

NOTE

QUERYTRACEON is a query hint used to apply a trace flag at the query level and was introduced in Chapter 1.

This shows the following output:

```
*** Converted Tree: ***
    LogOp_Project QCOL: [AdventureWorks2012].[Production].[Product].ProductID
    QCOL: [AdventureWorks2012].[Production].[Product].Name
        LogOp_Select
            LogOp_Get TBL: Production.Product Production.Product
            TableID=1973582069 TableReferenceID=0 IsRow: COL: IsBaseRow1001
            ScaOp_Comp x_cmpEq
                ScaOp_Identifier QCOL:
                [AdventureWorks2012].[Production].[Product].ProductID
                ScaOp_Const TI(int,ML=4) XVAR(int,Not Owned,Value=877)
        AncOp_PrjList
```

The output gets very verbose quickly, even for simple queries; unfortunately, there is no documented information to help understand these output trees and their operations. These operations are, in fact, relational algebra operations. For example, the Select operation, shown as LogOp_Select, selects the records that satisfy a given predicate and should not be confused with the SQL SELECT statement. The Select operation is more like the WHERE clause in a SQL statement. The Project operation, shown as LogOp_Project, is used to specify the columns required in the result. In the query, we are only requesting ProductID and name, and you can verify those columns on the LogOp_Project operation. You can read more about relational algebra operations in *Database System Concepts* by Abraham Silberschatz, Henry F. Korth, and S. Sudarshan (McGraw-Hill, 2010).

Now that we have a basic understanding of the created logical trees, in the next section, I show you how SQL Server will try to simplify the current input tree.

Simplification

Query rewrites or, more exactly, tree rewrites are performed in this stage to reduce the query tree into a simpler form in order to make the optimization process easier. Some of these simplifications include the following:

▶ Subqueries are converted into joins, but because a subquery does not always translate directly to an inner join, outer join and group-by operations may be added as necessary.

▶ Redundant inner and outer joins may be removed. A typical example is the Foreign Key Join elimination, which occurs when SQL Server can detect that some joins may not be needed, as foreign key constraints are available and only columns of the referencing table are requested. An example of Foreign Key Join elimination is shown later.

▶ Filters in WHERE clauses are pushed down in the query tree in order to enable early data filtering as well as potentially better matching of indexes and computed columns later in the optimization process (this simplification is known as *predicate pushdown*).

▶ Contradictions are detected and removed. Because these parts of the query are not executed at all, SQL Server saves resources such as I/O, locks, memory, and CPU, thus making the query execute faster. For example, the query optimizer may know that no records can satisfy a predicate even before touching any page of data. A contradiction may be related to a check constraint, or may be related to the way the query is written. Both scenarios will be shown in the next section.

The output of the simplification process is a simplified logical operator tree.

Contradiction Detection

Let's see a couple of examples of the simplification process, starting with contradiction detection. First, I need a table with a check constraint and, handily, the Employee table has the following check constraint definition (don't run the code; the constraint already exists):

```
ALTER TABLE HumanResources.Employee WITH CHECK ADD CONSTRAINT
    CK_Employee_VacationHours CHECK (VacationHours>=-40 AND
VacationHours<=240)
```

Figure 3-3   *Plan without contradiction detection*

This check constraint makes sure that the number of vacation hours is a number between −40 and 240. Therefore, if I request

```
SELECT * FROM HumanResources.Employee WHERE VacationHours > 80
```

SQL Server will use a Clustered Index Scan operator, as shown in Figure 3-3.

However, if I request all of the employees with more than 300 vacation hours, then because of this check constraint, the query optimizer must immediately know that no records qualify for predicate. Run the following query:

```
SELECT * FROM HumanResources.Employee WHERE VacationHours > 300
```

As expected, the query will return no records, but this time, it will show the execution plan shown in Figure 3-4.

Note that, this time, instead of a Clustered Index Scan, SQL Server is using a Constant Scan operator. The Constant Scan operator introduces one or more constant rows into a query and has virtually no cost. Because there is no need to access the table at all, SQL Server saves resources such as I/O, locks, memory, and CPU, thus making the query execute faster.

Now, let's see what happens if I disable the check constraint:

```
ALTER TABLE HumanResources.Employee NOCHECK CONSTRAINT CK_Employee_VacationHours
```

This time, running the previous SELECT query once again uses a Clustered Index Scan operator, as the query optimizer can no longer use the check constraint to guide its decisions. Don't forget to enable the constraint again by running the following statement:

```
ALTER TABLE HumanResources.Employee WITH CHECK CHECK CONSTRAINT
CK_Employee_VacationHours
```

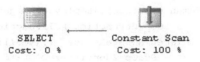

Figure 3-4   *Contradiction detection example*

A second type of contradiction case is when the query itself explicitly contains a contradiction. Take a look at the following query:

```
SELECT * FROM HumanResources.Employee WHERE VacationHours > 10
    AND VacationHours < 5
```

In this case, no check constraint is involved; both predicates are valid, and each will individually return records, but they contradict each other when they are run together. As a result, the query returns no records and the plan shows a Constant Scan operator similar to the plan in Figure 3-4. This may just look like a badly written query, but remember that some predicates may already be included in, for example, view definitions, and the developer of the query may be unaware of them. For example, in the previous query, a view may include the predicate VacationHours > 10, and a developer may call the view using the predicate VacationHours < 5. Because both predicates contradict each other, a Constant Scan operator will be used again instead. A contradiction may be also difficult to detect by the developer on some complex queries.

NOTE

You may try some simple similar queries on your own and not get a contradiction detection behavior. In some cases, a trivial plan may block this behavior.

Now, let's see the logical trees created during contradiction detection, again using the undocumented trace flag 8606:

```
SELECT * FROM HumanResources.Employee WHERE VacationHours > 300
OPTION (RECOMPILE, QUERYTRACEON 8606)
```

We get the following output (edited to fit the page):

```
*** Input Tree: ***
        LogOp_Project QCOL:[HumanResources].[Employee].BusinessEntityID
            LogOp_Select
                LogOp_Project
                    LogOp_Get TBL: HumanResources.Employee TableID=1237579447
                    TableReferenceID=0 IsRow: COL: IsBaseRow1001
                    AncOp_PrjList
                        AncOp_PrjEl QCOL:
                        [HumanResources].[Employee].OrganizationLevel
                            ScaOp_UdtFunction EClrFunctionType_UdtMethodGetLevel
                            IsDet NoDataAccess  TI(smallint,Null,ML=2)
                                ScaOp_Identifier QCOL:
                                [HumanResources].[Employee].OrganizationNode
```

```
        ScaOp_Comp x_cmpGt
            ScaOp_Identifier QCOL:
            [HumanResources].[Employee].VacationHours
            ScaOp_Const TI(smallint,ML=2)
        AncOp_PrjList
*** Simplified Tree: ***
        LogOp_ConstTableGet (0) COL: Chk1000  COL: IsBaseRow1001  QCOL:
        [HumanResources].[Employee].BusinessEntityID
```

As you can see, all the logical operators of the entire input tree are replaced by the simplified tree, consisting only of a LogOp_ConstTableGet operator, which will be later translated into the logical and physical Constant Scan operator we saw previously.

Foreign Key Join Elimination

Now I will show you an example of Foreign Key Join elimination. The following query joins two tables and shows the execution plan in Figure 3-5:

```
SELECT soh.SalesOrderID, c.AccountNumber
FROM Sales.SalesOrderHeader soh
JOIN Sales.Customer c ON soh.CustomerID = c.CustomerID
```

Let's see what happens if we comment out the AccountNumber column:

```
SELECT soh.SalesOrderID --, c.AccountNumber
FROM Sales.SalesOrderHeader soh
JOIN Sales.Customer c ON soh.CustomerID = c.CustomerID
```

If you run the query again, the Customer table and obviously the join operation are eliminated, as can be seen in the execution plan in Figure 3-6.

There are two reasons for this change. First, because the AccountNumber column is no longer required, no columns are requested from the Customer table. However, it seems like the Customer table is still needed because it is required as part of the equality operation on a join condition. That is, SQL Server needs to make sure that a Customer record exists for each related record in the Individual table.

Figure 3-5 *Original plan joining two tables*

Figure 3-6   *Foreign Key Join elimination example*

Actually, this validation is performed by the existing foreign key constraint, so the query optimizer realizes that there is no need to use the Customer table at all. This is the defined foreign key (again, there is no need to run this code):

```
ALTER TABLE Sales.SalesOrderHeader WITH CHECK ADD CONSTRAINT
FK_SalesOrderHeader_Customer_CustomerID FOREIGN KEY(CustomerID
REFERENCES Sales.Customer(CustomerID)
```

As a test, temporarily disable the foreign key by running the following statement:

```
ALTER TABLE Sales.SalesOrderHeader NOCHECK CONSTRAINT
FK_SalesOrderHeader_Customer_CustomerID
```

Now run the previous query again. Without the foreign key constraint, SQL Server has no choice but to perform the join operation to make sure that the join condition is executed. As a result, it will use a plan joining both tables again, similar to the one shown previously in Figure 3-5. Don't forget to reenable the foreign key by running the following statement:

```
ALTER TABLE Sales.SalesOrderHeader WITH CHECK CHECK CONSTRAINT
FK_SalesOrderHeader_Customer_CustomerID
```

Finally, you can also see this behavior on the created logical trees. To see this again, use the undocumented trace flag 8606, as shown next:

```
SELECT soh.SalesOrderID --, c.AccountNumber
FROM Sales.SalesOrderHeader soh
JOIN Sales.Customer c ON soh.CustomerID = c.CustomerID
OPTION (RECOMPILE, QUERYTRACEON 8606)
```

You can see an output similar to this, edited to fit the page:

```
*** Input Tree: ***
        LogOp_Project QCOL: [soh].SalesOrderID
            LogOp_Select
                LogOp_Join
                    LogOp_Project
```

```
            LogOp_Get TBL: Sales.SalesOrderHeader(alias TBL: soh)
            Sales.SalesOrderHeader TableID=1266103551
            TableReferenceID=0 IsRow: COL: IsBaseRow1001
            AncOp_PrjList
                AncOp_PrjEl QCOL: [soh].SalesOrderNumber
                    ScaOp_Intrinsic isnull
                        ScaOp_Arithmetic x_aopAdd
...
          LogOp_Project
              LogOp_Get TBL: Sales.Customer(alias TBL: c)
              Sales.Customer TableID=997578592 TableReferenceID=0
              IsRow: COL: IsBaseRow1003
              AncOp_PrjList
                  AncOp_PrjEl QCOL: [c].AccountNumber
                      ScaOp_Intrinsic isnull
                          ScaOp_Arithmetic x_aopAdd
                              ScaOp_Const TI(varchar collate
                              872468488,Var,Trim,ML=2)
                              ScaOp_Udf dbo.ufnLeadingZeros IsDet
                                  ScaOp_Identifier QCOL: [c].
CustomerID
...
*** Simplified Tree: ***
      LogOp_Join
          LogOp_Get TBL: Sales.SalesOrderHeader(alias TBL: soh)
          Sales.SalesOrderHeader TableID=1266103551 TableReferenceID=0
          IsRow: COL: IsBaseRow1001
          LogOp_Get TBL: Sales.Customer(alias TBL: c) Sales.Customer
          TableID=997578592 TableReferenceID=0 IsRow: COL: IsBaseRow1003
          ScaOp_Comp x_cmpEq
              ScaOp_Identifier QCOL: [c].CustomerID
              ScaOp_Identifier QCOL: [soh].CustomerID
*** Join-collapsed Tree: ***
      LogOp_Get TBL: Sales.SalesOrderHeader(alias TBL: soh)
      Sales.SalesOrderHeader TableID=1266103551 TableReferenceID=0 IsRow: COL:
      IsBaseRow1001
```

In the output, you can see that although the second tree was highly simplified (the input tree was edited to fit the page), both the input and the simplified tree still have logical Get operators, or LogOp_Get for the Sales.SalesOrderHeader and Sales.Customer tables. The join-collapsed tree has eliminated one of the tables, showing only Sales.SalesOrderHeader. Notice that the tree was simplified after the original input tree and, after that, the join was eliminated on the join-collapsed tree.

Trivial Plan

The optimization process may be expensive to initialize and run for simple queries that don't require any cost estimation. To avoid this expensive operation for simple queries, SQL Server uses the trivial plan optimization. In short, if there's only one way, or one obvious best way, to execute the query, depending on the query definition and available metadata, a lot of work can be avoided. For example, the following AdventureWorks2012 query will produce a trivial plan:

```
SELECT * FROM Sales.SalesOrderDetail
WHERE SalesOrderID = 43659
```

The execution plan will show whether a trivial plan optimization was performed; the Optimization Level entry in the Properties window of a graphical plan will show TRIVIAL, as shown in Figure 3-7. In the same way, an XML plan will show

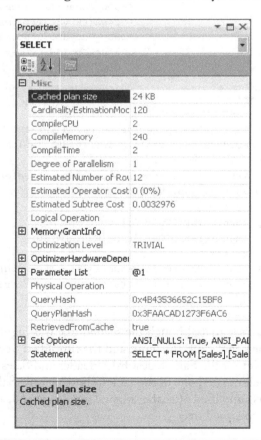

Figure 3-7 *Trivial plan properties*

the StatementOptmLevel attribute as TRIVIAL, as you can see in the next XML fragment:

```
<StmtSimple StatementCompId="1" StatementEstRows="12" StatementId="1"
StatementOptmLevel="TRIVIAL" StatementSubTreeCost="0.0032976"
StatementText="SELECT * FROM [Sales].[SalesOrderDetail] WHERE
[SalesOrderID]=@1"
StatementType="SELECT" QueryHash="0x801851E3A6490741"
QueryPlanHash="0x3E34C903A0998272" RetrievedFromCache="true">
```

As I mentioned at the start of this chapter, additional information regarding the optimization process can be shown using the sys.dm_exec_query_optimizer_info DMV, which will produce an output similar to the following for this query:

counter	occurrence	value
elapsed time	1	0.076
final cost	1	0.0032976
maximum DOP	1	0
optimizations	1	1
tables	1	1
trivial plan	1	1

The output shows that this is in fact a trivial plan optimization, using one table and a maximum DOP of 0, and it also displays the elapsed time and final cost. However, if we slightly change the query to the following, looking up on ProductID rather than SalesOrderID, we now get a full optimization:

```
SELECT * FROM Sales.SalesOrderDetail
WHERE ProductID = 870
```

In this case, the Optimization Level or StatementOptLevel property is FULL, which obviously means that the query did not qualify for a trivial plan, and a full optimization was performed instead. Full optimization is used for more complicated queries or queries using more complex features, which will require comparisons of candidate plans' costs in order to guide decisions; this will be explained in the next section. In this particular example, because the predicate ProductID = 870 can return zero, one, or more records, different plans may be created depending on cardinality estimations and the available navigation structures. This was not the case in the previous query using the SalesOrderID query, which is part of a unique index, and so it can return only zero or one record.

Finally, you can use an undocumented trace flag to disable the trivial plan optimization, which you can use for testing purposes; it is shown in the following example:

```
SELECT * FROM Sales.SalesOrderDetail
WHERE SalesOrderID = 43659
OPTION (RECOMPILE, QUERYTRACEON 8757)
```

If we use the sys.dm_exec_query_optimizer_info DMV again, we can see that now, instead of a trivial plan, we have a hint and the optimization goes to search 1, which will be explained later in the chapter.

counter	occurrence	value
elapsed time	1	0.001
final cost	1	0.0032976
Hints	1	1
maximum DOP	1	0
optimizations	1	1
search 1	1	1
search 1 tasks	1	131
search 1 time	1	0
tables	1	1
tasks	1	131

Transformation Rules

As I've mentioned previously, the SQL Server query optimizer uses transformation rules to explore the search space—that is, to explore the set of possible execution plans for a specific query. Transformation rules are based on relational algebra, taking a relational operator tree and generating equivalent alternatives, in the form of equivalent relational operator trees. At the most fundamental level, a query consists of logical expressions, and applying these transformation rules will generate equivalent logical and physical alternatives, which are stored in memory (in a structure called the Memo) for the entire duration of the optimization process. As explained later in this chapter, the query optimizer uses up to three optimization stages, and different transformation rules are applied in each stage.

Each transformation rule has a pattern and a substitute. The pattern is the expression to be analyzed and matched, and the substitute is the equivalent expression that is generated as an output. For example, for the commutativity rule, which is explained next, a transformation rule can be defined as

$$\text{Expr1 join Expr2} -> \text{Expr2 join Expr1}$$

which means that SQL Server will match the pattern Expr1 join Expr2, as in Individual join Customer, and will produce the equivalent expression, Expr2 join Expr1, or in our case, Customer join Individual. The two expressions are logically equivalent because both return exactly the same results.

Initially, the query tree contains only logical expressions, and transformation rules are applied to these logical expressions to generate either logical or physical expressions. As an example, a logical expression can be the definition of a logical join, whereas a physical expression could be an actual join implementation, such as a Merge Join or a Hash Join. Bear in mind that transformation rules cannot be applied to physical expressions.

The main types of transformation rules include simplification, exploration, and implementation rules. Simplification rules produce simpler logical trees as their outputs, and are mostly used during the simplification phase, before the full optimization, as explained previously. Exploration rules, also called logical transformation rules, generate logical equivalent alternatives. Finally, implementation rules, or physical transformation rules, are used to obtain physical alternatives. Both exploration and implementation rules are executed during the full optimization phase.

Examples of exploration rules include the commutativity and associativity rules, which are used in join optimization and shown in Figure 3-8. Commutativity and associativity rules are defined as

$$\text{A join B} -> \text{B join A}$$

and

$$\text{(A join B) join C} -> \text{B join (A join C)}$$

respectively. The commutativity rule (A join B – > B join A) means that A join B is equivalent to B join A, and joining the tables A and B in any order will return the

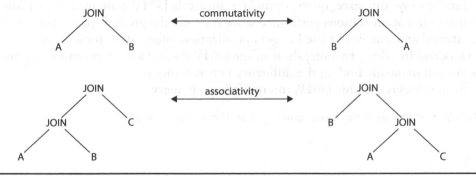

Figure 3-8 *Commutativity and associativity rules*

same results. Also note that applying the commutativity rule twice will generate the original expression again; that is, if you initially apply this transformation to obtain B join A, and then later apply the same transformation, you can obtain A join B again. However, the query optimizer can handle this problem in order to avoid duplicated expressions. In the same way, the associativity rule shows that (A join B) join C is equivalent to B join (A join C) because they also both produce the same results. An example of an implementation rule would be selecting a physical algorithm for a logical join, such as a Merge Join or a Hash Join.

So the query optimizer is using sets of transformation rules to generate and examine possible alternative execution plans. However, it's important to remember that applying rules does not necessarily reduce the cost of the generated alternatives, and the costing component still needs to estimate their costs. Although both logical and physical alternatives are kept in the Memo structure, only the physical alternatives have their costs determined. It's important, then, to bear in mind that although these alternatives may be equivalent and return the same results, their physical implementations may have very different costs. The final selection, as is hopefully clear now, will be the best (or, if you like, the "cheapest") physical alternative stored in the Memo.

For example, implementing A join B may have different costs depending on whether a Nested Loops Join or a Hash Join is selected. In addition, for the same physical join, implementing the A join B expression may have a different performance from B join A. As explained in Chapter 4, the performance of a join is different depending on which table is chosen as the inner or outer table in a Nested Loops Join, or the build and the probe inputs in a Hash Join. If you want to find out why the query optimizer might not choose a specific join algorithm, you can test using a hint to force a specific physical join and compare the cost of both the hinted and the original plans.

Those are the foundation principles of transformation rules, and the sys.dm_exec_query_transformation_stats DMV provides information about the existing transformation rules and how they are being used by the query optimizer. According to this DMV, SQL Server currently has 395 transformation rules, and more can be added in future versions of the product.

Similar to sys.dm_exec_query_optimizer_info, this DMV contains information regarding the optimizations performed since the time the given SQL Server instance was started and can also be used to get optimization information for a particular query or workload by taking two snapshots of the DMV (before and after optimizing your query) and manually finding the difference between them.

To start looking at this DMV, run the following query:

```
SELECT * FROM sys.dm_exec_query_transformation_stats
```

Here is some sample output from my test system using SQL Server 2014, showing the first few records out of 395 (edited to fit the page):

name	promise_total	promise_avg	promised	built_substitute	succeeded
JNtoNL	203352155	92.96051768	2187511	350792	285532
LOJNtoNL	35938188	449.0701754	80028	80028	79504
LSJNtoNL	40614706	450.6936171	90116	90116	90116
LASJNtoNL	4029039	451.6353548	8921	8921	8921
JNtoSM	366499276	418.7495941	875223	814754	441413
FOJNtoSM	6356	454	14	14	4
LOJNtoSM	11180944	443.3891422	25217	24996	17098
ROJNtoSM	11179128	443.3874589	25213	24992	17094
LSJNtoSM	4263232	443.2094812	9619	9453	1495
RSJNtoSM	4263232	443.2094812	9619	9453	6922

The sys.dm_exec_query_transformation_stats DMV includes what is known as the promise information, which tells the query optimizer how useful a given transformation rule might be. The first field in the results output is the name of the rule; for example, the first three rules listed are JNtoNL (Join to Nested Loops Join), LOJNtoNL (Left Outer Join to Nested Loops Join), and JNtoSM (Join to Sort Merge Join), where Sort Merge Join is the academic name of the SQL Server Merge Join operator.

The same issues shown for the sys.dm_exec_query_optimizer_info DMV regarding collecting data also apply to the sys.dm_exec_query_transformation_stats DMV, so the query shown in Listing 3-2 can help you to isolate the optimization information for a specific query while avoiding data from related queries as much as possible. The query is based on the succeeded column, which keeps track of the number of times a transformation rule was used and successfully produced a result.

Listing 3-2   *sys.dm_exec_query_transformation_stats Code*

```
-- optimize these queries now
-- so they do not skew the collected results
GO
SELECT *
INTO before_query_transformation_stats
FROM sys.dm_exec_query_transformation_stats
GO
SELECT *
INTO after_query_transformation_stats
FROM sys.dm_exec_query_transformation_stats
GO
DROP TABLE after_query_transformation_stats
```

```
DROP TABLE before_query_transformation_stats
-- real execution starts
GO
SELECT *
INTO before_query_transformation_stats
FROM sys.dm_exec_query_transformation_stats
GO
-- insert your query here
SELECT * FROM Sales.SalesOrderDetail
WHERE SalesOrderID = 43659
-- keep this to force a new optimization
OPTION (RECOMPILE)
GO
SELECT *
INTO after_query_transformation_stats
FROM sys.dm_exec_query_transformation_stats
GO
SELECT a.name, (a.promised - b.promised) as promised
FROM before_query_transformation_stats b
JOIN after_query_transformation_stats a
ON b.name = a.name
WHERE b.succeeded <> a.succeeded
DROP TABLE before_query_transformation_stats
DROP TABLE after_query_transformation_stats
```

For example, testing with a very simple AdventureWorks2012 query, such as

```
SELECT * FROM Sales.SalesOrderDetail
WHERE SalesOrderID = 43659
```

which is already included in the previous code, will show that the following transformation rules are being used:

name	promised
ProjectToComputeScalar	1
SelIdxToRng	1
SelPrjGetToTrivialScan	1
SelToTrivialFilter	1

The plan produced is a trivial plan. Let's again add the undocumented trace flag 8757 to avoid a trivial plan (just for testing purposes):

```
SELECT * FROM Sales.SalesOrderDetail
WHERE SalesOrderID = 43659
OPTION (RECOMPILE, QUERYTRACEON 8757)
```

We would then get the following output:

name	promised
AddCCPrjToGet	2
GetIdxToRng	1
GetToIdxScan	2
GetToScan	2
ProjectToComputeScalar	2
SelectToFilter	1
SelIdxToRng	1
SelToIdxStrategy	1

Let's now test a more complicated query. Include the following query in the code in Listing 3-2 to explore the transformation rules it uses:

```
SELECT c.CustomerID, COUNT(*)
FROM Sales.Customer c JOIN Sales.SalesOrderHeader o
ON c.CustomerID = o.CustomerID
GROUP BY c.CustomerID
```

As shown in the following output, 17 transformation rules were exercised during the optimization process:

name	promised
AppIdxToApp	0
EnforceSort	23
GbAggBeforeJoin	4
GbAggToHS	8
GbAggToStrm	8
GenLGAgg	2
GetIdxToRng	0
GetToIdxScan	4
GetToScan	4
ImplRestrRemap	3
JNtoHS	6
JNtoIdxLookup	6
JNtoSM	6

(Continued)

name	promised
JoinCommute	2
ProjectToComputeScalar	2
SelIdxToRng	6
SELonJN	1

Now, as I will explain in more detail in Chapter 10, hints may disable some of these transformation rules in order to obtain a specific desired behavior. As a way of experimenting with the effects of these rules, you can also use the undocumented statements DBCC RULEON and DBCC RULEOFF to enable or disable transformation rules, respectively, and thereby get additional insight into how the query optimizer works. However, before you do that, first be warned: because these statements impact the entire optimization process performed by the query optimizer, they should be used only in a test system for experimentation purposes.

To demonstrate the effects of these statements, the previous query would create the plan seen in Figure 3-9.

Here you can see, among other things, that SQL Server is pushing an aggregate below the join (a Stream Aggregate before the Merge Join). The query optimizer can push aggregations that significantly reduce cardinality estimation as early in the plan as possible. This is performed by the transformation rule GbAggBeforeJoin (or Group By Aggregate Before Join), which is included in the output shown previously. This specific transformation rule is used only if certain requirements are met—for example, when the GROUP BY clause includes the joining columns, which is the case in our example. Run the following statement to temporarily disable the use of the GbAggBeforeJoin transformation rule for the current session:

```
DBCC RULEOFF('GbAggBeforeJoin')
```

After disabling this transformation rule and running the query again, the plan, shown in Figure 3-10, will now show the aggregate after the join, which, according to the query optimizer, is a more expensive plan. You can verify this by looking at their estimated costs: 0.285331 and 0.312394, respectively. (These are not shown in the figures, but you can see them by hovering the mouse over the SELECT icon and examining the Estimated

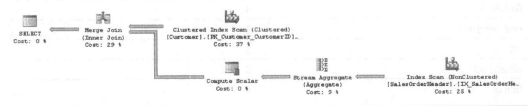

Figure 3-9   *Original execution plan*

Figure 3-10 *Plan with the GbAggBeforeJoin rule disabled*

Subtree Cost value, as explained before.) Note that, for this exercise, an optimization may need to be forced to see the new plan, perhaps using the OPTION (RECOMPILE) hint or one of the methods we've discussed to remove the plan from the cache, such as DBCC FREEPROCCACHE.

What's more, there are a couple of additional undocumented statements to show which transformation rules are enabled and disabled; these are DBCC SHOWONRULES and DBCC SHOWOFFRULES, respectively. By default, DBCC SHOWONRULES will list all the 395 transformation rules listed by the sys.dm_exec_query_transformation_stats DMV. To test it, try running the following code:

```
DBCC TRACEON (3604)
DBCC SHOWONRULES
```

We start this exercise enabling trace flag 3604, which, as explained earlier, instructs SQL Server to send the results to the client (in this case, your Management Studio session). After this, the output of DBCC SHOWONRULES, and later DBCC SHOWOFFRULES, the DBCC RULEON and DBCC RULEOFF statements will be conveniently available to us. The output is provided next (showing only a few of the possible rules to preserve space). The previously disabled rule will not be shown in this output.

```
DBCC execution completed. If DBCC printed error messages, contact your system
administrator.
Rules that are on globally:
JNtoNL
LOJNtoNL
LSJNtoNL
LASJNtoNL
JNtoSM
FOJNtoSM
LOJNtoSM
ROJNtoSM
LSJNtoSM
RSJNtoSM
LASJNtoSM
RASJNtoSM
```

In the same way, the following code will show the rules that are disabled:

```
DBCC SHOWOFFRULES
```

In our case, it will show that only one rule has been disabled:

```
Rules that are off globally:
GbAggBeforeJoin

DBCC execution completed. If DBCC printed error messages, contact your system
administrator.
```

To continue with our example of the effects of the transformation rules, we can disable the use of a Merge Join by disabling the rule JNtoSM (Join to Sort Merge Join) by running the following code:

```
DBCC RULEOFF('JNtoSM')
```

If you have followed the example, this time, DBCC RULEOFF will show some output indicating that the rule is off for some specific SPID. This also means that DBCC RULEON and DBCC RULEOFF work at the session level, but even in this case, your exercise may still impact the entire SQL Server instance because your created plans may be kept in the plan cache and potentially reused by other sessions. Running the sample query again will give us the totally new plan, using both a Hash Join and a Hash Aggregate, shown in Figure 3-11.

In Chapter 10, you will learn how to obtain this same behavior in your queries using hints.

Finally, before we finish, don't forget to reenable the GbAggBeforeJoin and JNtoSM transformation rules by running the following commands:

```
DBCC RULEON('JNtoSM')
DBCC RULEON('GbAggBeforeJoin')
```

Then verify that no transformation rules are still disabled by running this:

```
DBCC SHOWOFFRULES
```

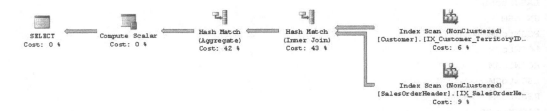

Figure 3-11 *Plan with the JNtoSM rule disabled*

You can also just close your current session because DBCC RULEON and DBCC RULEOFF work at the session level. You may also want to clear your plan cache (to make sure none of these experiment plans were left in memory) by once again running this:

```
DBCC FREEPROCCACHE
```

A second choice to obtain the same behavior is to use the (also undocumented) query hint QUERYRULEOFF. For example, the following code using the QUERYRULEOFF hint will disable the GbAggBeforeJoin rule only for the current optimization:

```
SELECT c.CustomerID, COUNT(*)
FROM Sales.Customer c JOIN Sales.SalesOrderHeader o
ON c.CustomerID = o.CustomerID
GROUP BY c.CustomerID
OPTION (RECOMPILE, QUERYRULEOFF GbAggBeforeJoin)
```

You can include more than one QUERYRULEOFF hint, like in the following example, to disable both the GbAggBeforeJoin and JNtoSM rules, as demonstrated before:

```
SELECT c.CustomerID, COUNT(*)
FROM Sales.Customer c JOIN Sales.SalesOrderHeader o
ON c.CustomerID = o.CustomerID
GROUP BY c.CustomerID
OPTION (RECOMPILE, QUERYRULEOFF GbAggBeforeJoin, QUERYRULEOFF JNtoSM)
```

Also, the query optimizer will obey disabled rules both at the session level and at the query level. There is no QUERYRULEON hint to enable a rule disabled at the session level. Because QUERYRULEOFF is a query hint, this effect lasts only for the optimization of the current query.

In both cases, DBCCRULEOFF and QUERYRULEOFF, you can be at a point where enough rules have been disabled that the query optimizer is not able to produce an execution plan. For example, if you run the query

```
SELECT c.CustomerID, COUNT(*)
FROM Sales.Customer c JOIN Sales.SalesOrderHeader o
ON c.CustomerID = o.CustomerID
GROUP BY c.CustomerID
OPTION (RECOMPILE, QUERYRULEOFF GbAggToStrm, QUERYRULEOFF GbAggToHS)
```

you would get the following error:

```
Msg 8622, Level 16, State 1, Line 1
Query processor could not produce a query plan because of the hints defined in
this query. Resubmit the query without specifying any hints and without using
SET FORCEPLAN.
```

In this particular example, I am disabling both the GbAggToStrm (Group by Aggregate to Stream) and GbAggToHS (Group by Aggregate to Hash) rules. At least one of those rules is required to perform an aggregation; GbAggToStrm would allow me to use a Stream Aggregate and GbAggToHS would allow me to use a Hash Aggregate.

Because the query processor knows the query is using hints, it asks you to resubmit the query without specifying any hints. Disabling both GbAggToStrm and GbAggToHS rules using DBCC RULEOFF, as explained earlier, and running the query without hints results in a more drastic error message:

```
Msg 8624, Level 16, State 1, Line 1
Internal Query Processor Error: The query processor could not produce a
query plan. For more information, contact Customer Support Services.
```

Finally, you can also obtain rules information using the undocumented trace flag 2373. Although it is verbose and provides memory information, it can also be used to find out the transformation rules used during the optimization of a particular query. For example,

```
SELECT c.CustomerID, COUNT(*)
FROM Sales.Customer c JOIN Sales.SalesOrderHeader o
ON c.CustomerID = o.CustomerID
GROUP BY c.CustomerID
OPTION (RECOMPILE, QUERYTRACEON 2373)
```

will show the following output (edited to fit the page):

```
Memory before rule NormalizeGbAgg: 27
Memory after rule NormalizeGbAgg: 27
Memory before rule IJtoIJSEL: 27
Memory after rule IJtoIJSEL: 28
Memory before rule MatchGet: 28
Memory after rule MatchGet: 28
Memory before rule MatchGet: 28
Memory after rule MatchGet: 28
Memory before rule JoinToIndexOnTheFly: 28
Memory after rule JoinToIndexOnTheFly: 28
Memory before rule JoinCommute: 28
Memory after rule JoinCommute: 28
Memory before rule JoinToIndexOnTheFly: 28
Memory after rule JoinToIndexOnTheFly: 28
Memory before rule GbAggBeforeJoin: 28
Memory after rule GbAggBeforeJoin: 28
Memory before rule GbAggBeforeJoin: 28
```

```
Memory after rule GbAggBeforeJoin: 30
Memory before rule IJtoIJSEL: 30
Memory after rule IJtoIJSEL: 30
Memory before rule NormalizeGbAgg: 30
Memory after rule NormalizeGbAgg: 30
Memory before rule GenLGAgg: 30
```

The Memo

The Memo structure was originally defined in "The Volcano Optimizer Generator" by Goetz Graefe and William McKenna in 1993. In the same way, the SQL Server query optimizer is based on the Cascades Framework, which was, in fact, a descendent of the Volcano Optimizer.

The Memo is a search data structure used to store the alternatives generated and analyzed by the query optimizer. These alternatives can be logical or physical operators, and are organized into groups of equivalent alternatives, such that each alternative in the same group produces the same results. Alternatives in the same group also share the same logical properties, and in the same way that operators can reference other operators on a relational tree, groups can also reference other groups in the Memo structure.

A new Memo structure is created for each optimization. The query optimizer first copies the original query tree's logical expressions into the Memo structure, placing each operator from the query tree in its own group, and then triggers the entire optimization process. During this process, transformation rules are applied to generate all the alternatives, starting with these initial logical expressions.

As the transformation rules produce new alternatives, these are added to their equivalent groups. Transformation rules may also produce a new expression that is not equivalent to any existing group, and that causes a new group to be created. As mentioned before, each alternative in a group is a simple logical or physical expression, such as a join or a scan, and a plan will be built using a combination of these alternatives. The number of these alternatives (and even groups) in a Memo structure can be huge.

Although there is the possibility that different combinations of transformation rules may end up producing the same expressions, as indicated earlier, the Memo structure is designed to avoid both the duplication of these alternatives and redundant optimizations. By doing this, it saves memory and is more efficient because it does not have to search the same plan alternatives more than once.

Although both logical and physical alternatives are kept in the Memo structure, only the physical alternatives are costed. Thus, at the end of the optimization process, the Memo contains all of the alternatives considered by the query optimizer, but only one plan is selected, based on the cost of their operations.

Now I will use some undocumented trace flags to show you how the Memo structure is populated and what its final state is after the optimization process has completed. We can use the undocumented trace flag 8608 to show the initial content of the Memo structure. Also, notice that a very simple query may not show anything, like in the following example (remember to enable trace flag 3604 first):

```
SELECT ProductID, name FROM Production.Product
OPTION (RECOMPILE, QUERYTRACEON 8608)
```

The previous query uses a trivial optimization that obviously requires no full optimization and no Memo structure, and therefore, creates a trivial plan. You can force a full optimization by using undocumented trace flag 8757 and running something like this:

```
SELECT ProductID, name FROM Production.Product
OPTION (RECOMPILE, QUERYTRACEON 8608, QUERYTRACEON 8757)
```

In this case, we can see a simple Memo structure like the following:

```
--- Initial Memo Structure ---
Root Group 0: Card=504 (Max=10000, Min=0)
   0 LogOp_Get
```

Let's try a simple query that does not qualify for a trivial plan and see its final logical tree using undocumented trace flag 8606:

```
SELECT ProductID, ListPrice FROM Production.Product
WHERE ListPrice > 90
OPTION (RECOMPILE, QUERYTRACEON 8606)
```

The final tree is this:

```
*** Tree After Project Normalization ***
    LogOp_Select
        LogOp_Get TBL: Production.Product Production.Product
        TableID=1973582069 TableReferenceID=0 IsRow: COL: IsBaseRow1001
        ScaOp_Comp x_cmpGt
            ScaOp_Identifier QCOL: Production].[Product].ListPrice
            ScaOp_Const TI(money,ML=8)
            XVAR(money,Not Owned,Value=(10000units)=(900000))
```

Now let's look at the initial Memo structure using undocumented trace flag 8608:

```
SELECT ProductID, ListPrice FROM Production.Product
WHERE ListPrice > 90
OPTION (RECOMPILE, QUERYTRACEON 8608)
```

We now have something like this:

```
--- Initial Memo Structure ---
Root Group 4: Card=216 (Max=10000, Min=0)
   0 LogOp_Select 0 3
Group 3:
   0 ScaOp_Comp  1 2
Group 2:
   0 ScaOp_Const
Group 1:
   0 ScaOp_Identifier
Group 0: Card=504 (Max=10000, Min=0)
   0 LogOp_Get
```

As you can see, the operators on the logical tree are copied to the Memo structure, and each operator is placed in its own group. We call group 4 the root group because it is the root operator of the initial plan (that is, the root node of the original query tree).

Finally, we can use the undocumented trace flag 8615 to see the Memo structure at the end of the optimization process:

```
SELECT ProductID, ListPrice FROM Production.Product
WHERE ListPrice > 90
OPTION (RECOMPILE, QUERYTRACEON 8615)
```

We would have a Memo structure with the following content:

```
--- Final Memo Structure ---
Root Group 4: Card=216 (Max=10000, Min=0)
   1 PhyOp_Filter 0.2 3.0  Cost(RowGoal 0,ReW 0,ReB 0,Dist 0,Total 0)= 0.0129672
   0 LogOp_Select 0 3
Group 3:
   0 ScaOp_Comp  1.0 2.0  Cost(RowGoal 0,ReW 0,ReB 0,Dist 0,Total 0)= 3
Group 2:
   0 ScaOp_Const    Cost(RowGoal 0,ReW 0,ReB 0,Dist 0,Total 0)= 1
Group 1:
   0 ScaOp_Identifier    Cost(RowGoal 0,ReW 0,ReB 0,Dist 0,Total 0)= 1
Group 0: Card=504 (Max=10000, Min=0)
   2 PhyOp_Range 1 ASC    Cost(RowGoal 0,ReW 0,ReB 0,Dist 0,Total 0)= 0.0127253
   0 LogOp_Get
```

Now let's look at a complete example. Running the following query:

```
SELECT ProductID, COUNT(*)
FROM Sales.SalesOrderDetail
GROUP BY ProductID
OPTION (RECOMPILE, QUERYTRACEON 8608)
```

This will create the following initial Memo structure:

```
--- Initial Memo Structure ---
Root Group 18: Card=266 (Max=133449, Min=0)
   0 LogOp_GbAgg 13 17
Group 17:
   0 AncOp_PrjList  16
Group 16:
   0 AncOp_PrjEl  15
Group 15:
   0 ScaOp_AggFunc  14
Group 14:
   0 ScaOp_Const
Group 13: Card=121317 (Max=133449, Min=0)
   0 LogOp_Get
Group 12:
   0 AncOp_PrjEl  11
Group 11:
   0 ScaOp_Intrinsic  9 10
Group 10:
   0 ScaOp_Const
Group 9:
   0 ScaOp_Arithmetic  6 8
Group 8:
   0 ScaOp_Convert  7
Group 7:
   0 ScaOp_Identifier
Group 6:
   0 ScaOp_Arithmetic  1 5
Group 5:
   0 ScaOp_Arithmetic  2 4
Group 4:
   0 ScaOp_Convert  3
Group 3:
   0 ScaOp_Identifier
Group 2:
   0 ScaOp_Const
Group 1:
   0 ScaOp_Convert  0
Group 0:
   0 ScaOp_Identifier
```

Now run the following query to look at the final Memo structure:

```
SELECT ProductID, COUNT(*)
FROM Sales.SalesOrderDetail
GROUP BY ProductID
OPTION (RECOMPILE, QUERYTRACEON 8615)
```

This will show the following output:

```
--- Final Memo Structure ---
Group 32: Card=266 (Max=133449, Min=0)
   0 LogOp_Project 30 31
Group 31:
   0 AncOp_PrjList  21
Group 30: Card=266 (Max=133449, Min=0)
   0 LogOp_GbAgg 25 29
Group 29:
   0 AncOp_PrjList  28
Group 28:
   0 AncOp_PrjEl  27
Group 27:
   0 ScaOp_AggFunc  26
Group 26:
   0 ScaOp_Identifier
Group 25: Card=532 (Max=133449, Min=0)
   0 LogOp_GbAgg 13 24
Group 24:
   0 AncOp_PrjList  23
Group 23:
   0 AncOp_PrjEl  22
Group 22:
   0 ScaOp_AggFunc  14
Group 21:
   0 AncOp_PrjEl  20
Group 20:
   0 ScaOp_Convert  19
Group 19:
   0 ScaOp_Identifier
Root Group 18: Card=266 (Max=133449, Min=0)
   4 PhyOp_StreamGbAgg 13.2 17.0  Cost(RowGoal 0,ReW 0,ReB 0,Dist 0,Total 0)=
       0.411876
   1 LogOp_RestrRemap 32
   0 LogOp_GbAgg 13 17
```

```
Group 17:
    0 AncOp_PrjList   16.0   Cost(RowGoal 0,ReW 0,ReB 0,Dist 0,Total 0)= 0
Group 16:
    0 AncOp_PrjEl   15.0   Cost(RowGoal 0,ReW 0,ReB 0,Dist 0,Total 0)= 0
Group 15:
    0 ScaOp_AggFunc   14.0   Cost(RowGoal 0,ReW 0,ReB 0,Dist 0,Total 0)= 2
Group 14:
    0 ScaOp_Const    Cost(RowGoal 0,ReW 0,ReB 0,Dist 0,Total 0)= 1
Group 13: Card=121317 (Max=133449, Min=0)
    2 PhyOp_Range 3 ASC    Cost(RowGoal 0,ReW 0,ReB 0,Dist 0,Total 0)= 0.338953
    0 LogOp_Get
Group 12:
    0 AncOp_PrjEl   11
Group 11:
    0 ScaOp_Intrinsic   9 10
Group 10:
    0 ScaOp_Const
Group 9:
    0 ScaOp_Arithmetic   6 8
Group 8:
    0 ScaOp_Convert   7
Group 7:
    0 ScaOp_Identifier
Group 6:
    0 ScaOp_Arithmetic   1 5
Group 5:
    0 ScaOp_Arithmetic   2 4
Group 4:
    0 ScaOp_Convert   3
Group 3:
    0 ScaOp_Identifier
Group 2:
    0 ScaOp_Const
Group 1:
    0 ScaOp_Convert   0
Group 0:
    0 ScaOp_Identifier
```

The initial Memo structure had 18 groups, and the final went to 32, meaning that 14 new groups were added during the optimization process. As explained earlier, during the optimization process, several transformation rules will be executed that will create new alternatives. If the new alternatives are equivalent to an existing operator, they are placed in the same group as this operator. If not, additional groups will be created. You can also see that group 18 was the root group.

Figure 3-12 *Plan showing operators selected*

Toward the end of the process, after some implementation rules are applied, equivalent physical operators will be added to the available Memo groups. After the cost for each operator is estimated, the query optimizer will look for the cheapest way to assemble a plan using the alternatives available. In this example, the plan selected is shown in Figure 3-12.

As we saw earlier, a group by aggregation requires either the GbAggToStrm (Group by Aggregate to Stream) or the GbAggToHS (Group by Aggregate to Hash) transformation rule. In addition, applying any of the techniques explained before, you can see that both rules were used on the optimization process; however, only the GbAggToStrm rule was able to create an alternative on group 18, adding the physical operator PhyOp_StreamGbAgg as an equivalent to the original logical operator LogOp_GbAgg. The PhyOp_StreamGbAgg operator is the Stream Aggregate operator that you can see in the final plan, shown in Figure 3-12. Group 18 shows cardinality estimation 266, indicated as Card=266, and an accumulated cost of 0.411876, which you can also verify on the final execution plan. An Index Scan is also shown in the plan, which corresponds to the PhyOp_Range and LogOp_Get operators shown in group 13.

As an additional test, you can see the Memo contents by forcing a Hash Aggregate by running the following query with a hint:

```
SELECT ProductID, COUNT(*)
FROM Sales.SalesOrderDetail
GROUP BY ProductID
OPTION (RECOMPILE, HASH GROUP, QUERYTRACEON 8615)
```

Statistics

To estimate the cost of an execution plan, the query optimizer needs to know, as precisely as possible, the number of records returned by a given query, and to help with this cardinality estimation, SQL Server uses and maintains optimizer statistics. Statistics contain statistical information describing the distribution of values in one or more columns of a table. Statistics will be explained in greater detail in Chapter 6.

You can use the undocumented trace flags 9292 and 9204 to show information about the statistics loaded during the optimization process. Take a look at the query

```
SELECT ProductID, name FROM Production.Product
WHERE ProductID = 877
OPTION (RECOMPILE, QUERYTRACEON 9292, QUERYTRACEON 9204)
```

which produces an output similar to this:

```
Stats header loaded: DbName: AdventureWorks2012, ObjName: Production.Product,
IndexId: 1, ColumnName: ProductID, EmptyTable: FALSE

Stats loaded: DbName: AdventureWorks2012, ObjName: Production.Product,
IndexId: 1, ColumnName: ProductID, EmptyTable: FALSE
```

To better understand how it works, let's create additional statistics objects:

```
CREATE STATISTICS stat1 ON Production.Product(ProductID)
CREATE STATISTICS stat2 ON Production.Product(ProductID)
CREATE STATISTICS stat3 ON Production.Product(ProductID)
CREATE STATISTICS stat4 ON Production.Product(ProductID)
```

Trace flag 9292 can be used to display the statistics objects that are considered interesting. Run the following query:

```
SELECT ProductID, name FROM Production.Product
WHERE ProductID = 877
OPTION (RECOMPILE, QUERYTRACEON 9292)
```

Here is the output:

```
Stats header loaded: DbName: AdventureWorks2012, ObjName: Production.Product,
IndexId: 1, ColumnName: ProductID, EmptyTable: FALSE

Stats header loaded: DbName: AdventureWorks2012, ObjName: Production.Product,
IndexId: 10, ColumnName: ProductID, EmptyTable: FALSE

Stats header loaded: DbName: AdventureWorks2012, ObjName: Production.Product,
IndexId: 11, ColumnName: ProductID, EmptyTable: FALSE

Stats header loaded: DbName: AdventureWorks2012, ObjName: Production.Product,
IndexId: 12, ColumnName: ProductID, EmptyTable: FALSE

Stats header loaded: DbName: AdventureWorks2012, ObjName: Production.Product,
IndexId: 13, ColumnName: ProductID, EmptyTable: FALSE
```

Trace flag 9204 can be used to display the statistics objects that were used to produce a cardinality estimate. Test the following code:

```
SELECT ProductID, name FROM Production.Product
WHERE ProductID = 877
OPTION (RECOMPILE, QUERYTRACEON 9204)
```

The output is

```
Stats loaded: DbName: AdventureWorks2012, ObjName: Production.Product,
IndexId: 1, ColumnName: ProductID, EmptyTable: FALSE
```

To clean up, drop the statistics object you've just created:

```
DROP STATISTICS Production.Product.stat1
DROP STATISTICS Production.Product.stat2
DROP STATISTICS Production.Product.stat3
DROP STATISTICS Production.Product.stat4
```

Full Optimization

As shown in the processing steps in Figure 3-13, if a query does not qualify for a trivial plan, SQL Server will run the cost-based optimization process, which uses transformation rules to generate alternative plans, stores these alternatives in the Memo structure, and uses cost estimation to select the best plan. This optimization process can be executed in up to three stages, with different transformation rules being applied at each stage.

Because some queries may have a huge number of possible query plans, it's sometimes not feasible to explore their entire search space—query optimization would take too long. So, in addition to applying transformation rules, a number of heuristics are used by the query optimizer to control the search strategy and to limit the number of alternatives generated, in order to quickly find a good plan. The query optimizer needs to balance the optimization time and the quality of the selected plan. For example, as explained in Chapter 10, optimizing join orders can create a huge number of possible alternatives. So a heuristic used by SQL Server creates an initial set of join orders based on their selectivity, as shown later in this section.

In addition, as introduced in Chapter 1, the optimization process can immediately finish if a good enough plan (relative to the query optimizer's internal thresholds) is found at the end of any of these three phases. However, if at the end of any given phase the best plan is still very expensive, the query optimizer will run the next phase, which will run an additional set of (usually more complex) transformation rules. These phases are called search 0, search 1, and search 2 on the sys.dm_exec_query_optimizer_info DMV and shown in Figure 3-13.

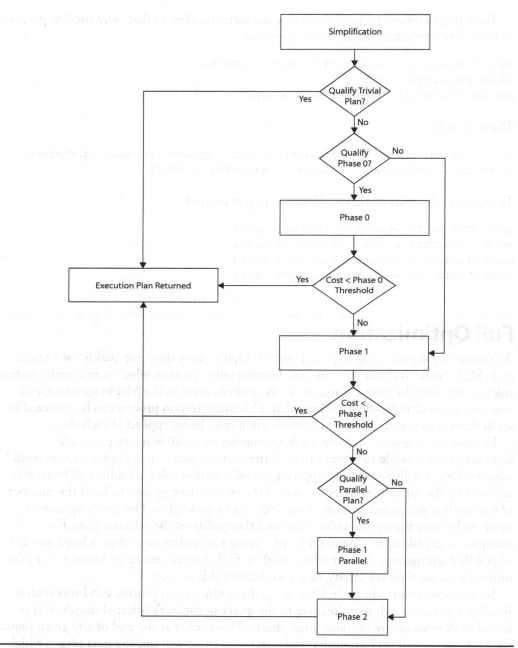

Figure 3-13 *The optimization process*

Search 0

Similar to the concept of the trivial plan, the first phase, search 0, will aim to find a plan as quickly as possible without trying sophisticated transformations. Search 0, called the transaction processing phase, is ideal for the small queries typically found on transaction-processing systems and it is used for queries with at least three tables. Before the full optimization process is started, the query optimizer generates the initial set of join orders based on heuristics. These heuristics begin by first joining the smallest tables or the tables that achieve the largest filtering based on their selectivity. Those are the only join orders considered on search 0. At the end of this phase, the query optimizer compares the cost of the best generated plan to an internal cost threshold, and if the plan is still very expensive, SQL Server will run the next phase.

Search 1

The next phase, search 1 (also called Quick Plan), uses additional transformation rules, limited join reordering, and is appropriate for more complex queries. At the end of this phase, SQL Server compares the cost of the cheapest plan to a second internal cost threshold; if the best plan is cheap enough, it is selected. If the query is still expensive and the system can run parallel queries, this phase is executed again to find a good parallel plan, but no plan is selected for execution at this point. At the end of this phase, the costs of the best serial and parallel plans are compared, and the cheapest one is used in the following phase, search 2, which we'll come to in just a moment.

As an example, the following query does not qualify for search 0 and will go directly to search 1:

```
SELECT * FROM Sales.SalesOrderDetail
WHERE ProductID = 870
```

Using the sys.dm_exec_query_optimizer_info DMV, as explained earlier in this chapter, you can display its optimization information seen next, which shows that only the search 1 phase was executed:

counter	occurrence	value
elapsed time	1	0.102
final cost	1	1.134781816
maximum DOP	1	0
optimizations	1	1
search 1	1	1
search 1 tasks	1	241

(Continued)

counter	occurrence	value
search 1 time	1	0.061
tables	1	1
tasks	1	241

The sys.dm_exec_query_optimizer_info DMV includes a counter named "gain stage 0 to stage 1," which shows the number of times search 1 was executed after search 0, and includes the average decrease in cost from one stage to the other, as defined by the following formula:

$$(MinimumPlanCost(\text{search } 0) - MinimumPlanCost(\text{search } 1)) / MinimumPlanCost(\text{search } 0)$$

For example, the query

```
SELECT soh.SalesOrderID, sod.SalesOrderDetailID, SalesReasonID
FROM Sales.SalesOrderHeader soh
JOIN Sales.SalesOrderDetail sod
    ON soh.SalesOrderID = soh.SalesOrderID
JOIN Sales.SalesOrderHeaderSalesReason sohsr
    ON sohsr.SalesOrderID = soh.SalesOrderID
WHERE soh.SalesOrderID = 43697
```

will provide the optimization information shown next:

counter	occurrence	value
elapsed time	1	0.002
final cost	1	1.413612922
gain stage 0 to stage 1	1	0.05339122
hints	1	1
maximum DOP	1	0
optimizations	1	1
search 0 tasks	1	158
search 0 time	1	0
search 1	1	1
search 1 tasks	1	101
search 1 time	1	0
tables	1	3
tasks	1	259

The output shows that the optimization process went through both the search 0 and search 1 stages and that a plan was found on the latter. It also shows a cost improvement of 5 percent by going from the search 0 stage to the search 1 stage.

Search 2

The last phase, search 2, is called full optimization, and is used for queries ranging from complex to very complex. A larger set of the potential transformation rules, parallel operators, and other advanced optimization strategies are considered in this phase. Because this is the last phase, an execution plan must be found here (perhaps with the exception of the timeout event, as explained later).

The sys.dm_exec_query_optimizer_info DMV includes another useful counter, named "gain stage 1 to stage 2," to show the number of times search 2 was executed after search 1, together with the average decrease in cost from one stage to the other, as defined by the following formula:

$$(\text{MinimumPlanCost(search 1)} - \text{MinimumPlanCost(search 2)}) / \text{MinimumPlanCost(search 1)}$$

We could also use the undocumented trace flags 8675 and 2372 to get additional information about these optimization phases. For example, run the following query:

```
SELECT DISTINCT pp.LastName, pp.FirstName
FROM Person.Person pp JOIN HumanResources.Employee e
    ON e.BusinessEntityID = pp.BusinessEntityID
JOIN Sales.SalesOrderHeader soh
    ON pp.BusinessEntityID = soh.SalesPersonID
JOIN Sales.SalesOrderDetail sod
    ON soh.SalesOrderID = soh.SalesOrderID
JOIN Production.Product p
    ON sod.ProductID = p.ProductID
WHERE ProductNumber = 'BK-M18B-44'
OPTION (RECOMPILE, QUERYTRACEON 8675)
```

It will create the optimization information shown next:

```
End of simplification, time: 0.003 net: 0.003 total: 0.003 net: 0.003
end exploration, tasks: 149 no total cost time: 0.005 net: 0.005 total: 0.009
end search(0),  cost: 13.884 tasks: 332 time: 0.002 net: 0.002 total: 0.011
end exploration, tasks: 926 Cost = 13.884 time: 0.01 net: 0.01 total: 0.021
end search(1),  cost: 3.46578 tasks: 1906 time: 0.009 net: 0.009 total: 0.031
end exploration, tasks: 3301 Cost = 3.46578 time: 0.008 net: 0.008 total: 0.04
*** Optimizer time out abort at task 4248 ***
```

```
end search(2),   cost: 0.832242 tasks: 4248 time: 0.013 net: 0.013 total: 0.053
*** Optimizer time out abort at task 4248 ***
End of post optimization rewrite, time: 0 net: 0 total: 0.053 net: 0.053
End of query plan compilation, time: 0 net: 0 total: 0.054 net: 0.054
```

The optimization information shows that this query went throughout all the three stages of optimization and had an optimization timeout on search 2. The optimization timeout concept was briefly introduced in Chapter 1 and will be explained next.

Running the same query with trace flag 2372 will show the following output, in which the search 0, 1, and 2 phases are named stage TP, QuickPlan, and Full, respectively:

```
Memory before NNFConvert: 25
Memory after NNFConvert: 25
Memory before project removal: 27
Memory after project removal: 29
Memory before simplification: 29
Memory after simplification: 58
Memory before heuristic join reordering: 58
Memory after heuristic join reordering: 65
Memory before project normalization: 65
Memory after project normalization: 65
Memory before stage TP: 68
Memory after stage TP: 84
Memory before stage QuickPlan: 84
Memory after stage QuickPlan: 126
Memory before stage Full: 126
Memory after stage Full: 172
Memory before copy out: 172
Memory after copy out: 173
```

As we've touched upon previously, the query optimizer has to find the best plan possible within the shortest amount of time. More to the point, it must eventually return a plan, even if that plan is not as efficient as it would like. To that end, the optimization process also includes the concept of an optimization cost budget. When this budget is exceeded, the search for the optimal plan is terminated, and the query optimizer will show an optimization timeout. This timeout is not a fixed amount of time, but is instead calculated based on the number of transformations applied together with the elapsed time.

When a timeout is found, the query optimizer stops the optimization process and returns the least expensive plan it has found so far. The best plan found so far could be a plan found during the current optimization stage, but most likely, it would be the best plan found in the previous stage. This obviously means that a timeout most likely will happen in the search 1 and search 2 stages. This timeout event is shown in the properties of a graphical plan as "Reason For Early Termination Of Statement Optimization" or in an XML plan as StatementOptmEarlyAbortReason. This event is also shown as the timeout counter on the sys.dm_exec_query_optimizer_info DMV. An example is shown in Figure 3-14, obtained by running the previous query in this section.

Finally, at the end of the optimization process, the chosen plan will be sent to the execution engine to be run, and the results will be sent back to the client.

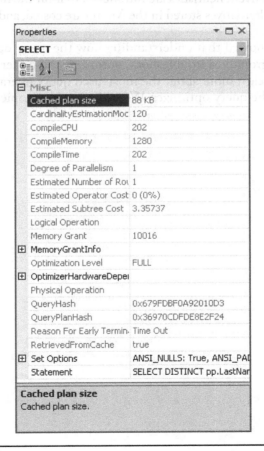

Figure 3-14 *Timeout example*

Summary

This chapter showed how the query optimizer works, explaining how your query goes from a SQL statement submitted to SQL Server, all the way to the selected execution plan, including parsing, binding, simplification, trivial plan, and the full optimization stages. Important concepts that are part of the query optimizer architecture, such as transformation rules and the Memo structure, were also introduced.

The query optimizer generates a solution space and selects the best possible execution plan from it, based on the plan cost. Transformation rules are used to generate these alternatives, which are stored in a memory structure called the Memo. Instead of exploring the search space exhaustively, heuristics are introduced to limit the number of possible solutions. Finally, the alternatives stored in the Memo are costed, and the best solution is returned for execution.

This chapter also showed that understanding how the query optimizer works can give you a great background to troubleshoot, optimize, and better tune your queries. But you still need to learn more about the most-used query operators employed on the plans created by the query optimizer. We will cover that topic in the next chapter.

Chapter 4

Query Operators

In This Chapter

The execution engine is, at its heart, a collection of physical operators that are software components performing the functions of the query processor. Their purpose is to execute your query in an efficient way. To look at it from the other direction, these operations implemented by the execution engine define the choices available to the query optimizer when building execution plans. The execution engine and its operators were briefly covered in previous chapters, and now we'll cover some of the most used operators, their algorithms, and their costs. In this chapter, I focus on operators related to data access, joins, aggregations, parallelism, and updates, as these are the ones most commonly used in queries, and also the ones more used in this book. Of course, many more operators are implemented by the execution engine, and you can find a complete list and description on SQL Server 2014 Books Online. This chapter illustrates how the query optimizer decides between the various choices of operators provided by the execution engine. For example, I show you how the query processor reasons about choosing between a Nested Loops Join and a Hash Join as well as between a Stream Aggregate and a Hash Aggregate operator.

This chapter starts with a look at the data access operations, including the operators to perform scans, seeks, and bookmark lookups on database structures, such as heaps, clustered indexes, and nonclustered indexes. The concepts of sorting and hashing are also explained, as well as how they impact some of the algorithms of both physical joins and aggregations, which are detailed later. In the same way, the section on joins presents the Nested Loops Join, Merge Join, and Hash Join physical operators. The next section focuses on aggregations and explains the Stream Aggregate and Hash Aggregate operators in detail. The chapter continues with parallelism and explains how it can help to reduce the response time of a query. Finally, the chapter concludes by explaining how the query processor handles update operations.

Data Access Operators

In this section, I show you the operations that directly access the database, using either a base table or an index, examples of which include scans and seeks. A scan reads an entire structure, which could be a heap, a clustered index, or a nonclustered index. A seek, on the other hand, does not scan an entire structure, but instead efficiently retrieves rows by navigating an index. Therefore, seeks can only be performed on a clustered or nonclustered index. Just to make the difference between these structures clear, a heap contains all of a table's columns, and its data is not stored sorted in any particular order. Conversely, in a clustered index, the data is stored logically, sorted by the clustering key and, in addition to the clustering key, the clustered index also contains the remaining columns of the table. On the other hand, a nonclustered index can be defined on a clustered index or a heap, and usually contains only a subset of the columns of the table. The operations on these structures are summarized in Table 4-1.

Structure	Scan	Seek
Heap	Table Scan	
Clustered index	Clustered Index Scan	Clustered Index Seek
Nonclustered index	Index Scan	Index Seek

Table 4-1 *Data Access Operators*

Scans

Let's start with the simplest example, by scanning a heap, which is performed by the Table Scan operator, as shown in Table 4-1. The following query on the AdventureWorks2012 database will use a Table Scan, as shown in Figure 4-1.

```
SELECT * FROM DatabaseLog
```

Similarly, the following query will show a Clustered Index Scan operator, as shown in the plan in Figure 4-2. The Table Scan and Clustered Index Scan operations are similar in that they both scan the entire base table, but the former is used for heaps and the latter for clustered indexes.

```
SELECT * FROM Person.Address
```

Sorting is something to consider when it comes to scans, because even when the data in a clustered index is stored sorted, using a Clustered Index Scan does not guarantee that the results will be sorted unless this is explicitly requested. By not automatically sorting the results, the storage engine has the option to find the most efficient way to access this data without worrying about returning it in an ordered set. Examples of these efficient methods used by the storage engine include using an allocation order scan based on Index Allocation Map (IAM) pages and using an index order scan based on the index linked list. In addition, an advanced scanning mechanism called "merry-go-round scanning" (an Enterprise edition-only feature) allows multiple query executions to share full table scans so that each execution may join the scan at a different location, thus saving the overhead of each query having to separately read the data.

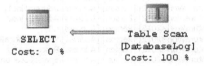

SELECT
Cost: 0 %

Table Scan
[DatabaseLog]
Cost: 100 %

Figure 4-1 *A Table Scan operator*

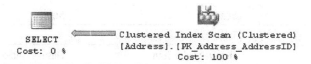

Figure 4-2 *A Clustered Index Scan operator*

If you want to know whether your data has been sorted, the Ordered property can show if the data was returned in a manner ordered by the Clustered Index Scan operator. So, for example, the clustering key of the Person.Address table is AddressID, and if you run the following query and look at the tooltip of the Clustered Index Scan operator, you will get something similar to what is shown in Figure 4-3.

```
SELECT * FROM Person.Address
ORDER BY AddressID
```

Clustered Index Scan (Clustered)	
Scanning a clustered index, entirely or only a range.	
Physical Operation	Clustered Index Scan
Logical Operation	Clustered Index Scan
Actual Execution Mode	Row
Estimated Execution Mode	Row
Storage	RowStore
Actual Number of Rows	19614
Actual Number of Batches	0
Estimated I/O Cost	0.257199
Estimated Operator Cost	0.278931 (100%)
Estimated Subtree Cost	0.278931
Estimated CPU Cost	0.0217324
Estimated Number of Executions	1
Number of Executions	1
Estimated Number of Rows	19614
Estimated Row Size	4241 B
Actual Rebinds	0
Actual Rewinds	0
Ordered	True
Node ID	0

Object
[AdventureWorks2012].[Person].[Address].
[PK_Address_AddressID]
Output List
[AdventureWorks2012].[Person].[Address].AddressID,
[AdventureWorks2012].[Person].[Address].AddressLine1,
[AdventureWorks2012].[Person].[Address].AddressLine2,
[AdventureWorks2012].[Person].[Address].City,
[AdventureWorks2012].[Person].[Address].StateProvinceID,
[AdventureWorks2012].[Person].[Address].PostalCode,
[AdventureWorks2012].[Person].[Address].SpatialLocation,
[AdventureWorks2012].[Person].[Address].rowguid,
[AdventureWorks2012].[Person].[Address].ModifiedDate

Figure 4-3 *Properties of the Clustered Index Scan operator*

Notice that the Ordered property shows True. If you run the same query without the ORDER BY clause, the Ordered property will, unsurprisingly, show False. In some cases, SQL Server can benefit from reading the table in the order specified by the clustered index. One example is shown later in this chapter in Figure 4-15, where a Stream Aggregate operator can benefit from the fact that a Clustered Index Scan operator can easily obtain the data already sorted.

Next, I show you an example of an Index Scan operator. This example uses a nonclustered index to cover a query; that is, it can solve the entire query without accessing the base table (bearing in mind that a nonclustered index usually contains only a few of the columns of the table). Run the following query, which will show the plan in Figure 4-4:

```
SELECT AddressID, City, StateProvinceID
FROM Person.Address
```

Note that the query optimizer was able to solve this query without even accessing the base table Person.Address, and instead decided to scan the IX_Address_AddressLine1_ AddressLine2_City_StateProvinceID_PostalCode index, which comprises fewer pages when compared to the clustered index. The index definition includes AddressLine1, AddressLine2, City, StateProvinceID, and PostalCode, so it can clearly cover columns requested in the query. However, you may wonder where the index is getting the AddressID column from. When a nonclustered index is created on a table with a clustered index, each nonclustered index row also includes the table clustering key. This clustering key is used to find which record from the clustered index is referred to by the nonclustered index row (a similar approach for nonclustered indexes on a heap will be explained later in this section). In this case, as I mentioned earlier, AddressID is the clustering key of the table, and it is stored in every row of the nonclustered index, which is why the index was able to cover this column in the previous query.

Seeks

Now let's look at Index Seeks. These can be performed by both the Clustered Index Seek and the Index Seek operators, which are used against clustered and nonclustered indexes, respectively. An Index Seek does not scan the entire index, but instead navigates the B-tree index structure to quickly find one or more records. The next query, together with the plan in Figure 4-5, shows an example of a Clustered Index Seek. A benefit of

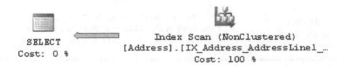

Figure 4-4   *An Index Scan operator*

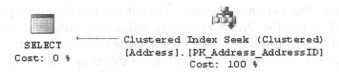

```
    SELECT          ◄──────── Clustered Index Seek (Clustered)
    Cost: 0 %                  [Address].[PK_Address_AddressID]
                                        Cost: 100 %
```

Figure 4-5 *A Clustered Index Seek operator*

a Clustered Index Seek, compared to a nonclustered Index Seek, is that the former can cover any column of the table. Of course, because the records of a clustered index are logically ordered by its clustering key, a table can only have one clustered index.

```
SELECT AddressID, City, StateProvinceID FROM Person.Address
WHERE AddressID = 12037
```

The next query and Figure 4-6 both illustrate a nonclustered Index Seek operator. It is interesting to note here that the base table was not used at all, and it was not even necessary to scan the entire index: there is a nonclustered index on the StateProvinceID and, as mentioned previously, it also contains the clustering key AddressID.

```
SELECT AddressID, StateProvinceID FROM Person.Address
WHERE StateProvinceID = 32
```

Although both examples shown return only one row, an Index Seek operation can also be used to find multiple rows with either equality or nonequality operators; this is called a partial ordered scan. The previous query just returned one row, but you can change it to a new parameter like in the following example:

```
SELECT AddressID, StateProvinceID FROM Person.Address
WHERE StateProvinceID = 9
```

In fact, the query has been auto-parameterized, and the same plan will be used with any other parameter. You can try to force a new optimization and plan (for example, using DBCC FREEPROCCACHE), but the same plan will be returned. In this case, the same plan shown in Figure 4-6 will be used, and 4,564 rows will be returned without the need to access the base table at all. A partial ordered scan works by using the index

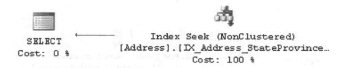

```
    SELECT          ◄──────── Index Seek (NonClustered)
    Cost: 0 %                  [Address].[IX_Address_StateProvince...
                                        Cost: 100 %
```

Figure 4-6 *An Index Seek operator*

to find the first row that qualifies and continues reading the remaining rows, which are all logically together in the same leaf pages of the index. More details about the index structure will be covered in Chapter 5.

A more complicated example of partial ordered scans involves using a nonequality operator or a BETWEEN clause, like in the following example:

```
SELECT AddressID, City, StateProvinceID FROM Person.Address
WHERE AddressID BETWEEN 10000 and 20000
```

Because the clustered index is defined using AddressID, a plan similar to Figure 4-5 will be used, where a Clustered Index Seek operation will be used to find the first row that qualifies to the filter predicate and will continue scanning the index, row by row, until the last row that qualifies is found. More accurately, the scan will stop on the first row that does not qualify.

Bookmark Lookup

The question that now comes up is what happens if a nonclustered index is useful to quickly find one or more records, but does not cover the query? In other words, what happens if the nonclustered index does not contain all of the columns requested by the query? In this case, the query optimizer has to decide if it is more efficient to use the nonclustered index to find these records quickly and then access the base table to obtain the additional fields, or if it is more optimal to just go straight to the base table and scan it, reading each row and testing to see if it matches the predicates. For example, in our previous query, an existing nonclustered index covers both AddressID and StateProvinceID columns. What if we also request the City and ModifiedDate columns on the same query? This is shown in the next query, which returns one record and produces the plan in Figure 4-7.

```
SELECT AddressID, City, StateProvinceID, ModifiedDate
FROM Person.Address
WHERE StateProvinceID = 32
```

As in the previous example, the query optimizer is choosing the index IX_Address_StateProvinceID to find the records quickly. However, because the index does not cover the additional columns, it also needs to use the base table (in this case, the clustered index) to get that additional information. This operation is called a *bookmark lookup*, and it is performed by the Key Lookup operator, which was introduced specifically to differentiate a bookmark lookup from a regular Clustered Index Seek. Actually, the Key Lookup operator only appears on a graphical plan (and then only from SQL Server 2005 Service Pack 2 and onward). Text and XML plans can show whether a Clustered

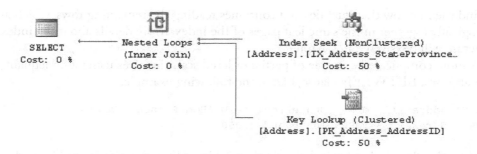

Figure 4-7 *A bookmark lookup example*

Index Seek operator is performing a bookmark lookup by looking at the LOOKUP keyword and Lookup attributes, as shown next. For example, run the following query:

```
SET SHOWPLAN_TEXT ON
GO
SELECT AddressID, City, StateProvinceID, ModifiedDate
FROM Person.Address
WHERE StateProvinceID = 32
GO
SET SHOWPLAN_TEXT OFF
GO
```

The output will show the following text plan, including a Clustered Index Seek operator with the LOOKUP keyword at the end:

```
|--Nested Loops(Inner Join, OUTER REFERENCES ...)
|--Index Seek(OBJECT:([Address].[IX_Address_StateProvinceID]),
    SEEK:([Address].[StateProvinceID]=(32)) ORDERED FORWARD)
|--Clustered Index Seek(OBJECT:([Address].[PK_Address_AddressID]),
    SEEK:([Address].[AddressID]=[Address].[AddressID]) LOOKUP ORDERED FORWARD)
```

The XML plan shows the same information in the following way:

```
<RelOp LogicalOp="Clustered Index Seek" PhysicalOp="Clustered Index Seek" ...>
...
<IndexScan Lookup="true" Ordered="true" ScanDirection="FORWARD" ...>
```

Keep in mind that although SQL Server 2000 implemented a bookmark lookup using a dedicated operator (called Bookmark Lookup), the operation is basically the same.

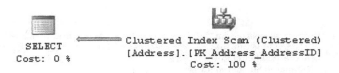

Figure 4-8 *Plan switching to a Clustered Index Scan*

Now run the same query, but this time, request StateProvinceID equal to 20. This will produce the plan shown in Figure 4-8.

```
SELECT AddressID, City, StateProvinceID, ModifiedDate
FROM Person.Address
WHERE StateProvinceID = 20
```

On this execution, the query optimizer has selected a Clustered Index Scan and the query has returned 308 records, compared to just a single record for the StateProvinceID 32. So the query optimizer is producing two different execution plans for the same query, with the only difference being the value of the StateProvinceID parameter. In this case, the query optimizer uses the value of the query's StateProvinceID parameter to estimate the cardinality of the predicate as it tries to produce an efficient plan for that parameter. I show this in more detail in Chapter 6.

This time, the query optimizer estimated that more records could be returned than when StateProvinceID was equal to 32, and it decided that it was cheaper to do a Table Scan than to perform many bookmark lookups. At this stage, you may be wondering at what point the query optimizer decides to change from one method to another. Because a bookmark lookup requires random I/O, which is very expensive, it would not take many records for the query optimizer to switch from a bookmark lookup to a Clustered Index Scan (or a Table Scan). We already know that when the query returned one record, for StateProvinceID 32, the query optimizer chose a bookmark lookup. We also saw that when we requested the records for StateProvinceID 20, which returned 308 records, it used a Clustered Index Scan. Logically, we can try requesting somewhere between 1 and 308 records to find this switchover point, right?

Actually, as you may already suspect, this is a cost-based decision that does not depend on the actual number of records returned by the query; rather, it is influenced by the estimated number of records. We can find these estimates by analyzing the histogram of the statistics object for the IX_Address_StateProvinceID index— something that will be covered in Chapter 6.

I performed this exercise and found that the highest estimated number of records to get a bookmark lookup for this particular example was 62, and the first one to have a Clustered Index Scan was 106. Let's look at both examples here, by running the query with the StateProvinceID values 163 and 71. We will get the plans shown in Figures 4-9 and 4-10, respectively.

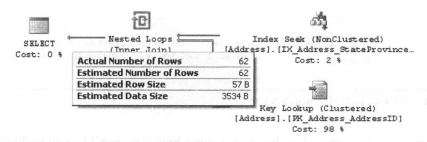

Figure 4-9 *Plan for the StateProvinceID = 163 predicate*

By looking at the plans, we can see that, for this specific example, the query optimizer selects a bookmark lookup for an estimated 62 records and changes to a Clustered Index Scan when that estimated number of records goes up to 106 (there are no estimated values between 62 and 106 for the histogram of this particular statistics object). Keep in mind that, although in this case both the actual and estimated number of rows are the same, the query optimizer makes its decision based on the estimated number of rows. The actual number of rows is only known after the execution plan is generated and executed, and the results returned.

Finally, because nonclustered indexes can exist on both heaps and clustered indexes, we can also have a bookmark lookup on a heap. To follow the next example, create an index on the DatabaseLog table, which is a heap, by running the following statement:

```
CREATE INDEX IX_Object ON DatabaseLog(Object)
```

Then run the following query, which will produce the plan in Figure 4-11:

```
SELECT * FROM DatabaseLog
WHERE Object = 'City'
```

Note that instead of the Key Lookup operator shown before, this plan displays an RID Lookup operator. This is because heaps do not have clustering keys like clustered indexes do, and instead they have row identifiers (RIDs). An RID is a row locator that includes

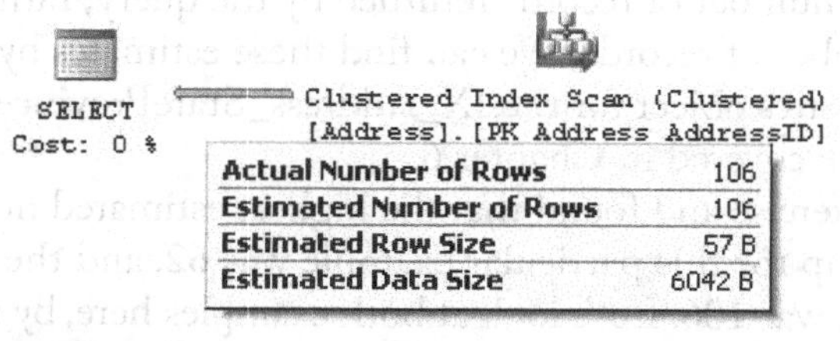

Figure 4-10 *Plan for the StateProvinceID = 71 predicate*

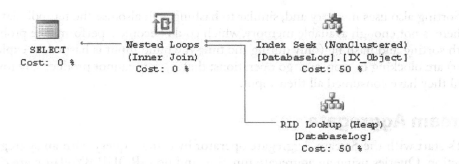

Figure 4-11 *An RID Lookup*

information such as the database file, page, and slot numbers to allow a specific record to
be easily located. Every row in a nonclustered index created on a heap contains the RID
of the corresponding heap record.

To clean up, simply remove the index you just created:

```
DROP INDEX DatabaseLog.IX_Object
```

Aggregations

Aggregations are used in databases to summarize information about some set of data.
The result can be a single value, such as the average salary for a company, or it can
be a per-group value, such as the average salary by department. SQL Server has two
operators to implement aggregations, Stream Aggregate and Hash Aggregate, and
they can be used to solve queries with aggregation functions (such as SUM, AVG, and
MAX), the GROUP BY clause, or the DISTINCT keyword.

Sorting and Hashing

Before introducing the remaining operators of this chapter, I would like to add a brief
discussion on sorting and hashing, both of which play a very important role in some of
the operators and algorithms of the execution engine. For example, two of the operators
covered in this chapter, Stream Aggregate and Merge Join, require data to be already
sorted. To provide sorted data, the query optimizer may employ an existing index, or
it may explicitly introduce a Sort operator. On the other hand, hashing is used by the
Hash Aggregate and Hash Join operators, both of which work by building a hash table
in memory. The Hash Join operator uses memory only for the smaller of its two inputs,
which is defined by the query optimizer.

Sorting also uses memory and, similar to hashing, will also use the tempdb database if there is not enough available memory, which could become a performance problem. Both sorting and hashing (only during the time the build input is hashed, as explained later) are blocking or stop-and-go operations; that is, they cannot produce any rows until they have consumed all their input.

Stream Aggregate

Let's start with the Stream Aggregate operator by using a query with an aggregation function. Queries using an aggregate function and no GROUP BY clause are called *scalar aggregates*, as they return a single value and are always implemented by the Stream Aggregate operator. To demonstrate, run the following query, which shows the plan in Figure 4-12:

```
SELECT AVG(ListPrice) FROM Production.Product
```

A text plan can be useful to show more details about both the Stream Aggregate and the Compute Scalar operators. Run the following query:

```
SET SHOWPLAN_TEXT ON
GO
SELECT AVG(ListPrice) FROM Production.Product
GO
SET SHOWPLAN_TEXT OFF
GO
```

Here is the displayed text plan:

```
|--Compute Scalar(DEFINE:([Expr1002]=CASE WHEN [Expr1003]=(0) THEN NULL ELSE
[Expr1004]/CONVERT_IMPLICIT(money,[Expr1003],0) END))
|--Stream Aggregate(DEFINE:([Expr1003]=Count(*), [Expr1004]=SUM([Product].
[ListPrice])))
|--Clustered Index Scan(OBJECT:([Product].[PK_Product_ProductID]))
```

The same information could be obtained from the graphical plan by selecting the Properties window (by pressing F4) of both the Stream Aggregate and Compute Scalar operators and then opening the Defined Values property, as shown in Figure 4-13.

SELECT
Cost: 0 %

Compute Scalar
Cost: 0 %

Stream Aggregate
(Aggregate)
Cost: 2 %

Clustered Index Scan (Clustered)
[Product].[PK_Product_ProductID]
Cost: 98 %

Figure 4-12 *A Stream Aggregate*

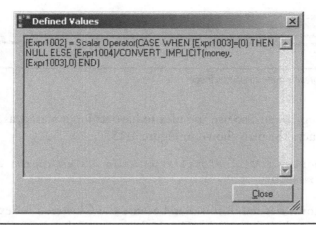

Figure 4-13 *Defined Values property of the Compute Scalar operator*

Note that in order to implement the AVG aggregation function, the Stream Aggregate is computing both a COUNT and a SUM aggregate, the results of which will be stored in the computed expressions Expr1003 and Expr1004, respectively. The Compute Scalar verifies that there is no division by zero by using a CASE expression. As you can see in the text plan, if Expr1003 (which is the value for the count) is zero, the Compute Scalar operator returns NULL; otherwise, it calculates and returns the average by dividing the sum by the count.

Now let's see an example of a query using the GROUP BY clause; the following query produces the plan in Figure 4-14:

```
SELECT ProductLine, COUNT(*) FROM Production.Product
GROUP BY ProductLine
```

A Stream Aggregate operator always requires its input to be sorted by the GROUP BY clause predicate, so in this case, the Sort operator shown in the plan will provide the data sorted by the ProductLine column. After the sorted input is received, the records for the same group will be next to each other so the Stream Aggregate operator can now easily count the records for each group. Note that although the first example in this section also used a Stream Aggregate, it did not require any sorted input: a query without a GROUP BY clause considers its entire input a single group.

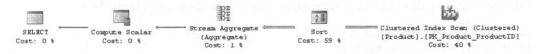

Figure 4-14 *Stream Aggregate using a Sort operator*

Figure 4-15 *Stream Aggregate using an existing index*

A Stream Aggregate can also use an index to have its input sorted, as in the following query, which produces the plan shown in Figure 4-15:

```
SELECT SalesOrderID, SUM(LineTotal) FROM Sales.SalesOrderDetail
GROUP BY SalesOrderID
```

No Sort operator is needed in this plan because the Clustered Index Scan provides the data already sorted by SalesOrderID, which is part of the clustering key of the SalesOrderDetail table. As in the previous example, the Stream Aggregate operator will consume the sorted data, but this time, it will calculate the sum of the LineTotal column for each group.

Because the purpose of the Stream Aggregate operator is to aggregate values based on groups, its algorithm relies on the fact that its input is already sorted by the GROUP BY clause predicate, and therefore, records from the same group are next to each other. Basically, in this algorithm, the first record read will create the first group, and its aggregate value will be initialized. Any record read after that will be checked to see if it matches the current group; if it does match, the record value will be aggregated to this group. On the other hand, if the record doesn't match the current group, a new group will be created, and its own aggregated value initialized. This process will continue until all the records are processed.

Hash Aggregate

Now let's take a look at the Hash Aggregate operator, shown as Hash Match (Aggregate) on the execution plans. This chapter describes two hash algorithms, Hash Aggregate and Hash Join, which work in a similar way and are, in fact, implemented by the same physical operator: Hash Match. I cover the Hash Aggregate operator in this section and the Hash Join operator in the "Joins" section.

The query optimizer can select a Hash Aggregate for big tables where the data is not sorted, there is no need to sort it, and its cardinality estimates only a few groups. For example, the SalesOrderHeader table has no index on the TerritoryID column, so the following query will use a Hash Aggregate operator, as shown in Figure 4-16:

```
SELECT TerritoryID, COUNT(*)
FROM Sales.SalesOrderHeader
GROUP BY TerritoryID
```

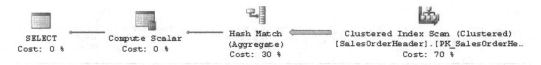

Figure 4-16 *A Hash Aggregate*

As mentioned earlier in this chapter, a hash operation builds a hash table in memory. The hash key used for this table is displayed on the Properties window of the Hash Aggregate operator as the Hash Keys Build property, which in this case is TerritoryID. Because this table is not sorted by the required column, TerritoryID, every row scanned can belong to any group.

The algorithm for the Hash Aggregate operator is similar to the Stream Aggregate, with the exceptions that, in this case, the input data does not have to be sorted, a hash table is created in memory, and a hash value is calculated for each row processed. For each hash value calculated, the algorithm will check whether a corresponding group already exists on the hash table; if it does not exist, the algorithm will create a new entry for it. In this way, the values for each record are aggregated in this entry on the hash table, and only one row for each group is stored in memory.

Note, again, that a Hash Aggregate helps when the data is not sorted. If you create an index that can provide sorted data, the query optimizer may select a Stream Aggregate instead. Run the following statement to create an index, and then execute the previous query again to verify that it uses a Stream Aggregate, as shown in the plan displayed in Figure 4-17:

```
CREATE INDEX IX_TerritoryID ON Sales.SalesOrderHeader(TerritoryID)
```

To clean up, drop the index using the following DROP INDEX statement:

```
DROP INDEX Sales.SalesOrderHeader.IX_TerritoryID
```

If the input is not sorted and order is explicitly requested in a query, the query optimizer may introduce a Sort operator and a Stream Aggregate, as shown previously, or it may decide to use a Hash Aggregate and then sort the results as in the following query, which produces the plan in Figure 4-18. The query optimizer will estimate which

Figure 4-17 *A Stream Aggregate operator using an index*

Figure 4-18 *A Hash Aggregate followed by a Sort operator*

operation is the least expensive: to sort the entire input and use a Stream Aggregate, or to use a Hash Aggregate and sort only the aggregated results.

```
SELECT TerritoryID, COUNT(*)
FROM Sales.SalesOrderHeader
GROUP BY TerritoryID
ORDER BY TerritoryID
```

Distinct Sort

Finally, a query using the DISTINCT keyword can be implemented by a Stream Aggregate, a Hash Aggregate, or a Distinct Sort operator. The Distinct Sort operator is used to both remove duplicates and sort its input. In fact, a query using DISTINCT can be rewritten as a GROUP BY query, and both can generate the same execution plan. If an index to provide sorted data is available, the query optimizer can use a Stream Aggregate operator. If no index is available, SQL Server can introduce a Distinct Sort operator or a Hash Aggregate operator. Let's look at all three cases here. The following two queries return the same data and produce the same execution plan, as shown in Figure 4-19:

```
SELECT DISTINCT(JobTitle)
FROM HumanResources.Employee
GO
SELECT JobTitle
FROM HumanResources.Employee
GROUP BY JobTitle
```

Note that the plan is using a Distinct Sort operator. This operator will sort the rows and eliminate duplicates.

Figure 4-19 *A Distinct Sort operator*

If we create an index, the query optimizer may instead use a Stream Aggregate operator because the plan can take advantage of the fact that the data is already sorted. To test it, run this:

```
CREATE INDEX IX_JobTitle ON HumanResources.Employee(JobTitle)
```

Then run the previous two queries again. Both queries will now produce a plan showing a Stream Aggregate operator. Drop the index before continuing by using this statement:

```
DROP INDEX HumanResources.Employee.IX_JobTitle
```

Finally, for a bigger table without an index to provide order, a Hash Aggregate may be used, as in the two following examples:

```
SELECT DISTINCT(TerritoryID)
FROM Sales.SalesOrderHeader
GO
SELECT TerritoryID
FROM Sales.SalesOrderHeader
GROUP BY TerritoryID
```

Both queries produce the same results and will use the same execution plan using a Hash Aggregate, as shown earlier in this chapter.

Joins

In this section, I talk about the three physical join operators that SQL Server uses to implement logical joins: the Nested Loops Join, the Merge Join, and the Hash Join. It is important to understand that no join algorithm is better than the others, and that the query optimizer will select the best join algorithm depending on the specific scenario, as I'll explain here.

Nested Loops Join

Let's start with a query listing employees who are also salespersons. This creates the plan in Figure 4-20, which uses a Nested Loops Join.

```
SELECT e.BusinessEntityID, TerritoryID
FROM HumanResources.Employee AS e
JOIN Sales.SalesPerson AS s ON e.BusinessEntityID = s.BusinessEntityID
```

The input shown at the top in a Nested Loops Join plan is known as the outer input, and the one at the bottom is the inner input. The algorithm for the Nested Loops Join

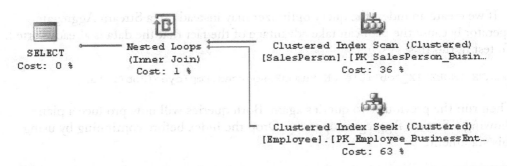

Figure 4-20 *A Nested Loops Join*

is very simple: the operator used to access the outer input is executed only once, and the operator used to access the inner input is executed once for every record that qualifies on the outer input. Note that in this example, the plan is scanning the SalesPerson table for the outer input. Because there is no filter on the SalesPerson table, all of its 17 records are returned; therefore, as dictated by the algorithm, the inner input (the Clustered Index Seek) is executed 17 times—once for each row from the outer table.

You can validate this information by looking at the operator properties. Figure 4-21 shows the Clustered Index Scan operator properties, where you can find the actual

Clustered Index Scan (Clustered)	
Scanning a clustered index, entirely or only a range.	
Physical Operation	Clustered Index Scan
Logical Operation	Clustered Index Scan
Actual Execution Mode	Row
Estimated Execution Mode	Row
Storage	RowStore
Actual Number of Rows	17
Actual Number of Batches	0
Estimated I/O Cost	0.003125
Estimated Operator Cost	0.0033007 (36%)
Estimated CPU Cost	0.0001757
Estimated Subtree Cost	0.0033007
Number of Executions	1
Estimated Number of Executions	1
Estimated Number of Rows	17
Estimated Row Size	15 B
Actual Rebinds	0
Actual Rewinds	0
Ordered	False
Node ID	1

Object
[AdventureWorks2012].[Sales].[SalesPerson].
[PK_SalesPerson_BusinessEntityID] [s]
Output List
[AdventureWorks2012].[Sales].
[SalesPerson].BusinessEntityID, [AdventureWorks2012].
[Sales].[SalesPerson].TerritoryID

Figure 4-21 *Properties of the Clustered Index Scan operator*

number of executions (which in this case is 1) and the actual number of rows (in this case, 17). Figure 4-22 shows the Clustered Index Seek operator properties, which demonstrate that both the actual number of rows and the number of executions is 17.

Let's change the query to add a filter by TerritoryID:

```
SELECT e.BusinessEntityID, HireDate
FROM HumanResources.Employee AS e
JOIN Sales.SalesPerson AS s ON e.BusinessEntityID = s.BusinessEntityID
WHERE TerritoryID = 1
```

This query produces a plan similar to the one shown previously using the SalesPerson as the outer input and a Clustered Index Seek on the Employee table as the inner input. The filter on the SalesPerson table is asking for TerritoryID equal to 1, and only three records qualify this time. As a result, the Clustered Index Seek, which is the operator on the inner input, is executed only three times. You can verify this information by looking at the properties of each operator, as we did for the previous query.

So, in summary, in the Nested Loops Join algorithm, the operator for the outer input will be executed once and the operator for the inner input will be executed once

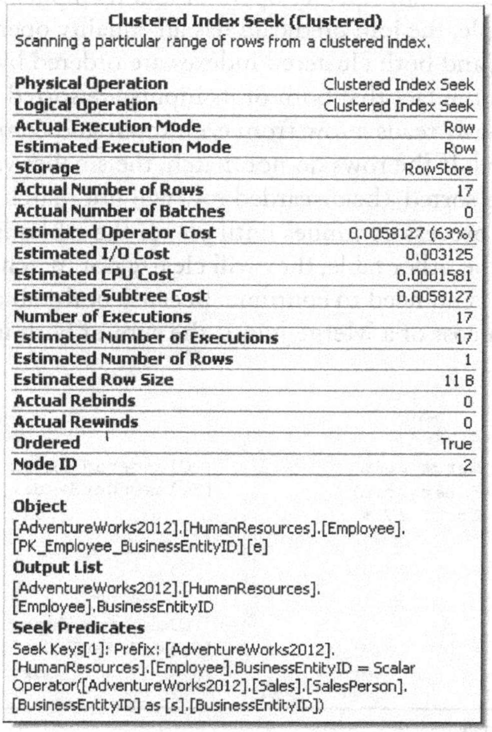

Clustered Index Seek (Clustered)	
Scanning a particular range of rows from a clustered index.	
Physical Operation	Clustered Index Seek
Logical Operation	Clustered Index Seek
Actual Execution Mode	Row
Estimated Execution Mode	Row
Storage	RowStore
Actual Number of Rows	17
Actual Number of Batches	0
Estimated Operator Cost	0.0058127 (63%)
Estimated I/O Cost	0.003125
Estimated CPU Cost	0.0001581
Estimated Subtree Cost	0.0058127
Number of Executions	17
Estimated Number of Executions	17
Estimated Number of Rows	1
Estimated Row Size	11 B
Actual Rebinds	0
Actual Rewinds	0
Ordered	True
Node ID	2

Object
[AdventureWorks2012].[HumanResources].[Employee].
[PK_Employee_BusinessEntityID] [e]
Output List
[AdventureWorks2012].[HumanResources].
[Employee].BusinessEntityID
Seek Predicates
Seek Keys[1]: Prefix: [AdventureWorks2012].
[HumanResources].[Employee].BusinessEntityID = Scalar
Operator([AdventureWorks2012].[Sales].[SalesPerson].
[BusinessEntityID] as [s].[BusinessEntityID])

Figure 4-22 *Properties of the Clustered Index Seek operator*

for every row that qualifies on the outer input. The result of this is that the cost of this algorithm is proportional to the size of the outer input multiplied by the size of the inner input. As such, the query optimizer is more likely to choose a Nested Loops Join when the outer input is small and the inner input has an index on the join key. This join type can be especially effective when the inner input is potentially large, as only a few rows, indicated by the outer input, will be searched.

Merge Join

Now let's take a look at a Merge Join example; run the following query. The execution plan is shown in Figure 4-23.

```
SELECT h.SalesOrderID, s.SalesOrderDetailID, OrderDate
FROM Sales.SalesOrderHeader h
JOIN Sales.SalesOrderDetail s ON h.SalesOrderID = s.SalesOrderID
```

One difference between this and a Nested Loops Join is that, in a Merge Join, both input operators are executed only once. You can verify this by looking at the properties of both operators, and you'll find that the number of executions is 1. Another difference is that a Merge Join requires an equality operator and its inputs sorted on the join predicate. In this example, the join predicate has an equality operator, which uses the SalesOrderID column, and both clustered indexes are ordered by SalesOrderID.

Taking benefit from the fact that both of its inputs are sorted on the join predicate, a Merge Join simultaneously reads a row from each input and compares them. If the rows match, they are returned. If the rows do not match, the smaller value can be discarded—because both inputs are sorted, the discarded row will not match any other row on the other input table. This process continues until one of the tables is completed. Even if there are still rows on the other table, they will clearly not match any rows on the fully scanned table, so there is no need to continue. Because both tables can potentially be scanned, the maximum cost of a Merge Join is the sum of both inputs.

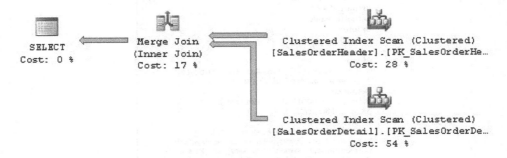

Figure 4-23 *A Merge Join example*

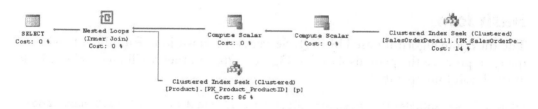

Figure 4-24 *A Nested Loops Join*

If the inputs are not already sorted, the query optimizer is not likely to choose a Merge Join. However, it might decide to sort one or even both inputs if it deems the cost is cheaper than the alternatives. Let's follow an exercise to see what happens if we force a Merge Join on, for example, a Nested Loops join plan. If you run the following query, you will notice that it uses a Nested Loops Join, as shown in Figure 4-24:

```
SELECT * FROM Sales.SalesOrderDetail s
JOIN Production.Product p ON s.ProductID = p.ProductID
WHERE SalesOrderID = 43659
```

In this case, a good plan is created using efficient Clustered Index Seek operators. If we force a Merge Join using a hint, as in the following query, the query optimizer has to introduce sorted sources such as Clustered Index Scan and Sort operators, both of which can be seen on the plan in Figure 4-25. Obviously, these additional operations are more expensive than a Clustered Index Seek, and they are only introduced because we instructed the query optimizer to do so.

```
SELECT * FROM Sales.SalesOrderdetail s
JOIN Production.Product p ON s.ProductID = p.ProductID
WHERE SalesOrderID = 43659
OPTION (MERGE JOIN)
```

In summary, given the nature of the Merge Join, the query optimizer is more likely to choose this algorithm when faced with medium to large inputs, where there is an equality operator on the join predicate, and the inputs are sorted.

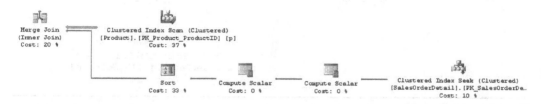

Figure 4-25 *Plan with a hint to use a Merge Join*

Hash Join

The third join algorithm used by SQL Server is the Hash Join. Run the following query to produce the plan displayed in Figure 4-26, and then we'll take a closer look at the Hash Join operator:

```
SELECT h.SalesOrderID, s.SalesOrderDetailID FROM Sales.SalesOrderHeader h
JOIN Sales.SalesOrderDetail s ON h.SalesOrderID = s.SalesOrderID
```

In the same way as the Merge Join, the Hash Join requires an equality operator on the join predicate, but unlike the Merge Join, it does not require its inputs to be sorted. In addition, the operations in both inputs are executed only once, which you can verify by looking at the operator properties, as shown before. However, a Hash Join works by creating a hash table in memory. The query optimizer will use cardinality estimation to detect the smaller of the two inputs, called the *build input,* and will use it to build a hash table in memory. If there is not enough memory to host the hash table, SQL Server can use a workfile in tempdb, which can impact the performance of the query. A Hash Join is a blocking operation, but only during the time the build input is hashed. After the build input is hashed, the second table, called the *probe input,* will be read and compared to the hash table using much the same mechanism as described in the "Hash Aggregate" section. If rows are matched, they will be returned and the results will be streamed through. On the execution plan, the table at the top will be used as the build input, and the table at the bottom as the probe input.

Finally, note that a behavior called "role reversal" may appear. If the query optimizer is not able to correctly estimate which of the two inputs is smaller, the build and probe roles may be reversed at execution time, and this will not be shown on the execution plan.

In summary, the query optimizer can choose a Hash Join for large inputs where there is an equality operator on the join predicate. Because both tables are scanned, the cost of a Hash Join is the sum of both inputs.

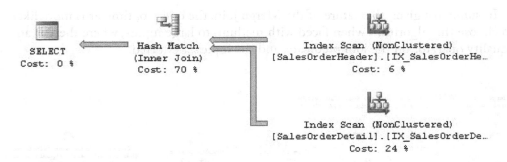

Figure 4-26 *A Hash Join example*

Parallelism

SQL Server can use parallelism to help some expensive queries execute faster by using several processors simultaneously. However, even when a query may get better performance by using parallel plans, it may still use more resources than a similar serial plan.

In order for the query optimizer to consider parallel plans, the SQL Server installation must have access to at least two processors or cores, or a hyper-threaded configuration. In addition, both the affinity mask and the max degree of parallelism advanced configuration options must allow the use of at least two processors. Finally, as explained later in this section, SQL Server will only consider parallelism for serial queries whose cost exceeds the configured cost threshold for parallelism (the default value is 5).

The affinity mask configuration option specifies which processors are eligible to run SQL Server threads, and the default value of 0 means that all the processors can be used. The max degree of parallelism configuration option is used to limit the number of processors that can be used in parallel plans, and its default value of 0 similarly allows all available processors to be used. As you can see, if you have the proper hardware, SQL Server allows parallel plans by default, with no additional configuration.

Parallelism will be considered by the query processor when the estimated cost of a serial plan is higher than the value defined in the cost threshold for the parallelism configuration parameter. However, this doesn't guarantee that parallelism will actually be employed in the final execution plan, as the final decision to parallelize a query (or not) will be based on cost reasons. That is, there is no guarantee that the best parallel plan found will have a lower cost than the best serial plan, so the serial plan may still end up being the better plan. Parallelism is implemented by the parallelism physical operator, also known as the exchange operator, which implements the Distribute Streams, Gather Streams, and Repartition Streams logical operations.

To create parallel plans, we need to create a couple of large tables in AdventureWorks2012 (and one of these tables will also be used in the next section). A simple way to do this is to copy the data from Sales.SalesOrderDetail a few times by running the following statements:

```
SELECT *
INTO #temp
FROM Sales.SalesOrderDetail
UNION ALL SELECT * FROM Sales.SalesOrderDetail
UNION ALL SELECT * FROM Sales.SalesOrderDetail
UNION ALL SELECT * FROM Sales.SalesOrderDetail
UNION ALL SELECT * FROM Sales.SalesOrderDetail
UNION ALL SELECT * FROM Sales.SalesOrderDetail
```

```
SELECT IDENTITY(int, 1, 1) AS ID, CarrierTrackingNumber, OrderQty, ProductID,
UnitPrice, LineTotal, rowguid, ModifiedDate
INTO dbo.SalesOrderDetail FROM #temp

SELECT IDENTITY(int, 1, 1) AS ID, CarrierTrackingNumber, OrderQty, ProductID,
UnitPrice, LineTotal, rowguid, ModifiedDate
INTO dbo.SalesOrderDetail2 FROM #temp

DROP TABLE #temp
```

The following query, using one of the tables we just created, will produce a parallel plan. Because this plan is too big to print in this book, only the parallel section is displayed in Figure 4-27.

```
SELECT ProductID, COUNT(*)
FROM dbo.SalesOrderDetail
GROUP BY ProductID
```

One benefit of the graphical plans, compared to text and XML plans, is that you can easily see which operators are being executed in parallel by looking at the parallelism symbol (a small yellow circle with arrows) included in the operator icon.

To see why a parallel plan was considered and selected, you can look at the cost of the serial plan. One way to do this is by using the MAXDOP hint to force a serial plan on the same query, as shown next:

```
SELECT ProductID, COUNT(*)
FROM dbo.SalesOrderDetail
GROUP BY ProductID
OPTION (MAXDOP 1)
```

The forced serial plan has a cost of 9.70746. Given that the default cost threshold for parallelism configuration option is 5, this clearly crosses that threshold. An interesting test you can perform in your test environment is to change the cost threshold for parallelism option to 10 by running the following statements:

```
EXEC sp_configure 'cost threshold for parallelism', 10
GO
RECONFIGURE
GO
```

Figure 4-27 *Part of a parallel plan*

If you run the same query again, this time without the MAXDOP hint, you will get a serial plan with the cost of 9.70746. Because the cost threshold for parallelism is now 10, the query optimizer did not even try to find a parallel plan. Do not forget to change the cost threshold for the parallelism configuration option back to the default value of 5 by running the following statement:

```
EXEC sp_configure 'cost threshold for parallelism', 5
GO
RECONFIGURE
GO
```

Keep in mind that we changed this value just for demonstration purposes; it is rarely necessary to adjust this advanced configuration setting.

The Exchange Operator

As mentioned earlier, parallelism is implemented by the parallelism physical operator, also known as the exchange operator. Parallelism in SQL Server works by splitting a task among two or more copies of the same operator, each copy running in its own scheduler. For example, if you would ask SQL Server to count the number of records on a small table, it may use a single Stream Aggregate operator to do that. But if you request to count the number of records in a very large table, SQL Server may use two or more Stream Aggregate operators, each to count the number of records of a part of the table. These Stream Aggregate operators would run in parallel, each one in a different scheduler and each performing part of the work. Obviously, this is a simplified explanation, but this section will explain the details soon.

The actual partitioning of data between these operators is handled, in most cases, by the Parallelism or Exchange operator. It is interesting that most of the operators do not need to be aware that they are being executed in parallel. For example, the Stream Aggregate operator we just mentioned only receives records, counts them, and returns the results without knowing that other Stream Aggregate operators are also performing the same operation with distinct records of a table. Of course, there are also parallel-aware operators such as the Parallel Scan, which we cover next. To see how it works, run the next query, which creates the parallel plan shown in Figure 4-28.

```
SELECT * FROM dbo.SalesOrderDetail
WHERE LineTotal > 3234
```

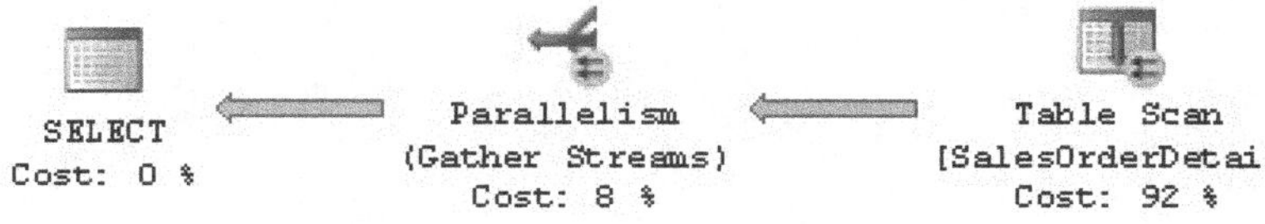

SELECT	Parallelism	Table Scan
Cost: 0 %	(Gather Streams)	[SalesOrderDetail]
	Cost: 8 %	Cost: 92 %

Figure 4-28 *A Parallel Scan query*

As mentioned earlier, the Parallel Scan is one of the few parallel-aware operators in SQL Server and is based on the work performed by the parallel page supplier, a storage engine process that assigns sets of pages to operators in the plan. In the plan shown, SQL Server will assign two or more Table Scan operators, and the parallel page supplier will provide them with sets of pages. A great advantage of this method is that it does not need to assign an equal number of pages per thread, but they are assigned on demand, which could help in cases where one CPU may be busy with some other system activities and may not be able to process many records, and thus does not slow down the entire process. For example, in my test execution, I see two threads—one processing 27,477 and the other 26,535 rows, as shown in the following XML plan fragment. (You can also see this information on the graphical plan by selecting the properties of the Table Scan operator and expanding the section Actual Number of Rows.)

```
<RunTimeInformation>
    <RunTimeCountersPerThread Thread="1" ActualRows="27477" … />
    <RunTimeCountersPerThread Thread="2" ActualRows="26535" … />
    <RunTimeCountersPerThread Thread="0" ActualRows="0" … />
</RunTimeInformation>
```

But obviously, this depends on the activity of each CPU. To simulate this, I ran another test while one of the CPUs was busy, and the plan showed one thread processing only 11,746 rows, while the second was processing 42,266. Notice that the plan also shows thread 0, which is the coordinator or main thread and does not process any rows.

Although the plan in Figure 4-28 only shows a Gather Streams exchange operator, the exchange operator can take three different functions or logical operations, as explained next.

Parallelism
(Gather Streams)

A Gather Streams exchange is also called a start parallelism exchange, and it is always at the beginning of a parallel plan or region, considering that execution starts from the far left of the plan. This operator consumes several input streams, combines them, and produces a single output stream of records. For example, in the plan shown in Figure 4-28, the Gather Streams exchange operator consumes the data produced by the two Table Scan operators running in parallel and sends all these records to its parent operator.

Opposite to a Gather Streams exchange, a Distribute Streams exchange is called a stop parallelism exchange, and takes a single input stream of records and produces multiple output streams.

Parallelism
(Distribute Streams)

The third exchange logical operation is the Repartition Streams exchange, which can consume multiple streams and produce multiple streams of records.

`Parallelism
(Repartition Streams)`

In the previous example, the Parallel Scan is a parallel-aware operator in which the parallel page supplier assigns sets of pages to operators in the plan. As indicated earlier, most of the time, operators are not aware they are running in parallel, and so it is the job of the exchange operator to send them rows using one of the partitioning types shown in Table 4-2. These types of partitioning are exposed to the user in the Partitioning Type property of execution plans, and they only make sense for Repartition Streams and Distribute Streams exchanges because, as shown in the plan in Figure 4-28, a Gather Streams exchange only routes the rows to a single consumer thread. A couple of examples of partitioning types will be shown later in this section.

Finally, another property of the exchange operators is they preserve the order of the input rows. When they do this, they are called *merging* or *order-preserving exchanges*. Otherwise, they are called *non-merging* or *non-order-preserving exchanges*. Merging exchanges do not perform any sort operation; rows must be already in sorted order. Because of this, this order-preserving operation only makes sense for Gather Streams and Repartition Streams exchanges. With a Distribute Streams exchange, there is only one producer, so there is nothing to merge. However, it is also worth mentioning that merging exchanges may not scale as well as non-merging exchanges. For example, compare the execution plans of these two versions of the first example on this section, the second one using an ORDER BY clause:

```
SELECT ProductID, COUNT(*)
FROM dbo.SalesOrderDetail
GROUP BY ProductID
GO
SELECT ProductID, COUNT(*)
FROM dbo.SalesOrderDetail
GROUP BY ProductID
ORDER BY ProductID
```

Partitioning Type	Description
Hash	Evaluates a hash function on one or more columns on the row to decide where to send each row.
Round Robin	Each packet of rows is sent to the next consumer in sequence.
Broadcast	All rows are sent to all consumer threads.
Demand	Each new row is sent to the consumer that asks for it. This is the only type of exchange that uses a pull rather than a push model for data flow.
Range	Evaluates a range function on one column on the row to decide where to send each row.

Table 4-2   *Types of Partitioning*

Although both plans are almost the same, the second one returns the results sorted by using an order-preserving exchange operator. You can verify that by looking at the properties of the Gather Streams exchange operator, which includes an Order By section, as you can see in Figure 4-29.

Hash partitioning is the most common partitioning type and can be used to parallelize a Merge Join or a Hash Join, like in the following example. Run the next query, which will get the plan shown in Figure 4-30, where you can see that hash partitioning is being used by the Repartition Streams exchanges, as also shown in the Partitioning Type property of one of these operators in Figure 4-31. In this case, hash partitioning distributes the build and probe rows among the individual Hash Join threads.

```
SELECT * FROM dbo.SalesOrderDetail s1 JOIN dbo.SalesOrderDetail2 s2
ON s1.id = s2.id
```

Finally, the following query, which includes a very selective predicate, produces the plan in Figure 4-32 and shows both a start parallelism operator or Gather Streams exchange, and a stop parallelism operator or Distribute Streams exchange. The Distribute Streams exchange operator uses broadcast partitioning, as you can verify in the properties of the operator in Figure 4-33. Broadcast partitioning sends the only row that qualifies from

Parallelism	
An operation involving parallelism.	
Physical Operation	Parallelism
Logical Operation	Gather Streams
Actual Execution Mode	Row
Estimated Execution Mode	Row
Actual Number of Rows	266
Actual Number of Batches	0
Estimated Operator Cost	0.03022 (0%)
Estimated I/O Cost	0
Estimated Subtree Cost	7.71224
Estimated CPU Cost	0.0302168
Number of Executions	1
Estimated Number of Executions	1
Estimated Number of Rows	266
Estimated Row Size	19 B
Actual Rebinds	0
Actual Rewinds	0
Node ID	2
Output List	
[AdventureWorks2012].[dbo].	
[SalesOrderDetail].ProductID, globalagg1005	
Order By	
[AdventureWorks2012].[dbo].	
[SalesOrderDetail].ProductID Ascending	

Figure 4-29 *Properties of the Parallelism operator*

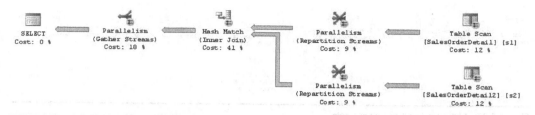

Figure 4-30 *A hash partitioning example*

table1 to all the Hash Join threads. A bitmap operator is also used to eliminate most of the rows from table2, which greatly improves the performance of the query.

```
SELECT * FROM dbo.SalesOrderDetail s1
JOIN dbo.SalesOrderDetail2 s2 ON s1.ProductID = s2.ProductID
WHERE s1.id = 123
```

Parallelism	
Repartition streams.	
Physical Operation	Parallelism
Logical Operation	Repartition Streams
Actual Execution Mode	Row
Estimated Execution Mode	Row
Actual Number of Rows	727902
Actual Number of Batches	0
Estimated I/O Cost	0
Estimated Operator Cost	4.24057 (9%)
Estimated CPU Cost	4.2406
Estimated Subtree Cost	10.1249
Estimated Number of Executions	1
Number of Executions	4
Estimated Number of Rows	727902
Estimated Row Size	95 B
Actual Rebinds	0
Actual Rewinds	0
Partitioning Type	Hash
Node ID	2

Output List
[AdventureWorks2012].[dbo].[SalesOrderDetail].ID,
[AdventureWorks2012].[dbo].
[SalesOrderDetail].CarrierTrackingNumber,
[AdventureWorks2012].[dbo].[SalesOrderDetail].OrderQty,
[AdventureWorks2012].[dbo].[SalesOrderDetail].ProductID,
[AdventureWorks2012].[dbo].[SalesOrderDetail].UnitPrice,
[AdventureWorks2012].[dbo].[SalesOrderDetail].LineTotal,
[AdventureWorks2012].[dbo].[SalesOrderDetail].rowguid,
[AdventureWorks2012].[dbo].
[SalesOrderDetail].ModifiedDate
Partition Columns
[AdventureWorks2012].[dbo].[SalesOrderDetail].ID

Figure 4-31 *Repartition Streams exchange operator properties*

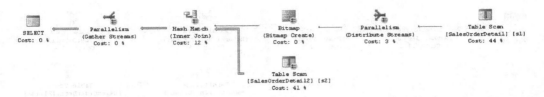

Figure 4-32 *A broadcast partitioning example*

I cover bitmap operators in more detail in Chapter 9, where you will see how they are used to optimize the performance of data warehouse queries.

Limitations

You may see cases when you have an expensive-enough query that is not parallelized. There are several SQL Server features that inhibit a parallel plan creating a serial plan instead:

► Scalar-valued user-defined functions

► CLR user-defined functions with data access

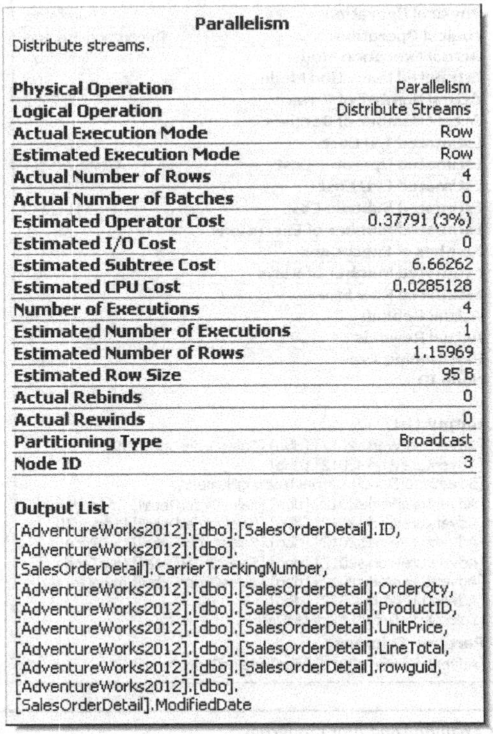

Parallelism	
Distribute streams.	
Physical Operation	Parallelism
Logical Operation	Distribute Streams
Actual Execution Mode	Row
Estimated Execution Mode	Row
Actual Number of Rows	4
Actual Number of Batches	0
Estimated Operator Cost	0.37791 (3%)
Estimated I/O Cost	0
Estimated Subtree Cost	6.66262
Estimated CPU Cost	0.0285128
Number of Executions	4
Estimated Number of Executions	1
Estimated Number of Rows	1.15969
Estimated Row Size	95 B
Actual Rebinds	0
Actual Rewinds	0
Partitioning Type	Broadcast
Node ID	3

Output List
[AdventureWorks2012].[dbo].[SalesOrderDetail].ID,
[AdventureWorks2012].[dbo].
[SalesOrderDetail].CarrierTrackingNumber,
[AdventureWorks2012].[dbo].[SalesOrderDetail].OrderQty,
[AdventureWorks2012].[dbo].[SalesOrderDetail].ProductID,
[AdventureWorks2012].[dbo].[SalesOrderDetail].UnitPrice,
[AdventureWorks2012].[dbo].[SalesOrderDetail].LineTotal,
[AdventureWorks2012].[dbo].[SalesOrderDetail].rowguid,
[AdventureWorks2012].[dbo].
[SalesOrderDetail].ModifiedDate

Figure 4-33 *Distribute Streams exchange operator properties*

▶ Miscellaneous built-in functions such as OBJECT_ID(), ERROR_NUMBER(), and @@TRANCOUNT

▶ Dynamic cursors

In a similar way, there are some other features that force a serial zone within a parallel plan, which can lead to performance problems. These features include the following:

▶ Multistatement, table-valued, user-defined functions

▶ TOP clause

▶ Global scalar aggregates

▶ Sequence functions

▶ Multiconsumer spool

▶ Backward scans

▶ System table scans

▶ Recursive queries

For example, the following code shows how the first parallel example in this section turns into a serial plan while using a simple user-defined function:

```
CREATE FUNCTION dbo.ufn_test(@ProductID int)
RETURNS int
AS
BEGIN
RETURN @ProductID
END
GO
SELECT dbo.ufn_test(ProductID), ProductID, COUNT(*)
FROM dbo.SalesOrderDetail
GROUP BY ProductID
```

As introduced in Chapter 1, the NonParallelPlanReason optional attribute of the QueryPlan element contains a high-level description of why a parallel plan may not be chosen for the optimized query, which in this case is CouldNotGenerateValidParallelPlan, as shown in the next XML plan fragment:

```
<QueryPlan … NonParallelPlanReason="CouldNotGenerateValidParallelPlan" … >
```

Finally, there is an undocumented and therefore unsupported trace flag that you could try to force a parallel plan. Trace flag 8649 can be used to set the cost overhead of parallelism to 0, encouraging a parallel plan, which could help in some cases (mostly cost related). Just for demonstration purposes, see the following example using a small table (note it is the SalesOrderDetail table on the Sales schema, not the bigger table on the dbo schema we created earlier):

```
SELECT ProductID, COUNT(*)
FROM Sales.SalesOrderDetail
GROUP BY ProductID
```

The previous query creates a serial plan with cost 0.429621. Using trace flag 8649, as shown next, will create a parallel plan with the slightly lower cost of 0.386606 units:

```
SELECT ProductID, COUNT(*)
FROM Sales.SalesOrderDetail
GROUP BY ProductID
OPTION (QUERYTRACEON 8649)
```

Updates

So far we have focused on how the query processor solves SELECT queries, so in this section, we will talk about update operations. Update operations are an intrinsic part of database operations, and they also need to be optimized so that they can be performed as quickly as possible. Keep in mind that when I say "updates" in this section, I am referring to any operation performed by the INSERT, DELETE, and UPDATE statements, as well as the MERGE statement, which was introduced in SQL Server 2008. In this chapter, I explain the basics of update operations and how they can quickly become complicated, as they need to update existing indexes, access multiple tables, and enforce existing constraints. I show how the query optimizer can select per-row and per-index plans to optimize UPDATE statements, and I describe the Halloween protection problem as well as how SQL Server avoids it.

Even when performing an update involves some other areas of SQL Server, such as transactions, concurrency control, or locking, update processing is still totally integrated within the SQL Server query processor framework. Update operations are also optimized so they can be performed as quickly as possible. So, in this section, I talk about updates from the query-processing point of view. As mentioned earlier, for the purposes of this section, I refer to any operations performed by the INSERT, DELETE, UPDATE, and MERGE statements as "updates."

Update plans can be complicated because they need to update existing indexes alongside data. Also, because of objects such as check constraints, referential integrity constraints, and triggers, those plans may also have to access multiple tables and enforce existing constraints. Updates may also require the updating of multiple tables when cascading referential integrity constraints or triggers are defined. Some of these operations, such as updating indexes, can have a big impact on the performance of the entire update operation, and we'll take a deeper look at that now.

Update operations are performed in two steps, which can be summarized as a read section followed by the update section. The first step provides the details of the changes to apply and which records will be updated. For INSERT operations, this includes the values to be inserted, and for DELETE operations, it includes obtaining the keys of the records to be deleted, which could be the clustering keys for clustered indexes or the RIDs for heaps. Just to keep you on your toes, for update operations, a combination of both the keys of the records to be updated and the data to be inserted is needed. In this first step, SQL Server may read the table to be updated just like in any other SELECT statement. In the second step, the update operations are performed, including updating indexes, validating constraints, and executing triggers. The update operation will fail and roll back if it violates a constraint.

Let me start with an example of a very simple update operation. Inserting a new record on the Person.CountryRegion table using the following query creates a very simple plan, as shown in Figure 4-34:

```
INSERT INTO Person.CountryRegion (CountryRegionCode, Name)
VALUES ('ZZ', 'New Country')
```

However, the operation gets complicated very quickly when you try to delete the same record by running the next statement, as shown on the plan in Figure 4-35:

```
DELETE FROM Person.CountryRegion
WHERE CountryRegionCode = 'ZZ'
```

As you can see in this plan, in addition to CountryRegion, three additional tables (StateProvince, CountryRegionCurrency, and SalesTerritory) are accessed. The reason behind this is that these three tables have foreign keys referencing CountryRegion, so SQL Server needs to validate that no records exist on these tables for this specific value of CountryRegionCode. Therefore, the tables are accessed and an Assert operator is included at the end of the plan to perform this validation. If a record with the CountryRegionCode to be deleted exists in any of these tables, the Assert operator

INSERT   Clustered Index Insert
Cost: 0 %   Cost: 100 %

Figure 4-34 *An insert example*

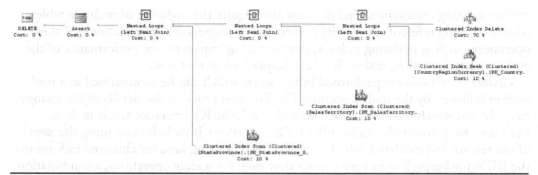

Figure 4-35 *A delete example*

will throw an exception and SQL Server will roll back the transaction, returning the following error message:

```
Msg 547, Level 16, State 0, Line 1
The DELETE statement conflicted with the REFERENCE constraint
"FK_CountryRegionCurrency_CountryRegion_CountryRegionCode". The conflict occurred
in database "AdventureWorks2012", table "Sales.CountryRegionCurrency", column
'CountryRegionCode'.
The statement has been terminated.
```

As you can see, the previous example shows how update operations can access some other tables not included in the original query—in this case, because of the definition of referential integrity constraints. The updating of nonclustered indexes is covered in the next section.

Per-Row and Per-Index Plans

An important operation performed by updates is the modifying and updating of existing nonclustered indexes, which is done by using per-row or per-index maintenance plans (also called narrow and wide plans, respectively). In a per-row maintenance plan, the updates to the base table and the existing indexes are performed by a single operator, one row at a time. On the other hand, in a per-index maintenance plan, the base table and each nonclustered index are updated in separate operations.

Except for a few cases where per-index plans are mandatory, the query optimizer can choose between a per-row and per-index plan based on performance reasons, and on an index-by-index basis. Although factors such as the structure and size of the table, as well as the other operations performed by the update statement, are all considered, choosing between per-index and per-row plans will mostly depend on the number of records being updated. The query optimizer is more likely to choose a per-row plan

Figure 4-36 *A per-row plan*

when a small number of records is being updated, and a per-index plan when the number of records to be updated increases because this choice scales better. A drawback with the per-row approach is that the storage engine updates the nonclustered index rows using the clustered index key order, which is not efficient when a large number of records needs to be updated.

The following query will create a per-row plan, which is shown in Figure 4-36. (Some additional queries may be shown on the plan due to the execution of an existing trigger.)

NOTE

Two queries in this section update data from the AdventureWorks2012 database, so perhaps you should request an estimated plan if you don't want the records to be updated. The BEGIN TRANSACTION and ROLLBACK TRANSACTION statements can also be used to create and roll back the transaction. Alternatively, you could perform a database backup before running these queries so that you will be able to restore the database later.

```
DELETE FROM Sales.SalesOrderDetail
WHERE SalesOrderDetailID = 61130
```

In addition to updating the clustered index, this delete operation will update two existing nonclustered indexes, IX_SalesOrderDetail_ProductID and AK_SalesOrderDetail_rowguid, which can be seen listed on the properties of the Clustered Index Delete operator, as shown in Figure 4-37.

To see a per-index plan, we need a table with a large number of rows, so we will be using the dbo.SalesOrderDetail table we created in the "Parallelism" section. Let's add two nonclustered indexes to the table:

```
CREATE NONCLUSTERED INDEX AK_SalesOrderDetail_rowguid
ON dbo.SalesOrderDetail (rowguid)
CREATE NONCLUSTERED INDEX IX_SalesOrderDetail_ProductID
ON dbo.SalesOrderDetail (ProductID)
```

When a large number of records is being updated, the query optimizer may choose a per-index plan, which the following query will demonstrate, by creating the per-index plan shown in Figure 4-38.

```
DELETE FROM dbo.SalesOrderDetail WHERE ProductID < 953
```

Clustered Index Delete

Delete rows from a clustered index.

Physical Operation	Clustered Index Delete
Logical Operation	Delete
Actual Execution Mode	Row
Estimated Execution Mode	Row
Actual Number of Rows	1
Actual Number of Batches	0
Estimated I/O Cost	0.03
Estimated Operator Cost	0.05184 (13%)
Estimated CPU Cost	0.000003
Estimated Subtree Cost	0.390793
Estimated Number of Executions	1
Number of Executions	1
Estimated Number of Rows	1.01239
Estimated Row Size	9 B
Actual Rebinds	0
Actual Rewinds	0
Node ID	0

Object
[AdventureWorks2012].[Sales].[SalesOrderDetail].
[PK_SalesOrderDetail_SalesOrderID_SalesOrderDetailID],
[AdventureWorks2012].[Sales].[SalesOrderDetail].
[AK_SalesOrderDetail_rowguid], [AdventureWorks2012].[Sales].
[SalesOrderDetail].[IX_SalesOrderDetail_ProductID]

Figure 4-37 *Properties of the Clustered Index Delete operator*

In this per-index update plan, the base table is updated using a Table Delete operator, while a Table Spool is used to read the data of the key values of the indexes to be updated and a Sort operator sorts the data in the order of the index. In addition, an Index Delete operator updates a specific nonclustered index in one operation (the name of which you can see in the properties of each operator). Although, the table spool is listed twice in the plan, it is actually the same operator being reused. Finally, the Sequence operator makes sure that each Index Delete operation is performed in sequence, as shown from top to bottom.

You can now delete the tables you have created for these exercises:

```
DROP TABLE dbo.SalesOrderDetail
DROP TABLE dbo.SalesOrderDetail2
```

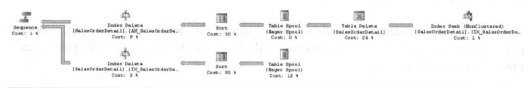

Figure 4-38 *A per-index plan*

For demonstration purposes only, you could use the undocumented and unsupported trace flag 8790 to force a per-index plan on a query, where the number of records being updated is not large enough to produce this kind of plan. For example, the following query on Sales.SalesOrderDetail requires this trace flag to produce a per-index plan; otherwise, a per-row plan would be returned instead:

```
DELETE FROM Sales.SalesOrderDetail
WHERE SalesOrderDetailID < 43740
OPTION (QUERYTRACEON 8790)
```

In summary, keep in mind that, except for a few cases where per-index plans are mandatory, the query optimizer can choose between a per-row and per-index plan on an index-by-index basis, so it is even possible to have both maintenance choices in the same execution plan.

Halloween Protection

Halloween protection refers to a problem that appears in certain update operations and was found more than 30 years ago by researchers working on the System R project at the IBM Almaden Research Center. The System R team was testing a query optimizer when they ran a query to update the salary column on an Employee table. The query was supposed to give a 10 percent raise to every employee with a salary of less than $25,000, but to their surprise, no employee had a salary under $25,000 after the update query was completed. They noticed that the query optimizer had selected the salary index and had updated some records multiple times until they reached the $25,000 salary. Because the salary index was used to scan the records, when the salary column was updated, some records were moved within the index and were then scanned again later, and those records were updated more than once. The problem was called the Halloween problem because it was discovered on Halloween, probably in 1976 or 1977.

As I mentioned at the beginning of this section, update operations have a read section followed by an update section, and that is a crucial distinction to bear in mind at this stage. To avoid the Halloween problem, the read and update sections must be completely separated; the read section must be completed in its entirety before the write section is run. I'll show you how SQL Server avoids the Halloween problem in the next example. Run the following statement to create a new table:

```
SELECT * INTO dbo.Product FROM Production.Product
```

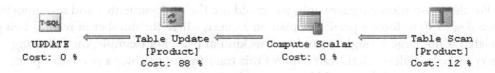

Figure 4-39 *An update without Halloween protection*

Run the following UPDATE statement, which produces the execution plan on Figure 4-39:

```
UPDATE dbo.Product SET ListPrice = ListPrice * 1.2
```

No Halloween protection is needed in this case because the statement updates the ListPrice column, which is not part of any index, so updating the data does not move any rows around. Now, to demonstrate the problem, let's create a clustered index on the ListPrice column, like so:

```
CREATE CLUSTERED INDEX CIX_ListPrice ON dbo.Product(ListPrice)
```

Run the previous UPDATE statement again. The query will show a similar plan, but this time including a Table Spool operator, which is a blocking operator, separating the read section from the write section. A blocking operator has to read all of the relevant rows before producing any output rows to the next operator. In this example, the table spool separates the Clustered Index Scan from the Clustered Index Update, as shown in Figure 4-40.

The spool operator scans the original data and saves a copy of it in a hidden spool table in tempdb before it is updated. A Table Spool operator is generally used to avoid the Halloween problem because it is a cheap operator. However, if the plan already includes another operator that can be used, such as a Sort, then the Table Spool operator is not needed, and the Sort can perform the same blocking job instead.

Finally, drop the table you have just created.

```
DROP TABLE dbo.Product
```

Figure 4-40 *An update with Halloween protection*

Summary

This chapter described the execution engine as a collection of physical operators, which also defines the choices that are available for the query optimizer to build execution plans with. Some of most commonly used operators of the execution engine were introduced, including their algorithms, relative costs, and the scenarios when the query optimizer is more likely to choose them. In particular, we've looked at operators for data access, aggregations, joins, parallelism, and update operations.

The concepts of sorting and hashing were also introduced as a mechanism used by the execution engine to match and process data. Data access operations included the scan of tables and indexes, index seeks, and bookmark lookup operations. Aggregation algorithms such as Stream Aggregate and Hash Aggregate were discussed, along with join algorithms such as the Nested Loops Join, Merge Join, and Hash Join. An introduction to parallelism was also presented, closing the chapter with update topics such as per-row and per-index plans and Halloween protection. Credit goes to Craig Freedman from the SQL Server team at Microsoft because he first documented most of what we know today about parallel query execution.

Understanding how these operators work, as well as what they are likely to cost, will give you a much stronger sense of what's actually happening under the hood when you investigate how your queries are being executed. This, in turn, will help you to find potential problems in your execution plans and to know when to resort to any of the techniques I describe later in the book.

Chapter 5

Indexes

In This Chapter

I ndexing is one of the most important techniques used in query tuning and optimization. By using the right indexes, SQL Server can speed up your queries and dramatically improve the performance of your applications. In this chapter, I introduce indexes, show you how SQL Server uses indexes, how you can provide better indexes, and how you can verify your execution plans to make sure these indexes are correctly used. There are several kinds of indexes in SQL Server. This chapter focuses on clustered and nonclustered indexes and discusses several topics, including covering indexes, filtered indexes, how to choose a clustered index key, and index fragmentation. Chapter 9 covers columnstore indexes in detail. Other types of indexes, such as XML, Spatial, and full-text indexes, are outside the scope of this book.

This chapter also includes sections about the Database Engine Tuning Advisor and the Missing Indexes feature, which will show how you can use the query optimizer itself to provide index-tuning recommendations. However, it is important to emphasize that, no matter what index recommendations these tools give, it is ultimately up to the database administrator or developer to do their own index analysis, test these recommendations thoroughly, and finally decide which of these recommendations to implement.

Finally, the sys.dm_db_index_usage_stats DMV is introduced as a tool to identify existing indexes that perhaps are not being used by your queries. Indexes that are not being used will provide no benefit to your databases, but will use valuable disk space and slow your update operations, so they should be considered for removal.

Introduction

As mentioned in Chapter 4, SQL Server can use indexes to perform seek and scan operations. Indexes can be used to speed up the execution of a query by quickly finding records without performing table scans, by delivering all the columns requested by the query without accessing the base table (that is, covering the query, which I'll return to in a moment), or by providing sorted order, which will benefit queries with GROUP BY, DISTINCT, or ORDER BY clauses.

Part of the query optimizer's job is to determine if an index can be used to resolve a predicate in a query. This is basically a comparison between an index key and a constant or variable. In addition, the query optimizer needs to determine if the index covers the query—that is, if the index contains all the columns required by the query (in which case it is referred to as a "covering index"). It needs to confirm this because a nonclustered index usually contains only a subset of the columns of the table.

SQL Server can also consider using more than one index and joining them to cover all the columns required by the query. This operation is called "index intersection." If it's not possible to cover all of the columns required by the query, SQL Server may need to access the base table, which could be a clustered index or a heap, to obtain the remaining columns. This is called a Bookmark Lookup operation (which could be a Key Lookup or an RID Lookup operation, as explained in Chapter 4). However, because a Bookmark Lookup requires random I/O, which is a very expensive operation, its usage can be effective only for a relatively small number of records.

Also keep in mind that although one or more indexes could be used, it does not mean that they will finally be selected in an execution plan, as this is always a cost-based decision. So, after creating an index, make sure you verify that the index is, in fact, used in a plan, and, of course, that your query is performing better, which is probably the primary reason why you are defining an index. An index that is not being used by any query will just take up valuable disk space, and may negatively affect the performance of update operations without providing any benefit. It is also possible that an index that was useful when it was originally created is no longer used by any query. This could be as a result of changes in the database, the data, or even the query itself. To help you avoid this situation, the last section in this chapter shows you how you can identify which indexes are no longer being used by any of your queries.

Creating Indexes

Let's start this section with a summary of some basic terminology used in indexes, some of which may be already used in previous chapters of the book:

▶ **Heap**   A heap is a data structure where rows are stored without a specified order. In other words, it is a table without a clustered index.

▶ **Clustered index**   In SQL Server, you can have the entire table logically sorted by a specific key in which the bottom, or leaf level, of the index contains the actual data rows of the table. Because of this, only one clustered index per table is possible. The data pages in the leaf level are linked in a doubly linked list (that is, each page has a pointer to the previous and next pages). Both clustered and nonclustered indexes are organized as B-trees.

▶ **Nonclustered index**   A nonclustered index row contains the index key values and a pointer to the data row on the base table. Nonclustered indexes can be created on both heaps and clustered indexes. Each table can have up to 999 nonclustered indexes, but usually, you should keep this number to a minimum. A nonclustered index can optionally contain non-key columns when using the INCLUDE clause, which are particularly useful when covering a query.

▶ **Unique index**   As the name suggests, a unique index does not allow two rows of data to have identical key values. A table can have one or more unique indexes, although it should not be very common. By default, unique indexes are created as nonclustered indexes unless you specify otherwise.

▶ **Primary key** A primary key is a key that uniquely identifies each record in the table and creates a unique index, which, by default, will also be a clustered index. In addition to the uniqueness property required for the unique index, its key columns are required to be defined as NOT NULL. By definition, only one primary key can be defined on a table.

Although creating a primary key is straightforward, something not everybody is aware of is that when a primary key is created, by default, it is created using a clustered index. This can be the case, for example, when using the Table Designer in SQL Server Management Studio (Table Designer is accessed when you right-click Tables and select New Table…) or when using the CREATE TABLE and ALTER TABLE statements, as shown next. If you run the following code to create a primary key, where the CLUSTERED or NONCLUSTERED keywords are not specified, the primary key will be created using a clustered index:

```
CREATE TABLE table1 (
    col1 int NOT NULL,
    col2 nchar(10) NULL,
    CONSTRAINT PK_table1 PRIMARY KEY(col1)
    )
```

Or

```
CREATE TABLE table1
    (
    col1 int NOT NULL,
    col2 nchar(10) NULL
    )
GO
ALTER TABLE table1 ADD CONSTRAINT
    PK_table1 PRIMARY KEY
    (
    col1
    )
```

The code generated by the Table Designer will explicitly request a clustered index for the primary key, as in the following code (but you usually don't see such code):

```
ALTER TABLE table1 ADD CONSTRAINT
    PK_table1 PRIMARY KEY CLUSTERED
    (
    col1
    )
```

Creating a clustered index along with a primary key can have some performance consequences, as I will show later in this chapter, so it is important to understand this is the default behavior. Obviously, it is also possible to have a primary key that is a nonclustered index, but this needs to be explicitly specified. Changing the previous code to create a nonclustered index will look like the following statement, where the CLUSTERED clause was changed to NONCLUSTERED:

```
ALTER TABLE table1 ADD CONSTRAINT
    PK_table1 PRIMARY KEY NONCLUSTERED
     (
    col1
     )
```

After the previous code is executed, PK_table1 will be created as a unique nonclustered index.

Although the previous code created an index as part of a constraint definition (in this case, a primary key), most likely you will be using the CREATE INDEX statement to define indexes. Next is a simplified version of the CREATE INDEX statement:

```
CREATE [UNIQUE ] [ CLUSTERED | NONCLUSTERED ] INDEX index_name
    ON <object> ( column [ ASC | DESC ] [ ,...n ] )
    [ INCLUDE ( column_name [ ,...n ] ) ]
    [ WHERE <filter_predicate> ]
    [ WITH ( <relational_index_option> [ ,...n ] ) ]
```

The UNIQUE clause creates a unique index in which no two rows are permitted to have the same index key value. CLUSTERED and NONCLUSTERED defines clustered and nonclustered indexes, respectively. The INCLUDE clause allows you to specify non-key columns to be added to the leaf level of the nonclustered index. The WHERE <filter_predicate> clause allows you to create a filter index that will also create filtered statistics. Filtered indexes and the INCLUDE clause will be explained in more detail later in this section. The WITH <relational_index_option> clause specifies the options to use when the index is created, such as FILLFACTOR, SORT_IN_ TEMPDB, DROP_EXISTING, or ONLINE.

In addition, the ALTER INDEX statement can be used to modify an index and perform operations such as disabling, rebuilding, and reorganizing indexes. The DROP INDEX statement will remove the specified index from the database. Using DROP INDEX with a nonclustered index will remove the index data pages from the database. Dropping a clustered index will not delete the index data but keep it stored as a heap instead.

Let's do a quick exercise to show some of these concepts and T-SQL statements mentioned in this section. Create a new table by running the following statement:

```
SELECT * INTO dbo.SalesOrderDetail
FROM Sales.SalesOrderDetail
```

Let's use the sys.indexes catalog view to inspect the table properties:

```
SELECT * FROM sys.indexes
WHERE object_id = OBJECT_ID('dbo.SalesOrderDetail')
```

As shown in the following results (not all the columns are listed), a heap will be created as described in the type and type_desc columns. A heap always has an index_id of 0.

object_id	name	index_id	type	type_desc	is_unique
1287675635	NULL	0	0	HEAP	0

Let's create a nonclustered index:

```
CREATE INDEX IX_ProductID ON dbo.SalesOrderDetail(ProductID)
```

sys.indexes now shows the following, where you can see that in addition to the heap, we now have a nonclustered index with index_id 2. Nonclustered indexes can have index_id values between 2 and 250 and between 256 and 1005. This range covers the maximum of 999 nonclustered indexes mentioned earlier. The values between 251 and 255 are reserved.

object_id	name	index_id	type	type_desc	is_unique
1287675635	NULL	0	0	HEAP	0
1287675635	IX_ProductID	2	2	NONCLUSTERED	0

Now create a clustered index:

```
CREATE CLUSTERED INDEX IX_SalesOrderID_SalesOrderDetailID
ON dbo.SalesOrderDetail(SalesOrderID, SalesOrderDetailID)
```

Note that instead of a heap, now we have a clustered index and the index_id is now 1. A clustered index always has an index_id of 1. Internally, the nonclustered index has been rebuilt to now use a cluster key pointer rather than a row identifier (RID).

object_id	name	index_id	type	type_desc	is_unique
1287675635	IX_SalesOrderID_SalesOrderDetailID	1	1	CLUSTERED	0
1287675635	IX_ProductID	2	2	NONCLUSTERED	0

Dropping the nonclustered index will remove the index pages entirely, leaving only the clustered index:

```
DROP INDEX dbo.SalesOrderDetail.IX_ProductID
```

object_id	name	index_id	type	type_desc	is_unique
1287675635	IX_SalesOrderID_SalesOrderDetailID	1	1	CLUSTERED	0

But notice that deleting the clustered index, which is considered the entire table, does not delete the underlying data, but simply changes the table structure to be a heap:

```
DROP INDEX dbo.SalesOrderDetail.IX_SalesOrderID_SalesOrderDetailID
```

object_id	name	index_id	type	type_desc	is_unique
1287675635	NULL	0	0	HEAP	0

For more details about the CREATE INDEX, ALTER INDEX, and DROP INDEX statements, refer to Books Online.

As shown in Figure 5-1, a clustered index is organized as a B-tree, which consists of a root node (the top node of the B-tree), leaf nodes (the bottom-level nodes, which contain the data pages of the table), and intermediate levels (the nodes between the root and leaf nodes). To find a specific record on a clustered index B-tree, SQL Server uses the root and intermediate-level nodes to navigate to the leaf node, as the root and intermediate nodes contain index pages and a pointer to either an intermediate-level page or a leaf node page. To put this in perspective, and based on the example in Figure 5-1, with only one intermediate level, SQL Server is required to read three pages to find a specific row. A table with a larger number of records could have more than one intermediate level, requiring SQL Server to read four or more pages to find a row. This is the operation performed by an Index Seek operator, and it is very effective when only one row is required or when a partial scan can be used to satisfy the query.

However, this operation can be very expensive when it needs to be performed for many records, each one requiring access to at least three pages. This is the problem we

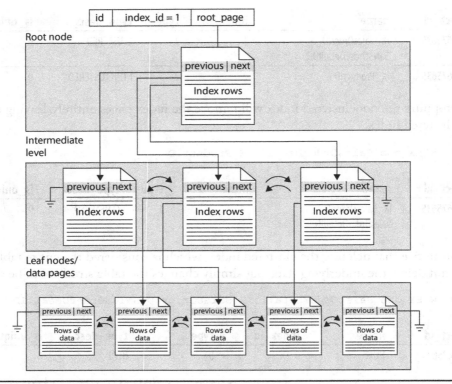

Figure 5-1 *Structure of a clustered index*

usually see when we have a nonclustered index that does not cover the query and needs to look at the clustered index for the remaining columns required by the table. In this case, SQL Server has to navigate on both the B-tree of the nonclustered index and the clustered index. The query optimizer places a high cost on these operations, and this is why sometimes when a large number of records are required by the query, SQL Server decides to instead perform a clustered index scan. More details of these operations are provided in Chapter 4.

Clustered Indexes vs. Heaps

One of the main decisions you have to make while creating a table is whether to use a clustered index or a heap. This is sometimes a topic for debate in the SQL Server community, and there is no right or wrong answer. Although the best solution may depend on your table definition and workload, it is usually recommended that each table be defined with a clustered index, and this section will show you why. Let's start with a summary of the advantages and disadvantages of organizing tables as clustered indexes or heaps. Some of the good reasons to leave a table as a heap are

▶ *When the heap is a very small table.* Although a clustered index could work fine for a small table too.

▶ *When an RID is smaller than a candidate clustered index key.* As introduced in Chapter 4, individual rows in a heap are identified by a row identifier (RID), which is a row locator that includes information such as the database file, page, and slot numbers to allow a specific record to be easily located. An RID uses 8 bytes and, in many cases, could be smaller than a clustered index key. Because every row in every nonclustered index contains the RID or the clustered index key to point to the corresponding record on the base table, a smaller size could greatly benefit the amount of resources used.

You definitely want to use a clustered index in the following cases:

▶ *You frequently need to return data in a sorted order or query ranges of data.* In this case, you would need to create the clustered index key on the column's desired order. You may need the entire table in a sorted order or only a range of the data. Examples of this last operation, called partial ordered scan, were provided in Chapter 4.

▶ *You frequently need to return data grouped together.* In this case, you would need to create the clustered index key on the columns used by the GROUP BY clause. As you learned in Chapter 4, to perform aggregate operations, SQL Server requires sorted data, and if it is not already sorted, a likely expensive sort operation may need to be added.

In the white paper "SQL Server Best Practices Article," available at http://technet .microsoft.com/en-us/library/cc917672.aspx, the authors performed a series of tests to show the difference in performance while using heaps and clustered indexes. Although these tests may or may not resemble your own schema, workload, or application, you could use it as a guideline to estimate the impact on your application.

The test used a clustered index with three columns as the clustered index key and no other nonclustered index to compare it to a heap with only one nonclustered index defined using exactly the same three columns. You can look at the paper for more details about the test, including the test scenarios. The interesting results shown by the six tests on the research are as follows:

▶ Performance of INSERT operations on a table with a clustered index was about 3 percent faster than performing the same operation on a heap with a corresponding nonclustered index. The reason for this difference is that even though inserting data into the heap had 62.8 percent fewer page splits/sec, writing into the clustered index required a single write operation, whereas inserting the data on the heap required two—one for the heap and the second one for the nonclustered index.

▶ Performance of UPDATE operations on a nonindexed column in a clustered index was 8.2 percent better than performing the same operation on a heap with a corresponding nonclustered index. The reason for this difference is that updating a row on the clustered index only required an Index Seek operation followed by an update of the data row, whereas for the heap, it required an Index Seek operation using the nonclustered index, followed by an RID lookup to find the corresponding row on the heap, and finally an update of the data row.

▶ Performance of DELETE operations on a clustered index was 18.25 percent faster than performing the same operation on a heap with a corresponding nonclustered index. The reason for this difference is that, similar to the previous UPDATE case, deleting a row on the clustered index only required an Index Seek operation followed by a delete of the data row, whereas for the heap, it required an Index Seek operation using the nonclustered index, followed by an RID lookup to find the corresponding row on the heap, and finally a delete. In addition, the row on the nonclustered index had to be deleted as well.

▶ Performance of a single-row SELECT operation on a clustered index was 13.8 percent faster than performing the same operation on a heap with a corresponding nonclustered index. This test assumes the search predicate is based on the index keys. Again, finding a row in a clustered index only requires a seek operation, and once the row is found, it contains all the required columns. In the case of the heap, once again, it required an Index Seek operation using the nonclustered index, followed by an RID lookup to find the corresponding row on the heap.

▶ Performance of a SELECT operation on a range of rows on a clustered index was 29.41 percent faster than performing the same operation on a heap with a corresponding nonclustered index. The specific query selected 228 rows. Once again, a Clustered Index Seek operation helped to find the first record quickly and, because the rows are stored in the order of the indexed columns, the remaining rows will be in the same or contiguous pages. As mentioned earlier, selecting a range of rows, called a partial ordered scan, is one of the cases where using a clustered index is definitely a superior choice to using a heap because fewer pages must be read. Also, keep in mind that for this scenario, the cost of performing multiple lookups may be so high in some cases that the query optimizer may decide to scan the entire heap instead. That is not the case for the clustered index, even if the specified range is large.

▶ On the disk utilization test following INSERT operations, the test showed little difference between the clustered index and a heap with a corresponding nonclustered index. However, on the disk utilization test following DELETE operations, the clustered index test showed a significant difference between the clustered index and a heap with a corresponding nonclustered index. The clustered index shrunk almost the same amount as the amount of data deleted, while the heap shrunk only a fraction of it. The reason for this difference is that empty extents are automatically deallocated in a clustered index, which is not the same for heaps, where the extents are held on to for later reuse. Recovering this unused disk space on a heap usually requires additional tasks, such as performing a table rebuild operation (using the ALTER TABLE REBUILD statement).

▶ On the concurrent INSERT operations, the test showed that as the number of processes that are concurrently inserting data increases, the amount of time per insert also increases, and this increase is more significant in the case of the clustered index compared to the heap. One of the main reasons for this was the contention found while inserting data in a particular location. The test showed that the page latch waits per second were 12 percent higher for the clustered index compared to the heap when 20 processes were concurrently inserting data, and this value grew to 61 percent when 50 concurrent processes inserted data. However, the test found that for the case of the 50 concurrent sessions, the overhead per insert was only an average of 1.2 milliseconds per insert operation and was not considered significant.

▶ Finally, because the heap required a nonclustered index to provide the same seek benefits as the clustered index, the disk space used by the clustered index was almost 35 percent smaller than the table organized as a heap.

The conclusion of the research of the paper was that, in general, the performance benefits of using a clustered index outweigh the negatives according to the tests performed. Finally, it is worth remembering that although clustered indexes are generally recommended, your performance may vary, depending on your own table schema, workload, and specific configuration, so you may want to test both choices carefully.

Clustered Index Key

Deciding which column or columns will be part of the clustered index key is also a very important design consideration because they need to be chosen carefully. In *Microsoft SQL Server 2008 Internals* (Microsoft Press, 2009), Kimberly Tripp defined that, as a best practice, indexes should be unique, narrow, static, and ever increasing. But remember that as other general recommendations, this may not apply to all cases, so you also test thoroughly for your database and workload. Let me explain why these may be important and how they may affect the performance of your database.

▶ **Unique**   If a clustered index is not defined using the UNIQUE clause, SQL Server will add a 4-byte uniquifier to each record, increasing the size of the clustered index key. As a comparison, an RID used by nonclustered indexes on heaps is only 8 bytes long.

▶ **Narrow**   As mentioned earlier in this chapter, because every row in every nonclustered index contains, in addition to the columns defining the index, the clustered index key to point to the corresponding row on the base table, a small size key could greatly benefit the amount of resources used. A small key size will require less storage and memory, which will also benefit performance. Again, as a comparison, an RID used by nonclustered indexes on heaps is only 8 bytes long.

▶ **Static or nonvolatile**   Updating a clustered index key can have some performance consequences, such as page splits and fragmentation created by the row relocation within the clustered index. In addition, because every nonclustered index contains the clustered index key, the changing rows in the nonclustered index will have to be updated as well to reflect the new clustered key value.

▶ **Ever increasing**   A clustered index key would benefit of having ever-increasing values instead of having more random values, like in a last name column, for example. Having to insert new rows based on random entry points creates page splits and therefore fragmentation. On the other side, you need to be aware that in some cases, having ever-increasing values can also cause contention, as multiple processes could be writing on the last page in a table.

Covering Indexes

A covering index is a very simple but a very important concept in query optimization, where an index can solve or is able to return all the columns requested by a query without accessing the base table at all. For example, the following query is already covered by an existing index, IX_SalesOrderHeader_CustomerID, as you can see in the plan in Figure 5-2:

```
SELECT SalesOrderID, CustomerID FROM Sales.SalesOrderHeader
WHERE CustomerID = 16448
```

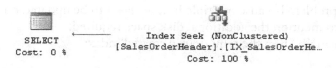

Figure 5-2   *A covering index*

On the plan, we can see that there is no need to access the base table at all. If we slightly change the query to also request the SalesPersonID column, this time, there is no index that covers the query and the plan in Figure 5-3 is produced instead:

```
SELECT SalesOrderID, CustomerID, SalesPersonID FROM Sales.SalesOrderHeader
WHERE CustomerID = 16448
```

The plan shows that the IX_SalesOrderHeader_CustomerID was used to quickly locate the required record, but because the index didn't include the SalesPersonID, a lookup operation to the clustered index was required as well. Keep in mind that trying to cover the query does not mean that you need to add another column to the index key unless you also must perform search operations using that column. Instead, you could use the INCLUDE clause of the CREATE or ALTER INDEX statement to add the additional column. At this point, you may decide to just update an existing index to include the required column, but for this example, we will create another one:

```
CREATE INDEX IX_SalesOrderHeader_CustomerID_SalesPersonID
ON Sales.SalesOrderHeader(CustomerID)
INCLUDE (SalesPersonID)
```

If you run the query again, the query optimizer will use a plan similar to the one shown previously in Figure 5-2, with just an Index Seek operation, this time with the new index IX_SalesOrderHeader_CustomerID_SalesPersonID and no need to access the base table at all. However, notice that creating many indexes on a table can also be

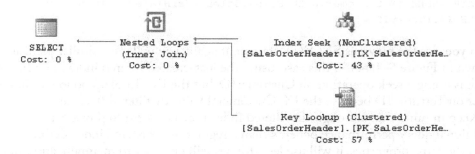

Figure 5-3   *A plan with a Key Lookup operation*

a performance problem because multiple indexes need to be updated on each update operation, not to mention the additional disk space required.

Finally, to clean up, drop the temporarily created index:

```
DROP INDEX Sales.SalesOrderHeader.IX_SalesOrderHeader_CustomerID_SalesPersonID
```

Filtered Indexes

You can use filtered indexes in queries where a column only has a small number of relevant values. This can be the case, for example, when you want to focus your query on some specific values in a table where a column has mostly NULL values and you need to query the non-NULL values. Handily, filtered indexes can also enforce uniqueness within the filtered data. Filtered indexes have the benefit of requiring less storage than regular indexes, and maintenance operations on them will be faster as well. In addition, a filter index will also create filtered statistics, which may have better quality than a statistics object created for the entire table, as a histogram will be created just for the specified range of values. As covered in more detail in Chapter 6, a histogram can have up to a maximum of 200 steps, which can be a limitation with a large number of distinct values. To create a filtered index, you need to specify a filter using the WHERE clause of the CREATE INDEX statement.

For example, if you look at the plan for the following query, you will see that it uses both the IX_SalesOrderHeader_CustomerID to filter on the CustomerID = 13917 predicate plus a Key Lookup operation to find the records on the clustered index and filter for TerritoryID = 4 (remember from Chapter 4 that in this case, a Key Lookup is really a Clustered Index Seek operator, which you can directly see if you use the SET SHOWPLAN_TEXT statement):

```
SELECT CustomerID, OrderDate, AccountNumber FROM Sales.SalesOrderHeader
WHERE CustomerID = 13917 AND TerritoryID = 4
```

Create the following filtered index:

```
CREATE INDEX IX_CustomerID ON Sales.SalesOrderHeader(CustomerID)
WHERE TerritoryID = 4
```

If you run the previous SELECT statement again, you will see a similar plan, as shown in Figure 5-4, but in this case, using the just-created filtered index. The Index Seek is doing a seek operation on CustomerID, but the Key Lookup no longer has to filter on TerritoryID because the IX_CustomerID already filtered that out.

Keep in mind that although the filtered index may not seem to provide any additional query performance benefits than a regular nonclustered index defined with the same properties, it will use less storage, will be easier to maintain, and can

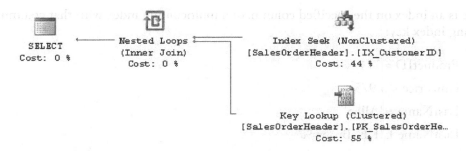

Figure 5-4   *Plan using a filtered index*

potentially provide better optimizer statistics because the filtered statistics will be more accurate since they cover only the rows in the filtered index.

However, a filtered index may not be used to solve a query when a value is not known, for example, when using variables or parameters. Because the query optimizer has to create a plan that can work for every possible value in a variable or parameter, the filtered index may not be selected. As introduced in Chapter 1, you may see the UnmatchedIndexes warning in an execution plan in these cases. Using our current example, the following query will show an UnmatchedIndexes warning indicating that the plan was not able to use the IX_CustomerID index, even when the value requested for TerritoryID was 4, the same used in the filtered index:

```
DECLARE @territory int
SET @territory = 4
SELECT CustomerID, OrderDate, AccountNumber FROM Sales.SalesOrderHeader
WHERE CustomerID = 13917 AND TerritoryID = @territory
```

Drop the index before continuing:

```
DROP INDEX Sales.SalesOrderHeader.IX_CustomerID
```

Index Operations

In a seek operation, SQL Server navigates throughout the B-tree index to quickly find the required records without the need for an index or table scan. This is similar to using an index at the end of a book to find a topic quickly, instead of reading the entire book. Once the first record has been found, SQL Server can then scan the index leaf level forward or backward to find additional records. Both equality and inequality operators can be used in a predicate, including =, <, >, <=, >=, <>, !=, !<, !>, BETWEEN, and IN. For example, the following predicates can be matched to an Index Seek operation if there is an index on the specified column, or a multicolumn index with that column as a leading index key:

- ► ProductID = 771
- ► UnitPrice < 3.975
- ► LastName = 'Allen'
- ► LastName LIKE 'Brown%'

As an example, look at the next query, which uses an Index Seek operator and produces the plan in Figure 5-5:

```
SELECT ProductID, SalesOrderID, SalesOrderDetailID
FROM Sales.SalesOrderDetail
WHERE ProductID = 771
```

The SalesOrderDetail table has a multicolumn index with ProductID as the leading column. The Index Seek operator properties, which you can see in Figure 5-6, include the following Seek predicate on the ProductID column, which shows that SQL Server was effectively able to use the index to seek on this column:

```
Seek Keys[1]: Prefix: [AdventureWorks].[Sales]. [SalesOrderDetail].ProductID =
Scalar Operator (CONVERT_IMPLICIT(int,[@1],0))
```

An index cannot be used to seek on some complex expressions, expressions using functions, or strings with a leading wildcard character, as in the following predicates:

- ► ABS(ProductID) = 771
- ► UnitPrice + 1 < 3.975
- ► LastName LIKE '%Allen'
- ► UPPER(LastName) = 'Allen'

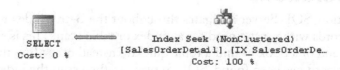

Figure 5-5 *Plan using an Index Seek*

Index Seek (NonClustered)
Scan a particular range of rows from a nonclustered index.

Physical Operation	Index Seek
Logical Operation	Index Seek
Actual Execution Mode	Row
Estimated Execution Mode	Row
Storage	RowStore
Actual Number of Rows	241
Actual Number of Batches	0
Estimated Operator Cost	0.0035471 (100%)
Estimated I/O Cost	0.003125
Estimated CPU Cost	0.0004221
Estimated Subtree Cost	0.0035471
Number of Executions	1
Estimated Number of Executions	1
Estimated Number of Rows	241
Estimated Row Size	19 B
Actual Rebinds	0
Actual Rewinds	0
Ordered	True
Node ID	0

Object
[AdventureWorks2012].[Sales].[SalesOrderDetail].
[IX_SalesOrderDetail_ProductID]
Output List
[AdventureWorks2012].[Sales].
[SalesOrderDetail].SalesOrderID, [AdventureWorks2012].
[Sales].[SalesOrderDetail].SalesOrderDetailID,
[AdventureWorks2012].[Sales].[SalesOrderDetail].ProductID
Seek Predicates
Seek Keys[1]: Prefix: [AdventureWorks2012].[Sales].
[SalesOrderDetail].ProductID = Scalar Operator
(CONVERT_IMPLICIT(int,[@1],0))

Figure 5-6   *Index Seek operator properties*

Compare the following query to the previous example; by adding an ABS function to the predicate, SQL Server is no longer able to use an Index Seek operator and chooses, instead, to do an Index Scan, as shown in the plan in Figure 5-7:

```
SELECT ProductID, SalesOrderID, SalesOrderDetailID
FROM Sales.SalesOrderDetail
WHERE ABS(ProductID) = 771
```

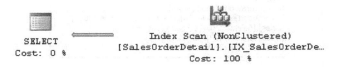

SELECT
Cost: 0 %

Index Scan (NonClustered)
[SalesOrderDetail].[IX_SalesOrderDe…
Cost: 100 %

Figure 5-7   *Plan using an Index Scan*

Note that in Figure 5-8, the following predicate is, however, still evaluated on the Index Scan operator:

```
abs([AdventureWorks].[Sales].[SalesOrderDetail].[ProductID]) =
CONVERT_IMPLICIT(int,[@1],0)
```

In the case of a multicolumn index, SQL Server can only use the index to seek on the second column if there is an equality predicate on the first column. So SQL Server can use a multicolumn index to seek on both columns in the following cases, supposing that a multicolumn index exists on both columns in the order presented:

▶ ProductID = 771 AND SalesOrderID > 34000

▶ LastName = 'Smith' AND FirstName = 'Ian'

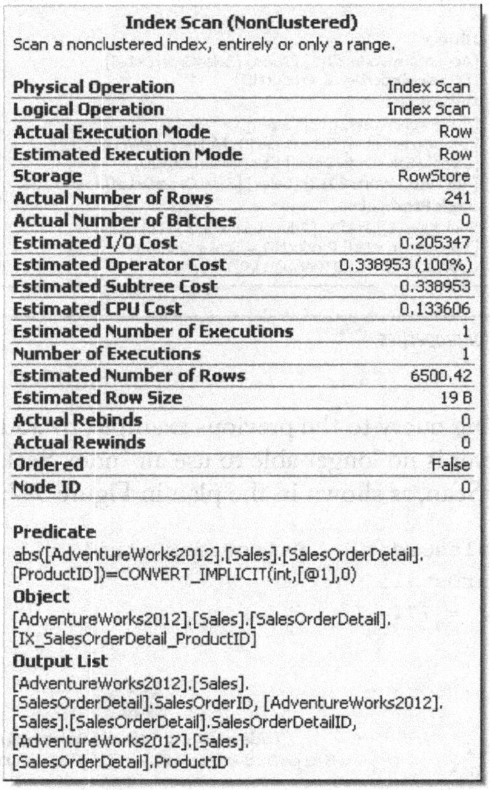

Index Scan (NonClustered)	
Scan a nonclustered index, entirely or only a range.	
Physical Operation	Index Scan
Logical Operation	Index Scan
Actual Execution Mode	Row
Estimated Execution Mode	Row
Storage	RowStore
Actual Number of Rows	241
Actual Number of Batches	0
Estimated I/O Cost	0.205347
Estimated Operator Cost	0.338953 (100%)
Estimated Subtree Cost	0.338953
Estimated CPU Cost	0.133606
Estimated Number of Executions	1
Number of Executions	1
Estimated Number of Rows	6500.42
Estimated Row Size	19 B
Actual Rebinds	0
Actual Rewinds	0
Ordered	False
Node ID	0

Predicate
abs([AdventureWorks2012].[Sales].[SalesOrderDetail].
[ProductID])=CONVERT_IMPLICIT(int,[@1],0)
Object
[AdventureWorks2012].[Sales].[SalesOrderDetail].
[IX_SalesOrderDetail_ProductID]
Output List
[AdventureWorks2012].[Sales].
[SalesOrderDetail].SalesOrderID, [AdventureWorks2012].
[Sales].[SalesOrderDetail].SalesOrderDetailID,
[AdventureWorks2012].[Sales].
[SalesOrderDetail].ProductID

Figure 5-8   *Index Scan operator properties*

That being said, if there is no equality predicate on the first column, or if the predicate cannot be evaluated on the second column, as is the case in a complex expression, then SQL Server may still only be able to use a multicolumn index to seek on just the first column, as in the following examples:

► ProductID < 771 AND SalesOrderID = 34000

► LastName > 'Smith' AND FirstName = 'Ian'

► ProductID = 771 AND ABS(SalesOrderID) = 34000

However, SQL Server is not able to use a multicolumn index for an Index Seek in the following examples because it is not even able to search on the first column:

► ABS(ProductID) = 771 AND SalesOrderID = 34000

► LastName LIKE '%Smith' AND FirstName = 'Ian'

Finally, take a look at the following query and the Index Seek operator properties in Figure 5-9:

```
SELECT ProductID, SalesOrderID, SalesOrderDetailID
FROM Sales.SalesOrderDetail
WHERE ProductID = 771 AND ABS(SalesOrderID) = 45233
```

The seek predicate is using only the ProductID column, as shown here:

```
Seek Keys[1]: Prefix: [AdventureWorks].[Sales].[SalesOrderDetail].ProductID =
Scalar Operator (CONVERT_IMPLICIT(int,[@1],0)
```

An additional predicate on the SalesOrderID column is evaluated like any other scan predicate, as listed here:

```
abs([AdventureWorks].[Sales].[SalesOrderDetail].[SalesOrderID])=[@2]
```

In summary, this shows that, as we expected, SQL Server was able to perform a seek operation on the ProductID column, but, because of the use of the ABS function, was not able to do the same for SalesOrderID. The index was used to navigate directly to find the rows that satisfy the first predicate, but then had to continue scanning to validate the second predicate.

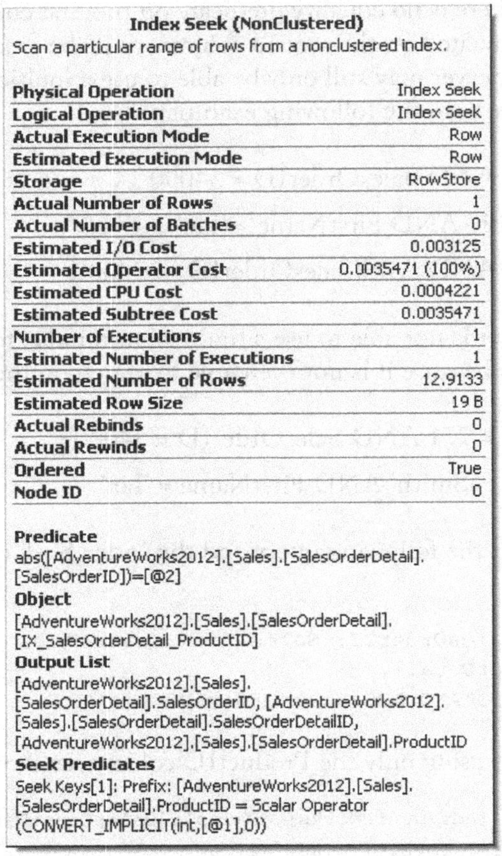

Index Seek (NonClustered)	
Scan a particular range of rows from a nonclustered index.	
Physical Operation	Index Seek
Logical Operation	Index Seek
Actual Execution Mode	Row
Estimated Execution Mode	Row
Storage	RowStore
Actual Number of Rows	1
Actual Number of Batches	0
Estimated I/O Cost	0.003125
Estimated Operator Cost	0.0035471 (100%)
Estimated CPU Cost	0.0004221
Estimated Subtree Cost	0.0035471
Number of Executions	1
Estimated Number of Executions	1
Estimated Number of Rows	12.9133
Estimated Row Size	19 B
Actual Rebinds	0
Actual Rewinds	0
Ordered	True
Node ID	0

Predicate
abs([AdventureWorks2012].[Sales].[SalesOrderDetail].
[SalesOrderID])=[@2]
Object
[AdventureWorks2012].[Sales].[SalesOrderDetail].
[IX_SalesOrderDetail_ProductID]
Output List
[AdventureWorks2012].[Sales].
[SalesOrderDetail].SalesOrderID, [AdventureWorks2012].
[Sales].[SalesOrderDetail].SalesOrderDetailID,
[AdventureWorks2012].[Sales].[SalesOrderDetail].ProductID
Seek Predicates
Seek Keys[1]: Prefix: [AdventureWorks2012].[Sales].
[SalesOrderDetail].ProductID = Scalar Operator
(CONVERT_IMPLICIT(int,[@1],0))

Figure 5-9   *Index Seek operator showing both seek and predicate properties*

The Database Engine Tuning Advisor

Currently, all major commercial database vendors include a physical database design tool to help with the creation of indexes. However, when these tools were first developed, there were just two main architectural approaches considered for how the tools should recommend indexes. The first approach was to build a stand-alone tool with its own cost model and design rules. The second approach was to build a tool that could use the query optimizer cost model.

A problem with building a stand-alone tool is the requirement for duplicating the cost module. On top of that, having a tool with its own cost model, even if it's better than the query optimizer's cost model, may not be a good idea because the optimizer still chooses its plan based on its own model.

The second approach, using the query optimizer to help with physical database design, was proposed in the database research community as far as back as 1988. Because it's the optimizer that chooses the indexes for an execution plan, it makes sense to use the optimizer itself to help find which missing indexes would benefit existing queries. In this scenario, the physical design tool would use the optimizer to evaluate the cost of queries given a set of candidate indexes. An additional benefit of this approach is that, as the optimizer cost model evolves, any tool using its cost model can automatically benefit from it.

SQL Server was the first commercial database product to include a physical design tool, in the shape of the Index Tuning Wizard, which shipped with SQL Server 7.0, and which was later replaced by the Database Engine Tuning Advisor (DTA) in SQL Server 2005. Both tools use the query optimizer cost model approach and were created as part of the AutoAdmin project at Microsoft, the goal of which was to reduce the total cost of ownership (TCO) of databases by making them self-tuning and self-managing. In addition to indexes, the DTA can help with the creation of indexed views and table partitioning.

However, creating real indexes in a DTA tuning session is not feasible; its overhead could affect operational queries and degrade the performance of your database. So how does the DTA estimate the cost of using an index that does not yet exist? Actually, even during a regular query optimization, the query optimizer does not use indexes to estimate the cost of a query. The decision on whether to use an index or not relies only on some metadata and the statistical information regarding the columns of the index. Index data itself is not needed during query optimization, but will, of course, be required during query execution if the index is chosen.

So, to avoid creating real indexes during a DTA session, SQL Server uses a special kind of indexes called hypothetical indexes, which were also used by the Index Tuning Wizard. As the name implies, hypothetical indexes are not real indexes; they only contain statistics and can be created with the undocumented WITH STATISTICS_ONLY option of the CREATE INDEX statement. You may not be able to see these indexes during a DTA session because they are dropped automatically when they are no longer needed. However, you could see the CREATE INDEX WITH STATISTICS_ONLY and DROP INDEX statements if you run a SQL Server Profiler session to see what the DTA is doing.

Let's take a quick tour of some of these concepts. To get started, create a new table on the AdventureWorks database:

```
SELECT * INTO dbo.SalesOrderDetail
FROM Sales.SalesOrderDetail
```

Copy the following query and save it to a file:

```
SELECT * FROM dbo.SalesOrderDetail
WHERE ProductID = 897
```

Open a new DTA session. The DTA is found in the Performance Tools menu under Microsoft SQL Server 2014 with the full name "SQL Server 2014 Database Engine Tuning Advisor." You can optionally run a SQL Server Profiler session if you want to inspect what the DTA is doing. On the Workload File option, select the file containing the SQL statement that you just created and then specify AdventureWorks2012 as both the database to tune and the database for workload analysis. Click the Start Analysis button and, when the DTA analysis finishes, run this query to inspect the contents of the msdb..DTA_reports_query table:

```
SELECT * FROM msdb..DTA_reports_query
```

Running that query shows the following output (edited for space):

StatementString	CurrentCost	RecommendedCost
SELECT * FROM dbo.SalesOrderDetail WHERE ProductID = 897	1.24414	0.00333398

Notice that the query returns information such as the query that was tuned, as well as the current and recommended cost. The current cost, 1.24414, is easy to obtain by directly requesting an estimated execution plan for the query, as shown in Figure 5-10.

Since the DTA analysis was completed, the required hypothetical indexes were already dropped. To obtain the indexes recommended by the DTA, click the Recommendations tab and look at the Index Recommendations section, where you can find the code to create any recommended index by clicking the Definition column. In our example, it will show the following code:

```
CREATE CLUSTERED INDEX [_dta_index_SalesOrderDetail_c_5_1440724185__K5]
ON [dbo].[SalesOrderDetail]
(
	[ProductID] ASC
)WITH (SORT_IN_TEMPDB = OFF, DROP_EXISTING = OFF, ONLINE = OFF) ON [PRIMARY]
```

In the next statement, and for demonstration purposes only, I will go ahead and create the index recommended by the DTA. However, instead of a regular index, I will create it as a hypothetical index by adding the WITH STATISTICS_ONLY clause. Keep in mind that hypothetical indexes cannot be used by your queries and are only useful to the DTA.

```
CREATE CLUSTERED INDEX cix_ProductID ON dbo.SalesOrderDetail(ProductID)
WITH STATISTICS_ONLY
```

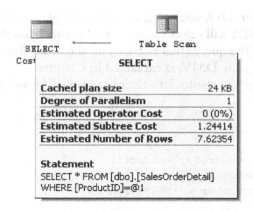

SELECT	
Cached plan size	24 KB
Degree of Parallelism	1
Estimated Operator Cost	0 (0%)
Estimated Subtree Cost	1.24414
Estimated Number of Rows	7.62354

Statement
SELECT * FROM [dbo].[SalesOrderDetail]
WHERE [ProductID]=@1

Figure 5-10   *Plan showing total cost*

You can validate that a hypothetical index was created by running the next query:

```
SELECT * FROM sys.indexes
WHERE object_id = OBJECT_ID('dbo.SalesOrderDetail')
AND name = 'cix_ProductID'
```

The output is shown next (note that the is_hypothetical field shows that this is, in fact, just a hypothetical index):

object_id	name	index_id	type	type_desc	is_hypothetical
1607676775	cix_ProductID	3	1	CLUSTERED	1

Remove the hypothetical index by running this statement:

```
DROP INDEX dbo.SalesOrderDetail.cix_ProductID
```

Finally, implement the DTA recommendation, creating the _dta_index_SalesOrd erDetail_c_5_1440724185__K5 index, as indicated before. After implementing the recommendation and running the query again, the clustered index is, in fact, now being used by the query optimizer. This time, the plan shows a Clustered Index Seek operator and an estimated cost of 0.0033652, which is very close to the recommended cost listed previously when querying the msdb..DTA_reports_query table.

Tuning a Workload Using the Plan Cache

In addition to the traditional options for tuning a workload using the File or Table choice, which allows you to specify a script or a table containing the T-SQL statements to tune, starting with SQL Server 2012, you can also specify the plan cache as a workload to tune. In this case, the DTA will select the top 1,000 events from the plan cache based on total elapsed time of the query (that is, based on the total_elapsed_time column of the sys.dm_exec_query_stats DMV, as explained in Chapter 2). Let's try an example, and to make it easy to see the results, let's clear the plan cache and run only one query in Management Studio:

```
DBCC FREEPROCCACHE
GO
SELECT SalesOrderID, OrderQty, ProductID
FROM dbo.SalesOrderDetail
WHERE CarrierTrackingNumber = 'D609-4F2A-9B'
```

After the query is executed, most likely, it will be kept in the plan cache. Open a new DTA session. In the Workload option, select Plan Cache and specify AdventureWorks2012 as both the database to tune and the database for workload analysis. Click the Start Analysis button. After the analysis is completed, you can select the Recommendations tab and select Index Recommendations, which will include the following recommendations (which you can see by looking at the Definition column):

```
CREATE NONCLUSTERED INDEX [_dta_index_SalesOrderDetail_5_807673925__K3_1_4_5]
ON [dbo].[SalesOrderDetail]
(
    [CarrierTrackingNumber] ASC
)
INCLUDE ([SalesOrderID],
    [OrderQty],
    [ProductID]) WITH (SORT_IN_TEMPDB = OFF, DROP_EXISTING = OFF, ONLINE = OFF)
ON [PRIMARY]
```

Finally, drop the table you just created by running the following statement:

```
DROP TABLE dbo.SalesOrderDetail
```

Offload of Tuning Overhead to Test Server

One of the most interesting and perhaps less known features of the DTA is that you can use it with a test server to tune the workload of a production server. As I mentioned earlier, the DTA relies on the query optimizer to make its tuning recommendations, and you can use it to make these optimizer calls to a test server instance without affecting the performance of the production server.

To better understand how this works, let's first review what kind of information the query optimizer needs to optimize a query. Basically, the most important information it needs to perform an optimization is

▶ The database metadata (that is, table and column definitions, indexes, constraints, and so on)

▶ Optimizer statistics (index and column statistics)

▶ Table size (number of rows and pages)

▶ Available memory and number of processors

The DTA can gather the database metadata and statistics from the production server and use it to create a similar database, with no data, on a different server. This database is called a shell database. The DTA can also obtain the available memory and number of processors on the production server by using the extended stored procedure xp_msver, and use this information for the optimization process. It is important to remember that no data is needed for the optimization process. This process is summarized in Figure 5-11.

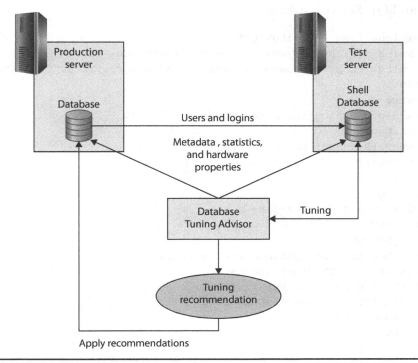

Figure 5-11   *Using a test server and a shell database with the DTA*

This process provides the following benefits:

▶ There is no need to do an expensive optimization on the production server, which can affect its resources usage. The production server is only used to gather initial metadata and the required statistics.

▶ There is no need to copy the entire database to a test server either (which is especially important for big databases), thus saving disk space and time to copy the database.

▶ There are no problems where test servers are not as powerful as production servers because the DTA tuning session will consider the available memory and number of processors on the production server.

Now I am going to show an example of how to run a tuning session. First of all, the use of a test server is not supported by the DTA graphical user interface, so the use of the dta utility (the command-prompt version of DTA) is required. Configuring a test server also requires an XML input file containing the dta input information. I am using the following input file (saved as input.xml) for this example. You will need to change "production_instance" and "test_instance" where appropriate. These must also be different SQL Server instances.

```xml
<?xml version="1.0" encoding="utf-16" ?>
<DTAXML xmlns:xsi="http://www.w3.org/2001/XMLSchema-instance"
        xmlns="http://schemas.microsoft.com/sqlserver/2004/07/dta">
  <DTAInput>
    <Server>
      <Name>production_instance</Name>
      <Database>
        <Name>AdventureWorks2012</Name>
      </Database>
    </Server>
    <Workload>
      <File>workload.sql</File>
    </Workload>
    <TuningOptions>
      <TestServer>test_instance</TestServer>
      <FeatureSet>IDX</FeatureSet>
      <Partitioning>NONE</Partitioning>
      <KeepExisting>NONE</KeepExisting>
    </TuningOptions>
  </DTAInput>
</DTAXML>
```

The Server and Database elements of the XML file include the production SQL Server instance and database. The Workload element includes the definition of a script containing the workload to tune. TuningOptions includes the TestServer subelement, which is used to include the name of the test SQL Server instance.

Create the workload.sql file containing a simple query like this:

```
SELECT * FROM AdventureWorks2012.Sales.SalesOrderDetail
WHERE ProductID = 898
```

Run the following command (note the difference in –S and –s because case is important here):

```
dta -ix input.xml -S production_instance -s session1
```

A successful execution will show an output similar to this:

```
Microsoft (R) SQL Server Microsoft SQL Server Database Engine Tuning Advisor
command line utility
Version 12.0.2000.8 ((SQL14_RTM).140220-1832 )
Copyright (c) 2014 Microsoft. All rights reserved.
Tuning session successfully created. Session ID is 3.
Total time used: 00:00:49
Workload consumed:  100%, Estimated improvement:   88%
Tuning process finished.
```

This example creates an entire copy of AdventureWorks2012 (with no data) and performs the requested optimization. The shell database is automatically deleted after the tuning session is completed. Optionally, you can keep the shell database (for example, if you want to use it again on another tuning exercise) by using the RetainShellDB in the TuningOptions element, as in the following XML fragment:

```
<TuningOptions>
  <TestServer>test_instance</TestServer>
  <FeatureSet>IDX</FeatureSet>
  <Partitioning>NONE</Partitioning>
  <KeepExisting>NONE</KeepExisting>
  <RetainShellDB>1</RetainShellDB>
</TuningOptions>
```

If the shell database already exists when you request a tuning session, the database creation process will be skipped. However, you will have to manually delete this database when it is no longer needed.

Once the tuning session is completed, you can use the DTA graphical user interface as usual to see the recommendations. To do this, open the DTA, open the session you used by double-clicking its session name (session1 in our example), and choose the Recommendations tab if it is not already selected.

Although the DTA automatically gathers the metadata and statistics to build the shell database, I am going to show you how to script the required objects and statistics to tune a simple query. This can be helpful in cases where you don't want to script the entire database. Scripting database objects is a fairly simple process well known by SQL Server professionals. Something that may be new for many, though, is how to script the statistics. Created scripts make use of the undocumented STATS_ STREAM, ROWCOUNT, and PAGECOUNT options of the CREATE/UPDATE STATISTICS statement.

As an example, to optimize the simple query shown previously, try the following in Management Studio:

1. Select Databases.
2. Right-click the AdventureWorks2012 database, select Tasks | Generate Scripts, and then click Next.
3. Select "Select specific database objects."
4. Expand Tables.
5. Select Sales.SalesOrderDetail and click Next.
6. Click Advanced.
7. Look for the Script Statistics choice and select "Script statistics and histograms."
8. Choose True on Script Indexes.

Your Advanced Scripting Options window should look similar to Figure 5-12.

Click OK to finish the wizard and generate the scripts. You will get a script with a few UPDATE STATISTICS statements similar to this (with the STAT_STREAM value shortened to fit in this page):

```
UPDATE STATISTICS [Sales].[SalesOrderDetail]([IX_SalesOrderDetail_ProductID])
WITH STATS_STREAM = 0x01000000030000000000000000000000041858B2900000000141A00 …,
ROWCOUNT = 121317, PAGECOUNT = 274
```

These UPDATE STATISTICS statements are used to update the statistics of existing indexes (obviously, the related CREATE INDEX statements were scripted as well). If the table also has column statistics, it will include CREATE STATISTICS statements instead.

Finally, I will show you an example of how to use the scripted statistics to obtain plans and cost estimates on an empty table. Running the following query on the regular

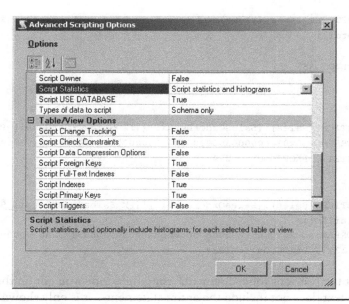

Figure 5-12   *Advanced Scripting Options window*

AdventureWorks2012 database creates the following plan with an estimated number of rows of 9 and a cost of 0.0296836:

```
SELECT * FROM Sales.SalesOrderDetail
WHERE ProductID = 898
```

Let's produce the same plan on a new and empty database. First, create the Sales schema:

```
CREATE SCHEMA Sales
```

Following the procedure described before, you can script the Sales.SalesOrderDetail table. You will end with multiple statements, including the following (again shortened to fit in this space). Although the script created many statements, these are the minimum statements required for this exercise.

```
CREATE TABLE [Sales].[SalesOrderDetail](
     [SalesOrderID] [int] NOT NULL,
...
) ON [PRIMARY]
GO
```

```
CREATE NONCLUSTERED INDEX [IX_SalesOrderDetail_ProductID] ON [Sales].
[SalesOrderDetail]
(
      [ProductID] ASC
)
GO

UPDATE STATISTICS [Sales].[SalesOrderDetail]([IX_SalesOrderDetail_ProductID])
WITH STATS_STREAM = 0x0100000003000000000000000000000041858B2900000000141A00 …,
ROWCOUNT = 121317, PAGECOUNT = 274
GO

UPDATE STATISTICS [Sales].[SalesOrderDetail]([PK_SalesOrderDetail_SalesOrderID_
SalesOrderDetailID])
WITH STATS_STREAM = 0x0100000002000000000000000000000051752A6300000000431500 …,
ROWCOUNT = 121317, PAGECOUNT = 1237
```

Run at least the previous four statements using the scripts you got on the previous step (note that this text does not include the entire statement—it is only shown for reference). After implementing the script on an empty database and running the sample query, you will again get the plan with a cost of 0.0296836 and estimated number of rows of 9.

Missing Indexes

SQL Server does provide a second approach that can help you find useful indexes for your existing queries. Although not as powerful as the DTA, this option, called the Missing Indexes feature, does not require the database administrator to decide when tuning is needed, to explicitly identify what workload represents the load to tune, or to run any tool. This is a lightweight feature that is always on and, like the DTA, was also introduced with SQL Server 2005. Let's take a look at what it does.

During optimization, the query optimizer defines what the best indexes for a query are and, if these indexes don't exist, it will make this index information available in the query XML plan (which is also available in a graphical plan in SQL Server Management Studio 2008 or later). Alternatively, it will aggregate this information for queries optimized since the instance was started, and make it all available on the sys.dm_db_missing_index DMVs. Note that just by displaying this information, the query optimizer is not only warning you that it might not be selecting an efficient plan; it is also showing you which indexes may help to improve the performance of your query. In addition, database administrators and developers should be aware of the limitations of this feature, as described on the Books Online entry "Limitations of the Missing Indexes Feature," at http://msdn.microsoft.com/en-us/library/ms345485(v=sql.105).aspx.

So, with all that in mind, let's take a quick look to see how this feature works. Create the dbo.SalesOrderDetail table on the AdventureWorks2012 database by running the following statement:

```
SELECT * INTO dbo.SalesOrderDetail
FROM Sales.SalesOrderDetail
```

Run this query and request a graphical or XML execution plan:

```
SELECT * FROM dbo.SalesOrderDetail
WHERE SalesOrderID = 43670 AND SalesOrderDetailID > 112
```

This query could benefit from an index on the SalesOrderID and SalesOrderDetailID columns, but no missing indexes information is shown this time. One limitation of the Missing Indexes feature that this example has revealed is that it does not work with a trivial plan optimization. You can verify that this is a trivial plan by looking at the graphical plan properties, shown as Optimization Level TRIVIAL, or by looking at the XML plan, where the StatementOptmLevel is shown as TRIVIAL. You can avoid the trivial plan optimization in several ways, as I explained in Chapter 3. In our case, we're just going to create a nonrelated index by running the following statement:

```
CREATE INDEX IX_ProductID ON dbo.SalesOrderDetail(ProductID)
```

What is significant about this is that, although the index created will not be used by our previous query, the query no longer qualifies for a trivial plan. Run the query again, and this time the XML plan will contain the following entry:

```
<MissingIndexes>
  <MissingIndexGroup Impact="99.7142">
    <MissingIndex Database="[AdventureWorks2012]" Schema="[dbo]"
      Table="[SalesOrderDetail]">
      <ColumnGroup Usage="EQUALITY">
        <Column Name="[SalesOrderID]" ColumnId="1" />
      </ColumnGroup>
      <ColumnGroup Usage="INEQUALITY">
        <Column Name="[SalesOrderDetailID]" ColumnId="2" />
      </ColumnGroup>
    </MissingIndex>
  </MissingIndexGroup>
</MissingIndexes>
```

The MissingIndexes entry in the XML plan can show up to three groups—equality, inequality, and included—and the first two are shown in this example using the

ColumnGroup attribute. The information contained in these groups can be used to create the missing index; the key of the index can be built by using the equality columns, followed by the inequality columns, and the included columns can be added using the INCLUDE clause of the CREATE INDEX statement. Management Studio (versions SQL Server 2008 and later) can build the CREATE INDEX statement for you. In fact, if you look at the graphical plan, you can see a Missing Index warning at the top, including a CREATE INDEX command, as shown in Figure 5-13.

Notice the impact value of 99.7142. Impact is a number between 0 and 100 that gives you an estimate of the average percentage benefit that the query could obtain if the proposed index were available. You can right-click the graphical plan and select Missing Index Details to see the CREATE INDEX command that can be used to create this desired index, as shown next:

```
/*
Missing Index Details from SQLQuery1.sql - (local).AdventureWorks2012
The Query Processor estimates that implementing the following index could
improve the query cost by 99.7142%.
*/


/*
USE [AdventureWorks2012]
GO
CREATE NONCLUSTERED INDEX [<Name of Missing Index, sysname,>]
ON [dbo].[SalesOrderDetail] ([SalesOrderID],[SalesOrderDetailID])

GO
*/
```

Create the recommended index, after you provide a name for it, by running the following statement:

```
CREATE NONCLUSTERED INDEX IX_SalesOrderID_SalesOrderDetailID
ON [dbo].[SalesOrderDetail]([SalesOrderID], [SalesOrderDetailID])
```

```
Query 1: Query cost (relative to the batch): 100%
SELECT * FROM [dbo].[SalesOrderDetail] WHERE [SalesOrderID]=@1 AND [SalesOrderDetailID]>@2
Missing Index (Impact 99.7142): CREATE NONCLUSTERED INDEX [<Name of Missing Index, sysname,>] …

SELECT          Table Scan
Cost: 0 %      [SalesOrderDetail]
                Cost: 100 %
```

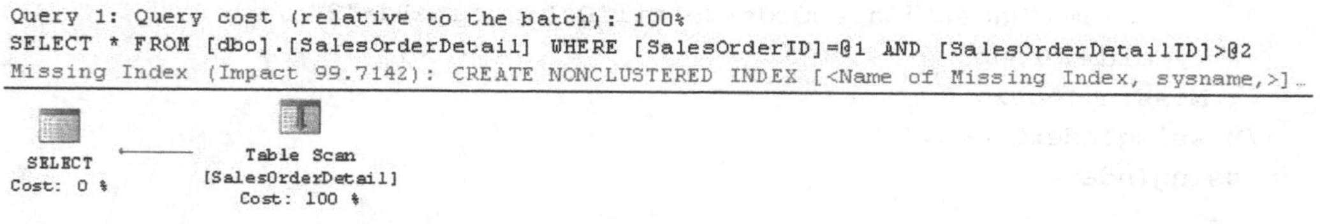

Figure 5-13 *Plan with a Missing Index warning*

If you run our previous SELECT statement again and look at the execution plan, this time you'll see an Index Seek operator using the index you've just created, and both the Missing Index warning and the MissingIndex element of the XML plan are gone.

Finally, remove the dbo.SalesOrderDetail table you've just created by running the following statement:

```
DROP TABLE dbo.SalesOrderDetail
```

Index Fragmentation

Although SQL Server automatically maintains indexes after any INSERT, UPDATE, DELETE, or MERGE operation, some index maintenance activities on your databases may still be required, mostly due to index fragmentation. Fragmentation happens when the logical order of pages in an index does not match the physical order in the data file. Because fragmentation can affect the performance of some queries, you need to monitor the fragmentation level of your indexes and, if required, perform reorganize or rebuild operations on them.

It is also worth clarifying that fragmentation may affect only queries performing scans or range scans; queries performing index seeks may not be affected at all. The query optimizer does not consider fragmentation either, so the plans it produces will be the same whether you have high fragmentation or no fragmentation at all. That is, the query optimizer does not consider whether the pages in an index are in physical order or not. However, one of the inputs for the query optimizer is the number of pages used by a table or index, and this number of pages may increase when there is a lot of unused space.

You can use the sys.dm_db_index_physical_stats DMF to analyze the fragmentation level of your indexes, where you can query this information for a specific partition or index, or look at all the indexes on a table, database, or even the entire SQL Server instance. The following example will return fragmentation information for the Sales.SalesOrderDetail of the AdventureWorks2012 database:

```
SELECT a.index_id, name, avg_fragmentation_in_percent, fragment_count,
    avg_fragment_size_in_pages
FROM sys.dm_db_index_physical_stats (DB_ID('AdventureWorks2012'),
    OBJECT_ID('Sales.SalesOrderDetail'), NULL, NULL, NULL) AS a
JOIN sys.indexes AS b ON a.object_id = b.object_id AND a.index_id = b.index_id
```

In my copy of AdventureWorks2012, I got the following output (not all the columns shown to fit the page):

index_id	name	avg_fragmentation_in_percent
1	PK_SalesOrderDetail_SalesOrderID_SalesOrderDetailID	36.13581245
2	AK_SalesOrderDetail_rowguid	2.643171806
3	IX_SalesOrderDetail_ProductID	25.83892617

Although the level of fragmentation considered a problem may vary and depend on your database and application, a best practice is to reorganize indexes with more than 10 percent and up to 30 percent fragmentation. An index rebuild operation could be more appropriate if you have fragmentation greater than 30 percent. Fragmentation 10 percent or less should not be considered a problem.

An index reorganization operation defragments the leaf level of clustered and nonclustered indexes and is always an online operation. While rebuilding an index, you can optionally use the ONLINE = ON clause to perform an online operation for most of the index rebuild operation (a very short phase at the beginning and the end of the operation will not allow concurrent user activity). Rebuilding an index drops and re-creates the index and removes fragmentation by compacting the index pages based on the specified or existing fill factor configuration. The fill factor is a value from 1 to 100 that specifies a percentage that indicates how full the leaf level of each index page must be during index creation or alteration.

To rebuild all the indexes on the SalesOrderDetail table, use the following statement:

```
ALTER INDEX ALL ON Sales.SalesOrderDetail REBUILD
```

Here is the fragmentation in my copy of AdventureWorks2012 after running the previous statement:

index_id	name	avg_fragmentation_in_percent
1	PK_SalesOrderDetail_SalesOrderID_SalesOrderDetailID	0.24291498
2	AK_SalesOrderDetail_rowguid	0
3	IX_SalesOrderDetail_ProductID	0

In case you need to reorganize the index, which is not the case here, you can use a command like this:

```
ALTER INDEX ALL ON Sales.SalesOrderDetail REORGANIZE
```

As mentioned earlier, fragmentation can also be removed from a heap by using the ALTER TABLE REBUILD statement. However, it could be an expensive operation because it causes all the nonclustered indexes to be rebuilt as the heap RIDs obviously change. Rebuilding an index also has an impact on statistics maintenance. For more details about index and statistics maintenance, see Chapter 6.

Unused Indexes

I'll end this chapter on indexes by introducing the functionality of the sys.dm_db_index_usage_stats DMV, which you can use to learn about the operations performed by your indexes. It is especially helpful in discovering indexes that are not used by any query, or are only minimally used. As we've already discussed, indexes that are not being used will provide no benefit to your databases, but will use valuable disk space, slow your update operations, and should be considered for removal.

The sys.dm_db_index_usage_stats DMV stores the number of seek, scan, lookup, and update operations performed by both user and system queries, including the last time each type of operation was performed, and its counters are reset when the SQL Server service starts. Keep in mind that this DMV, in addition to nonclustered indexes, will also include heaps, listed as index_id equal to 0, and clustered indexes, listed as index_id equal to 1. For the purposes of this section, you may want to just focus on nonclustered indexes, which include index_id values 2 or greater. Because heaps and clustered indexes contain the table's data, they may not even be candidates for removal in the first place.

By inspecting the user_seeks, user_scans, and user_lookup values of your nonclustered indexes, you can see how your indexes are being used, and you can also look at the user_updates values to see the amount of updates performed on the index. All of this information will help to give you a sense as to how useful an index actually is. Bear in mind that all I'll be demonstrating is how to call up information from this DMV and what sort of situations will trigger different updates to the information it returns.

As an example, run the following code to create a new table with a nonclustered index:

```
SELECT * INTO dbo.SalesOrderDetail
FROM Sales.SalesOrderDetail
CREATE NONCLUSTERED INDEX IX_ProductID ON dbo.SalesOrderDetail(ProductID)
```

If you want to keep track of the values for this example, follow these steps carefully, because every query execution may change the index usage statistics. When you run the following query, it will initially contain only one record, which was created because of table access performed when the IX_ProductID index was created:

```
SELECT DB_NAME(database_id) AS database_name,
    OBJECT_NAME(s.object_id) AS object_name, i.name, s.*
FROM sys.dm_db_index_usage_stats s JOIN sys.indexes i
    ON s.object_id = i.object_id AND s.index_id = i.index_id
AND OBJECT_ID('dbo.SalesOrderDetail') = s.object_id
```

However, the values that we will be inspecting in this exercise—user_seeks, user_scans, user_lookups, and user_updates—are all set to 0. Now run the following query, let's say, three times:

```
SELECT * FROM dbo.SalesOrderDetail
```

This query is using a Table Scan operator, so, if you rerun our previous query using the sys.dm_db_index_usage_stats DMV, it will show the value 3 on the user_scans column. Note that the column index_id is 0, denoting a heap, and the name of the table is also listed (as a heap is just a table with no clustered index). Run the next query, which uses an Index Seek, twice. After the query is executed, a new record will be added for the nonclustered index, and the user_seeks counter will show a value of 2.

```
SELECT ProductID FROM dbo.SalesOrderDetail
WHERE ProductID = 773
```

Now, run the following query four times, and it will use both Index Seek and RID Lookup operators. Because the user_seeks for the nonclustered index had a value of 2, it will be updated to 6, and the user_lookups value for the heap will be updated to 4.

```
SELECT * FROM dbo.SalesOrderDetail
WHERE ProductID = 773
```

Finally, run the following query once:

```
UPDATE dbo.SalesOrderDetail
SET ProductID = 666
WHERE ProductID = 927
```

Note that the UPDATE statement is doing an Index Seek and a Table Update, so user_seek will be updated for the index, and user_updates will be updated once for both the nonclustered index and the heap. Here is the final output of our query using the sys.dm_db_index_usage_stats DMV (edited for space):

name	index_id	user_seeks	user_scans	user_lookups	user_updates
NULL	0	0	3	4	1
IX_ProductID	2	7	0	0	1

Finally, drop the table you just created:

```
DROP TABLE dbo.SalesOrderDetail
```

Summary

This chapter introduced indexing as one of the most important techniques used in query tuning and optimization and covered clustered and nonclustered indexes along with related topics such as how SQL Server uses indexes, how to choose a clustered index key, and how to fix index fragmentation.

This chapter also explained how you can define the key of your indexes so that they are likely to be considered for seek operations, which can improve the performance of your queries by finding records more quickly. Predicates were analyzed in the contexts of both single- and multicolumn indexes, and we also covered how to verify an execution plan to validate that indexes were selected and properly used by SQL Server.

The Database Engine Tuning Advisor and the Missing Indexes feature, both introduced with SQL Server 2005, were presented to show how the query optimizer itself can be used to provide index-tuning recommendations.

Finally, the sys.dm_db_index_usage_stats DMV was introduced, together with its ability to provide valuable information regarding your nonclustered indexes usage. Although we didn't have time to discuss all the practicalities of using this DMV, we covered enough for you to be able to easily find nonclustered indexes that are not being used by your SQL Server instance.

Chapter 6

Statistics

In This Chapter

The SQL Server query optimizer is a cost-based optimizer; therefore, the quality of the execution plans it generates is directly related to the accuracy of its cost estimations. In the same way, the estimated cost of a plan is based on the algorithms or operators used as well as their cardinality estimations. For this reason, to correctly estimate the cost of an execution plan, the query optimizer needs to estimate, as precisely as possible, the number of records returned by a given query.

During query optimization, SQL Server explores many candidate plans, estimates their relative costs, and selects the most efficient one. As such, incorrect cardinality and cost estimation may cause the query optimizer to choose inefficient plans, which can have a negative impact on the performance of your database.

In this chapter I discuss the statistics used by the query optimizer, how to make sure you are providing it with the best possible quality of statistics, and what to do in cases where bad cardinality estimations are inevitable. Query optimizer statistics contain three major pieces of information: the histogram, the density information, and the string statistics, all of which help with different parts of the cardinality estimation process. I show you how statistics are created and maintained, and how they are used by the query optimizer. I also provide you with information on how to detect cardinality estimation errors that can negatively impact the quality of your execution plans, as well as recommendations on how to fix them.

I also cover the new cardinality estimator introduced with SQL Server 2014, including details and differences with the old cardinality estimator. The chapter ends with an overview of the costing module, which estimates the I/O and CPU cost for each operator, to finally obtain the total cost of the query plan.

Statistics

SQL Server creates and maintains statistics to allow the query optimizer to calculate cardinality estimation. A *cardinality estimate* is the estimated number of rows that will be returned by a query or by a specific query operation such as a join or a filter. *Selectivity* is a concept similar to cardinality estimation, which can be described as the fraction of rows in a set that satisfy a predicate, and it is always a value between 0 and 1, inclusive. A highly selective predicate returns a small number of rows. Rather than say any more on the subject here, we'll dive into more detail about these concepts later in this chapter.

Creating and Updating Statistics

To get started, let's take a look at the various ways statistics can be created and updated. Statistics are created in several ways: automatically by the query optimizer (if the default option to automatically create statistics, AUTO_CREATE_STATISTICS, is on), when an index is created, and explicitly (for example, via the CREATE STATISTICS statement). Statistics can be created on one or more columns, and both the index and explicit creation methods support single- and multicolumn statistics. However, the statistics that are automatically generated by the query optimizer are always single-column statistics. As I've already mentioned briefly, the components of statistics objects are the histogram, the density information, and the string statistics. Both histograms and string statistics are created only for the first column of a statistics object, the latter only if the column is of a string data type.

Density information, which I discuss in plenty of detail later in this chapter, is calculated for each set of columns, forming a prefix in the statistics object. Filtered statistics, on the other hand, are not created automatically by the query optimizer, but only when a filtered index is created or when a CREATE STATISTICS statement with a WHERE clause is issued. Both filtered indexes and statistics are a feature introduced in SQL Server 2008. Filtered indexes were covered in Chapter 5, and we will touch on filtered statistics later in this chapter.

With the default configuration (if AUTO_UPDATE_STATISTICS is on), the query optimizer automatically updates statistics when they are out of date. As noted before, the query optimizer does not automatically create multicolumn or filtered statistics, but once they are created, by using any of the methods described earlier, they can be automatically updated. Alternatively, index rebuild operations and statements such as UPDATE STATISTICS can also be used to update statistics. Because both the auto-create and auto-update default choices will give you good quality statistics most of the time, it is strongly recommended that you keep these defaults. Naturally you also have the choice to use some other statements if you need more control over the quality of the statistics.

So, by default, statistics may be automatically created (if nonexistent) and automatically updated (if out of date) as necessary during query optimization. By "out of date" we refer to the data being changed and therefore the statistics not being representative of the underlying data (more on the exact mechanism later). If an execution plan for a specific query exists in the plan cache and the statistics that were used to build the plan are now out of date, then the plan is discarded, the statistics are updated, and a new plan is created. In a similar way, updating statistics, either manually or automatically, invalidates any existing execution plan that used those statistics, and will cause a new optimization the next time the query is executed.

When it comes to determining the quality of your statistics, a fact to consider is the size of the sample of the target table used to calculate said statistics. The query optimizer determines a statistically significant sample by default when it creates or updates statistics, and the minimum sample size is 8MB (1,024 pages) or the size of the table if it's smaller than 8MB. The sample size will increase for bigger tables, but it may still only be a small percentage of the table.

If needed, you can use the CREATE STATISTICS and UPDATE STATISTICS statements to explicitly request a bigger sample or scan the entire table to have better quality statistics. In order to do that you need to specify a sample size or use the WITH FULLSCAN option to scan the entire table. A sample size can be specified as number of rows or percentage and, because the query optimizer has to scan all the rows on a data page, these values are approximate. Using WITH FULLSCAN or using a larger sample can be of benefit, especially with data that is not randomly distributed throughout the table. Scanning the entire table will naturally give you the most accurate statistics possible. Consider that if statistics are built after scanning 50 percent of a table, then SQL Server will assume that the 50 percent of data that it has not seen is statistically exactly the same as the 50 percent it has seen. In fact, given that statistics are always created alongside a new index, and given that this operation scans the entire table anyway, index statistics are initially created with the equivalent of the WITH FULLSCAN option. However, if the query optimizer needs to automatically update these index statistics, it has to go back to a default sample because it may take too long to scan the entire table again.

By default, SQL Server needs to wait for the update statistics operation to complete before optimizing and executing the query; that is, statistics are updated synchronously. A database configuration option introduced with SQL Server 2005, AUTO_UPDATE_STATISTICS_ASYNC, can be used to change this default and let the statistics be updated asynchronously. As you might have guessed, with asynchronous statistics update, the query optimizer does not wait for the update statistics operation to complete, and instead just uses the current statistics for the optimization process. This can help in situations where applications experience timeouts caused by delays related to the automatic update of statistics. Although the current optimization will use the out-of-date statistics, they will be updated in the background and will be used by any later query optimization. However, asynchronous statistics updates usually only benefit OLTP workloads and may not be a good solution for more expensive queries, where getting a better plan is more important than an infrequent delay in statistics update.

SQL Server defines when statistics are out of date by using column modification counters, or colmodctrs, which count the total number of modifications for the leading statistics column since the last time statistics were updated. Basically, for tables bigger than 500 rows, a statistics object is considered out of date if the colmodctr value of the leading column has changed by more than 500 plus 20 percent of the number of rows in the table. The same formula is used by filtered statistics, but, because they are built only from a subset of the records of the table, the colmodctr value is first multiplied by the selectivity of the filter. colmodctrs are exposed in the modification_counter column of the sys.dm_db_stats_properties DMF, which is available starting with SQL Server

2008 R2 Service Pack 2 and SQL Server 2012 Service Pack 1. (Previously, colmodctrs were only available using a dedicated administrator connection and looking at the rcmodified column of the sys.sysrscols base system table in SQL Server 2008 or the sysrowset columns for SQL Server 2005.)

> **NOTE**
>
> *SQL Server 2000 used rowmodctrs, or row modification counters, instead to keep track of the number of changes in a table or index. The main difference with colmodctrs is that rowmodctrs track any change to the row, whereas colmodctrs only track changes to the leading column of the statistics object. Currently, the sp_updatestats statement, which is another way to update statistics, is still based on rowmodctrs, whose values are available as the rowmodctr column of the sys.sysindexes compatibility view.*

Trace flag 2371 was introduced with SQL Server 2008 R2 Service Pack 1 as a way to automatically update statistics in a lower and dynamic percentage rate, instead of the mentioned 20 percent threshold. With this dynamic percentage rate, the higher the number of rows in a table, the lower this threshold will become to trigger an automatic update of statistics. Tables with less than 25,000 records will still use the 20 percent threshold, but as the number of records in the table increase, this threshold will be lower and lower. For more details about this trace flag, see the article "Changes to Automatic Update Statistics in SQL Server – Traceflag 2371."

The density information on multicolumn statistics might improve the quality of execution plans in the case of correlated columns or statistical correlations between columns. As mentioned previously, density information is kept for all the columns in a statistics object, in the order that they appear in the statistics definition. By default, SQL Server assumes columns are independent; therefore, if a relationship or dependency exists between columns, multicolumn statistics can help with cardinality estimation problems in queries that are using these columns. Density information will also help on filters and GROUP BY operations, as we'll see in the "Density" section later on. Filtered statistics, which are also explained later in this chapter, can also be used for cardinality estimation problems with correlated columns. More details about the independency assumption are covered later in the section "The New Cardinality Estimator."

Inspecting Statistics Objects

Let's look at an example of a statistics object and inspect the data it stores. But first make sure you are using the new cardinality estimator by running the following statement:

```
ALTER DATABASE AdventureWorks2012
SET COMPATIBILITY_LEVEL = 120
```

Existing statistics for a specific object can be displayed using the sys.stats catalog view, as used in the following query:

```
SELECT * FROM sys.stats
WHERE object_id = OBJECT_ID('Sales.SalesOrderDetail')
```

An output similar to the following (edited to fit the page) will be shown:

object_id	name	stats_id
1154103152	PK_SalesOrderDetail_SalesOrderID_SalesOrderDetailID	1
1154103152	AK_SalesOrderDetail_rowguid	2
1154103152	IX_SalesOrderDetail_ProductID	3

One record for each statistics object is shown. You can use the DBCC SHOW_ STATISTICS statement to display the details of a statistics object by specifying the column name or the name of the statistics object.

For example, run the following statement to verify that there are no statistics on the UnitPrice column of the Sales.SalesOrderDetail table:

```
DBCC SHOW_STATISTICS ('Sales.SalesOrderDetail', UnitPrice)
```

If no statistics object exists, which is the case for a fresh installation of the AdventureWorks2012 database, you will receive the following error message:

```
Msg 2767, Level 16, State 1, Line 1
Could not locate statistics 'UnitPrice' in the system catalogs.
DBCC execution completed. If DBCC printed error messages, contact your system
administrator.
```

By then running the following query, the query optimizer will automatically create statistics on the UnitPrice column, which is used in the query predicate:

```
SELECT * FROM Sales.SalesOrderDetail
WHERE UnitPrice = 35
```

Running the previous DBCC SHOW_STATISTICS statement again will now show a statistics object similar to the following output (displayed as text and edited to fit the page).

```
Name                     Updated              Rows      Rows Sampled Steps
------------------------  -------------------  --------  ------------ -----
_WA_Sys_00000007_44CA3770 Jan 6 2014 11:55PM   121317    110388       200
```

```
All density    Average Length Columns
-------------  -------------- ----------------
0.003205128    8              UnitPrice


RANGE_HI_KEY      RANGE_ROWS    EQ_ROWS       DISTINCT_RANGE_ROWS  AVG_RANGE_ROWS
----------------  ------------  ------------  -------------------- --------------
1.3282            0             1             0                    1
1.374             35.19722      142.3062      0                    370.2226
2.29              35.19722      2747.751      0                    370.2226
2.994             417.5509      341.9168      3                    123.5255
3.975             35.19722      1             0                    370.2226
3.99              35.19722      2061.052      0                    370.2226
```

The output is separated into three result sets called the header, the density vector, and the histogram, although the header information has been truncated to fit onto the page, and only a few rows of the histogram are shown. Let's look at the columns of the header using the previous statistics object example, bearing in mind that some of the columns I'll describe are not visible in the previous output.

▶ **Name: _WA_Sys_00000007_44CA3770** This is the name of the statistics object, and will probably be different in your SQL Server instance. All automatically generated statistics have a name that starts with _WA_Sys. The 00000007 value is the column_id of the column on which these statistics are based, as can be seen on the sys.columns catalog, and 44CA3770 is the hexadecimal equivalent of the object_id value of the table (which can be easily verified using the calculator program available in Windows). WA stands for Washington, the state in the United States where the SQL Server development team is located.

▶ **Updated: Jan 6 2014 11:55PM** This is the date and time when the statistics object was created or last updated.

▶ **Rows: 121317** This is the number of rows that existed in the table when the statistics object was created or last updated.

▶ **Rows Sampled: 110388** This is the number of rows sampled when the statistics object was created or last updated.

▶ **Steps: 200** This is the number of steps of the histogram, which will be explained in the next section.

▶ **Density: 0.06236244** Density of all the values sampled except the RANGE_HI_KEY values (RANGE_HI_KEY will be explained later in the "Histogram" section). This density value is no longer used by the query optimizer, and it is only included for backward compatibility.

▶ **Average key length: 8** This is the average number of bytes for the columns of the statistics object.

- ▶ **String Index: NO**   This value indicates if the statistics object contains string statistics, and the only choices are YES or NO. String statistics contain the data distribution of substrings in a string column and can be used to estimate the cardinality of queries with LIKE conditions. As indicated before, string statistics are only created for the first column, and only when the column is of a string data type.

- ▶ **Filter Expression and Unfiltered Rows**   These columns will be explained in the "Filtered Statistics" section, later in the chapter.

Below the header you'll find the density vector, which includes a wealth of potentially useful density information and will be explained in the next section.

Density

To better explain the density vector, run the following statement to inspect the statistics of the existing index, IX_SalesOrderDetail_ProductID:

```
DBCC SHOW_STATISTICS ('Sales.SalesOrderDetail', IX_SalesOrderDetail_ProductID)
```

This will display the following density vector, which shows the densities for the ProductID column, as well as a combination of columns ProductID, SalesOrderID, and then ProductID, SalesOrderID, and SalesOrderDetailID:

```
All density    Average Length Columns
-------------- -------------- ---------------------------------------------------------
0.003759399    4              ProductID
8.242868E-06   8              ProductID, SalesOrderID
8.242868E-06   12             ProductID, SalesOrderID, SalesOrderDetailID
```

Density, which is defined as 1 / "number of distinct values," is listed in the All density field, and it is calculated for each set of columns, forming a prefix for the columns in the statistics object. For example, the statistics object listed was created for the columns ProductID, SalesOrderID, and SalesOrderDetailID, and so the density vector will show three different density values: one for ProductID, another one for ProductID and SalesOrderID combined, and a third one for the combination of ProductID, SalesOrderID, and SalesOrderDetailID. The names of the analyzed columns will be displayed in the Columns field, and the Average Length column will show the average number of bytes for each density value. In the previous example, all the columns were defined using the int data type, so the average lengths for each of the density values will be 4, 8, and 12 bytes, respectively. Now that we've seen how density information is structured, let's take a look at how it's used.

Density information can be used to improve the query optimizer's estimates for GROUP BY operations, and on equality predicates where a value is unknown, as in the case of a query using local variables. To see how this is done, let's consider, for example, the number of distinct values for ProductID on the Sales.SalesOrderDetail table: 266. Density can be calculated, as mentioned earlier, as 1 / "number of distinct values," which in this case would be 1 / 266, which is 0.003759399, as shown on the first density value in the previous example.

So, the query optimizer can use the density information to estimate the cardinality of GROUP BY queries. GROUP BY queries can benefit from the estimated number of distinct values, and this information is already available in the density value. If you have this density information, then all you have to do is find the estimated number of distinct values by calculating the reciprocal of the density value. For example, to estimate the cardinality of the following query using GROUP BY ProductID, we can calculate the reciprocal of the ProductID density shown in the following statement. In this case, we have 1 / 0.003759399, which gives us 266, which is the estimated number of rows shown in the plan in Figure 6-1.

```
SELECT ProductID FROM Sales.SalesOrderDetail
GROUP BY ProductID
```

In a similar way, to test GROUP BY ProductID, SalesOrderID, we would need 1 / 8.242868E-06, which gives us an answer of 121,317. That is to say that in the sampled data there are 121,317 unique combinations of ProductID and SalesOrderID. You can also verify by obtaining that query's graphical plan.

Next is an example of how the density can be used to estimate the cardinality of a query using local variables:

```
DECLARE @ProductID int
SET @ProductID = 921
SELECT ProductID FROM Sales.SalesOrderDetail
WHERE ProductID = @ProductID
```

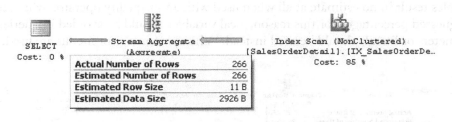

Actual Number of Rows	266
Estimated Number of Rows	266
Estimated Row Size	11 B
Estimated Data Size	2926 B

Figure 6-1   *Cardinality estimation example using a GROUP BY clause*

```
                                                  ⛁
                              Index Seek (NonClustered)
   SELECT  ⟵────────         [SalesOrderDetail].[IX_SalesOrderDe…
   Cost: 0 %
                          ┌────────────────────────────────────┐
                          │ Actual Number of Rows        3095  │
                          │ Estimated Number of Rows  456.079  │
                          │ Estimated Row Size           11 B  │
                          │ Estimated Data Size        5017 B  │
                          └────────────────────────────────────┘
```

Figure 6-2   *Cardinality estimation example using a local variable*

In this case, the query optimizer does not know the value of the @ProductID local variable at optimization time, so it is not able to use the histogram (which we'll discuss shortly) and will use the density information instead. The estimated number of rows is obtained using the density multiplied by the number of records in the table, which in our example is 0.003759399 * 121317, or 456.079, as shown in Figure 6-2.

Actually, because the query optimizer does not know the value of @ProductID at optimization time, the value 921 in the previous listing does not matter; any other value will give exactly the same estimated number of rows and execution plan, this being the average number of rows per value. Finally, run this query with an inequality operator:

```
DECLARE @pid int = 897
SELECT * FROM Sales.SalesOrderDetail
WHERE ProductID < @pid
```

Just as before, the value 897 does not matter; any other value will give you the same estimated number of rows and execution plan. However, this time, the query optimizer is not able to use the density information and instead is using the standard guess of 30 percent selectivity for inequality comparisons. This means that the estimated number of rows is always 30 percent of the total number of records for an inequality operator; in this case, 30 percent of 121,317 is 36,395.1, as shown in Figure 6-3.

However, the use of local variables in a query limits the quality of the cardinality estimate when using the density information with equality operators. Worse, local variables result in no estimate at all when used with an inequality operator, which results in a guessed percentage. For this reason, local variables should be avoided in queries, and parameters or literals should be used instead. When parameters or literals are used, the

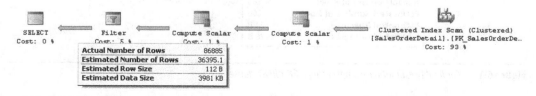

Figure 6-3   *Cardinality estimation example using a 30 percent guess*

query optimizer is able to use the histogram, which will provide better-quality estimates than the density information on its own.

As it happens, the last section of the DBCC SHOW_STATISTICS output is the histogram, which I will now explain.

Histogram

In SQL Server, histograms are created only for the first column of a statistics object, and they compress the information of the distribution of values in that column by partitioning that information into subsets called buckets or steps. The maximum number of steps in a histogram is 200, but even if the input has 200 or more unique values, a histogram may still have fewer than 200 steps. To build the histogram, SQL Server finds the unique values in the column and tries to capture the most frequent ones using a variation of the maxdiff algorithm, so that the most statistically significant information is preserved. Maxdiff is one of the available histograms whose purpose is to accurately represent the distribution of data values in relational databases.

NOTE

You can find a simplified version of the algorithm used to build the histogram in the Microsoft white paper "Statistics Used by the Query Optimizer in Microsoft SQL Server 2008," by Eric Hanson and Yavor Angelov.

To see how the histogram is used, run the following statement to display the current statistics of the IX_SalesOrderDetail_ProductID index on the Sales.SalesOrderDetail table:

```
DBCC SHOW_STATISTICS ('Sales.SalesOrderDetail', IX_SalesOrderDetail_ProductID)
```

Both the multicolumn index and statistics objects include the columns ProductID, SalesOrderID, and SalesOrderDetailID, but because the histogram is only for the first column, this data is only available for the ProductID column.

Next, I will show you some examples of how the histogram may be used to estimate the cardinality of some simple predicates. Let's take a look at a section of the histogram, as shown in the following output:

RANGE_HI_KEY	RANGE_ROWS	EQ_ROWS	DISTINCT_RANGE_ROWS	AVG_RANGE_ROWS
826	0	305	0	1
831	110	198	3	36.66667
832	0	256	0	1

RANGE_HI_KEY is the upper boundary of a histogram step; the value 826 is the upper boundary for the first step displayed, and 831 is the upper boundary for the second step shown. This means that the second step may contain only values from 827 to 831. The RANGE_HI_KEY values are usually the more frequent values in the distribution.

With that in mind, and to better understand the rest of the histogram structure and how the histogram information was aggregated, run the following query to obtain the real number of records for ProductIDs 827 to 831, and we'll compare them against the histogram:

```
SELECT ProductID, COUNT(*) AS Total
FROM Sales.SalesOrderDetail
WHERE ProductID BETWEEN 827 AND 831
GROUP BY ProductID
```

This produces the following result:

ProductID	Total
827	31
828	46
830	33
831	198

Going back to the histogram, EQ_ROWS is the estimated number of rows whose column value equals RANGE_HI_KEY. So, in our example, for the RANGE_HI_KEY value of 831, EQ_ROWS shows 198, which we know is also the actual number of existing records for ProductID 831.

RANGE_ROWS is the estimated number of rows whose column value falls inside the range of the step, excluding the upper boundary. In our example, this is the number of records with values from 827 to 830 (831, the upper boundary or RANGE_HI_KEY, is excluded). The histogram shows 110 records, and we could obtain the same value by getting the sum of 31 records for ProductID 827, 46 records for ProductID 828, 0 records for ProductID 829, and 33 records for ProductID 830.

DISTINCT_RANGE_ROWS is the estimated number of rows with a distinct column value inside this range, once again excluding the upper boundary. In our example, we have records for three distinct values (827, 828, and 830), so DISTINCT_RANGE_ROWS is 3. There are no records for ProductID 829, and 831, which is the upper boundary, is again excluded.

Finally, AVG_RANGE_ROWS is the average number of rows per distinct value, excluding the upper boundary, and it is simply calculated as RANGE_ROWS / DISTINCT_RANGE_ROWS. In our example, we have a total of 110 records for 3 DISTINCT_RANGE_ROWS, which gives us 110 / 3 = 36.6667, also shown in the

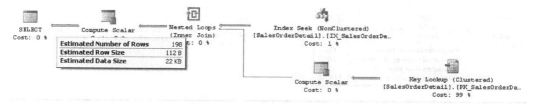

Figure 6-4   *Cardinality estimation example using a RANGE_HI_KEY value*

second step of the histogram shown previously. Basically the histogram assumes the value 110 is evenly split between all three ProductIDs.

Now let's see how the histogram is used to estimate the selectivity of some queries. Let's look at the first query:

```
SELECT * FROM Sales.SalesOrderDetail
WHERE ProductID = 831
```

Because 831 is the RANGE_HI_KEY on the second step of the histogram shown previously, the query optimizer will use the EQ_ROWS value (the estimated number of rows whose column value equals RANGE_HI_KEY) directly, and the estimated number of rows will be 198, as shown in Figure 6-4.

Now run the same query, with the value set to 828. This time, the value is inside the range of the second step but is not a RANGE_HI_KEY value inside the histogram, so the query optimizer uses the value calculated for AVG_RANGE_ROWS (the average number of rows per distinct value), which is 36.6667, as shown in the histogram. The plan for this query is shown in Figure 6-5 and, unsurprisingly, we get the same estimated number of rows for any of the other values within the range (except for the RANGE_HI_KEY, obviously). This even includes the value 829, for which there are no rows inside the table.

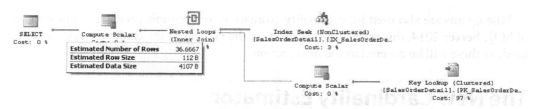

Figure 6-5   *Cardinality estimation example using an AVG_RANGE_ROWS value*

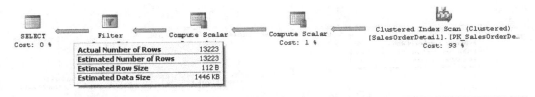

Actual Number of Rows	13223
Estimated Number of Rows	13223
Estimated Row Size	112 B
Estimated Data Size	1446 KB

Figure 6-6   *Cardinality estimation example using an inequality operator*

Let's now use an inequality operator and try to find the records with a ProductID less than 714. Because this requires all the records, both inside the range of a step and the upper boundary, we need to calculate the sum of the values of both the RANGE_ROWS and EQ_ROWS columns for steps 1 through 7, as shown in the following histogram, which give us a total of 13,223 rows:

RANGE_HI_KEY	RANGE_ROWS	EQ_ROWS	DISTINCT_RANGE_ROWS	AVG_RANGE_ROWS
707	0	3083	0	1
708	0	3007	0	1
709	0	188	0	1
710	0	44	0	1
711	0	3090	0	1
712	0	3382	0	1
713	0	429	0	1
714	0	1218	0	1
715	0	1635	0	1

The following is the query in question, and the estimated number of rows is shown in the execution plan in Figure 6-6:

```
SELECT * FROM Sales.SalesOrderDetail
WHERE ProductID < 714
```

Histograms are also used for cardinality estimations on multiple predicates; however, as of SQL Server 2014, this estimation depends on the version of the cardinality estimation used, so these will be covered in the next section.

The New Cardinality Estimator

As mentioned in the introduction, SQL Server 2014 includes a new cardinality estimator, and in this version, the old cardinality estimator is still available. This section explains what a cardinality estimator is, why a new cardinality estimator was built, and how to enable the new and the old cardinality estimators.

The cardinality estimator is the component of the query processor whose job it is to estimate the number of rows returned by relational operations in a query. This information, along with some other data, is used by the query optimizer to select an efficient execution plan. Cardinality estimation is inherently inexact because it is a mathematical model that relies on statistical information. It is also based on several assumptions that, although not documented, have been known over the years—some of them include the uniformity, independence, containment, and inclusion assumptions. A brief description of these assumptions follows:

▶ **Uniformity**   Used when the distribution for an attribute is unknown—for example, inside of range rows in a histogram step or when a histogram is not available.

▶ **Independence**   Used when the attributes in a relation are independent, unless a correlation between them is known.

▶ **Containment**   Used when two attributes might be the same; in this case, they are assumed to be the same.

▶ **Inclusion**   Used when comparing an attribute with a constant; it is assumed there is always a match.

The current cardinality estimator was written along with the entire query processor for SQL Server 7.0, which was released back in December 1998. Obviously this component has faced multiple changes during several years and multiple releases of SQL Server, including fixes, adjustments, and extensions to accommodate cardinality estimation for new T-SQL features. So you may be thinking, why replace a component that has been successfully used for about the last 15 years?

In the paper "Testing Cardinality Estimation Models in SQL Server" by Campbell Fraser et al., the authors explain some of the reasons for the redesign of the cardinality estimator, including the following:

▶ To accommodate the cardinality estimator to new workload patterns.

▶ Changes made to the cardinality estimator over the years made the component difficult to "debug, predict, and understand."

▶ Trying to improve on the current model was difficult using the current architecture, so a new design was created, focused on the separation of tasks of (a) deciding how to compute a particular estimate, and (b) actually performing the computation.

I was also surprised to read in the paper that the authors admit that, according to their experience in practice, the previously listed assumptions are "frequently incorrect."

A major concern that comes to mind with such a huge change inside the query optimizer is plan regressions. The fear of plan regressions has been considered the biggest obstacle to query optimizer improvements. Regressions are problems introduced after a fix has been applied to the query optimizer and are sometimes referred to as the classic "two wrongs make a right." This can happen when two bad estimations—for example, one overestimating a value and the second one underestimating it—cancel each other out, luckily giving a good estimate. Correcting only one of these values may now lead to a bad estimation, which may negatively impact the choice of plan selection, thus causing a regression.

To help avoid regressions related to the new cardinality estimator, SQL Server provides a way to enable or disable it, depending on the database compatibility level. This can be changed using the ALTER DATABASE statement, as indicated earlier. Setting a database to the compatibility level 120 will use the new cardinality estimator, whereas a compatibility level less than 120 will use the old cardinality estimator. In addition, once you are using a specific cardinality estimator, there are two trace flags you can use to change to the other. Trace flag 2312 can be used to enable the new cardinality estimator, whereas trace flag 9481 can be used to disable it. You can even use the trace flags for a specific query using the QUERYTRACEON hint. Both trace flags and their use with the QUERYTRACEON hint are documented and supported.

NOTE

The compatibility level of a database is changed several times in this chapter for demonstration purposes to show the behaviors of the old and new cardinality estimators. In a production environment, a database compatibility level should be static and never or rarely changed.

Finally, SQL Server includes several new extended events we can use to troubleshoot problems with cardinality estimation, or just to explore how it works. These events include query_optimizer_estimate_cardinality, inaccurate_cardinality_estimate, query_optimizer_force_both_cardinality_estimation_behaviors, and query_rpc_set_cardinality.

Examples

This section shows the difference in estimations between the new and old cardinality estimators regarding AND'ed and OR'ed predicates, known as conjunctions and disjunctions, respectively. Some other sections in the chapter explain the difference in other topics (for example, in the use of statistics on ascending keys).

First, let's look at the traditional behavior. For that, make sure you are using the old cardinality estimator by running the following statement on the AdventureWorks2012 database:

```
ALTER DATABASE AdventureWorks2012 SET COMPATIBILITY_LEVEL = 110
```

Then run this statement:

```
SELECT * FROM Person.Address WHERE City = 'Burbank'
```

By looking at the execution plan, as shown previously, we can see an estimate of 196 records. In a similar way, the following statement will get an estimate of 194:

```
SELECT * FROM Person.Address WHERE PostalCode = '91502'
```

Both estimations of single predicates use the histogram, as explained earlier. If we use both predicates, we have the following query, which will have an estimated 1.93862 number of rows:

```
SELECT * FROM Person.Address
WHERE City = 'Burbank' AND PostalCode = '91502'
```

Because SQL Server does not know anything about any data correlation between both predicates, it assumes they are independent and again uses the histograms, as I showed before, to find the intersection between both sets of records, multiplying the selectivity of both clauses. The selectivity of the predicate City = 'Burbank' is calculated as 196 / 19614 (where 19614 is the total number of rows in the table), or 0.009992862. The selectivity of the predicate PostalCode = '91502' is calculated as 194 / 19614, or 0.009890894. In order to get the intersection of these sets, we need to multiply the selectivity values of both predicate clauses, 0.009992862 and 0.009890894, to get 9.88383E-05. Finally, the calculated selectivity is multiplied by the total number of records to obtain the estimate 9.88383E-05 * 19614, obtaining 1.93862. A more direct formula could be to simply use (196 * 194) / 19614.0 to get the same result.

Let's see the same estimations using the new cardinality estimator:

```
ALTER DATABASE AdventureWorks2012 SET COMPATIBILITY_LEVEL = 120
GO
SELECT * FROM Person.Address WHERE City = 'Burbank' AND PostalCode = '91502'
```

Running the same statement again will give an estimate of 19.3931 rows, as shown in Figure 6-7.

The new formula used in this case is

```
selectivity of most selective filter * SQRT(selectivity of next most
selective filter)
```

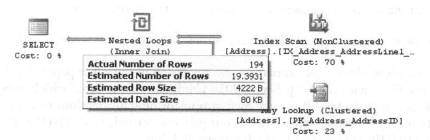

Figure 6-7   *AND'ed predicates with the new cardinality estimator*

or (194/19614) * SQRT(196/19614) * 19614, which gives 19.393. If there were a third (or more) predicate, the formula would be extended by adding a SQRT operation for each predicate, such as in

```
selectivity of most selective filter * SQRT(selectivity of next most
selective filter) * SQRT(SQRT(selectivity of next most selective filter))
```

and so on.

Now keep in mind that the old cardinality estimator is using the original independence assumption. The new cardinality estimator is using a new formula, relaxing this assumption, which is now called the exponential backoff. This new formula does not assume total correlation either, but at least the new estimation is better than the original. Finally, note that the query optimizer is not able to know if the data is correlated, so it will be using these formulas, regardless of whether or not the data is correlated. In our example, the data is correlated; the ZIP code 91502 corresponds to the city of Burbank, California.

Now let's test the same example using OR'ed predicates, first using the old cardinality estimator:

```
ALTER DATABASE AdventureWorks2012 SET COMPATIBILITY_LEVEL = 110
GO
SELECT * FROM Person.Address WHERE City = 'Burbank' OR PostalCode = '91502'
```

By definition, an OR'ed predicate is the union of the sets of rows of both clauses, without duplicates. That is, this should be the rows estimated for the predicate City = 'Burbank' plus the rows estimated for PostalCode = '91502', but if there are any rows that may belong to both sets, then they should be included only once. As indicated in the previous example, the estimated number of rows for the predicate City = 'Burbank' alone is 196 rows, and the estimated number of rows for the predicate PostalCode = '91502' alone is 194 rows. The estimated number of records that belong to both sets is the AND'ed predicate we saw previously: 1.93862 rows. Therefore, the estimated number of rows for the OR'ed predicate is 196 + 194 − 1.93862, or 388.061.

Testing the same example for the new cardinality estimator would return an estimate of 292.269 rows, as shown in Figure 6-8.

```
ALTER DATABASE AdventureWorks2012 SET COMPATIBILITY_LEVEL = 120
GO
SELECT * FROM Person.Address WHERE City = 'Burbank' OR PostalCode = '91502'
```

The formula to obtain this estimation was suggested in the white paper "Optimizing Your Query Plans with the SQL Server 2014 Cardinality Estimator," which indicates that SQL Server "calculates this value by first transforming disjunctions to a negation of conjunctions." In this case, we can update our previous formula to (1-(1-(196/19614)) * SQRT(1-(194/19614))) * 19614, which returns 292.269.

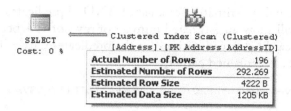

Clustered Index Scan (Clustered)	
[Address].[PK_Address_AddressID]	
Actual Number of Rows	196
Estimated Number of Rows	292.269
Estimated Row Size	4222 B
Estimated Data Size	1205 KB

Figure 6-8   *OR'ed predicates with the new cardinality estimator*

If you have enabled the new cardinality estimator at the database level but want to disable it for a specific query to avoid plan regression, you can use trace flag 9481, as explained earlier:

```
ALTER DATABASE AdventureWorks2012 SET COMPATIBILITY_LEVEL = 120
GO
SELECT * FROM Person.Address WHERE City = 'Burbank' AND PostalCode = '91502'
OPTION (QUERYTRACEON 9481)
```

NOTE

As indicated in Chapter 1, the QUERYTRACEON query hint is used to apply a trace flag at the query level, and currently it is only supported in a limited number of scenarios, including the trace flags 2312 and 9481 mentioned in this section.

Finally, since starting with SQL Server 2014, two cardinality estimators are available, figuring out which one was used by a specific optimization will now be required, especially for troubleshooting purposes. You can find this information on execution plans by looking at the CardinalityEstimationModelVersion property of a graphical plan or the CardinalityEstimationModelVersion attribute of the StmtSimple element in an XML plan, as in the following XML fragment:

```
<StmtSimple ... CardinalityEstimationModelVersion="120" ...>
```

A value of 120 means the new cardinality estimator is used. All other database compatibility levels possible in SQL Server 2014, such as 90, 100, and 110, will return a CardinalityEstimationModelVersion value of 70, which means the old cardinality estimator is used.

Trace Flag 4137

Finally, trace flag 4137 can be used as another choice to help with correlated AND predicates. Trace flag 4137 (which was originally released as a fix for SQL Server 2008 Service Pack 2, SQL Server 2008 R2 Service Pack 1, and SQL Server 2012 RTM) will select the lowest cardinality estimation of a list of AND'ed predicates. For example, the following code will show an estimated number of rows of 194, because 194 is the smallest of both cardinality estimations for the predicates City = 'Burbank' and PostalCode = '91502', as explained earlier.

```
ALTER DATABASE AdventureWorks2012 SET COMPATIBILITY_LEVEL = 110
GO
SELECT * FROM Person.Address
WHERE City = 'Burbank' AND PostalCode = '91502'
OPTION (QUERYTRACEON 4137)
```

NOTE

Using trace flag 4137 with QUERYTRACEON is documented and totally supported.

To make things a little bit more confusing, trace flag 4137 does not work with the new cardinality estimator, and trace flag 9471 needs to be used instead. Another difference with trace flag 9471 is that it impacts both conjunctive and disjunctive predicates, whereas trace flag 4137 only works with conjunctive predicates.

Finally, filtered statistics, which are covered in a section later in this chapter, may be helpful in some cases when data is totally correlated.

Cardinality Estimation Errors

Cardinality estimation errors can lead to the query optimizer making poor choices as to how best to execute a query and, therefore, to badly performing execution plans. Fortunately, you can easily check whether you have cardinality estimation errors by comparing the estimated against the actual number of rows, as shown in graphical or XML execution plans, or by using the SET STATISTICS PROFILE statement. In the next query, I show you how to use the SET STATISTICS PROFILE statement with one of our previous examples, where SQL Server is making a blind guess regarding the selectivity of certain columns:

```
SET STATISTICS PROFILE ON
GO
SELECT * FROM Sales.SalesOrderDetail
WHERE OrderQty * UnitPrice > 10000
GO
SET STATISTICS PROFILE OFF
GO
```

This is the resulting output, with the EstimateRows column manually moved just after the Rows column, and edited to fit the page:

```
Rows    EstimateRows StmtText
------  ------------ ----------------------------------------------------------
772     36395.1      SELECT * FROM [Sales].[SalesOrderDetail] WHERE [OrderQty] *[U
772     36395.1      |--Filter(WHERE:([Expr1003]>($10000.0000)))
0       121317         |--Compute Scalar(DEFINE:([AdventureWorks2012].[Sales]
0       121317           |--Compute Scalar(DEFINE:([AdventureWorks2012].[S
121317  121317            |--Clustered Index Scan(OBJECT:([AdventureWo
```

Using this output, you can easily compare the actual number of rows, shown on the Rows column, against the estimated number of records, shown on the EstimateRows column, for each operator in the plan. Introduced with SQL Server 2012, the inaccurate_cardinality_estimate extended event can also be used to detect inaccurate cardinality estimations by identifying which query operators output significantly more rows than those estimated by the query optimizer.

Because each operator relies on previous operations for its input, cardinality estimation errors can propagate exponentially throughout the query plan. For example, a cardinality estimation error on a Filter operator can impact the cardinality estimation of all the other operators in the plan that consume the data produced by that operator. If your query is not performing well and you find cardinality estimation errors, check for problems such as missing or out-of-date statistics, very small samples being used, correlation between columns, use of scalar expressions, guessing selectivity issues, and so on.

Recommendations to help with these issues have been provided throughout this chapter and include topics such as using the auto-create and auto-update statistics default configurations, updating statistics using WITH FULLSCAN, avoiding local variables in queries, avoiding non-constant-foldable or complex expressions on predicates, using computed columns, and considering multicolumn or filtered statistics, among other things. In addition, parameter-sniffing and parameter-sensitive queries are covered in more detail in Chapter 8. That's a fairly long list, but it should help convince you that you are already armed with pragmatically useful information.

Some SQL Server features, such as table variables, have no statistics, so you might want to consider instead using a temporary table or a standard table if you're having performance problems related to cardinality estimation errors. Multistatement table-valued user-defined functions have no statistics either. In this case, you can consider using a temporary table or a standard table as a temporary holding place for their results. In both these cases (table variables and multistatement table-valued user-defined functions), the query optimizer will guess at one row (which has been updated to 100 rows for multistatement table-valued user-defined functions in SQL Server 2014). In addition, for complex queries that are not performing well because of cardinality estimation errors, you may want to consider breaking down the query into two or more steps while storing the intermediate results in temporary tables. This will allow SQL

Server to create statistics on the intermediate results, which will help the query optimizer to produce a better execution plan. More details about breaking down complex queries will be covered in Chapter 10.

> **NOTE**
> *A new trace flag has been introduced with SQL Server 2012 Service Pack 2, which provides better cardinality estimation while using table variables. This trace flag is also expected to be implemented in SQL Server 2014. For more details, see http://support.microsoft.com/kb/2952444.*

Incremental Statistics

A major problem with updating statistics in large tables in SQL Server was that the entire table always had to be sampled, even if only recent data had changed. This was also true when partitioning was being used: even if only the newest partition had changed since the last time statistics were updated, updating statistics again required sampling the entire table, including all the partitions that haven't changed. Incremental statistics, a new SQL Server 2014 feature, can help with this problem.

Using incremental statistics, you can update only the statistics on the partition or partitions that have been modified, and the information on these partitions will be merged with the existing information to create the final statistics object. Another advantage of incremental statistics is that the percentage of data changes required to trigger an automatic update of statistics now works at the partition level, which basically means that now only 20 percent of rows changed (changes on the leading statistics column) per partition is required. Unfortunately, the histogram is still limited to 200 steps for the entire statistics object in this version of SQL Server.

Let's look at an example of how can you update statistics at a partition level to explore its behavior. First, we need to create a partitioned table using the AdventureWorks2012 database:

```
CREATE PARTITION FUNCTION TransactionRangePF1 (datetime)
AS RANGE RIGHT FOR VALUES
(
    '20071001', '20071101', '20071201', '20080101',
    '20080201', '20080301', '20080401', '20080501',
    '20080601', '20080701', '20080801'
)
GO
CREATE PARTITION SCHEME TransactionsPS1 AS PARTITION TransactionRangePF1 TO
(
  [PRIMARY], [PRIMARY], [PRIMARY], [PRIMARY], [PRIMARY],
  [PRIMARY], [PRIMARY], [PRIMARY], [PRIMARY], [PRIMARY],
  [PRIMARY], [PRIMARY], [PRIMARY]
)
```

```
GO
CREATE TABLE dbo.TransactionHistory
(
  TransactionID int NOT NULL,
  ProductID int NOT NULL,
  ReferenceOrderID int NOT NULL,
  ReferenceOrderLineID int NOT NULL DEFAULT (0),
  TransactionDate datetime NOT NULL DEFAULT (GETDATE()),
  TransactionType nchar(1) NOT NULL,
  Quantity int NOT NULL,
  ActualCost money NOT NULL,
  ModifiedDate datetime NOT NULL DEFAULT (GETDATE()),
  CONSTRAINT CK_TransactionType
    CHECK (UPPER(TransactionType) IN (N'W', N'S', N'P'))
)
ON TransactionsPS1 (TransactionDate)
GO
```

NOTE

For details about partitioning and the CREATE PARTITION FUNCTION / SCHEME statements, refer to "Partitioned Tables and Indexes" in Books Online.

We currently have data to populate 12 partitions. Let's start by first populating only 11:

```
INSERT INTO dbo.TransactionHistory
SELECT * FROM Production.TransactionHistory
WHERE TransactionDate < '2008-08-01'
```

If required, you can use the following statement to inspect the contents of the partitions:

```
SELECT * FROM sys.partitions
WHERE object_id = OBJECT_ID('dbo.TransactionHistory')
```

Let's create an incremental statistics object using the CREATE STATISTICS statement with the new INCREMENTAL clause set to ON (OFF is the default):

```
CREATE STATISTICS incrstats ON dbo.TransactionHistory(TransactionDate)
WITH FULLSCAN, INCREMENTAL = ON
```

You can also create incremental statistics while creating an index using the new STATISTICS_INCREMENTAL clause of the CREATE INDEX statement. You can inspect the created statistics object using the following query:

```
DBCC SHOW_STATISTICS('dbo.TransactionHistory', incrstats)
```

Among other things, you will notice that the created histogram has 200 steps (only the last three shown here):

	RANGE_HI_KEY	RANGE_ROWS	EQ_ROWS	DISTINCT_RANGE_ROWS
198	2008-07-25 00:00:00.000	187	100	2
199	2008-07-27 00:00:00.000	103	101	1
200	2008-07-31 00:00:00.000	281	131	3

So we already have the maximum number of steps in a statistics object. What would happen if we add data to a new partition? Let's add data to partition 12:

```
INSERT INTO dbo.TransactionHistory
SELECT * FROM Production.TransactionHistory
WHERE TransactionDate >= '2008-08-01'
```

Now, we update the statistics object using the following statement:

```
UPDATE STATISTICS dbo.TransactionHistory(incrstats)
WITH RESAMPLE ON PARTITIONS(12)
```

Note the new syntax specifying the partition, where you can specify multiple partitions, separated by commas. The UPDATE STATISTICS statement reads the specified partitions and then merges their results with the existing statistics object to build the global statistics. Note the RESAMPLE clause; this is required because partition statistics objects need to have the same sample rates to be merged to build the global statistics objects. Although only the specified partition was scanned, you can see that SQL Server has rearranged the histogram. The last three steps now show data for the added partition. You can also compare the original with the new histogram for other minor differences:

	RANGE_HI_KEY	RANGE_ROWS	EQ_ROWS	DISTINCT_RANGE_ROWS
197	2008-07-31 00:00:00.000	150	131	2
198	2008-08-12 00:00:00.000	300	36	9
199	2008-08-22 00:00:00.000	229	43	7
200	2008-09-03 00:00:00.000	363	37	11

If you want to disable the incremental statistics object for any reason, you can use the following statement to go back to the original behavior (or optionally just drop the statistics object and create a new one):

```
UPDATE STATISTICS dbo.TransactionHistory(incrstats)
WITH FULLSCAN, INCREMENTAL = OFF
```

After disabling the incremental statistics, trying to update a partition, as shown previously, will return the following error message:

```
Msg 9111, Level 16, State 1, Line 1
UPDATE STATISTICS ON PARTITIONS syntax is not supported for non-incremental
statistics.
```

Finally, you can also enable incremental statistics for your automatic statistics at the database level, if needed. This requires the INCREMENTAL = ON clause in the ALTER DATABASE statement, and obviously also requires AUTO_CREATE_ STATISTICS set to ON.

To clean up the objects created for this exercise, run the following statements:

```
DROP TABLE dbo.TransactionHistory
DROP PARTITION SCHEME TransactionsPS1
DROP PARTITION FUNCTION TransactionRangePF1
```

Statistics on Computed Columns

Another interesting step performed during query optimization is the automatic matching of computed columns. Although computed columns have been available in previous versions of SQL Server, the automatic matching feature was only introduced with SQL Server 2005. In this section, I show you how this feature works and explain how computed columns can help improve the performance of your queries.

A problem faced by some queries using scalar expressions is that they usually cannot benefit from statistics, and without statistics, the query optimizer will use the 30 percent selectivity guess on inequality comparisons, which may produce inefficient execution plans. A solution to this problem is the use of computed columns because SQL Server can automatically create and update statistics on these columns. A great benefit of this solution is that you don't need to specify the name of the computed column in your queries for SQL Server to use its statistics. The query optimizer automatically matches the computed column definition to an existing scalar expression in a query, so your applications do not need to be changed.

To see an example, run this query, which creates the plan shown in Figure 6-9:

```
SELECT * FROM Sales.SalesOrderDetail
WHERE OrderQty * UnitPrice > 10000
```

The estimated number of rows is 36,395.1, which is 30 percent of the total number of rows (121,317), although the query returns only 772 records. SQL Server is obviously using a selectivity guess because it cannot estimate the selectivity of the expression OrderQty * UnitPrice > 10000.

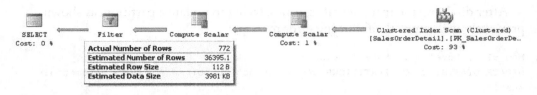

Figure 6-9 *Cardinality estimation example using a 30 percent guess*

Now create a computed column:

```
ALTER TABLE Sales.SalesOrderDetail
ADD cc AS OrderQty * UnitPrice
```

Run the previous SELECT statement again, and note that, this time, the estimated number of rows has changed and is close to the actual number of rows returned by the query, as shown in Figure 6-10. You can optionally test replacing the 10,000 with some other value, such as 10, 100, 1,000, or 5,000, and compare the actual and the estimated number of rows returned.

Note that creating the computed column does not create statistics; these statistics are created the first time the query is optimized, and you can run the next query to display the information about the statistics objects for the Sales.SalesOrderDetail table:

```
SELECT * FROM sys.stats
WHERE object_id = OBJECT_ID('Sales.SalesOrderDetail')
```

The newly created statistics object will most likely be at the end of the list. Copy the name of the object, and use the following command to display the details about the statistics object (I've used the name of my local object, but you should replace that as appropriate):

```
DBCC SHOW_STATISTICS ('Sales.SalesOrderDetail', _WA_Sys_0000000E_44CA3770)
```

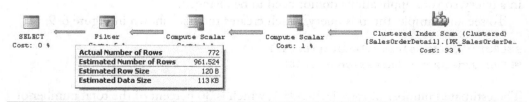

Figure 6-10 *Cardinality estimation example using computed columns*

You can also use "cc" as the name of the object to get the same results. The "cc" column should be shown on the Columns field in the density section. In any case, the number of rows is estimated using the histogram of the created statistics object, as explained earlier for inequality comparisons.

```
DBCC SHOW_STATISTICS ('Sales.SalesOrderDetail', cc)
```

Unfortunately, for automatic matching to work, the expression must be exactly the same as the computed column definition. So, if I change the query to UnitPrice * OrderQty, instead of OrderQty * UnitPrice, the execution plan will show an estimated number of rows of 30 percent again, as this query will demonstrate:

```
SELECT * FROM Sales.SalesOrderDetail
WHERE UnitPrice * OrderQty > 10000
```

Finally, drop the created computed column:

```
ALTER TABLE Sales.SalesOrderDetail
DROP COLUMN cc
```

Filtered Statistics

Filtered statistics are statistics created on a subset of records in a table. Filtered statistics are automatically created when filtered indexes are created, but they can also be created manually by specifying a WHERE clause on the CREATE STATISTICS statement, in which case a filtered index is not required. As you might imagine, filtered statistics can help with queries accessing specific subsets of data. They can also be useful in situations such as correlated columns, especially when one of these columns has a small number of unique values, and you can create multiple filtered statistics for each one of these distinct values. As shown in the "Histogram" section previously, when using multiple predicates, SQL Server assumes that each clause in a query is independent. If the columns used in this query were correlated, then the cardinality estimation would be incorrect. Even with the exponential backoff behavior of the new cardinality estimator, you can still get better cardinality estimation with filter statistics because each statistics object has its own histogram. Filtered statistics may also help with huge tables where a large number of unique values are not accurately represented in the 200-step limitation currently enforced on histograms.

Next, I show you how you can use filtered statistics to help in a problem with correlated columns. Running the following query will correctly estimate the number of rows to be 93:

```
SELECT * FROM Person.Address
WHERE City = 'Los Angeles'
```

In the same way, running the next query will correctly estimate 4,564 rows:

```
SELECT * FROM Person.Address
WHERE StateProvinceID = 9
```

However, because StateProvinceID 9 corresponds to the state of California (which you can verify by looking at the Person.StateProvince table), it is possible for somebody to run this query, which in this case will show a less precise estimate of 44.8614 rows (this is using the new cardinality estimator, or 21.6403 using the old one), as shown in the plan in Figure 6-11.

```
SELECT * FROM Person.Address
WHERE City = 'Los Angeles' AND StateProvinceID = 9
```

Because of the assumption of independence, SQL Server will multiply the cardinality of both predicates, as explained earlier in this chapter. The calculation, abbreviated as (93 * 4,564) / 19,614, will give us the value 21.6403 for the old cardinality estimator (19,614 is the total number of rows in the table). In the case of the exponential backoff used by the new cardinality estimator, the calculation would be (93 / 19,614) * SQRT(4,564 / 19,614) * 19,614, which will be roughly 44.861 rows.

However, both the independence assumption and the exponential backoff are incorrect in this example because the columns are statistically correlated. To help with this problem, you can create a filtered statistics object for the state of California, as shown in the next statement:

```
CREATE STATISTICS california
ON Person.Address(City)
WHERE StateProvinceID = 9
```

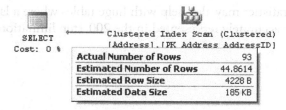

	Clustered Index Scan (Clustered)
SELECT	[Address].[PK_Address_AddressID]
Cost: 0 %	

Actual Number of Rows	93
Estimated Number of Rows	44.8614
Estimated Row Size	4228 B
Estimated Data Size	185 KB

Figure 6-11   *Cardinality estimate with exponential backoff*

Clearing the cache and running the previous query again will now give a better estimate, as shown in the plan in Figure 6-12.

```
DBCC FREEPROCCACHE
GO
SELECT * FROM Person.Address
WHERE City = 'Los Angeles' AND StateProvinceID = 9
```

Let's now inspect the filtered statistics object by running the following statement:

```
DBCC SHOW_STATISTICS('Person.Address', california)
```

This will produce the following output (edited here to fit the page), showing the estimate of 93 rows for Los Angeles on the EQ_ROWS column:

Name	Rows	Rows Sampled	Filter Expression	Unfiltered Rows
california	4564	4564	([StateProvinceID]=(9))	19614

RANGE_HI_KEY	RANGE_ROWS	EQ_ROWS	DISTINCT_RANGE_ROWS	AVG_RANGE_ROWS
Alhambra	0	1	0	1
Alpine	0	1	0	1
Altadena	0	2	0	1
Auburn	0	1	0	1
Baldwin Park	0	1	0	1
Barstow	0	2	0	1
...				
Los Angeles	0	93	0	1

Notice that the filter definition is shown on the Filter Expression field, and that the Unfiltered Rows field shows the total number of records in the table when the filtered statistics were created. Also note that, this time, the Rows column number is less than the total number of rows in the table, and corresponds to the number of records that satisfied the filter predicate when the statistics object was created. The filter definition

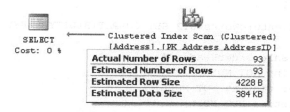

Figure 6-12   *Cardinality estimate with filtered statistics*

can also be seen on the filter_definition column of the sys.stats catalog view. Also notice that the histogram only shows cities for California, according to the filter definition (only a few steps are shown).

Finally, drop the statistics object you have just created by running the following statement:

```
DROP STATISTICS Person.Address.california
```

Statistics on Ascending Keys

Statistics on ascending keys presents a cardinality estimation problem that has been present in all versions of SQL Server since version 7. Using trace flags 2389 and 2390 has been the best solution to this problem. As of SQL Server 2014, you can also use the new cardinality estimator to obtain exactly the same estimation, but without having to use these trace flags.

But first let me explain what the problem is. As we saw earlier, SQL Server builds a histogram on the first column of each statistics object. With statistics on ascending or descending key columns, such as IDENTITY and real-time timestamp columns, new inserted values usually fall outside the range of values covered by the histogram. In addition, the number of records added might be too small to trigger an automatic update of statistics. Because recently added rows are not covered in the histogram when in fact a significant number of rows should be included, running a query using those values may result in inaccurate cardinality estimates, which may also result in poorly performing plans.

The traditional recommendation from Microsoft to fix this problem has been to manually update statistics after loading data, but unfortunately, this may also require more frequent statistics updates, which may not always be feasible. Trace flags 2389 and 2390, which were first published by Ian Jose from Microsoft in his article "Ascending Keys and Auto Quick Corrected Statistics," were also introduced as of SQL Server 2005 Service Pack 1 to help with this problem.

To show you what the problem is and how these trace flags work, let's start by creating a table in AdventureWorks2012. But first, make sure you are using the old cardinality estimator:

```
ALTER DATABASE AdventureWorks2012 SET COMPATIBILITY_LEVEL = 110
GO
CREATE TABLE dbo.SalesOrderHeader (
    SalesOrderID int NOT NULL,
    RevisionNumber tinyint NOT NULL,
    OrderDate datetime NOT NULL,
    DueDate datetime NOT NULL,
    ShipDate datetime NULL,
```

```
      Status tinyint NOT NULL,
      OnlineOrderFlag dbo.Flag NOT NULL,
      SalesOrderNumber nvarchar(25) NOT NULL,
      PurchaseOrderNumber dbo.OrderNumber NULL,
      AccountNumber dbo.AccountNumber NULL,
      CustomerID int NOT NULL,
      SalesPersonID int NULL,
      TerritoryID int NULL,
      BillToAddressID int NOT NULL,
      ShipToAddressID int NOT NULL,
      ShipMethodID int NOT NULL,
      CreditCardID int NULL,
      CreditCardApprovalCode varchar(15) NULL,
      CurrencyRateID int NULL,
      SubTotal money NOT NULL,
      TaxAmt money NOT NULL,
      Freight money NOT NULL,
      TotalDue money NOT NULL,
      Comment nvarchar(128) NULL,
      rowguid uniqueidentifier NOT NULL,
      ModifiedDate datetime NOT NULL
)
```

Populate the table with some initial data and create an index on it (notice that both tables have the same name, but in the dbo and Sales schemas):

```
INSERT INTO dbo.SalesOrderHeader SELECT * FROM Sales.SalesOrderHeader
WHERE OrderDate < '2008-07-20 00:00:00.000'
CREATE INDEX IX_OrderDate ON SalesOrderHeader(OrderDate)
```

After creating the index, SQL Server will also create a statistics object for it, so a query like this will have a good cardinality estimate of 35 rows (as there is data for July 19, and it is captured on the last step of the statistics histogram object, which you can verify by using the DBCC SHOW_STATISTICS statement).

```
SELECT * FROM dbo.SalesOrderHeader WHERE OrderDate = '2008-07-19 00:00:00.000'
```

Now, let's suppose we add new data for July 20:

```
INSERT INTO dbo.SalesOrderHeader SELECT * FROM Sales.SalesOrderHeader
WHERE OrderDate = '2008-07-20 00:00:00.000'
```

So let's change the query to look for records for July 20:

```
SELECT * FROM dbo.SalesOrderHeader WHERE OrderDate = '2008-07-20 00:00:00.000'
```

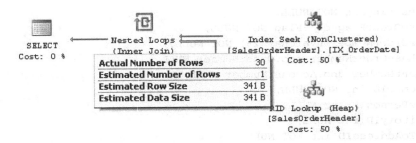

Figure 6-13   *Bad cardinality estimate after new records are added*

Because the number of rows added is not enough to trigger an automatic update of statistics, the value July 20 is not represented on the existing histogram. This anomaly means that SQL Server will use an estimate of 1, as shown in Figure 6-13.

Although the plans for both queries in this example are very similar, a bad cardinality estimate may produce bad plans in some more realistic scenarios and queries.

Trace Flag 2389

Now let's see how trace flag 2389 helps with this problem. Run the next statements (notice that trace flag 2388 has not been mentioned before and will be explained shortly):

```
DBCC TRACEON (2388)
DBCC TRACEON (2389)
```

Trace flag 2389, which was introduced with SQL Server 2005 Service Pack 1, begins to track the nature of columns via subsequent operations of updating statistics. When the statistics are seen to increase three times in a row, the column is branded "Ascending." Trace flag 2388 is not required to enable the behavior described in this article, but enables the display of previously hidden metadata that is useful to show how trace flags 2389 and 2390 work and determine if a column has been branded "Ascending." The trace flag changes the output of the DBCC SHOW_STATISTICS statement to show you a historical look at the most recent statistics update operations.

Trace flag 2390 enables a similar behavior to 2389, even if the ascending nature of the column is not known, but I will not cover it here. Run DBCC SHOW_STATISTICS:

```
DBCC SHOW_STATISTICS ('dbo.SalesOrderHeader', 'IX_OrderDate')
```

The statement shows the following output (condensed to fit the page):

Updated	Rows Above	Rows Below	Inserts Since Last Update	Deletes Since Last Update	Leading column Type
Jan 11 2014 2:12PM	NULL	NULL	NULL	NULL	Unknown

Not much data for now. However, I'll show you this output after three consecutive batches of inserting data and updating statistics. Run the following statement to update statistics, including the data you just added for February 20:

```
UPDATE STATISTICS dbo.SalesOrderHeader WITH FULLSCAN
```

DBCC SHOW_STATISTICS now shows

Updated	Rows Above	Rows Below	Inserts Since Last Update	Deletes Since Last Update	Leading column Type
Jan 11 2014 2:13PM	30	0	30	0	Unknown
Jan 11 2014 2:12PM	NULL	NULL	NULL	NULL	NULL

where Rows Above and Inserts Since Last Update accounts for the 30 rows added previously (you may need to scroll to the right). Now run the second batch:

```
INSERT INTO dbo.SalesOrderHeader SELECT * FROM Sales.SalesOrderHeader
WHERE OrderDate = '2008-07-21 00:00:00.000'
```

Again, running this query will verify the one-row estimate in the plan:

```
SELECT * FROM dbo.SalesOrderHeader WHERE OrderDate = '2008-07-21 00:00:00.000'
```

Now update statistics again:

```
UPDATE STATISTICS dbo.SalesOrderHeader WITH FULLSCAN
```

DBCC SHOW_STATISTICS now shows this. Notice a new record with Inserts Since Last Update and Rows Above, with a value of 27. Leading column Type still shows "Unknown."

Updated	Rows Above	Rows Below	Inserts Since Last Update	Deletes Since Last Update	Leading column Type
Jan 11 2014 2:15PM	27	0	27	0	Unknown
Jan 11 2014 2:13PM	30	0	30	0	NULL
Jan 11 2014 2:12PM	NULL	NULL	NULL	NULL	NULL

Now for a third batch:

```
INSERT INTO dbo.SalesOrderHeader SELECT * FROM Sales.SalesOrderHeader
WHERE OrderDate = '2008-07-22 00:00:00.000'
```

Update statistics one last time:

```
UPDATE STATISTICS dbo.SalesOrderHeader WITH FULLSCAN
```

DBCC SHOW_STATISTICS now shows this:

Updated	Rows Above	Rows Below	Inserts Since Last Update	Deletes Since Last Update	Leading column Type
Jan 11 2014 2:16PM	32	0	32	0	Ascending
Jan 11 2014 2:15PM	27	0	27	0	NULL
Jan 11 2014 2:13PM	30	0	30	0	NULL
Jan 11 2014 2:12PM	NULL	NULL	NULL	NULL	NULL

In addition to the new record accounting for the 32 rows added, now you can notice that the branding was changed to "Ascending." Once the column is branded "Ascending," SQL Server will be able to give you a better cardinality estimate, without having to manually update statistics.

To test it, try this batch:

```
INSERT INTO dbo.SalesOrderHeader SELECT * FROM Sales.SalesOrderHeader
WHERE OrderDate = '2008-07-23 00:00:00.000'
```

Now run the following query:

```
SELECT * FROM dbo.SalesOrderHeader WHERE OrderDate = '2008-07-23 00:00:00.000'
```

This time we get a better cardinality estimate. Notice that no UPDATE STATISTICS was required this time.

Instead of the estimate of one row, now we get 27.9677. But where is this value coming from? The query optimizer is now using the density information of the statistics object. As explained earlier, the definition of density is 1 / "number of distinct values," and the estimated number of rows is obtained using the density multiplied by the number of records in the table, which in this case is 0.000896861 * 31184, or 27.967713424, as shown in the plan. Also notice that density information is only used for values not covered in the histogram (you can see the density information using the same DBCC SHOW_STATISTICS statement, but in another session where trace flag 2388 is not enabled).

In addition, if we look for data that does not exist, we still get the one-row estimate, which is always adequate because it will return 0 records.

```
SELECT * FROM dbo.SalesOrderHeader WHERE OrderDate = '2008-07-24 00:00:00.000'
```

Notice that branding a column "Ascending" requires statistics to increase three times in a row. If later we insert older data, breaking the ascending sequence, the column Leading column Type will show "Stationary" and the query processor will be back to the original cardinality estimate behavior. Three new additional updates in a row with increasing values can brand it as "Ascending" again.

Finally, you could use the trace flags on a query without defining them at the session or global level using the QUERYTRACEON hint, as shown next:

```
SELECT * FROM dbo.SalesOrderHeader WHERE OrderDate = '2008-07-23 00:00:00.000'
OPTION (QUERYTRACEON 2389, QUERYTRACEON 2390)
```

Trace flags 2389 and 2390 are no longer needed if you are using the new cardinality estimator, and you will get exactly the same behavior and estimation. To see how it works, drop the dbo.SalesOrderHeader table:

```
DROP TABLE dbo.SalesOrderHeader
```

Disable trace flags 2388 and 2389, as shown next, or open a new session:

```
DBCC TRACEOFF (2388)
DBCC TRACEOFF (2389)
```

NOTE

You can also make sure that the trace flags are not enabled by running DBCC TRACESTATUS.

Create the dbo.SalesOrderHeader, as indicated at the beginning of this section. Insert some data again and create an index, as shown next:

```
INSERT INTO dbo.SalesOrderHeader SELECT * FROM Sales.SalesOrderHeader
WHERE OrderDate < '2008-07-20 00:00:00.000'
CREATE INDEX IX_OrderDate ON SalesOrderHeader(OrderDate)
```

Now add new data for July 20:

```
INSERT INTO dbo.SalesOrderHeader SELECT * FROM Sales.SalesOrderHeader
WHERE OrderDate = '2008-07-20 00:00:00.000'
```

Same as before, because the number of rows added is too small, it is not enough to trigger an automatic update of statistics. Running the following query with the old cardinality estimator will estimate one row, as we saw earlier:

```
ALTER DATABASE AdventureWorks2012 SET COMPATIBILITY_LEVEL = 110
GO
SELECT * FROM dbo.SalesOrderHeader WHERE OrderDate = '2008-07-20 00:00:00.000'
```

Running the same query with the new cardinality estimator will give a better estimate of 27.9631, without the need to use trace flags 2390 and 2390:

```
ALTER DATABASE AdventureWorks2012 SET COMPATIBILITY_LEVEL = 120
GO
SELECT * FROM dbo.SalesOrderHeader WHERE OrderDate = '2008-07-20 00:00:00.000'
```

The value 27.9631 is estimated exactly the same way as explained earlier, using the density multiplied by the number of records in the table, which in this case is 0.0008992806 * 31095, or 27.9631302570. But remember to use the DBCC SHOW_STATISTICS against this new version of the table to obtain the new density.

UPDATE STATISTICS with ROWCOUNT and PAGECOUNT

The undocumented ROWCOUNT and PAGECOUNT options of the UPDATE STATISTICS statement are used by the Data Engine Tuning Advisor (DTA) to script and copy statistics when you want to configure a test server to tune the workload of a production server. You can also see these statements in action if you script a statistics object. As an example, try the following in Management Studio: select Databases, right-click the AdventureWorks2012 database, select Tasks, Generate Scripts …, click Next, select "Select specific database objects," expand Tables, select Sales.SalesOrderDetail, click Next, click Advanced, look for the Script Statistics choice, and select "Script statistics and histograms." Finally, choose True on Script Indexes. Click OK and finish the wizard to generate the scripts. You will get a script with a few UPDATE STATISTICS statements similar to this (with the STATS_STREAM value shortened to fit this page):

```
UPDATE STATISTICS [Sales].[SalesOrderDetail]([IX_SalesOrderDetail_ProductID])
WITH STATS_STREAM = 0x010000000300000000000000 …, ROWCOUNT = 121317,
PAGECOUNT = 274
```

In this section I show how you can use the ROWCOUNT and PAGECOUNT options of the UPDATE STATISTICS statement in cases where you want to see which execution plans would be generated for huge tables (with millions of records), but then test those plans in small or even empty tables. As you can imagine, these options can be helpful for testing in some scenarios where you may not want to spend time or disk space creating big tables.

By using this method you are asking the query optimizer to generate execution plans using cardinality estimations as if the table really had millions of records, even if your table is actually tiny. Note that this option, available since SQL Server 2005, only helps in creating the execution plan for your queries. Actually running the query will use the real data in your test table, which will, of course, execute faster than a table with millions of records.

Using these UPDATE STATISTICS options does not change the table statistics but only the counters for the numbers of rows and pages of a table. As I will show shortly, the query optimizer uses this information to estimate the cardinality of queries. Finally, before we look at examples, keep in mind that these are undocumented and unsupported options and should not be used in a production environment.

So, let's look at an example. Run the following query to create a new table on the AdventureWorks2012 database:

```
SELECT * INTO dbo.Address
FROM Person.Address
```

Inspect the number of rows by running the following query; the row_count column should show 19,614 rows:

```
SELECT * FROM sys.dm_db_partition_stats
WHERE object_id = OBJECT_ID('dbo.Address')
```

Now run the following query and inspect the graphical execution plan:

```
SELECT * FROM dbo.Address
WHERE City = 'London'
```

Running this query will create a new statistics object for the City column and will show the plan in Figure 6-14. Note that the estimated number of rows is 434, and it's using a simple Table Scan operator.

We can discover where the query optimizer is getting the estimated number of rows by inspecting the statistics object. Using the methodology shown earlier in the "Histogram" section, you can find out the name of the statistics object and then use DBCC SHOW_STATISTICS to show its histogram. By looking at the histogram, you can find the value 434 on EQ_ROWS for the RANGE_HI_KEY value 'London'.

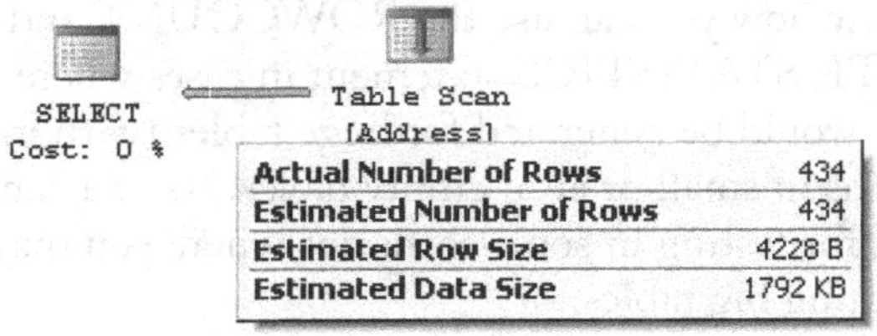

Figure 6-14 *Cardinality estimation example using a small table*

Now run the following UPDATE STATISTICS WITH ROWCOUNT, PAGECOUNT statement (you can specify any other value for ROWCOUNT and PAGECOUNT):

```
UPDATE STATISTICS dbo.Address WITH ROWCOUNT = 1000000, PAGECOUNT = 100000
```

If you inspect the number of rows from sys.dm_db_partition_stats again, as shown previously, it will now show 1,000,000 rows (the new number of pages is also shown by the column in_row_data_page_count). Clear the plan cache and run the query again.

```
DBCC FREEPROCCACHE
GO
SELECT * FROM dbo.Address WHERE City = 'London'
```

Note that the estimated number of rows has changed from 434 to 22,127.1, as shown in Figure 6-15.

However, if you look at the statistics object again, using DBCC SHOW_STATISTICS as shown before, you'll see that the histogram has not changed. One way to obtain the estimated number of rows shown in the new execution plan is by calculating the percentage (or fraction) of rows for the value 'London' from the statistics sample, which in this case is 19,614. So the fraction is 434 / 19,614, or 0.022127052. Next, we apply the same percentage to the new "current" number of rows, which results in 1,000,000 * 0.022127052, and we get 22,127.1, which is the estimated number of rows displayed in the plan in Figure 6-15.

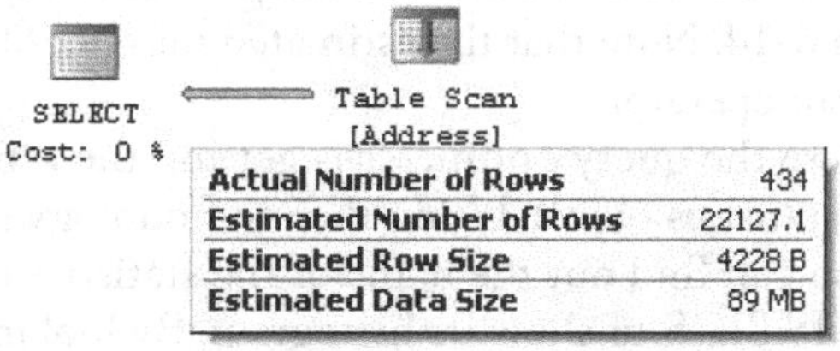

Figure 6-15 *Cardinality estimation using ROWCOUNT and PAGECOUNT*

Finally, if you want to restore the real values for rows and pages, perhaps to perform additional testing, you can use the DBCC UPDATEUSAGE statement. DBCC UPDATEUSAGE can be used to correct pages and row count inaccuracies in the catalog views. Run the following statement:

```
DBCC UPDATEUSAGE(AdventureWorks2012, 'dbo.Address') WITH COUNT_ROWS
```

However, after you finish your testing, it is recommended that you drop this table to avoid any pages and row count inaccuracies left by mistake.

```
DROP TABLE dbo.Address
```

Statistics on Linked Servers

A known problem when connecting to linked servers on instances running SQL Server 2012 RTM and older is that the query processor is not able to get the required optimizer statistics from the remote instance due to the user permissions used by the linked server. In those versions, in order to obtain all available statistics, the user must own the table or be a member of the sysadmin fixed server role, the db_owner fixed database role, or the db_ddladmin fixed database role on the linked server. With SQL Server 2012 Service Pack 1 and later, it is now possible to access these statistics, basically running DBCC SHOW_STATISTICS, with only SELECT permissions. Although this is also the default behavior in SQL Server 2014, you still need to be aware of this issue if you are connecting to older versions of SQL Server or if you may have a regression in a particular scenario and need to go back to the old behavior.

So let's see how it works using a linked server (here just called remote) by connecting to a SQL Server 2012 RTM or older instance.

```
SELECT l.SalesOrderID, l.CustomerID
FROM AdventureWorks2012.Sales.SalesOrderHeader l
JOIN [remote].AdventureWorks2012.Sales.SalesOrderHeader r
ON l.SalesOrderID = r.SalesOrderID
WHERE r.CustomerID = 11000
```

My test configuration uses a linked server relying on a login with read-only permissions on the data (for example, db_datareader). Running the previous query against a remote SQL Server instance installed returns a bad cardinality estimate and the plan shown in Figure 6-16, using a Hash Join. Because the local query processor does not have access to the statistics on the remote server, it has to rely on a guess (in this case, estimating 177.384 records). You can notice a big difference between the actual and estimated number of rows.

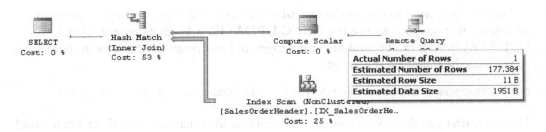

	Actual Number of Rows	1
	Estimated Number of Rows	177.384
	Estimated Row Size	11 B
	Estimated Data Size	1951 B

Figure 6-16 *Bad cardinality estimate with a linked server*

If we run the same query against a SQL Server 2012 Service Pack 1 or later remote server, we get a better cardinality estimate, and the query optimizer is able to make a better decision. In this case, we would get a new plan using a Nested Loops Join, which is more appropriate for a small number of records. Although the new behavior is enabled by default on linked server targets SQL Server 2012 Service Pack 1 and later, you also have the choice of disabling it by using trace flag 9485, which you can use in case of regressions in scenarios where the performance of some queries may be getting worse. Enabling trace flag 9485 reverts the new permission check to the original behavior.

Run the following statement to enable trace flag 9485:

```
DBCC TRACEON (9485)
```

Running the query again will produce the original plan with the Hash Join and the 177.384 cardinality estimate. You may also need to use a statement to clear the current plan or force a new optimization during your testing (for example, DBCC FREEPROCCACHE).

Statistics Maintenance

As mentioned already, the query optimizer will, by default, automatically update statistics when they are out of date. Statistics can also be updated with the UPDATE STATISTICS statement, which you can schedule to run as a maintenance job. Another statement commonly used, sp_updatestats, also runs UPDATE STATISTICS behind the scenes.

There are two important benefits of updating statistics in a maintenance job. The first is that your queries will use updated statistics without having to wait for the automatic update of statistics to be completed, thus avoiding delays in the optimization of your queries (although asynchronous statistics updates can also be used to partially help with this problem). The second benefit is that you can use a bigger sample than the query optimizer will use, or you can even scan the entire table. This can give you better-quality statistics for big tables, especially for those where data is not randomly distributed in their data pages. Manually updating statistics can also be a benefit after operations such as batch data loads, which update large amounts of data, are performed.

On the other hand, also note that the update of statistics will cause a recompiling of plans already in the plan cache that are using these statistics, so you may not want to update statistics too frequently, either.

An additional consideration for manually updating statistics in a maintenance job is how they relate to index rebuild maintenance jobs, which also update the index statistics. Keep the following items in mind when combining maintenance jobs for both indexes and statistics, remembering that there are both index and nonindex column statistics, and that index operations obviously may impact only the first of these:

▶ Rebuilding an index (for example, by using the ALTER INDEX … REBUILD statement) will also update index statistics by scanning all the rows in the table, which is the equivalent of using UPDATE STATISTICS WITH FULLSCAN. Rebuilding indexes does not update any column statistics.

▶ Reorganizing an index (for example, using the ALTER INDEX … REORGANIZE statement) does not update any statistics, not even index statistics.

▶ By default, the UPDATE STATISTICS statement updates both index and column statistics. Using the INDEX option will update index statistics only, and using the COLUMNS option will update nonindexed column statistics only.

Therefore, depending on your maintenance jobs and scripts, several scenarios can exist. The simplest maintenance plan is if you want to rebuild all the indexes and update all the statistics. As mentioned before, if you rebuild all your indexes, then all the index statistics will also be automatically updated by scanning all the rows in the table. Then you just need to update your nonindexed column statistics by running UPDATE STATISTICS WITH FULLSCAN, COLUMNS. Because the index rebuild job updates only index statistics, and the second one updates only column statistics, it does not matter which one is executed first.

Of course, more complicated maintenance plans can exist—for example, when indexes are rebuilt or reorganized depending on their fragmentation level, a topic covered in more detail in Chapter 5. You should keep in mind the items mentioned previously so that you can avoid problems such as updating the index statistics twice, which could occur when both index rebuild and update statistics operations are performed. You should also avoid discarding previously performed work—for example, when you rebuild the indexes of a table, which also updates statistics by scanning the entire table—and later running a job updating the statistics with a default or smaller sample. In this case, previously updated statistics are replaced with statistics that have potentially less quality.

Let me show you how these commands work, with some examples. Create a new table called dbo.SalesOrderDetail:

```
SELECT * INTO dbo.SalesOrderDetail FROM Sales.SalesOrderDetail
```

The next query uses the sys.stats catalog view to show that there are no statistics objects for the new table:

```
SELECT name, auto_created, STATS_DATE(object_id, stats_id) AS update_date
FROM sys.stats
WHERE object_id = OBJECT_ID('dbo.SalesOrderDetail')
```

Now run the following query:

```
SELECT * FROM dbo.SalesOrderDetail
WHERE SalesOrderID = 43670 AND OrderQty = 1
```

Use the previous query using sys.stats to verify that two statistics objects were created: one for the SalesOrderID column and a second for the OrderQty column. Now create the following index and run the sys.stats query again to verify that a new statistics object for the ProductID column has been created:

```
CREATE INDEX IX_ProductID ON dbo.SalesOrderDetail(ProductID)
```

This will be the output of the sys.stats query so far:

name	auto_created	update_date
_WA_Sys_00000004_4DD47EBD	1	1/11/2014 8:11:34 PM
_WA_Sys_00000001_4DD47EBD	1	1/11/2014 8:11:34 PM
IX_ProductID	0	1/11/2014 8:14:31 PM

Notice how the value of the auto_created column, which indicates whether the statistics were created by the query optimizer, is 0 for the IX_ProductID statistics object. Run the next command to update just the column statistics:

```
UPDATE STATISTICS dbo.SalesOrderDetail WITH FULLSCAN, COLUMNS
```

You can validate that only the column statistics were updated by comparing the update_date column with the previous output. The update_date column uses the STATS_DATE function to display the last point in time when the statistics were updated, as shown in the following output:

name	auto_created	update_date
_WA_Sys_00000004_4DD47EBD	1	1/11/2014 8:16:54 PM
_WA_Sys_00000001_4DD47EBD	1	1/11/2014 8:16:55 PM
IX_ProductID	0	1/11/2014 8:14:31 PM

This command will do the same for just the index statistics:

```
UPDATE STATISTICS dbo.SalesOrderDetail WITH FULLSCAN, INDEX
```

And these commands will update both the index and column statistics:

```
UPDATE STATISTICS dbo.SalesOrderDetail WITH FULLSCAN
UPDATE STATISTICS dbo.SalesOrderDetail WITH FULLSCAN, ALL
```

As mentioned earlier, if you run the sys.stats query after each of the next two queries, you'll see how an ALTER INDEX REBUILD statement only updates index statistics:

```
ALTER INDEX ix_ProductID ON dbo.SalesOrderDetail REBUILD
```

And you can verify that reorganizing an index does not update any statistics:

```
ALTER INDEX ix_ProductID on dbo.SalesOrderDetail REORGANIZE
```

Finally, for good housekeeping, remove the table you have just created:

```
DROP TABLE dbo.SalesOrderDetail
```

Cost Estimation

As I've established, the quality of the execution plans the query optimizer generates is directly related to the accuracy of its costing estimates. Even when the query optimizer is able to enumerate low-cost plans, an incorrect cost estimation may result in the query optimizer choosing inefficient plans, which can negatively impact the performance of your database. During query optimization, the query optimizer explores many candidate plans, estimates their cost, and then selects the most efficient one.

Costs are estimated for any partial or complete plan, as shown in Chapter 3 when we explored the content of the Memo structure. Cost computation is done per operator, and the total plan cost is the sum of the costs of all the operators in that plan. The cost of each operator depends on its algorithm and the estimated number of records it returns.

Some operators, such as Sort and Hash Join, also consider the available memory in the system. A high-level overview of the cost of the algorithms for some of the most used operators was provided in Chapter 4.

So, each operator has an associated CPU cost, some of them will also have some I/O cost, and the cost of the operator as a whole is the sum of these costs. An operator such as a Clustered Index Scan has both CPU and I/O costs, whereas some other operators, such as Stream Aggregate, will only have a CPU cost. Because it is not documented how these costs are calculated, I will show you a basic example of how the cost of a plan is estimated.

To demonstrate this in an example, let's look at the largest table in the AdventureWorks database. Run the following query and look at the estimated CPU and I/O costs for the Clustered Index Scan operator, as shown in Figure 6-17:

```
SELECT * FROM Sales.SalesOrderDetail
WHERE LineTotal = 35
```

Note that in an older version of SQL Server the cost used to mean the estimated time in seconds that a query would take to execute on a specific hardware configuration, but currently, this value is meaningless as an objective unit of measurement, and should not be interpreted as one. Its purpose is solely to be used internally to pick between different candidate plans.

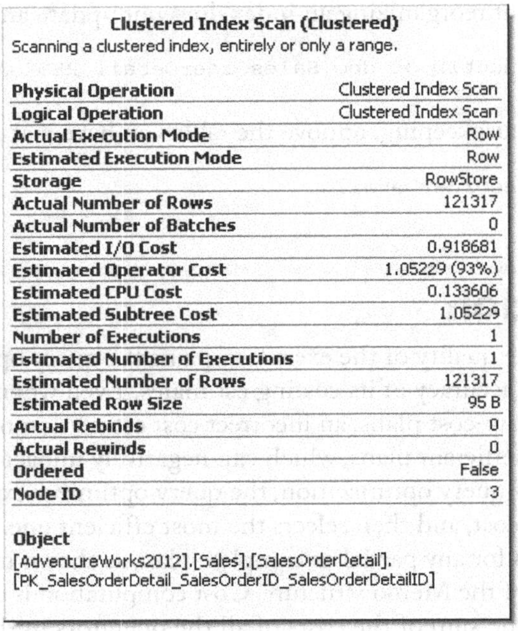

Clustered Index Scan (Clustered)	
Scanning a clustered index, entirely or only a range.	
Physical Operation	Clustered Index Scan
Logical Operation	Clustered Index Scan
Actual Execution Mode	Row
Estimated Execution Mode	Row
Storage	RowStore
Actual Number of Rows	121317
Actual Number of Batches	0
Estimated I/O Cost	0.918681
Estimated Operator Cost	1.05229 (93%)
Estimated CPU Cost	0.133606
Estimated Subtree Cost	1.05229
Number of Executions	1
Estimated Number of Executions	1
Estimated Number of Rows	121317
Estimated Row Size	95 B
Actual Rebinds	0
Actual Rewinds	0
Ordered	False
Node ID	3

Object
[AdventureWorks2012].[Sales].[SalesOrderDetail].
[PK_SalesOrderDetail_SalesOrderID_SalesOrderDetailID]

Figure 6-17 *Clustered Index Scan operator properties*

For a Clustered Index Scan operator, I observed that the CPU cost is 0.0001581 for the first record, plus 0.0000011 for any additional record after that. Because in this specific case we have an estimated 121,317 records, we can calculate 0.0001581 + 0.0000011 * (121317 − 1), which comes to 0.133606, which is the value shown as Estimated CPU Cost in Figure 6-17. In a similar way, I noticed that the minimum I/O cost is 0.003125 for the first database page, and then it grows in increments of 0.00074074 for every additional page. Because this operator scans the entire table, I can use the next query to find the number of database pages (which turns out to be 1,237):

```
SELECT in_row_data_page_count, row_count
FROM sys.dm_db_partition_stats
WHERE object_id = OBJECT_ID('Sales.SalesOrderDetail')
AND index_id = 1
```

In this case I have 0.003125 + 0.00074074 * (1234 − 1), which comes to roughly 0.918681, which is the value shown as Estimated I/O Cost.

Finally, we add both costs, 0.133606 + 0.918681, to get 1.05229, which is the total estimated cost of the operator. In the same way, adding the cost of all the operators will give the total cost of the plan. In this case, the cost of the Clustered Index Scan (1.05229) plus the cost of the first Compute Scalar operator (0.01213), the second Compute Scalar operator (0.01213), and the Filter operator (0.05823) will give the total cost of the plan: 1.13478.

Summary

In this chapter you have seen how statistics are used by SQL Server to estimate the cardinality as well as the cost of operators and execution plans. The most important elements of a statistics object—namely the histogram, the density information, and string statistics—were introduced and explained. Examples of how to use histograms were shown, including queries with equality and inequality operators and both AND'ed and OR'ed predicates. The use of density information was shown in GROUP BY operations as well as in cases when the query optimizer is not able to use a histogram, such as in the case of local variables.

Maintenance of statistics was also explained, with some emphasis on how to proactively update statistics to avoid delays during query optimization, and how to improve the quality of statistics by scanning the entire table instead of a default sample. We also discussed how to detect cardinality estimation errors, which can negatively impact the quality of your execution plans, and we looked at recommendations on how to fix them.

Chapter 7

In-Memory OLTP aka Hekaton

It has been suggested recently by the database research community that because relational database management systems were originally architected in the late 1970s, when hardware was vastly different, a new design and architectural approach should be required with the new hardware available today. Relational database management systems were originally designed assuming that memory was limited and expensive and that databases were many times larger than the main memory, so because of that, data should reside on disk. With current hardware having memory sizes and disk volumes thousands of times larger, and processors thousands of times faster, these assumptions are no longer true. In addition, disk access has been subject to physical limits since its introduction, has not increased at a similar pace, and continues to be the slowest part of the system. Although memory capacity has grown dramatically—which is not the same case for the size of OLTP databases—one of the new design considerations is that an OLTP engine should be memory based instead of disk oriented, because most OLTP databases already fit into main memory.

In addition, an analysis performed early on for the Hekaton project at Microsoft showed that even with the current hardware available today, a 10 to 100 times performance improvement could not be achieved using current SQL Server mechanisms; instead, it would require dramatically changing the way data management systems are designed. SQL Server is already highly optimized, so using current techniques could not deliver dramatic performance gains or orders of magnitude speedup. Even after a main memory engine was built, there was still significant time spent in query processing, so they realized they needed to drastically reduce the number of instructions executed. Taking benefit of this available memory is not just a matter of reading more of the existing disk pages to memory, but rather involves redesigning data management systems using a different approach to gain the most possible benefit of this new hardware. In addition, standard concurrency control mechanisms available today do not scale up to the high transaction rates achievable by an in-memory optimized database, so locking becomes the next bottleneck.

Specialized in-memory database engines have appeared on the market, including Oracle TimesTen and IBM SolidDB. Microsoft also started shipping in-memory technologies with the xVelocity in-memory analytics engine as part of SQL Server Analysis Services and the xVelocity memory optimized columnstore indexes integrated into the SQL Server engine. Now, with SQL Server 2014, Microsoft introduces In-Memory OLTP, code-named Hekaton, as a new OLTP database engine. Hekaton's performance improvement is based in three major architecture areas: optimization for main memory access, compiling procedures to native code, and latches and lock elimination. We will look at these three major areas next.

In this chapter I cover Hekaton, an Enterprise Edition–only feature. xVelocity memory optimized columnstore indexes will be covered in Chapter 9. Because Hekaton is a new feature in SQL Server 2014, I will try to cover this technology as much as possible in this chapter; however, because this book is focused on query tuning and optimization, topics such as transactions and concurrency control may not be covered in detail. Also, to differentiate the Hekaton engine terminology from the standard SQL Server engine covered in the rest of the book, this chapter will call memory-optimized tables and natively compiled stored procedures to Hekaton tables and stored procedures. Standard tables and procedures will be called disk-based tables and regular or interpreted stored procedures.

Architecture

One of the main strategic decisions made during the Hekaton project was to build a new database engine fully integrated into SQL Server instead of creating a separate new product as other vendors did. This could give users several advantages, such as enabling existing applications to run without code changes, and no need to buy and learn a separate product. As mentioned earlier, Hekaton can provide several orders of magnitude performance increase based on the following:

▶ **Optimized tables and indexes for main memory data access** Hekaton tables and indexes are designed and optimized for memory. They are not stored as database pages, and they do not use a memory buffer pool either.

▶ **Procedures compiled to native code** Stored procedures can be first optimized by the SQL Server query optimizer, like any regular stored procedure, and then compiled into highly efficient machine code.

▶ **Locks and latches elimination** Hekaton implements a new optimistic multiversion concurrency control (MVCC) mechanism, which uses new data structures to eliminate traditional locks and latches, so there is no waiting because of blocking.

The lack of a locking/latching mechanism does not mean that chaos will ensue as Hekaton uses MVCC to provide snapshot, repeatable read, and serializable transaction isolation, as covered later. The Hekaton database engine has three major components, which are shown in Figure 7-1.

▶ **Hekaton storage engine** This component manages tables and indexes while providing support for storage, transactions, recoverability, high availability, and so on.

▶ **Hekaton compiler** This component compiles procedures and tables into native code, which is loaded as DLLs into the SQL Server process.

▶ **Hekaton runtime system** This component provides integration with other SQL Server resources.

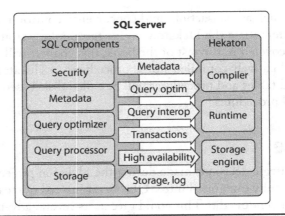

Figure 7-1 *The Hekaton database engine*

Hekaton memory-optimized tables are stored in memory all the time using new data structures completely different from disk-based tables. Obviously, they are also kept in disk, but only for durability purposes, so they are only read from disk during database recovery, for example, when the SQL Server instance starts. Hekaton tables are fully ACID—that is, they guarantee the Atomicity, Consistency, Isolation, Durability properties—although a nondurable version of the tables is available as well, in which data is not persisted on disk. Hekaton tables must have at least one index, and there is no data structure equivalent to a heap. SQL Server uses the same transaction log to log operations for both disk-based and Hekaton tables. Hekaton indexes are maintained only in memory, never persisted on disk, and as a consequence, its operations are never logged. Indexes are rebuilt when data is loaded into memory at SQL Server restart.

Although natively compiled stored procedures can only access memory-optimized tables, SQL Server provides operators for accessing and updating Hekaton tables, which can be used by interpreted T-SQL. This functionality is provided by a new component called the query interop, which can also allow accessing and updating both memory-optimized and regular tables in the same transaction.

Hekaton can help in applications experiencing CPU, I/O, and locking bottlenecks. Through the use of natively compiled stored procedures, fewer instructions are executed than with a traditional stored procedure, thus helping in cases where the execution time is dominated by the stored procedure code. Except logging, no I/O is required during normal database operations, and Hekaton even requires less logging than operations with regular disk-based tables. Applications with concurrency issues, such as contention in locks, latches, and spinlocks, can also greatly benefit from Hekaton because it does not take latches when accessing data.

NOTE

A particular scenario where Hekaton can greatly improve performance is with the last-page insert problem, where latch contention is caused when all threads continually attempt to update the last page of an index due to the use of incremental keys. By eliminating latches and locks, Hekaton can make these operations extremely fast.

However, Hekaton cannot be used to improve performance if your application has memory or network bottlenecks. Hekaton requires that all the tables defined as memory-optimized actually fit in memory, so your installation must have enough RAM to fit them all. Finally, Hekaton is only available in the 64-bit version of SQL Server 2014 and is an Enterprise Edition–only feature.

Tables and Indexes

As explained earlier, Hekaton tables can be accessed either by natively compiled stored procedures or by standard T-SQL, such as ad hoc queries or standard stored procedures. Tables are stored in memory, and each row can potentially have multiple versions. Versions are kept in memory instead of tempdb as the versioning mechanism of the standard database engine does. Versions that are no longer needed—that is, that are no longer visible to any transaction—are deleted to avoid filling up the available memory. This process is known as *garbage collection*.

Chapter 5 introduced indexes for traditional tables. Memory-optimized tables also benefit from indexes, and in this section, I talk about these indexes and how they are different from their disk-based counterparts. As explained earlier, Hekaton indexes are never persisted to disk; they exist only in memory, and because of that, their operations are not logged in the transaction log. Only index metadata is persisted, and indexes are rebuilt when data is loaded into memory at SQL Server restart.

Two different kinds of indexes exist on Hekaton: hash and range indexes, both of which are lock-free implementations. Hash indexes support index seeks on equality predicates, but they cannot be used with inequality predicates or to return sorted data. Range indexes can be used for range scans, ordered scans, and operations with inequality predicates. Range indexes can also be used for index seeks on equality predicates, but hash indexes offer far better performance and are the recommended choice for this kind of operation.

NOTE

Range indexes are being called just "nonclustered indexes" or "memory-optimized nonclustered indexes" in the latest updates of the SQL Server documentation. Keep that in mind in case the name "range indexes" is no longer used in future documentation.

Hash indexes are not ordered indexes; scanning them would return records in random order. Both kinds of indexes are covering indexes; the index contains memory pointers to the table rows where all the columns can be retrieved. There is no direct access to a record without using an index, so at least one index is required to locate the data in memory.

Although the concepts of fragmentation and fillfactor, as explained in Chapter 5, do not apply to Hekaton indexes, we may see that we can get a similar but new behavior with the bucket count configuration: it is possible for a hash index to have empty buckets, resulting in wasted space and impacting the performance of index scans, or to have a large number of records in a single bucket, which may impact the performance of search operations. In addition, updating and deleting records can create a new kind of fragmentation on the underlying data disk storage.

Creating Hekaton Tables

Creating a memory-optimized table requires a memory-optimized filegroup. The following error is returned if you try to create a table and you do not have one:

```
Msg 41337, Level 16, State 0, Line 22
The MEMORY_OPTIMIZED_DATA filegroup does not exist or is empty. Memory optimized
tables cannot be created for database until it has one MEMORY_OPTIMIZED_DATA
filegroup that is not empty.
```

You can either create a new database with a memory-optimized filegroup or add one to an existing database. The following statement shows the first scenario:

```
CREATE DATABASE Test
ON PRIMARY (NAME = Test_data,
FILENAME = 'C:\DATA\Test_data.mdf', SIZE=500MB),
FILEGROUP Test_fg CONTAINS MEMORY_OPTIMIZED_DATA
(NAME = Test_fg, FILENAME = 'C:\DATA\Test_fg')
LOG ON (NAME = Test_log, Filename='C:\DATA\Test_log.ldf', SIZE=500MB)
COLLATE Latin1_General_100_BIN2
```

The following code shows how you can add a memory-optimized data filegroup to an existing database:

```
CREATE DATABASE Test
ON PRIMARY (NAME = Test_data,
FILENAME = 'C:\DATA\Test_data.mdf', SIZE=500MB)
LOG ON (NAME = Test_log, Filename='C:\DATA\Test_log.ldf', SIZE=500MB)
COLLATE Latin1_General_100_BIN2
GO
ALTER DATABASE Test ADD FILEGROUP Test_fg CONTAINS MEMORY_OPTIMIZED_DATA
GO
ALTER DATABASE Test ADD FILE (NAME = Test_fg, FILENAME = N'C:\DATA\Test_fg')
    TO FILEGROUP Test_fg
GO
```

NOTE

You may have noticed the COLLATE clause on both CREATE DATABASE statements. There are some considerations to keep in mind regarding database collations when working with Hekaton. More details later in this section.

Once you have a database with a memory-optimized filegroup, you are ready to create your first Hekaton table. For this exercise you will copy data from AdventureWorks2012 to the newly created Test database. You might notice that scripting any of the AdventureWorks2012 tables and using the resulting code to create a new memory-optimized table will immediately show the first limitations of Hekaton: not all table properties are supported on the initial release, as I will explain later. You could also use the Memory Optimization Advisor to help you in migrating disk-based tables to memory-optimized tables. The Memory Optimization Advisor is covered later in this chapter.

Creating a Hekaton table requires the MEMORY_OPTIMIZED clause, which needs to be set to ON. Explicitly defining DURABILITY as SCHEMA_AND_DATA is also recommended, although this is its default value if the DURABILITY clause is not specified.

You can try to create a table defining only MEMORY_OPTIMIZED, as shown next:

```
CREATE TABLE TransactionHistoryArchive (
      TransactionID int NOT NULL,
      ProductID int NOT NULL,
      ReferenceOrderID int NOT NULL,
      ReferenceOrderLineID int NOT NULL,
      TransactionDate datetime NOT NULL,
      TransactionType nchar(1) NOT NULL,
      Quantity int NOT NULL,
      ActualCost money NOT NULL,
      ModifiedDate datetime NOT NULL
) WITH (MEMORY_OPTIMIZED = ON)
```

But you get the following error:

```
Msg 41321, Level 16, State 7, Line 17
The memory optimized table 'TransactionHistoryArchive' with
DURABILITY=SCHEMA_AND_DATA must have a primary key.
Msg 1750, Level 16, State 0, Line 17
Could not create constraint or index. See previous errors.
```

Because the error indicates that a memory-optimized table must have a primary, you could define one by changing the following line:

```
      TransactionID int NOT NULL PRIMARY KEY,
```

However, you still get the following message:

```
Msg 12317, Level 16, State 76, Line 17
Clustered indexes, which are the default for primary keys, are not
supported with memory optimized tables.
```

Change the previous line to specify a nonclustered index:

```
TransactionID int NOT NULL PRIMARY KEY NONCLUSTERED,
```

The statement finally succeeds and creates a table with a range index.

A hash index could also be created for the primary key if you explicitly use the HASH clause, as specified in the following example, which also requires the BUCKET_COUNT option. First let's drop the new table by using DROP TABLE in exactly the same way as with a disk-based table:

```
DROP TABLE TransactionHistoryArchive
```

Then we can create the table:

```
CREATE TABLE TransactionHistoryArchive (
    TransactionID int NOT NULL PRIMARY KEY NONCLUSTERED HASH WITH
        (BUCKET_COUNT = 100000),
    ProductID int NOT NULL,
    ReferenceOrderID int NOT NULL,
    ReferenceOrderLineID int NOT NULL,
    TransactionDate datetime NOT NULL,
    TransactionType nchar(1) NOT NULL,
    Quantity int NOT NULL,
    ActualCost money NOT NULL,
    ModifiedDate datetime NOT NULL
) WITH (MEMORY_OPTIMIZED = ON)
```

So a memory-optimized table must also have a primary key, which could be a hash or a range index. The maximum number of indexes currently is eight, and obviously, we can have both hash and range indexes on the same table, as shown in the following example (again, dropping the previous table if needed):

```
CREATE TABLE TransactionHistoryArchive (
    TransactionID int NOT NULL PRIMARY KEY NONCLUSTERED HASH WITH
        (BUCKET_COUNT = 100000),
    ProductID int NOT NULL,
```

```
        ReferenceOrderID int NOT NULL,
        ReferenceOrderLineID int NOT NULL,
        TransactionDate datetime NOT NULL,
        TransactionType nchar(1) NOT NULL,
        Quantity int NOT NULL,
        ActualCost money NOT NULL,
        ModifiedDate datetime NOT NULL,
        INDEX IX_ProductID NONCLUSTERED (ProductID)
) WITH (MEMORY_OPTIMIZED = ON)
```

The previous code creates a hash index on the TransactionID column, which is also the table primary key, and a range index on the ProductID column. The NONCLUSTERED keyword is optional for range indexes in this example. Once the table is created, we are ready to populate it by copying data from AdventureWorks2012. However, the following will not work:

```
INSERT INTO TransactionHistoryArchive
SELECT * FROM AdventureWorks2012.Production.TransactionHistoryArchive
```

We get the following error message:

```
Msg 41317, Level 16, State 3, Line 28
A user transaction that accesses memory optimized tables or natively
compiled procedures cannot access more than one user database or
databases model and msdb, and it cannot write to master.
```

As indicated in the error message, a user transaction that accesses memory-optimized tables cannot access more than one user database. For the same reason, the following code joining two tables from two user databases will not work either:

```
SELECT * FROM TransactionHistoryArchive tha
JOIN AdventureWorks2012.Production.TransactionHistory ta
    ON tha.TransactionID = ta.TransactionID
```

But you can copy this data in some other ways, such as using the Import and Export Wizard or using a temporary table like in the following code:

```
SELECT * INTO #temp
FROM AdventureWorks2012.Production.TransactionHistoryArchive
GO
INSERT INTO TransactionHistoryArchive
SELECT * FROM #temp
```

However, as explained earlier, a user transaction accessing memory-optimized tables and disk-based tables on the same database is perfectly supported (except in the case of natively compiled stored procedures). The following example will create a disk-based table and join both a memory-optimized and a disk-based table:

```
CREATE TABLE TransactionHistory (
     TransactionID int,
     ProductID int)
GO
SELECT * FROM TransactionHistoryArchive tha
JOIN TransactionHistory ta ON tha.TransactionID = ta.TransactionID
```

As shown earlier, the minimum requirements to create a memory-optimized table is to use the MEMORY_OPTIMIZED clause and to define a primary key, which itself requires an index. A second and optional clause, DURABILITY, is also commonly used and supports the options SCHEMA_AND_DATA and SCHEMA_ONLY. SCHEMA_AND_DATA, which is the default, allows both schema and data to be persisted on disk. SCHEMA_ONLY means that the table data will not be persisted on disk upon instance restart; only the table schema is persisted. SCHEMA_ONLY creates nondurable tables, which can improve the performance transaction by significantly reducing the I/O impact of the workload and can be used in some scenarios such as session state management and staging tables used in ETL processing.

Finally, as indicated earlier, there are some items to take into account regarding database collations when working with Hekaton. Memory-optimized tables and natively compiled stored procedures have the following restrictions:

▶ Char and varchar columns in memory-optimized tables must use code page 1252 collation. Note that this limitation does not apply to the nchar and nvarchar data types. You can get a list of the supported collations using code page 1252 by running the following query:

```
SELECT * FROM sys.fn_helpcollations()
WHERE COLLATIONPROPERTY(name, 'codepage') = 1252
```

Trying to use a different code page in a char or varchar column will return the following error message:

```
Msg 12329, Level 16, State 107, Line 10
The data types char(n) and varchar(n) using a collation that has a code page
other than 1252 are not supported with memory optimized tables.
```

▶ Indexes on string columns (char, nchar, varchar, or nvarchar) can only be specified using BIN2 collations. You can get a list of such collations by running the following query:

```
SELECT * FROM sys.fn_helpcollations() WHERE name like '%BIN2'
```

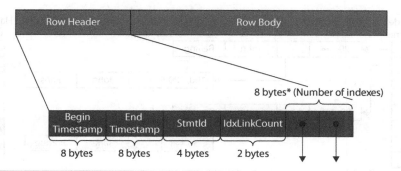

Figure 7-2   *Structure of a Hekaton row*

Similarly, trying to create an index on a character column not using a BIN2 collation will return the following error message:

```
Msg 12328, Level 16, State 106, Line 10
Indexes on character columns that do not use a *_BIN2 collation are
not supported with indexes on memory optimized tables.
```

▶ Finally, comparison, sorting, and manipulation of character strings inside natively compiled stored procedures must also use BIN2 collations. Not following this recommendation will get you the following error message:

```
Msg 12327, Level 16, State 105, Procedure test, Line 44
Comparison, sorting, and manipulation of character strings that do
not use a *_BIN2 collation is not supported with natively compiled
stored procedures.
```

Figure 7-2 shows the structure of a record in which we can identify two main parts: a row header and a row body or payload. The row header starts with a begin and end timestamp, which is used to identify where the record is valid for a transaction, as explained later in this section.

Next is the StmtId, which is the statement ID value of the statement that created the row. The last section of the header consists of index pointers, one per each index available on the table. The row body is the record itself, containing the index key columns along with the remaining columns of the row. Because the row body contains all the columns of the record, we could say that in Hekaton there is no need to define covering indexes as with traditional indexes: a memory-optimized index is a covering index, meaning that all the columns are included in the index. An index contains a memory pointer to the actual row in the table.

Hash Indexes

Hash indexes were introduced previously. Now let's take a look at them in more detail. Figure 7-3 shows an example of hash indexes containing three records: the "Susan" row,

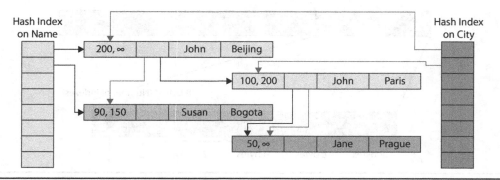

Figure 7-3   *Example of Hekaton rows and indexes*

the "Jane" row, and the "John" row. Notice that "John" has two versions, the complexities and relationships of which will be explained shortly. Two hash indexes are defined: the first one on the column Name and the second on the column City, so a hash table is allocated for each index, with each box representing a different hash bucket. The first part of the record (for example, 90, 150) is the begin and end timestamp shown previously in Figure 7-2. The infinity symbol (∞) at the end timestamp means that this is the currently valid version of the row. For simplicity, the example assumes that each hash bucket contains records based on the first letter of the key, either Name or City, although this is not how the hash function really works, as explained later.

Because the table has two indexes, each record has two pointers, one for each index, as represented in Figure 7-2. The first hash bucket for the Name index has a chain of three records: two versions for John and one version for Jane. The links between these records are shown with black arrows. The second hash bucket for the Name index only has a chain of one record, the Susan record, and so no links are shown. In the same way, Figure 7-3 shows two buckets for the City index—the first one with two records for Beijing and Bogota, and the second for Paris and Prague. The links are shown in gray arrows. The record "John, Beijing" has a valid time from 200 to infinity, which means it was created by a transaction that committed at time 200 and the record is still valid. The other version ("John, Paris") was valid from time 100 to 200, when it was updated to "John, Beijing". In the MVCC system, UPDATEs are treated as effectively INSERTs and DELETEs. Rows are only visible from the begin timestamp and up until (but not including) the end timestamp, so in this case, the existing version was expired by setting the end timestamp, and a new version with an infinity end timestamp was created.

A transaction started at time 150 would then see the "John, Paris" version, but one started at 220 would find the latest version of "John, Beijing". But how does SQL Server find the records using the index? This is where the hash function comes into play.

For the statement,

```
SELECT * FROM Table WHERE City = 'Beijing',
```

SQL Server will apply the hash function to the predicate. Remember that for simplicity, our hash function example was based on the first letter of the string, so in this case the result is "B." SQL Server will then look directly into the hash bucket and pull the pointer to the first row. Looking at the first row, it will now compare the strings; if they are the same, it will return the required row details. Then it will walk the chain of index pointers, comparing values and returning rows where appropriate.

Finally, notice that the example uses two hash indexes, but the same example works if we had used, for example, a hash index on Name and a range index on City, or both range indexes.

BUCKET_COUNT controls the size of the hash table, so this value should be chosen carefully. The recommendation is to have it two times the maximum expected number of distinct values in the index key, rounded up to the nearest power of two, although Hekaton will round up for you if needed. An inadequate BUCKET_COUNT value can lead to performance problems: a value too large can lead to many empty buckets in the hash table. This can cause higher memory usage as each bucket uses 8 bytes. Also, scanning the index will be more expensive because it has to scan those empty buckets. However, a large BUCKET_COUNT value does not affect the performance of index seeks. On the other hand, a BUCKET_COUNT value too small can lead to long chains of records that will cause searching for a specific record to be more expensive because the engine has to traverse multiple values to find a specific row.

Let's see some examples of how BUCKET_COUNT works, starting with an empty table. Drop the existing TransactionHistoryArchive table:

```
DROP TABLE TransactionHistoryArchive
```

Now create the table again with a BUCKET_COUNT of 100,000:

```
CREATE TABLE TransactionHistoryArchive (
    TransactionID int NOT NULL PRIMARY KEY NONCLUSTERED HASH WITH
        (BUCKET_COUNT = 100000),
    ProductID int NOT NULL,
    ReferenceOrderID int NOT NULL,
    ReferenceOrderLineID int NOT NULL,
    TransactionDate datetime NOT NULL,
    TransactionType nchar(1) NOT NULL,
    Quantity int NOT NULL,
    ActualCost money NOT NULL,
    ModifiedDate datetime NOT NULL
) WITH (MEMORY_OPTIMIZED = ON)
```

You can use the sys.dm_db_xtp_hash_index_stats DMV to show statistics about hash indexes. Run this:

```
SELECT * FROM sys.dm_db_xtp_hash_index_stats
```

You get the following output:

object_id	table_name	index_id	index_name	total_bucket_count	empty_bucket_count	avg_chain_len	max_chain_len
309576141	Transaction HistoryArchive	2	PK__Transact__ 55433A4A5BA80FBC	131072	131072	0	0

We can see that instead of 100,000 buckets, SQL Server rounded up to the nearest power of two (in this case, $2 \wedge 17$, or 131,072), as shown on the total_bucket_count column.

Insert the same data again by running the following statements:

```
DROP TABLE #temp
GO
SELECT * INTO #temp
FROM AdventureWorks2012.Production.TransactionHistoryArchive
GO
INSERT INTO TransactionHistoryArchive
SELECT * FROM #temp
```

This time, 89,253 records are inserted. Run the sys.dm_db_xtp_hash_index_stats DMV again. This time you get data similar to the following:

object_id	table_name	index_id	index_name	total_bucket_count	empty_bucket_count	avg_chain_len	max_chain_len
309576141	Transaction HistoryArchive	2	PK__Transact__ 55433A4A5BA80FBC	131072	91881	2	4

We can note several things. The total number of buckets (131,072) minus the empty buckets (91,881), shown as empty_bucket_count, gives us the number of buckets used (39,191). Because we inserted 89,253 records in 39,191 buckets, this give us 2.28 records per bucket on average, which is represented by the value avg_chain_len of 2, documented as the average length of the row chains over all the hash buckets in the index. max_chain_len is the maximum length of the row chains in the hash buckets.

Just to show an extreme case where performance may be impaired, run the same exercise, but request only 1,024 as BUCKET_COUNT. After inserting the 89,253 records, we could get the following output:

object_id	table_name	index_id	index_name	total_bucket_count	empty_bucket_count	avg_chain_len	max_chain_len
373576369	Transaction HistoryArchive	2	PK__Transact__ 55433A4A89A2F661	1024	0	87	89

In this case, we have 89,253 records divided by 1,024 (or 87.16 records per bucket). Hash collisions occur when two or more index keys are mapped to the same hash bucket, like in this example, and a large number of hash collisions can impact the performance of lookup operations.

The other extreme case is having too many buckets compared to the number of records. Running the same example for 1,000,000 buckets and inserting the same number of records would give us this:

object_id	table_name	index_id	index_name	total_bucket_count	empty_bucket_count	avg_chain_len	max_chain_len
405576483	Transaction HistoryArchive	2	PK__Transact__ 55433A4A0A843683	1048576	959323	1	1

This example has 91.49 percent unused buckets, which will both use more memory and impact the performance of scan operations by having to read many unused buckets.

Wondering what the behavior is if we have the same number of buckets as records? Change the previous code to create 65,536 buckets. Then run this:

```
DROP TABLE #temp
GO
SELECT TOP 65536 * INTO #temp
FROM AdventureWorks2012.Production.TransactionHistoryArchive
GO
INSERT INTO TransactionHistoryArchive
SELECT * FROM #temp
```

We get the following output:

object_id	table_name	index_id	index_name	total_bucket_count	empty_bucket_count	avg_chain_len	max_chain_len
437576597	Transaction HistoryArchive	2	PK__Transact__ 55433A4AFB5FAACA	65536	47828	3	7

So after looking at these extreme cases, it is worth reminding ourselves that the recommendation is to configure the BUCKET_COUNT as two times the maximum expected number of distinct values in the index key, keeping in mind that changing the BUCKET_COUNT is not a trivial matter and requires the table to be dropped and re-created.

SQL Server uses the same hashing function for all the hash indexes, and this function is deterministic, which means that the same index key will always be mapped to the same bucket in the index. Finally, as we were able to see in the examples, multiple index keys can also be mapped to the same hash bucket, and because key values are not evenly distributed in the buckets, there can be a number of empty buckets, and used buckets may contain one or more records.

Range Indexes

Although hash indexes support index seeks on equality predicates and are the best choice for point lookups, index seeks on inequality predicates, like the ones using the operators >, <, <=, and >=, are not supported on this kind of index. In addition, because all index key columns are used to compute the hash value, index seeks on a hash index cannot be used when only a subset of these index key columns are used in an equality predicate. For example, if the hash index is defined as lastname, firstname, you cannot use it in an equality predicate using only lastname or only firstname. Hash indexes cannot be used to retrieve the records sorted by the index definition either. Range indexes can be used to help in all these scenarios and have the additional benefit that they don't require you to define a number of buckets. However, although range indexes have several advantages over hash indexes, keep in mind that range indexes could lead to suboptimal performance for Index Seek operations where hash indexes are recommended instead.

Range indexes are a new form of B-tree, called a Bw-tree, designed for new hardware taking advantage of the cache of modern multicore processors. They are in-memory structures that achieve outstanding performance via latch-free techniques and were originally described by Microsoft Research in the paper "The Bw-Tree: A B-tree for New Hardware Platforms," by Justin Levandoski, et al. Figure 7-4 shows the general structure of a Bw-tree.

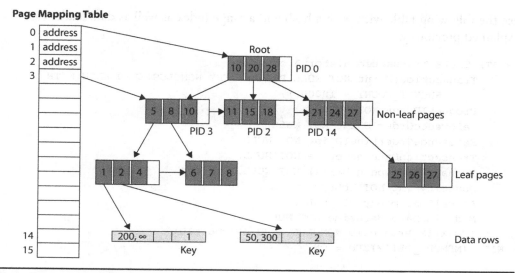

Figure 7-4   *Structure of a Bw-tree*

Similar to a regular B-tree, as explained in Chapter 5, in a Bw-tree the root and non-leaf pages point to index pages at the next level of the tree, and the leaf pages contain a set of ordered key values with pointers that point to the data rows. Each non-leaf page has a logical page ID (PID), and a page mapping table contains the mapping of these PIDs to their physical memory address. For example, in Figure 7-4, the top entry of the page mapping table has the number 0 and points to the page with PID 0. Keys on non-leaf pages contain the highest value possible that this page references. Leaf pages do not have a PID, only memory addresses pointing to the data rows. So to find the row with key equal to 2, SQL Server would start with the root page (PID 0), follow the link for key = 10 (because 10 is greater than 2), which points to the page with PID 3, and then follow the link for key = 5 (which again is greater than 2). The pointed leaf page contains the key 2, which has the memory address pointing to the required record. For more details about the internals of these new memory structures, you may want to refer to the research paper previously listed.

Examples

Let's now run some queries to get a basic understanding of how these indexes work and what kind of execution plans they create. In this section, I use ad hoc T-SQL, which in Hekaton is said to use the query interop capabilities. The examples in this section use the following table with both a hash and a range index as well as data loaded, as explained previously.

```
CREATE TABLE TransactionHistoryArchive (
    TransactionID int NOT NULL PRIMARY KEY NONCLUSTERED HASH WITH
        (BUCKET_COUNT = 100000),
    ProductID int NOT NULL,
    ReferenceOrderID int NOT NULL,
    ReferenceOrderLineID int NOT NULL,
    TransactionDate datetime NOT NULL,
    TransactionType nchar(1) NOT NULL,
    Quantity int NOT NULL,
    ActualCost money NOT NULL,
    ModifiedDate datetime NOT NULL,
    INDEX IX_ProductID NONCLUSTERED (ProductID)
) WITH (MEMORY_OPTIMIZED = ON)
```

First, run the following query:

```
SELECT * FROM TransactionHistoryArchive
WHERE TransactionID = 8209
```

Because we defined a hash index on the TransactionID column, we get the plan shown in Figure 7-5, which uses an Index Seek operator.

The index used is named PK__Transact__55433A4A7EB94404. The name was given automatically but it is also possible to specify a name, if required, as shown in an example later. As mentioned previously, hash indexes are efficient for point lookups, but they do not support index seeks on inequality predicates. If you change the previous query to use an inequality predicate, as shown next, it will create a plan with an Index Scan, as shown in Figure 7-6.

```
SELECT * FROM TransactionHistoryArchive
WHERE TransactionID > 8209
```

Now let's try a different query:

```
SELECT * FROM TransactionHistoryArchive
WHERE ProductID = 780
```

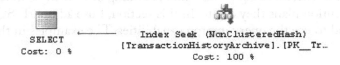

Figure 7-5 *Index Seek operation on a hash index*

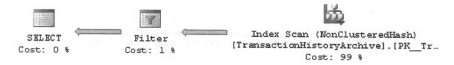

Figure 7-6   *Index Scan operation on a hash index*

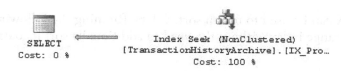

Figure 7-7   *Index Seek operation on a range index*

Because we have a range index defined on ProductID, an Index Seek operation will be used on that index, IX_ProductID, as shown in Figure 7-7. Now let's try an inequality operation on the same column.

```
SELECT * FROM TransactionHistoryArchive
WHERE ProductID < 780
```

This time the range index can be used to access the data, without the need of an Index Scan operation. The resulting plan can be seen in Figure 7-8.

Hash indexes cannot be used to return data sorted because their rows are stored in random order. The following query will use a Sort operation to sort the requested data, as shown in Figure 7-9.

```
SELECT * FROM TransactionHistoryArchive
ORDER BY TransactionID
```

Figure 7-8   *Index Seek operation on a hash index with an inequality predicate*

Figure 7-9   *Sort operation used to sort data with a hash index*

Figure 7-10   *Using a range index to return sorted data*

A range index can be used to return sorted data. Running the following query will simply scan the range index without the need to additionally sort its data, as shown in Figure 7-10.

```
SELECT * FROM TransactionHistoryArchive
ORDER BY ProductID
```

However, unlike disk-based indexes, range indexes are unidirectional, which might surprise you. Therefore, requesting the same query using ORDER BY ProductID DESC will not be able to use the index-sorted data and will instead use a plan with an Index Scan and a Sort, similar to the one shown in Figure 7-9.

Finally, let's look at an example of a hash index with two columns. Let's assume you have the following version of the TransactionHistoryArchive table, which uses a hash index with both TransactionID and ProductID columns:

```
CREATE TABLE TransactionHistoryArchive (
    TransactionID int NOT NULL,
    ProductID int NOT NULL,
    ReferenceOrderID int NOT NULL,
    ReferenceOrderLineID int NOT NULL,
    TransactionDate datetime NOT NULL,
    TransactionType nchar(1) NOT NULL,
    Quantity int NOT NULL,
    ActualCost money NOT NULL,
    ModifiedDate datetime NOT NULL,
    CONSTRAINT PK_TransactionID_ProductID PRIMARY KEY NONCLUSTERED
            HASH (TransactionID, ProductID) WITH (BUCKET_COUNT = 100000)
) WITH (MEMORY_OPTIMIZED = ON)
```

Because all the index key columns are required to compute the hash value, as explained earlier, SQL Server will be able to use an Index Seek on the PK_TransactionID_ProductID in the following query:

```
SELECT * FROM TransactionHistoryArchive
WHERE TransactionID = 7173 AND ProductID = 398
```

But not in the following query, which will resort to an Index Scan:

```
SELECT * FROM TransactionHistoryArchive
WHERE TransactionID = 7173
```

Although the execution plans showed in this section use the familiar Index Scan and Index Seek operations, keep in mind that these indexes and data are in memory and there is no disk access at all. In this case, the table and indexes used are in memory and use totally different structures. So how do you identify them when you see them in execution plans, especially when you query both memory-optimized and disk-based tables? You can look at the Storage property in the operator properties and see a value of MemoryOptimized, as shown in Figure 7-11. Although you can see NonClusteredHash after the name of the operator for hash indexes, range indexes just show NonClustered, which is the same shown for regular disk-based nonclustered indexes.

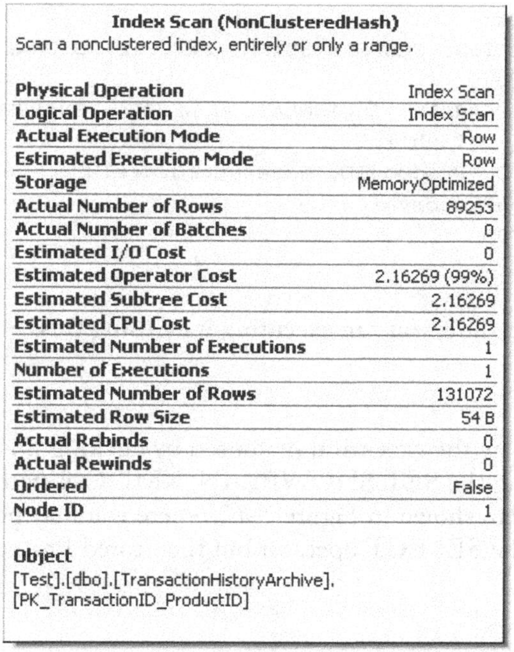

Index Scan (NonClusteredHash)	
Scan a nonclustered index, entirely or only a range.	
Physical Operation	Index Scan
Logical Operation	Index Scan
Actual Execution Mode	Row
Estimated Execution Mode	Row
Storage	MemoryOptimized
Actual Number of Rows	89253
Actual Number of Batches	0
Estimated I/O Cost	0
Estimated Operator Cost	2.16269 (99%)
Estimated Subtree Cost	2.16269
Estimated CPU Cost	2.16269
Estimated Number of Executions	1
Number of Executions	1
Estimated Number of Rows	131072
Estimated Row Size	54 B
Actual Rebinds	0
Actual Rewinds	0
Ordered	False
Node ID	1
Object	
[Test].[dbo].[TransactionHistoryArchive]. [PK_TransactionID_ProductID]	

Figure 7-11   *Index Scan properties on a Hash Index*

Natively Compiled Stored Procedures

As previously mentioned, to create natively compiled stored procedures, Hekaton leverages the SQL Server query optimizer to produce an efficient query plan, which is later compiled into native code and loaded as DLLs into the SQL Server process. You may want to use natively compiled stored procedures mostly in performance-critical parts of an application or in procedures that are frequently executed. However, you need to be aware of the limitations of the T-SQL supported features on natively compiled stored procedures for SQL Server 2014, which are also covered in a section later in this chapter.

Creating Natively Compiled Stored Procedures

Let's now create a natively compiled stored procedure, which, as shown in the following example, requires the NATIVE_COMPILATION clause:

```
CREATE PROCEDURE test
WITH NATIVE_COMPILATION, SCHEMABINDING, EXECUTE AS OWNER
AS
BEGIN ATOMIC WITH (TRANSACTION ISOLATION LEVEL = SNAPSHOT,
    LANGUAGE = 'us_english')
SELECT TransactionID, ProductID, ReferenceOrderID
FROM dbo.TransactionHistoryArchive
WHERE ProductID = 780
END
```

After creating the procedure, you can executing it by using this:

```
EXEC test
```

You could also display the execution plan used by clicking Display Estimated Execution Plan or using the SET SHOWPLAN_XML ON statement. In either case, we get the graphical plan shown in Figure 7-12, where you may notice that the root of the plan no longer is the SELECT operator but the Stored Procedure operator.

Figure 7-12 *Execution plan of a natively compiled stored procedure*

In addition to NATIVE_COMPILATION, the code shows other required clauses: SCHEMABINDING, EXECUTE AS, and BEGIN ATOMIC. Leaving any of these out will produce an error. These choices must be set at compile time and are aimed at minimizing the number of runtime checks and operations that must be performed at execution time, thus helping with the performance of the execution.

SCHEMABINDING refers to the fact that natively compiled stored procedures must be schema bound, which means that tables referenced by the procedure cannot be dropped. This helps to avoid costly schema stability locks before execution. Trying to delete the dbo.TransactionHistoryArchive table we created earlier would produce the following error:

```
Msg 3729, Level 16, State 1, Line 65
Cannot DROP TABLE 'dbo.TransactionHistoryArchive' because it is being
referenced by object 'test'.
```

The EXECUTE AS requirement focuses on avoiding permission checks at execution time. In natively compiled stored procedures, the default EXECUTE AS CALLER is not supported, so you have to use any of the other three choices available: EXECUTE AS SELF, EXECUTE AS OWNER, or EXECUTE AS user_name.

BEGIN ATOMIC is part of the ANSI SQL standard, and in SQL Server, it's used to define an atomic block in which either the entire block succeeds or all the statements in the block are rolled back. If the procedure is invoked outside the context of an active transaction, BEGIN ATOMIC will start a new transaction and the atomic block will define the beginning and end of the transaction. However, if a transaction is already started when the atomic block begins, the transaction borders will be defined by the BEGIN TRANSACTION, COMMIT TRANSACTION, and ROLLBACK TRANSACTION statements. BEGIN ATOMIC supports five options: TRANSACTION ISOLATION LEVEL and LANGUAGE, which are required, and DELAYED_DURABILITY, DATEFORMAT, and DATEFIRST, which are optional.

TRANSACTION ISOLATION LEVEL defines the transaction isolation level to be used by the natively compiled stored procedure, and the supported values are SNAPSHOT, REPEATABLEREAD, and SERIALIZABLE. LANGUAGE defines the language used by the stored procedure and determines the date and time formats and system messages. Languages are defined in sys.syslanguages. DELAYED_ DURABILITY is used to specify the durability of the transaction and, by default, is OFF, meaning that transactions are fully durable. When DELAYED_DURABILITY is enabled, transaction commits are asynchronous and can improve the performance of transactions by writing log records to the transaction log in batches, but can lead to data loss in the case of a system failure.

NOTE

Delayed transaction durability is a new SQL Server 2014 feature that can also be used outside Hekaton and is useful in cases where you have performance issues due to latency in transaction log writes and you can tolerate some data loss. For more details about delayed durability, see http://msdn.microsoft.com/en-us/library/dn449490(v=sql.120).aspx.

As mentioned earlier, Hekaton tables support the SNAPSHOT, REPEATABLE READ, and SERIALIZABLE isolation levels and utilize an MVCC mechanism. The isolation level can be specified in the ATOMIC clause, as was done earlier, or directly in interpreted T-SQL using the SET TRANSACTION ISOLATION LEVEL statement. It is interesting to note that although multiversioning is also supported on disk-based tables, they only use the SNAPSHOT and READ_COMMITTED_SNAPSHOT isolation levels. In addition, versions in Hekaton are not maintained in tempdb, as is the case with disk-based tables, but rather in memory as part of the memory-optimized data structures. Finally, there is no blocking on memory-optimized tables. It is an optimistic assumption that there will be no conflicts, so if two transactions try to update the same row, a write-write conflict is generated. Because Hekaton does not use locks, locking hints are not supported with memory-optimized tables either.

Finally, it is recommended that you manually update your table's statistics before creating your natively compiled stored procedures. As mentioned later in this chapter, although statistics are automatically created in memory-optimized tables, they are not automatically updated as data changes, as they are in a default configuration with disk-based tables. This means that when you originally create a table, no statistics information exists because the table is empty, and the same is true as data is loaded or written to the table.

For example, running the following statement after the TransactionHistoryArchive is created will get the output shown in Figure 7-13:

```
DBCC SHOW_STATISTICS(TransactionHistoryArchive, PK_TransactionID_ProductID)
```

	Name	Updated	Rows	Rows Sampled	Steps	Density	Average key length	String Index	Filter Expression	Unfiltered Rows
1	PK_TransactionID_ProductID	NULL	NULL	NULL	NULL	NULL	NULL	NULL	NULL	NULL

All density	Average Length	Columns

RANGE_HI_KEY	RANGE_ROWS	EQ_ROWS	DISTINCT_RANGE_ROWS	AVG_RANGE_ROWS

Figure 7-13 *DBCC SHOW_STATISTICS output for the TransactionHistoryArchive table*

	Name	Updated	Rows	Rows Sampled	Steps	Density	Average key length	String Index	Filter Expression	Unfiltered Rows
1	PK_TransactionID_ProductID	Apr 9 2014 11:22PM	89253	89253	3	1	8	NO	NULL	89253

	All density	Average Length	Columns
1	1.120411E-05	4	TransactionID
2	1.120411E-05	8	TransactionID, ProductID

	RANGE_HI_KEY	RANGE_ROWS	EQ_ROWS	DISTINCT_RANGE_ROWS	AVG_RANGE_ROWS
1	1	0	1	0	1
2	89252	89250	1	89250	1
3	89253	0	1	0	1

Figure 7-14 *DBCC SHOW_STATISTICS output after statistics were updated*

Because statistics are not automatically updated, you will get the same output no matter how much data is loaded or written to the table. To update the statistics, run the following UPDATE STATISTICS statement:

```
UPDATE STATISTICS TransactionHistoryArchive WITH FULLSCAN, NORECOMPUTE
```

DBCC SHOW_STATISTICS will now return better statistics information, as shown in Figure 7-14.

Note that the FULLSCAN and NORECOMPUTE clauses are required with memory-optimized tables.

DLLs

The Hekaton engine uses some SQL Server engine components for compilation of native procedures—namely, the query-processing stack we discussed in Chapters 1 and 3 for parsing, binding, and query optimization. But because the final purpose is to produce native code, other operations are added to create a DLL.

Translating the plan created by the query optimizer to C code is not a trivial task, and additional steps are required to perform this operation. Keep in mind that native code is also produced when a table is created. Table operations such as computing a hash function on a key, comparing two records, or serializing a record into a log buffer are compiled into native code.

First, the created plan is used to create a data structure called the Mixed Abstract Tree (MAT), which is later transformed into a structure that can be more easily converted to C code, called the Pure Imperative Tree (PIT). Later on, the required C code is generated using the PIT, and in the final step, a C/C++ compiler and linker are used to produce a DLL. The Microsoft C/C++ Optimizing Compiler and Microsoft Incremental Linker are used in this process and can be found as cl.exe and link.exe as part of the SQL Server 2014 installation.

Several files created in these steps will be available at the file system, as shown later, including the C code. All these steps are performed automatically, and the process is transparent to the user—you only have to create the memory-optimized table or natively compiled stored procedure as indicated before. Once the DLL is created, it is loaded into the SQL Server address space where it can be executed. These steps and the architecture of the Hekaton compiler are shown in Figure 7-15.

DLLs for both memory-optimized tables and natively compiled stored procedures are recompiled during recovery every time the SQL Server instance is started. SQL Server maintains the information required to re-create these DLLs in each database metadata.

It is interesting to note that the generated DLLs are not kept in the database but in the file system, and you can find them, along with some other intermediate files, by looking at the location returned by the following query:

```
SELECT name, description FROM sys.dm_os_loaded_modules
where description = 'XTP Native DLL'
```

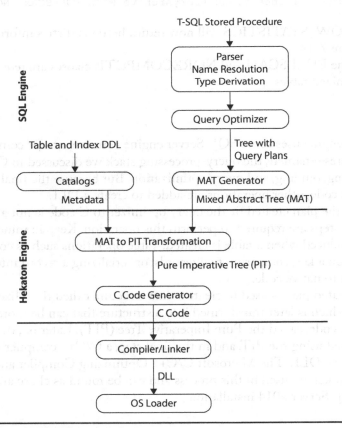

Figure 7-15 *Architecture of the Hekaton compiler*

I got the following output:

name	description
C:\Program Files\Microsoft SQL Server\MSSQL12.MSSQLSERVER\MSSQL\DATA\xtp\7\xtp_t_7_885578193.dll	XTP Native DLL
C:\Program Files\Microsoft SQL Server\MSSQL12.MSSQLSERVER\MSSQL\DATA\xtp\7\xtp_p_7_917578307.dll	XTP Native DLL

A directory is created in the xtp directory named after the database ID, in this case, 7. Next, the names of the DLL files start with "xtp," followed by "t" for tables and "p" for stored procedures. Again, we have the database ID on the name (in this case, 7), followed by the object ID, which is 885578193 for the TransactionHistoryArchive table and 917578307 for the test natively compiled stored procedure.

You can inspect the listed directories and find the DLL file, the C source code, and several other files, as you can see in Figure 7-16.

There is no need to maintain these files because SQL Server automatically removes them when they are no longer needed. If you drop both the table and procedure we just created, all these files will be automatically deleted by the garbage collector, although it may not happen immediately, especially for tables. Run the following to test it:

```
DROP PROCEDURE test
DROP TABLE TransactionHistoryArchive
```

Also notice that you would need to delete the procedure first to avoid error 3729, as explained earlier.

Having those files on the file system does not represent a security risk (for example, in the case that they could be manually altered). Every time Hekaton has to load the DLLs

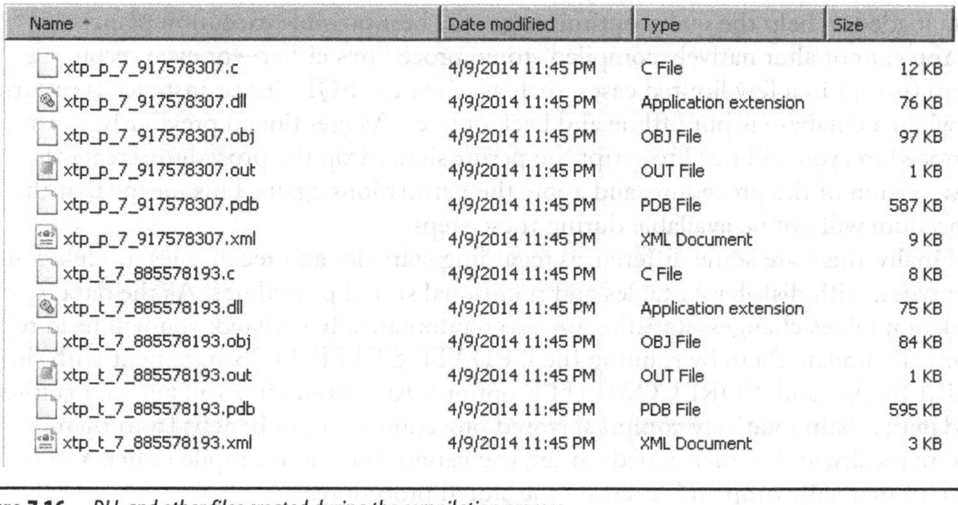

Name ▲	Date modified	Type	Size
xtp_p_7_917578307.c	4/9/2014 11:45 PM	C File	12 KB
xtp_p_7_917578307.dll	4/9/2014 11:45 PM	Application extension	76 KB
xtp_p_7_917578307.obj	4/9/2014 11:45 PM	OBJ File	97 KB
xtp_p_7_917578307.out	4/9/2014 11:45 PM	OUT File	1 KB
xtp_p_7_917578307.pdb	4/9/2014 11:45 PM	PDB File	587 KB
xtp_p_7_917578307.xml	4/9/2014 11:45 PM	XML Document	9 KB
xtp_t_7_885578193.c	4/9/2014 11:45 PM	C File	8 KB
xtp_t_7_885578193.dll	4/9/2014 11:45 PM	Application extension	75 KB
xtp_t_7_885578193.obj	4/9/2014 11:45 PM	OBJ File	84 KB
xtp_t_7_885578193.out	4/9/2014 11:45 PM	OUT File	1 KB
xtp_t_7_885578193.pdb	4/9/2014 11:45 PM	PDB File	595 KB
xtp_t_7_885578193.xml	4/9/2014 11:45 PM	XML Document	3 KB

Figure 7-16   *DLL and other files created during the compilation process*

again, such as when an instance is restarted or a database is put offline and then back online, SQL Server will compile the DLLs again, and those existing files are never used.

Limitations

Without a doubt, the main limitation of Hekaton, at least as of SQL Server 2014, is that tables cannot be altered: a new table with the required changes will have to be created instead. This is the case for any change you want to make to a table, such as adding a new column or a new index or changing the bucket count of a hash index. Obviously, creating a new table would need several other operations as well, such as first copying its data to another location, dropping the table, creating the new table with the needed changes, and copying the data back, which would require some downtime for the application. This limitation will probably be the biggest challenge to deployed applications, which will, of course, demand serious thinking and architecture design to avoid or minimize changes once the required memory-optimized tables are in production.

Because memory is not immediately freed after a table is dropped, additional memory would also be needed even if a regular table is used to temporarily copy this data. A new memory-optimized table could also be used as the temporary table, but this will further increase the required memory.

In addition, dropping and creating a table will usually also imply some other operations, such as scripting all its permissions. And because natively compiled stored procedures are schema bound, this also means that they need to be dropped first before the table can be dropped. That is, you need to script these procedures, drop them, and create them again once the new table is created. Similar to tables, you may need to script the permissions of the procedures as well. Updating statistics with the FULLSCAN option is also highly recommended after the table is created and all the data loaded to help the query optimizer get the best possible execution plan.

You cannot alter natively compiled stored procedures either—or even recompile them (except in a few limited cases, such as when the SQL Server instance is restarted or when a database is put offline and back online). As mentioned previously, to alter a procedure, you will need to script the permissions, drop the procedure, create the new version of the procedure, and apply the permissions again. This means that the procedure will not be available during these steps.

Finally, there are some differences regarding statistics and recompiles in Hekaton compared with disk-based tables and traditional stored procedures. As the data in Hekaton tables changes, statistics are never automatically updated; you will need to manually update them by running the UPDATE STATISTICS statement with the FULLSCAN and NORECOMPUTE options. Also, even after you get your statistics updated, existing natively compiled stored procedures cannot benefit from them automatically, and as mentioned earlier, you cannot force a recompile either. You will have to manually drop and re-create the stored procedures.

Hekaton tables and stored procedures do not support the full T-SQL surface area that is supported by disk-based tables and regular stored procedures. For example, the following features are not supported on memory-optimized tables:

▶ IDENTITY columns are only partially supported. For more details, see http://msdn.microsoft.com/en-us/library/dn247640(v=sql.120).aspx.

▶ FOREIGN KEY constraints

▶ CHECK constraints

▶ DEFAULT constraints

▶ Computed columns

▶ DML triggers

▶ Some data types

Finally, for an entire list of unsupported T-SQL constructs on Hekaton tables and stored procedures, see http://msdn.microsoft.com/en-us/library/dn246937(v=sql.120).aspx.

AMR Tool

SQL Server 2014 includes a tool to help you decide which tables and stored procedures you can move to Hekaton or In-Memory OLTP. In this section, I give you a quick tour of this tool, the AMR (Analysis, Migration, and Reporting). The AMR tool is integrated with the SQL Server Data Collector, and to enable it, you have to enable the new Transaction Performance Collection Sets on the Configure Data Collection Wizard, as shown in Figure 7-17. The Data Collector was introduced in Chapter 2.

This will create two new collection sets—Stored Procedure Usage Analysis and Table Usage Analysis—in addition to the three system data collection sets previously available with the Data Collector.

Once you configure the Transaction Performance Collection Sets on the Data Collector, you are ready to test the AMR tool. First, you need to create some database activity. In this case, we are testing the following stored procedures on a copy of AdventureWorks2012:

```
CREATE PROCEDURE test1
AS
SELECT * FROM Sales.SalesOrderHeader soh
     JOIN Sales.SalesOrderDetail sod ON soh.SalesOrderID = sod.SalesOrderID
WHERE ProductID = 870

CREATE PROCEDURE test2
AS
SELECT ProductID, SalesOrderID, COUNT(*)
FROM Sales.SalesOrderDetail
GROUP BY ProductID, SalesOrderID
```

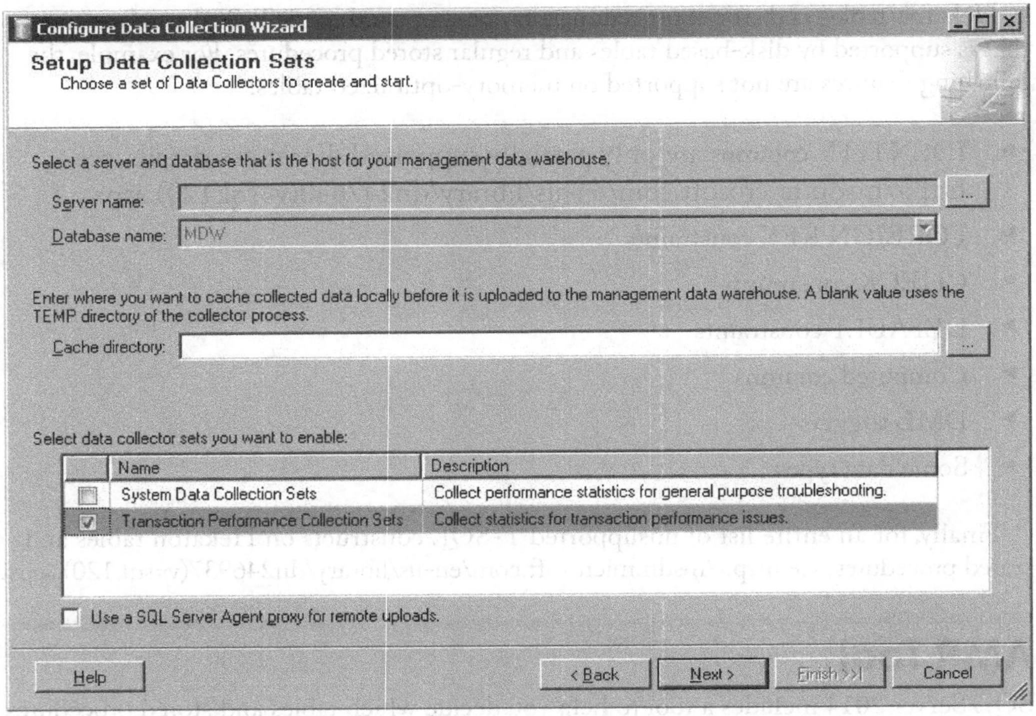

Figure 7-17   *Configuring the AMR tool on the Data Collection Wizard*

Execute the procedures multiple times:

```
EXEC test1
GO
EXEC test2
GO
```

After you create some database activity, you may have to wait for the next Data Collector upload job to execute. For example, the Stored Procedure Usage Analysis upload job runs every 30 minutes, and the Table Usage Analysis runs every 15 minutes. You could also run these jobs (collection_set_5_upload and collection_set_6_upload, respectively) manually.

To access the AMR reports, right-click your MDW database, select Reports, Management Data Warehouse, and Transaction Performance Analysis Overview. The main AMR tool report is shown in Figure 7-18.

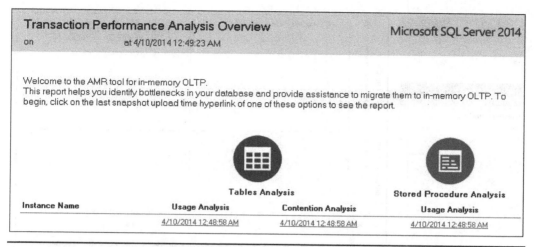

Figure 7-18   *Transaction Performance Analysis Overview report*

Clicking Usage Analysis in the Tables Analysis section will show the Recommended Tables Based on Usage report, as shown in Figure 7-19, which lists the top candidate tables for memory optimization based on the access patterns of the workload. The report graph shows the performance benefits on memory optimization, along with the migration effort required to move tables to In-Memory OLTP based on how many unsupported features the table uses.

Selecting Tables Analysis, Contention Analysis on the main report will show the Recommended Tables Based on Contention report shown in Figure 7-20.

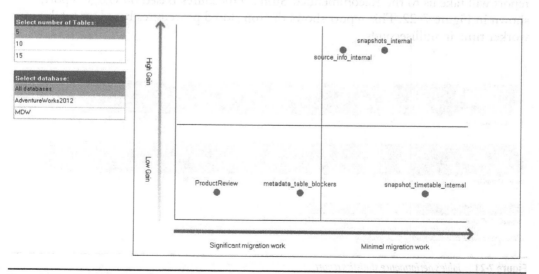

Figure 7-19   *Recommended Tables Based on Usage report*

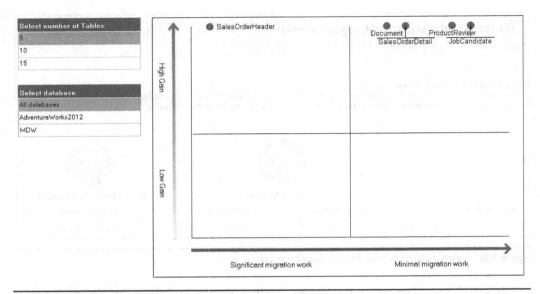

Figure 7-20 *Recommended Tables Based on Contention report*

In both cases, the reports recommend to prioritize the tables in the top-right corner of the graph. Clicking a table name in any of the previous reports will show the table performance statistics details, including both table usage and contention statistics. An example is shown in Figure 7-21.

On the other hand, selecting Stored Procedure Analysis, Usage Analysis on the main report will take us to the Recommended Stored Procedures Based on Usage report, shown in Figure 7-22. This report shows the top stored procedures based on total worker time in milliseconds.

| Table Name | % of total accesses | Lookup Statistics | | Range Scan Statistics | | Interop Gain | | Native Gain | |
		Count	Average per Transaction	Count	Average per Transaction	Lookup	Range	Lookup	Range
SalesOrderDetail	0.8	0	0	736	27.26	1.5X-2.5X	1X-4X	2.5X	1X-4X

| Table Name | % of total waits | Latch Statistics | | | Lock Statistics | | |
		Page latch wait count	Average wait time per latch wait (ms)	Page lock count	Page lock wait count	Average wait time per lock wait (ms)
SalesOrderDetail	0	0	0	556048	0	0

Table Name	Number of Migration Blockers
SalesOrderDetail	11

See information for all user tables in database: AdventureWorks2012

Figure 7-21 *Table's performance statistics report*

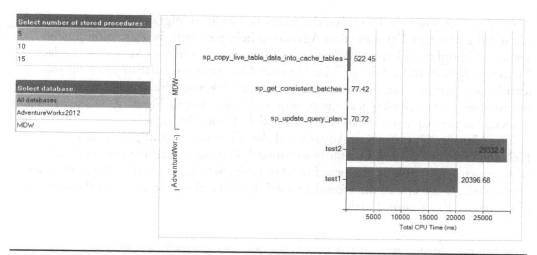

Figure 7-22 *Recommended Stored Procedures Based on Usage report*

Similarly, clicking a specific stored procedure will show the stored procedure execution statistics detail and the tables it references. An example for the test2 stored procedure is shown in Figure 7-23.

You can also click the listed tables to get the table's performance statistics report shown previously.

In summary, the AMR tool, which can be used against instances of SQL Server 2008 or later, will be very helpful in providing recommendations as to which tables and stored procedures you might want to consider migrating into Hekaton. You could also upgrade your database to SQL Server 2014 and run this tool for analysis of your real performance data and iteratively move tables and stored procedures to In-Memory OLTP as required.

Stored Procedure's Execution Statistics

Cached Time	Total CPU Time (ms)	Total Execution Time (ms)	Total Cache Missed	Execution Count
4/10/2014 12:17:44 AM	29332.8	319281.76	289	422

Stored Procedure's Table References:

Referenced Server	Referenced Database	Referenced Schema	Referenced Table
	AdventureWorks2012		
		Sales	SalesOrderDetail

Figure 7-23 *Stored procedure's execution statistics report*

Finally, once you have identified the tables you want to migrate to Hekaton, you can use the Memory Optimization Advisor to help you with the migration process. To access it, right-click the table you want to migrate in Object Explorer and select Memory Optimization Advisor. The Memory Optimization Advisor can help you identify any features that are incompatible with a Hekaton table, giving you additional information on which changes may be required. For example, Figure 7-24 shows such a screen for the AdventureWorks2012.Sales.SalesOrderDetail table.

The Memory Optimization Advisor will also allow you to configure your new Hekaton table by defining a memory-optimized filegroup, renaming your original table, copying this table to the new Hekaton table, defining a primary key, and other operations. At the end of the wizard, you will have the choice to script all the selections or to execute them immediately.

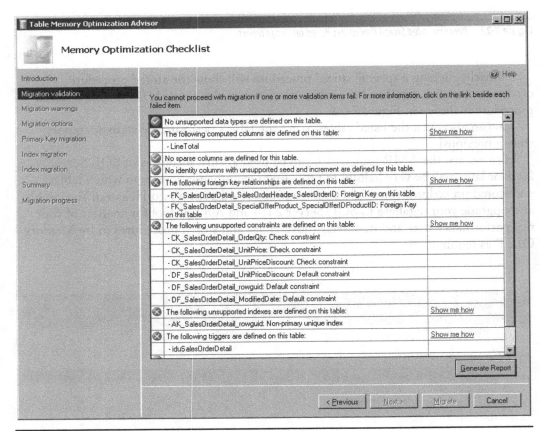

Figure 7-24   *Memory Optimization Checklist of the Memory Optimization Advisor*

In a similar way, the Native Compilation Advisor can be used to identify T-SQL elements that are not supported in natively compiled stored procedures. To access this, right-click the stored procedure that you want to analyze in Object Explorer and select Native Compilation Advisor. The advisor will generate a list of unsupported T-SQL elements that the stored procedure may contain.

Summary

This chapter covered In-Memory OLTP, also known as Hekaton, without a doubt the most important new feature of SQL Server 2014. The Hekaton OLTP database engine is a response to a new design and architectural approach looking to achieve the most benefit of the new hardware available today. Although optimization for main memory access has been its main feature, and is even part of its name, Hekaton performance improvement is also complemented by other major architecture areas, such as compiling procedures to native code, as well as latches and lock elimination.

This chapter covered the Hekaton architecture and its main components—memory-optimized tables, hash and range indexes, and natively compiled stored procedures were explained in great detail. Finally, the AMR tool, which can help you decide which tables and stored procedures you can move to In-Memory OLTP, was explained. Although Hekaton includes several limitations on its first release in SQL Server 2014, Microsoft has said those limitations will be lifted in future releases.

Chapter 8

Plan Caching

In This Chapter

We have covered how the optimization process produces a query plan. This chapter deals with what happens to those plans. Understanding how the plan cache works is extremely important for the performance of your queries and SQL Server in general. Query optimization is a relatively expensive operation, so if plans can be cached and reused, this optimization cost will be avoided. Trying to minimize this cost saves on optimization time and server resources such as CPU. Plan caching also needs to be balanced with keeping the plan cache size to a minimum so memory resources can be used by your queries.

However, there might be cases when reusing a plan is not appropriate and would instead create a performance problem. This chapter shows how to identify those performance problems and what the available solutions are. Although parameter sniffing is sometimes seen as something bad, it is, in fact, a performance optimization that allows SQL Server to optimize a query for the particular parameter values initially passed in. The fact that it does not work fine in all cases is what has given it somewhat of a bad reputation, and is usually referred to as the parameter-sniffing problem.

Batch Compilation and Recompilation

As mentioned in Chapter 1, every time a batch is submitted to SQL Server for execution, SQL Server first checks the plan cache to see if an execution plan for that batch already exists. Query optimization is a relatively expensive operation, so if a valid plan is available in the plan cache and can be used, the optimization process can be skipped and the associated cost of this step, in terms of optimization time, CPU resources, and so on, can be avoided. If a plan is not found, the batch is compiled to generate an execution plan for all queries in the stored procedure, the trigger, or the dynamic SQL batch.

The query optimizer begins by loading all the "interesting" statistics and also validating whether any of these statistics are outdated. It then updates any outdated statistics, except in cases where the AUTO_UPDATE_STATISTICS_ASYNC configuration option is used, in which case the query optimizer will use the existing statistics, even if they are out of date. In this case, the statistics are updated asynchronously, ready for the next query optimization that may require them. The query optimizer then proceeds with the optimization process, which was explained in detail in Chapter 3.

If a plan is found in the plan cache or a new one is created, it can now be executed. Query execution technically begins at this point, as shown in Figure 8-1, but the plan is still validated for correctness-related reasons, which includes schema changes. If the schema is not valid, the plan is discarded and the batch or individual query is compiled again. If the schema is valid, the query optimizer then checks for data statistics changes, looking for new applicable statistics or outdated statistics. If newer statistics are available, the plan is discarded and the batch or individual query is compiled again. Such compilations are known as "recompilations." As you may have noticed, recompilations are performed for good reasons—both to ensure plan correctness and plan optimality (that is, to obtain potentially faster query execution plans). Recompilations may also need to be monitored to make sure they are not occurring too frequently and causing performance issues. The entire compilation and recompilation process is summarized in Figure 8-1.

You can look for excessive compiles and recompiles using the SQL Compilations/sec and SQL Re-Compilations/sec counters of the SQLServer:SQL Statistics object in Windows System Monitor. SQL Compilations/sec allows you to see the number of compilations per second. Because plans are cached and reused, after SQL Server user activity is stable, this value should reach a steady state. SQL Re-Compilations/sec allows you to see the number of recompiles per second. As shown earlier, recompilations are performed for good reasons, but generally you want the number of recompiles to be low.

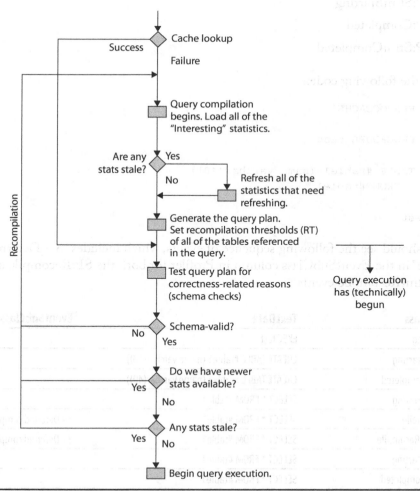

Figure 8-1   *Compilation and recompilation process*

Once you know you have a high number of recompiles, you can use the SP:Recompile and SQL:StmtRecompile trace events or the sql_statement_recompile extended event to troubleshoot and get additional information. As an example, let's look at the following exercise. Start a Profiler session on your test instance and select the following trace events (some of which were covered in Chapter 2). These are located in the Stored Procedures event class and the TSQL event class.

▶ SP:Recompile

▶ SQL:StmtRecompile

▶ SP:Starting

▶ SP:StmtStarting

▶ SP:Completed

▶ SP:StmtCompleted

Run the following code:

```
DBCC FREEPROCCACHE
GO
CREATE PROCEDURE test
AS
CREATE TABLE #table1 (name varchar(40))
SELECT * FROM #table1
GO
EXEC test
```

You should see the following sequence of events, which includes "3 – Deferred compile" in the EventSubClass column in Profiler for both the SP:Recompile and SQL:StmtRecompile events.

EventClass	TextData	EventSubClass
SP:Starting	EXEC test	
SP:StmtStarting	CREATE TABLE #table1 (name varchar(40))	
SP:StmtCompleted	CREATE TABLE #table1 (name varchar(40))	
SP:StmtStarting	SELECT * FROM #table1	
SP:Recompile	SELECT * FROM #table1	3 - Deferred compile
SQL:StmtRecompile	SELECT * FROM #table1	3 - Deferred compile
SP:StmtStarting	SELECT * FROM #table1	
SP:StmtCompleted	SELECT * FROM #table1	
SP:Completed	EXEC test	

The captured events show a deferred compile caused by the SELECT statement as the reason for the recompiles. Remember that when a stored procedure is executed for the first time, it is also optimized and an execution plan is created as a result. A plan certainly can be created for the CREATE TABLE statement inside the stored procedure. However, the SELECT statement cannot be optimized at this moment because it references the table #table1, which does not exist yet. Remember that this is still the optimization process, and in order to create the object #table1, the resulting plan should be first executed. Only after table #table1 is created during the execution of the stored procedure will SQL Server finally be able to optimize the SELECT statement, but this time it will show as a recompile.

Deferred compile is one of the possible values for EventSubClass. You can find the other documented values by running the following query:

```
SELECT map_key, map_value FROM sys.dm_xe_map_values
WHERE name = 'statement_recompile_cause'
```

Running the previous query shows the following output. The descriptions of these values are taken from the "Plan Caching and Recompilation in SQL Server 2012" Microsoft white paper.

SubclassName	SubclassValue	Detailed Reason for Recompilation
Schema changed	1	Schema, bindings, or permissions changed between compile and execute.
Statistics changed	2	Statistics changed.
Deferred compile	3	Recompile because of DNR (Deferred Name Resolution). Object not found at compile time, deferred check to runtime.
Set option change	4	Set option changed in batch.
Temp table changed	5	Temp table schema, binding, or permission changed.
Remote rowset changed	6	Remote rowset schema, binding, or permission changed.
For browse permissions changed	7	Permissions changed in FOR BROWSE (deprecated DBLIB option).
Query notification environment changed	8	Query notification environment changed.
Partition view changed	9	SQL Server sometimes adds data-dependent implied predicates to WHERE clauses of queries in some indexed views. If the underlying data changes, such implied predicates become invalid, and the associated cached query plan needs recompilation.
Cursor options changed	10	Change in cursor options.

(Continued)

SubclassName	SubclassValue	Detailed Reason for Recompilation
Option (Recompile) requested	11	Recompile was requested.
Parameterized plan flushed	12	Parameterized plan was flushed from cache (SQL Server 2008 and later).
Test plan linearization	13	For internal test only (SQL Server 2008 and later).
Plan affecting database version changed	14	For internal test only (SQL Server 2008 and later).
QDS plan forcing policy changed	15	For internal test only (SQL Server 2014).
QDS plan forcing failed	16	For internal test only (SQL Server 2014).

Exploring the Plan Cache

As you saw in Chapter 2, you can use the sys.dm_exec_query_stats DMV to return aggregate performance statistics for cached query plans in SQL Server, where each entry represents a query statement within the cached plan. You saw examples of how to find the most expensive queries using different criteria such as CPU, logical reads, physical reads, logical writes, CLR time, or elapsed time. We also indicated that to get the same information in the past, you would have to capture a usually expensive server trace and analyze the collected data using third-party tools or your own created methods, which was a very time-consuming process. However, although the information of the sys.dm_exec_query_stats DMV is available automatically without any required configuration, it also has a few limitations—mainly that not every query gets cached or that a cached plan can be removed at any time. Despite these limitations, using this DMV is still a huge improvement over running server traces manually.

In addition, as covered in Chapter 5, the Database Engine Tuning Advisor (DTA) can use the information on this DMV when you specify the plan cache as a workload to tune, which uses the most expensive queries based on the query elapsed time. This means that you don't even have to search for the most expensive queries and input them on the DTA—everything is available directly with only a few mouse clicks.

Regardless of the method you are using to capture the most expensive queries in your system, you should always take into account cases where a query alone may not use many resources (for example, CPU cycles), but the cumulative cost could be very high because it is so frequently executed.

Another DMV useful for looking at the plan cache is sys.dm_exec_cached_plans, which returns a row for each query plan that is cached by SQL Server. We will use this DMV to explore the plan cache in the remaining sections of the chapter, where we will focus mostly on the following three columns:

- **usecounts**   Number of times the cache object has been looked up.
- **cacheobjtype**   The type of object in the plan cache, which can be one of the following:
  - Compiled Plan
  - Compiled Plan Stub
  - Parse Tree   As mentioned in Chapter 3, a query processor component called the algebrizer produces a tree that represents the logical structure of a query. This structure is called an algebrizer tree, although it sometimes may be referred to as a parse tree or a normalized tree, and is later handed off to the query optimizer, which uses it to produce an execution plan. Because the produced execution plan is cached, there is no need to cache these algebrizer trees—the only exception being the trees for views, defaults, and constraints—because they can be referenced by many different queries.
  - Extended Proc   Cached objects that track metadata for an extended stored procedure.
  - CLR Compiled Func
  - CLR Compiled Proc
- **objtype**   The type of object, which can be one of the following:
  - Proc (stored procedure)
  - Prepared (prepared statement)
  - Adhoc (ad hoc query)
  - ReplProc (replication-filter procedure)
  - Trigger
  - View
  - Default
  - UsrTab (user table)
  - SysTab (system table)
  - Check (check constraint)
  - Rule

You can use the sys.dm_os_memory_cache_counters DMV to provide runtime information about the number of entries in the plan cache, along with the amount of memory allocated and in use. The following query provides a quick summary of what you can see in detail on the sys.dm_exec_cached_plans DMV:

```
SELECT * FROM sys.dm_os_memory_cache_counters
WHERE type IN ('CACHESTORE_OBJCP', 'CACHESTORE_SQLCP', 'CACHESTORE_PHDR',
    'CACHESTORE_XPROC')
```

Notice that we are filtering the query to the following four cache stores:

▶ **CACHESTORE_OBJCP**   Used for stored procedures, functions, and triggers

▶ **CACHESTORE_SQLCP**   Used for ad hoc and prepared queries

▶ **CACHESTORE_PHDR**   Used for algebrizer trees of views, defaults, and constraints

▶ **CACHESTORE_XPROC**   Used for extended procedures

Finally, although not directly related to the plan cache, new with SQL Server 2014 (and only on the Enterprise edition), SQL Server allows using nonvolatile storage, usually solid-state drives (SSD), as an extension to the memory subsystem rather than the disk subsystem. This feature is known as the "buffer pool extension" and is configured using the new BUFFER POOL EXTENSION clause of the ALTER SERVER CONFIGURATION statement. In addition, you can use the is_in_bpool_extension column of the sys.dm_os_buffer_descriptors DMV to return information about all the data pages currently in the SQL Server buffer pool that are also being used by the buffer pool extension feature. For more details about this new feature, refer to Books Online.

How to Remove Plans

So far in this book we have made extensive use of the DBCC FREEPROCCACHE statement because it makes it very easy to clean the entire plan cache for testing purposes, and by this point you should be aware that you need to be extremely careful about using it in a production environment. Along with this are some other statements that can allow you to be more selective when cleaning the plan cache, which is an instance-wide resource. You may clean the plans for a specific database, a resource governor pool, or even an individual plan. Here is a summary of these statements:

▶ `DBCC FREEPROCCACHE [ ( { plan_handle | sql_handle | pool_name } ) ]`

This statement can be used to remove all the cache entries from the plan cache, a particular plan by specifying a plan handle or SQL handle, or all the plans associated with a specified resource pool.

▶ DBCC FREESYSTEMCACHE ('ALL' [, pool_name])

This statement releases all unused cache entries from all caches, in addition to the plan cache. ALL can be used to specify all supported caches, and pool_name can be used to specify a resource governor pool cache.

▶ DBCC FLUSHPROCINDB(db_id)

This statement can be used to remove all the cache entries for a specific database.

In addition, you need to be aware that many other statements that you run in a SQL Server instance can remove the plans for the entire instance or a specific database. For example, detaching or restoring a database or changing some SQL Server configuration options can remove all the plans for the entire cache. Some ALTER DATABASE choices may remove all the plans for a specific database. For an entire list, refer to Books Online.

Parameterization

We briefly introduced autoparameterization in Chapter 2 while covering the query_ hash and plan_hash values. To understand how SQL Server caches a plan, along with the different mechanisms by which a plan can be reused, you need to understand parameterization in more detail. Parameterization allows an execution plan to be reused by automatically replacing literal values in statements with parameters. Let's examine those queries again, but this time using the sys.dm_exec_cached_plans DMV, which you can use to return each query plan presently cached by SQL Server. One particular column, usecounts, will be useful because it returns the number of times a specific cache object has been looked up in the plan cache, basically indicating the number of times the plan has been reused. The cacheobjtype and objtype columns, which were introduced in the previous section, will be used as well.

Let's take a look at the following query:

```
DBCC FREEPROCCACHE
GO
SELECT * FROM Person.Address
WHERE StateProvinceID = 79
GO
SELECT * FROM Person.Address
WHERE StateProvinceID = 59
GO
SELECT * FROM sys.dm_exec_cached_plans
CROSS APPLY sys.dm_exec_sql_text(plan_handle)
WHERE text like '%Person%'
```

We get the following output, abbreviated to fit the page. You can ignore the first two result sets showing the data from the Person.Address table and the query using the sys .dm_exec_cached_plans itself, which appears in the third result set.

usecounts	cacheobjtype	objtype	text
1	Compiled Plan	Adhoc	SELECT * FROM Person.Address WHERE StateProvinceID = 59
1	Compiled Plan	Adhoc	SELECT * FROM Person.Address WHERE StateProvinceID = 79

In this case we see that each sentence or batch was compiled into its own execution plan, even when they only differ on the value for StateProvinceID. SQL Server is, by default, very conservative about deciding when to autoparameterize a query, so in this case, no plan was reused because it is not safe to do it ("not safe" meaning that by doing it there is a potential for performance degradation). In fact, if you take a look at the plan (for example, by using the sys.dm_exec_query_plan DMF, introduced in Chapter 1) and the plan_handle column of the sys.dm_exec_cached_plans, as shown in the following query, you could see that they are different execution plans—one using an Index Seek/ Key Lookup combination and the second one using a Clustered Index Scan. The query will return the query text along with a link that you can click to show the graphical plan.

```
SELECT text, query_plan FROM sys.dm_exec_cached_plans
CROSS APPLY sys.dm_exec_sql_text(plan_handle)
CROSS APPLY sys.dm_exec_query_plan(plan_handle)
WHERE text like '%Person%'
```

As mentioned in Chapter 2, because a filter with an equality comparison on StateProvinceID could return zero, one, or more rows, it is not considered safe for SQL Server to autoparameterize the query. That is, if the query optimizer decides that if for different parameters different execution plans may be produced, then it is not safe to parameterize.

Autoparameterization

However, if we use the second version of the queries, like in

```
DBCC FREEPROCCACHE
GO
SELECT * FROM Person.Address
WHERE AddressID = 12
GO
SELECT * FROM Person.Address
WHERE AddressID = 37
GO
SELECT * FROM sys.dm_exec_cached_plans
```

```
CROSS APPLY sys.dm_exec_sql_text(plan_handle)
WHERE text like '%Person%'
```

we get the following output, again abbreviated to fit the page:

usecounts	cacheobjtype	objtype	text
1	Compiled Plan	Adhoc	SELECT * FROM Person.Address WHERE AddressID = 37
1	Compiled Plan	Adhoc	SELECT * FROM Person.Address WHERE AddressID = 12
2	Compiled Plan	Prepared	(@1 tinyint)SELECT * FROM [Person].[Address] WHERE [AddressID]=@1

Because in this case AddressID is part of a unique index, an equality predicate on AddressID will always return a maximum of one record, so it is safe for the query optimizer to autoparameterize the query and reuse the same plan, as shown in the last row, with a usecounts value of 2 and objtype of Prepared. Autoparameterization is also called "simple parameterization" and is usually applied to those queries whose parameterized form would result in a trivial plan. The first two rows in this example are really considered shell queries and do not contain a full execution plan, which you can verify by using the sys.dm_exec_query_plan DMF, as shown earlier.

The Optimize for Ad Hoc Workloads Option

Optimize for Ad Hoc Workloads is a configuration option introduced with SQL Server 2008 that can be very helpful in cases where you have a large number of ad hoc queries with a low or no possibility of reuse. When this option is used, SQL Server will store a small compiled plan stub in the plan cache when a query is optimized for the first time instead of the full execution plan. Only after a second optimization, the plan stub is replaced with the full execution plan. Avoiding plans that are never reused can help to minimize the size of the plan cache and therefore free up system memory. In fact, there is basically no downside to using this option, so you may consider enabling it for every SQL Server installation.

Let's look at an example using sp_configure to enable this option. Execute the following statements:

```
EXEC sp_configure 'optimize for ad hoc workloads', 1
RECONFIGURE
DBCC FREEPROCCACHE
GO
SELECT * FROM Person.Address
WHERE StateProvinceID = 79
GO
SELECT * FROM sys.dm_exec_cached_plans
CROSS APPLY sys.dm_exec_sql_text(plan_handle)
WHERE text like '%Person%'
```

At this moment, we have enabled the Optimize for Ad Hoc Workloads configuration option at the instance level, and after the execution of the first SELECT statement, we see the following output:

usecounts	size_in_bytes	cacheobjtype	objtype	text
1	352	Compiled Plan Stub	Adhoc	SELECT * FROM Person.Address WHERE StateProvinceID = 79

As you can see, the compiled plan stub is a small object using a small number of bytes (in this case, 352). The usecounts column is always 1 for a compiled plan stub because it is never reused. It is also worth clarifying that a plan stub is not the same as the shell query mentioned earlier in this section.

Now execute the following statements:

```
SELECT * FROM Person.Address
WHERE StateProvinceID = 79
GO
SELECT * FROM sys.dm_exec_cached_plans
CROSS APPLY sys.dm_exec_sql_text(plan_handle)
WHERE text like '%Person%'
```

We get the following output:

usecounts	size_in_bytes	cacheobjtype	objtype	text
1	16384	Compiled Plan	Adhoc	SELECT * FROM Person.Address WHERE StateProvinceID = 79

After the query is optimized the second time, the compiled plan stub is replaced with a full execution plan, as shown on the cacheobjtype column. Also notice that the size of the plan is considerable larger than the plan stub (in this case, 16,384 bytes).

However, keep in mind that although this configuration option can be useful in scenarios where you may not have control over the queries submitted to SQL Server, it does not mean that writing a large number of ad hoc queries is recommended or encouraged. Using explicit parameterization (for example, with stored procedures) is recommended instead. Finally, although it is recommended to keep this configuration option enabled in your environments, don't forget to disable it to continue testing the remaining code in the book using the default configuration.

```
EXEC sp_configure 'optimize for ad hoc workloads', 0
RECONFIGURE
```

Forced Parameterization

Remember the first example in this section, using the StateProvinceID = 79 predicate, when it was not safe for SQL Server to parameterize? There might be some special cases where you want to parameterize similar queries if you know that using the same plan can provide better performance. Although you could create stored procedures to do just that, if your application generates ad hoc SQL calls, there is an option introduced with SQL Server 2008 that can help you do that—and without changing a single line of application source code. This option is forced parameterization, which can be set at the database level or for a specific query. Forced parameterization applies to SELECT, INSERT, UPDATE, and DELETE statements, and it is subject to certain limitations, which are documented in Books Online.

To enable this feature and test how it works, enable forced parameterization at the database level by running the following statement:

```
ALTER DATABASE AdventureWorks2012 SET PARAMETERIZATION FORCED
```

Then run the following queries again:

```
DBCC FREEPROCCACHE
GO
SELECT * FROM Person.Address
WHERE StateProvinceID = 79
GO
SELECT * FROM Person.Address
WHERE StateProvinceID = 59
GO
SELECT * FROM sys.dm_exec_cached_plans
CROSS APPLY sys.dm_exec_sql_text(plan_handle)
WHERE text like '%Person%'
```

Different from our first example, when we got two distinct plans, one customized for each query, this time we get only one, as shown in the following output:

usecounts	cacheobjtype	objtype	text
1	Compiled Plan	Adhoc	SELECT * FROM Person.Address WHERE StateProvinceID = 59
1	Compiled Plan	Adhoc	SELECT * FROM Person.Address WHERE StateProvinceID = 79
2	Compiled Plan	Prepared	(@0 int)select * from Person . Address where StateProvinceID = @0

In this case we have only one plan, as shown on the third row. The first two rows are not really execution plans but rather shell queries, as indicated earlier in this section.

You may remember that the original plans created in the first example of this section included one with a Clustered Index Scan and the other with an Index/Key Lookup combination. You may be wondering which plan was selected to be shared for both executions. If you have made it this far in the book, you might easily guess that this plan is defined in the first optimization. If you use the query with the StateProvinceID = 79 predicate first, you will get a plan with a Clustered Index Scan for both executions, whereas if you use the query with StateProvinceID = 59, you get the Index/Key Lookup combination, again for both executions. Using some other values of StateProvinceID may even produce different execution plans.

However, because all the similar queries will be using the same plan, this may not be adequate in all scenarios and should be tested thoroughly in your application to verify that, in fact, it is producing better query performance. In fact, the following section in this chapter talks about problems with queries sensitive to parameters, or what many SQL Server users call the "parameter-sniffing problem."

Finally, there is also the PARAMETERIZATION SIMPLE and PARAMETERIZATION FORCED query hints, which can be used to override the current database-level parameterization setting and can only be used inside a plan guide. For example, if you define the use of ALTER DATABASE AdventureWorks2012 SET PARAMETERIZATION FORCED, as shown earlier, you can define a plan guide including OPTION (PARAMETERIZATION SIMPLE) to override this behavior for a particular query.

Again, don't forget to disable forced parameterization by running the following statement to return to the default parameterization setting:

```
ALTER DATABASE AdventureWorks2012 SET PARAMETERIZATION SIMPLE
```

Stored Procedures

Finally, if you want to explicitly take benefit of parameterization, you have a few choices, which include using stored procedures, user-defined scalar functions, and multistatement table-valued functions. All these objects are designed to promote plan reuse and will show the value Proc on the objtype column of the sys.dm_exec_cached_plans DMV. Therefore, let's take a look and see what happens if you use a query that was not automatically parameterized in a stored procedure using a parameter. Create the following stored procedure:

```
CREATE PROCEDURE test (@stateid int)
AS
SELECT * FROM Person.Address
WHERE StateProvinceID = @stateid
```

And run the following code:

```
DBCC FREEPROCCACHE
GO
exec test @stateid = 79
GO
```

```
exec test @stateid = 59
GO
SELECT * FROM sys.dm_exec_cached_plans
CROSS APPLY sys.dm_exec_sql_text(plan_handle)
WHERE text like '%Person%'
```

We get the following output:

usecounts	cacheobjtype	objtype	text
2	Compiled Plan	Proc	CREATE PROCEDURE test (@stateid int) AS ...

Similar to the case with forced parameterization, where it was important to know which query was optimized first, in the case of a stored procedure, it is also critical to understand that the first optimization will use the parameter provided at that moment to produce the execution plan. In this case, where the parameter 79 is first used, you will notice that both plans are the same and use a Clustered Index Scan operator. You can run the following code, where the parameter 59 is used first, in which case the plan created will use an Index Seek/Key Lookup combination:

```
DBCC FREEPROCCACHE
GO
exec test @stateid = 59
GO
exec test @stateid = 79
GO
SELECT * FROM sys.dm_exec_cached_plans
CROSS APPLY sys.dm_exec_sql_text(plan_handle)
WHERE text like '%Person%'
```

But why are different plans created on each case? We mentioned earlier that in the case of the predicate using AddressID, it is safe for the query optimizer to use the same plan because this column is part of a unique index, and an equality predicate on AddressID will always return a maximum of one record. However, the StateProvinceID is not part of a unique index and has a wide data distribution, which you can see by running the following query:

```
SELECT StateProvinceID, COUNT(*) AS cnt
FROM Person.Address
GROUP BY StateProvinceID
ORDER BY cnt
```

An abbreviated output showing the extremes of the table is provided next, where you can see that for some values of StateProvinceID, only one record was found, whereas for other values, a few thousand records were returned.

StateProvinceID	cnt
32	1
41	1
44	1
59	1
118	1
...	
50	1588
14	1954
79	2636
9	4564

Obviously, in this case the query optimizer will decide which operations to use in the resulting execution plan based on the cardinality estimation of each operation.

Parameter Sniffing

In the previous section we talked about parameterization and plan reuse. In this section we cover in more detail the cases in which reusing a plan can create performance problems. As you saw in Chapter 6, SQL Server can use the histogram of statistics objects to estimate the cardinality of a query, and then use this information to try to produce an optimal execution plan. The query optimizer accomplishes this by first inspecting the values of the query parameters. This behavior is called "parameter sniffing," and it is a very good thing: getting an execution plan tailored to the current parameters of a query naturally improves the performance of your applications. This chapter has explained that the plan cache can store these execution plans so that they can be reused the next time the same query needs to be executed. This saves optimization time and CPU resources because the query does not need to be optimized again.

However, although the query optimizer and the plan cache work well together most of the time, some performance problems can occasionally appear. Given that the query optimizer can produce different execution plans for syntactically identical queries, depending on their parameters, caching and reusing only one of these plans may create a performance issue for alternative instances of this query that would benefit from a better plan. This is a known problem with T-SQL code using explicit parameterization, such as stored procedures. In this section, I'll show you more details about this problem, along with a few recommendations on how to fix it.

To see an example, let's write a simple stored procedure using the Sales.SalesOrderDetail table on the AdventureWorks2012 database (at this point you may have to drop a previous version of the test procedure, if it exists):

```
CREATE PROCEDURE test (@pid int)
AS
SELECT * FROM Sales.SalesOrderDetail
WHERE ProductID = @pid
```

Run the following statement to execute the stored procedure:

```
EXEC test @pid = 897
```

The query optimizer estimates that only a few records will be returned by this query, and it produces the execution plan shown in Figure 8-2, which uses an Index Seek operator to quickly find the records on an existing nonclustered index, and a Key Lookup operator to search on the base table for the remaining columns requested by the query.

This combination of Index Seek and Key Lookup operators was a good choice because, although it's a relatively expensive combination, the query was highly selective. However, what if a different parameter is used, producing a less selective predicate? For example, try the following query, including a SET STATISTICS IO ON statement to display the amount of disk activity generated by the query:

```
SET STATISTICS IO ON
GO
EXEC test @pid = 870
GO
```

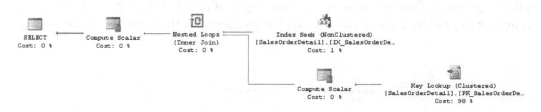

Figure 8-2   *Plan using Index Seek and Key Lookup operators*

The Messages tab will show the following output:

```
Table 'SalesOrderDetail'. Scan count 1, logical reads 18038, physical reads 57,
read-ahead reads 447, lob logical reads 0, lob physical reads 0,
lob read-ahead reads 0.
```

As you can see, on this execution alone, SQL Server is performing 18,038 logical reads when the base table only has 1,246 pages; therefore, it's using over 14 times more I/O operations than just simply scanning the entire table. As you saw in Chapter 4, performing Index Seeks plus Key Lookups on the base table, which uses random I/Os, is a very expensive operation. Note that you may get slightly different values in your own copy of the AdventureWorks2012 database.

Now clear the plan cache to remove the execution plan currently held in memory and then run the stored procedure again, using the same parameter, as shown next:

```
DBCC FREEPROCCACHE
GO
EXEC test @pid = 870
GO
```

This time, you'll get a totally different execution plan. The I/O information now will show that only 1,246 pages were read, and the execution plan will include a Clustered Index Scan, as shown in Figure 8-3. Because this time, there was no optimized version of the stored procedure in the plan cache, SQL Server optimized it from scratch using the new parameter and created a new optimal execution plan.

Of course, this doesn't mean you're not supposed to trust your stored procedures any more or that maybe all your code is incorrect. This is just a problem that you need to be aware of and research, especially if you have queries where performance changes dramatically when different parameters are introduced. If you happen to have this problem, you have a few choices available, which we'll explore next.

Another related problem is that you don't have control over the lifetime of a plan in the cache, so every time a plan is removed from the cache, the newly created execution plan may depend on whichever parameter happens to be passed next. Some of the following choices allow you to have a certain degree of plan stability by asking the query optimizer to produce a plan based on a typical parameter or the average column density.

Figure 8-3   *Plan using a Clustered Index Scan*

Optimize for a Typical Parameter

There might be cases when most of the executions of a query use the same execution plan and you want to avoid an ongoing optimization cost by reusing that plan. In these cases, you can use a hint introduced with SQL Server 2005 called OPTIMIZE FOR, which is useful when an optimal plan can be generated for the majority of values used in a specific parameter and in addition can provide more plan stability. As a result, only the few executions using an atypical parameter may not have an optimal plan.

Suppose that almost all the executions of our stored procedure would benefit from the previous plan using an Index Seek and a Key Lookup operator. To take advantage of that, you could write the stored procedure as shown next:

```
ALTER PROCEDURE test (@pid int)
AS
SELECT * FROM Sales.SalesOrderDetail
WHERE ProductID = @pid
OPTION (OPTIMIZE FOR (@pid = 897))
```

When you run the stored procedure for the first time, it will be optimized for the value 897, no matter what parameter value was actually specified for the execution. If you want to check, test the case by running the following:

```
EXEC test @pid = 870
```

You can find the following entry close to the end of the XML plan (or the Parameter List property in a graphical plan):

```
<ParameterList>
  <ColumnReference Column="@pid" ParameterCompiledValue="(897)"
    ParameterRuntimeValue="(870)" />
</ParameterList>
```

This entry clearly shows which parameter value was used during optimization and which one was used during execution. In this case, the stored procedure is optimized only once, and the plan is stored in the plan cache and reused as many times as needed. The benefit of using this hint, in addition to avoiding optimization cost, is that you have total control over which plan is produced during the query optimization and stored in the plan cache. The OPTIMIZE FOR query hint can also allow you to use more than one parameter, separated by commas.

Optimize on Every Execution

If using different parameters produces different execution plans and you want the best performance for every query, the solution might be to optimize for every execution. You will get the best possible plan on every execution, but will end up paying for the optimization cost, so you'll need to decide if that's a worthwhile trade-off. To do this, use the RECOMPILE hint, as shown next:

```
ALTER PROCEDURE test (@pid int)
AS
SELECT * FROM Sales.SalesOrderDetail
WHERE ProductID = @pid
OPTION (RECOMPILE)
```

Using OPTION (RECOMPILE) can also allow the values of local variables to be sniffed, as shown in the next section. Not surprisingly, this option will return "Option (Recompile) requested" in the EventSubClass column in SQL Trace for both the SP:Recompile and SQL:StmtRecompile events, as you saw earlier in this chapter.

Local Variables and the OPTIMIZE FOR UNKNOWN Hint

Another solution that has been traditionally implemented in the past is the use of local variables in queries instead of parameters. As mentioned in Chapter 6, the query optimizer is not able to see the values of local variables at optimization time because these values are only known at execution time. However, by using local variables, you are disabling parameter sniffing, which basically means that the query optimizer will not be able to access the statistics histogram to find an optimal plan for the query. Instead, it will rely on just the density information of the statistics object, a subject also covered in Chapter 6.

This solution will simply ignore the parameter values and use the same execution plan for all the executions, but at least you're getting a consistent plan every time. A variation of the OPTIMIZE FOR hint shown previously is the OPTIMIZE FOR UNKNOWN hint. This hint was introduced with SQL Server 2008 and has the same effect as using local variables. A benefit of the OPTIMIZE FOR UNKNOWN hint compared with OPTIMIZE FOR is that it does not require you to specify a value for a parameter. Also, you don't have to worry if a specified value becomes atypical over time.

Running the following two versions of our stored procedure will have equivalent outcomes and will produce the same execution plan. The first version uses local variables, and the second one uses the OPTIMIZE FOR UNKNOWN hint.

```
ALTER PROCEDURE test (@pid int)
AS
DECLARE @p int = @pid
```

```
SELECT * FROM Sales.SalesOrderDetail
WHERE ProductID = @p

ALTER PROCEDURE test (@pid int)
AS
SELECT * FROM Sales.SalesOrderDetail
WHERE ProductID = @pid
OPTION (OPTIMIZE FOR UNKNOWN)
```

In this case, the query optimizer will create the plan using the Clustered Index Scan shown previously, no matter which parameter you use to execute the stored procedure. Note that the OPTIMIZE FOR UNKNOWN query hint will apply to all the parameters used in a query unless you use the following syntax to target only a specific parameter:

```
ALTER PROCEDURE test (@pid int)
AS
SELECT * FROM Sales.SalesOrderDetail
WHERE ProductID = @pid
OPTION (OPTIMIZE FOR (@pid UNKNOWN))
```

Finally, keep in mind that parameter sniffing is a desired optimization, and you would only want to disable it when you have any of the problems mentioned in this section and if it improves the general performance of your query.

It is interesting to note that as of SQL Server 2005, where statement-level compilation was introduced to allow the optimization of an individual statement, it was technically possible to sniff the value of local variables in the same way as with a parameter. However, this behavior was not implemented because there was already a lot of code using local variables to explicitly disable parameter sniffing. Local variables, however, can be sniffed while using the RECOMPILE query hint explained earlier. For example, let's use the following code with both local variables and the OPTION (RECOMPILE) hint:

```
ALTER PROCEDURE test (@pid int)
AS
DECLARE @p int = @pid
SELECT * FROM Sales.SalesOrderDetail
WHERE ProductID = @p
OPTION (RECOMPILE)
```

And then run the following:

```
EXEC test @pid = 897
```

The query optimizer will be able to see the value of the local variable (in this case, 897) and get a plan optimized for that specific value (in this case, the plan with the Index Seek/ Key Lookup operations, instead of the plan with the Clustered Index Scan, shown earlier when no value could be sniffed).

Although Chapter 6 explained how to use the histogram and the density vector of the statistics object to estimate the cardinality of a query, let's review this again here from the point of view of disabling parameter sniffing. Any of the stored procedures at the beginning of this section—either using local variables or the OPTIMIZE FOR UNKNOWN hint—will return the plan in Figure 8-4, with an estimated cardinality of 456.079.

Let's see how SQL Server is obtaining the value 456.079 and what the reasoning behind this is. As explained in Chapter 6, density is defined as follows:

1 / number of distinct values

The SalesOrderDetail table has 266 distinct values for ProductID, so the density is calculated as 1 / 266, or 0.003759399, which you can verify by looking at the statistics object (for example, using the DBCC SHOW_STATISTICS statement). One assumption in the statistics mathematical model used by SQL Server is the uniformity assumption, and because in this case SQL Server cannot use the histogram, the uniformity assumption tells us that for any given value, the data distribution is the same. To obtain the estimated number of records, SQL Server will multiply the density by the current total number of records (0.003759399 * 121,317, or 456.079), as shown in the plan. This is also the same as dividing the total number of records by the number of distinct values (121,317 / 266, which also equals 456.079).

Finally, the benefit of using the OPTIMIZE FOR UNKNOWN hint is that you only need to optimize the query once and can reuse the produced plan many times. Also, there is no need to specify a value like in the OPTIMIZE FOR hint.

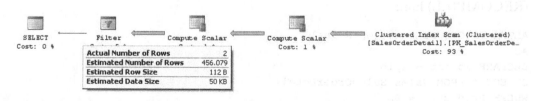

Figure 8-4   *Cardinality estimate with parameter sniffing disabled*

Disabling Parameter Sniffing

As mentioned in the previous section, when you use local variables in a query to avoid using a stored procedure parameter or when you use the OPTIMIZE FOR UNKNOWN query hint, you are basically disabling parameter sniffing. Microsoft has also published trace flag 4136 to disable parameter sniffing at the instance level. As described in Microsoft Knowledge Base article 980653, this trace flag was first introduced as a cumulative update for older versions of SQL Server such as SQL Server 2005 SP3, SQL Server 2008 SP1, and SQL Server 2008 R2, and it is available on the latest versions as well, including SQL Server 2014. There are still three cases where this trace flag has no effect:

▶ Queries using the OPTIMIZE FOR query hint

▶ Queries using the OPTION (RECOMPILE) hint

▶ Queries in a stored procedure using the WITH RECOMPILE option

As with using forced parameterization at the database level, this should be considered an extreme option that can only be used on some limited cases and should be used with caution, making sure you test your application thoroughly to validate that, in fact, it improves performance. In addition, you could use this trace flag if the majority of your queries benefit from disabling parameter sniffing and still use any of the three exceptions listed before for queries that may not. At least Microsoft has recommended that users of their Dynamics AX application consider using this trace flag, as documented at http://blogs.msdn.com/b/axperf/archive/2010/05/07/important-sql-server-change-parameter-sniffing-and-plan-caching.aspx.

Parameter Sniffing and SET Options That Affect Plan Reuse

One interesting problem I've been asked to troubleshoot is when a stored procedure is taking too long to execute or is timing out on a web application but returning immediately when executed directly in SQL Server Management Studio—even for the same parameters. Although there could be a few reasons for a performance problem like this, including blocking, the most frequent reason for this happening is related to a behavior where two different plans were created with different SET options, and at least one of those plans was optimized using a combination of parameters that produced a "bad" plan for some other executions of the same stored procedure with different parameters. Although you may be tempted just to run sp_recompile to force a new optimization and allow the application to continue working, this does not really fix the problem, and it may eventually come back. You might also encounter a similar scenario where you have updated statistics, rebuilt an index, or changed something else to find out that suddenly the problem seems to be fixed. It is not. Those changes probably just forced a new optimization with the "good" parameter you were just testing. Obviously, the best thing to do for this kind of problem is to capture the "bad" plan for further analysis in order to provide a permanent solution. In this section, I show you how to do that.

Remember that, in general, query optimization is an expensive operation, and in order to avoid this optimization cost, the plan cache will try to keep the generated execution plans in memory so they can be reused. However, if a new connection running the same stored procedure has different SET options, it may generate a new plan instead of reusing one already in the plan cache. This new plan can then be reused by later executions of the same stored procedure, but only if the same connection settings are used. A new plan is needed because some of these SET options may impact the choice of an execution plan due to the fact that they affect the results of evaluating constant expressions during the optimization process. Another connection setting, FORCEPLAN, acts similar to a hint, requesting the query optimizer both to preserve the join order as specified on the query syntax and to use nested loop joins only. The following SET options will affect the reuse of execution plans:

- ANSI_NULL_DFLT_OFF
- ANSI_NULL_DFLT_ON
- ANSI_NULLS
- ANSI_PADDING
- ANSI_WARNINGS
- ARITHABORT
- CONCAT_NULL_YIELDS_NULL
- DATEFIRST
- DATEFORMAT
- FORCEPLAN
- LANGUAGE
- NO_BROWSETABLE
- NUMERIC_ROUNDABORT
- QUOTED_IDENTIFIER

> **NOTE**
>
> *The ANSI_NULLS OFF, ANSI_PADDING OFF, and CONCAT_NULL_YIELDS_NULL OFF SET statements and database options have been deprecated. In a future version of SQL Server, these SET statements and database options will always be set to ON.*

Unfortunately, management and development tools such as SQL Server Management Studio, the ADO.NET framework, and even the sqlcmd utility have different SET options in their default configuration. You will find that often the problem is that one of the options, ARITHABORT, is OFF by default in ADO.NET and ON by default in Management Studio. Therefore, it may be possible that, in our example, Management Studio and the web application are actually using distinct cached plans, but the plan created for the web application was not good for some other executions of the same stored procedure with different parameters.

Now let's see how to prove that optimizing with different parameters is, in fact, the problem for your specific instance of the issue. We'll look at how to extract the plans to inspect both the parameters and the SET options used during optimization. Because AdventureWorks2012 does not have the default SET options of a new database, we'll create our own database, copy some data from AdventureWorks2012, and create a new stored procedure. Run the following code to do that:

```
CREATE DATABASE Test
GO
USE Test
GO
SELECT * INTO dbo.SalesOrderDetail
FROM AdventureWorks2012.Sales.SalesOrderDetail
GO
CREATE NONCLUSTERED INDEX IX_SalesOrderDetail_ProductID
ON dbo.SalesOrderDetail(ProductID)
GO
CREATE PROCEDURE test (@pid int)
AS
SELECT * FROM dbo.SalesOrderDetail
WHERE ProductID = @pid
```

Let's test two different applications, executing the stored procedure from both SQL Server Management Studio and a .NET application (see the upcoming sidebar, "C# Code for SET Options Test," for code and instructions to build this application). For the purposes of this test, we want to assume that a plan with a table scan is a bad plan and a plan using an Index Seek/RID Lookup is the optimal one.

Start with a clean plan cache by running the following command:

```
DBCC FREEPROCCACHE
```

Run the .NET application from a command prompt window and provide the value 870 as a parameter. Note that the only purpose of this .NET application is to run the test stored procedure we created earlier.

```
C:\TestApp\test
Enter ProductID: 870
```

At this time, we can start inspecting the plan cache to see the plans available in memory. Run the following script from the Test database (we will be running this script again later during this exercise):

```
SELECT plan_handle, usecounts, pvt.set_options
FROM (
    SELECT plan_handle, usecounts, epa.attribute, epa.value
    FROM sys.dm_exec_cached_plans
        OUTER APPLY sys.dm_exec_plan_attributes(plan_handle) AS epa
    WHERE cacheobjtype = 'Compiled Plan') AS ecpa
PIVOT (MAX(ecpa.value) FOR ecpa.attribute IN ("set_options", "objectid")) AS pvt
WHERE pvt.objectid = OBJECT_ID('dbo.test')
```

You should get an output similar to this:

plan_handle	usecounts	set_options
0x050007002255970F9042B8F801000000010000000000000000000000000 ...	1	251

The output shows that we have one execution plan in the plan cache, it has been used once (as indicated by the usecounts value), and the set_options value (taken from the sys.dm_exec_plan_attributes DMF) is 251. Because this was the first execution of the stored procedure, it was optimized using the parameter 870, which in this case created a plan using a table scan (here, considered a "bad" plan). Now run the application again using a parameter that returns only a few records and that should benefit from an Index Seek/RID Lookup plan:

```
C:\TestApp\test
Enter ProductID: 898
```

If you inspect the plan cache again, you will notice that the plan has been used twice, as noted by the usecounts column; unfortunately, this time it was not good for the second parameter used. In a real production database, this second execution may not perform as expected, taking too long to execute, and it might trigger the developer to try to troubleshoot the problem by running the stored procedure in Management Studio using something like this:

```
EXEC test @pid = 898
```

Now the developer may be confused by the fact that SQL Server is returning a good execution plan and the query is returning its results immediately. Inspecting the plan cache again will show something similar to this:

plan_handle	usecounts	set_options
0x050007002255970FB049B8F801000000001000000000000000000000000 ...	1	4347
0x050007002255970F9042B8F801000000001000000000000000000000000 ...	2	251

You can see that a new plan was added for the Management Studio execution, with a different value for set_options (in this case, 4347).

What to do next? It is time to inspect the plans and look at the SET options and parameters used during the optimization. Select the plan_handle of the first plan created (the one with the set_options value 251 in your own example) and use it to run the following query:

```
SELECT * FROM sys.dm_exec_query_plan(0x050007002255970F9042B
8F801000000001000000000000000000000 …)
```

You can find the SET options at the beginning of the XML plan (also available using the properties window of a graphical execution plan):

```
<StatementSetOptions QUOTED_IDENTIFIER="true" ARITHABORT="false"
CONCAT_NULL_YIELDS_NULL="true" ANSI_NULLS="true" ANSI_PADDING="true"
ANSI_WARNINGS="true" NUMERIC_ROUNDABORT="false" />
```

And you can find the used parameters at the end (also available on the graphical execution plan):

```
<ParameterList>
    <ColumnReference Column="@pid" ParameterCompiledValue="(870)" />
</ParameterList>
```

Do the same for the second plan, and you will get the following information for the SET options:

```
<StatementSetOptions QUOTED_IDENTIFIER="true" ARITHABORT="true"
CONCAT_NULL_YIELDS_NULL="true" ANSI_NULLS="true" ANSI_PADDING="true"
ANSI_WARNINGS="true" NUMERIC_ROUNDABORT="false" />
```

And you will get the following parameter information:

```
<ParameterList>
    <ColumnReference Column="@pid" ParameterCompiledValue="(898)" />
</ParameterList>
```

This information shows that the ARITHABORT SET option has a different value on these plans and that the parameter used to optimize the query on the web application was 870. You can also verify the operators used in the plan—the first one used a table scan and the second one an Index Seek/RID Lookup combination. Now that you have captured the plans, you can force a new optimization so that the application can use a better plan immediately (keeping in mind that this is not a permanent solution). Try this:

```
sp_recompile test
```

You could optionally use the following script to display the configured SET options for a specific set_options value:

```
DECLARE @set_options int = 4347
IF ((1 & @set_options) = 1) PRINT 'ANSI_PADDING'
IF ((4 & @set_options) = 4) PRINT 'FORCEPLAN'
IF ((8 & @set_options) = 8) PRINT 'CONCAT_NULL_YIELDS_NULL'
IF ((16 & @set_options) = 16) PRINT 'ANSI_WARNINGS'
IF ((32 & @set_options) = 32) PRINT 'ANSI_NULLS'
IF ((64 & @set_options) = 64) PRINT 'QUOTED_IDENTIFIER'
IF ((128 & @set_options) = 128) PRINT 'ANSI_NULL_DFLT_ON'
IF ((256 & @set_options) = 256) PRINT 'ANSI_NULL_DFLT_OFF'
IF ((512 & @set_options) = 512) PRINT 'NoBrowseTable'
IF ((4096 & @set_options) = 4096) PRINT 'ARITH_ABORT'
IF ((8192 & @set_options) = 8192) PRINT 'NUMERIC_ROUNDABORT'
IF ((16384 & @set_options) = 16384) PRINT 'DATEFIRST'
IF ((32768 & @set_options) = 32768) PRINT 'DATEFORMAT'
IF ((65536 & @set_options) = 65536) PRINT 'LanguageID'
```

This will return the following output for the set_options value 4347:

```
ANSI_PADDING
CONCAT_NULL_YIELDS_NULL
ANSI_WARNINGS
ANSI_NULLS
QUOTED_IDENTIFIER
ANSI_NULL_DFLT_ON
ARITH_ABORT
```

Now that you have identified that this is, in fact, a problem related to parameter sniffing, you can apply any of the techniques shown earlier in this section.

C# Code for SET Options Test

Use the following code for this test:

```
using System;
using System.Data;
using System.Data.SqlClient;

class Test
{
    static void Main()
    {
        SqlConnection cnn = null;
        SqlDataReader reader = null;

        try
        {
            Console.Write("Enter ProductID: ");
            string pid = Console.ReadLine();

            cnn = new SqlConnection("Data Source=(local);Initial Catalog=Test;
                Integrated Security=SSPI");
            SqlCommand cmd = new SqlCommand();
            cmd.Connection = cnn;
            cmd.CommandText = "dbo.test";
            cmd.CommandType = CommandType.StoredProcedure;
            cmd.Parameters.Add("@pid", SqlDbType.Int).Value = pid;
            cnn.Open();
            reader = cmd.ExecuteReader();
            while (reader.Read())
            {
                Console.WriteLine(reader[0]);
            }
            return;
        }
        catch (Exception e)
        {
            throw e;
        }
        finally
```

(*continued*)

```
        {
            if (cnn != null)
            {
                if (cnn.State != ConnectionState.Closed)
                    cnn.Close();
            }
        }
    }
}
```

Same as with the C# code shown in Chapter 2, to compile this code, you need to run the following in a command prompt window, assuming the code was saved in a file named test.cs:

```
csc test.cs
```

Visual Studio is not required to compile this code, just the Microsoft .NET Framework, which is needed to install SQL Server. Therefore, it will be already installed on your system. You may need to find the location of the .csc executable, though, if it is not included on the system PATH (although it is usually inside the C:\Windows\Microsoft.NET directory). The connection string in the code assumes you are connecting to a default instance of SQL Server using Windows authentication, so you may need to change these values if they are different in your installation.

Summary

This chapter covered plan caching and focused on what you need to know to efficiently reuse query plans. Query optimization is a relatively expensive operation, so if a query can be optimized once and the created plan reused many times, it can greatly improve the performance of your applications. We covered the batch compilation and recompilation process in detail and showed how to identify problems with excessive compilations and recompilations.

Plan reuse is based on query parameterization, so this topic was also covered in detail. We looked at cases where SQL Server decides to automatically parameterize your queries as well as cases when it has to be explicitly defined, through either the use of the forced parameterization configuration option or the use of objects such as stored procedures, user-defined scalar functions, and multistatement table-valued functions.

However, although looking at the parameters of a query helps the query optimizer to produce better execution plans, the occasional reuse of some of these plans can also be a performance problem because they may not be optimal for the same query executed with different parameters. We showed that parameter sniffing is, in fact, a performance optimization, but we also covered solutions to the cases when reusing such plans may not be adequate.

Chapter 9

Data Warehouses

In This Chapter

▶ Data Warehouses
▶ Star Join Query Optimization
▶ Columnstore Indexes
▶ Summary

When we read about high-performing applications in a SQL Server book or article, we usually assume they are talking about transactional applications and obviously OLTP databases. In fact, although I haven't mentioned data warehouses so far in this book, most of the content applies to both OLTP and data warehouse databases. The SQL Server query optimizer can automatically identify and optimize data warehouse queries without any required configuration, so the concepts explained in this book about query optimization, query operators, indexes, statistics, and most of the other topics apply to data warehouses as well.

In this chapter I cover topics specific to data warehouses only. Describing what a data warehouse is also provides us with an opportunity to define OLTP systems and what the differences between both are. I describe how the query optimizer identifies data warehouse queries and cover some of the data warehouse optimizations introduced in the last few versions of SQL Server.

Bitmap filtering, an optimization used in star join queries since SQL Server 2008, can be used to filter out rows from a fact table very early during query processing, thus significantly improving the performance of data warehouse queries. Bitmap filtering is based on Bloom filters, originally conceived by Burton Bloom in 1970.

Columnstore indexes, a feature available since SQL Server 2012, introduces us two new paradigms: columnar-based storage and new batch-processing algorithms. Although this feature had some limitations when it was originally released—mostly the fact that the indexes were not updatable and only nonclustered indexes could be created—these limitations have been addressed in the current release, SQL Server 2014. The star join query optimizations and xVelocity memory-optimized columnstore indexes are Enterprise Edition–only features.

Finally, although outside the scope of this book, it is interesting to mention how new trends such as increasing data volumes and new sources and types of data are changing the traditional data warehouse landscape, and how concepts such as Big Data and solutions such as Apache Hadoop are becoming more popular every day.

Data Warehouses

The information in an organization is usually kept in two forms—in an operational system and in an analytic system—both of which have very different purposes. Although the purpose of an operational system, also known as an online transaction processing (OLTP) system, is to support the execution of a business process, the purpose of an analytic system or data warehouse is to help with the measurement of a business process and business decision making. OLTP systems are based on small, high-performance transactions consisting of INSERT, DELETE, UPDATE, and SELECT statements, whereas a data warehouse is based on large and complex queries of aggregated data. The degree of normalization is another main difference between these systems: whereas an OLTP system will usually be in third normal form, a data warehouse will use a denormalized dimensional model called a star schema. The third normal form used by OLTP systems helps with data integrity and data redundancy problems because update operations need to be updated in one place only. A data warehouse dimensional model is more appropriate for ad hoc complex queries.

In *Star Schema: The Complete Reference* (McGraw-Hill Professional, 2010), Christopher Adamson provides a great summary of the differences between operational and analytic systems, as detailed in Table 9-1.

A dimensional design, when implemented in a relational database such as in SQL Server, is called a star schema. Data warehouses using a star schema use fact and dimension tables, where fact tables contain the business's facts or numerical measures, which can participate in calculations, and dimension tables contain the attributes or descriptions of the facts. Not everything that is numeric is a fact, which can be the case with numeric data such as phone numbers, age, and size information. Additional normalization is sometimes performed within dimension tables in a star schema, which is called a snowflake schema.

SQL Server includes a sample data warehouse database, AdventureWorksDW2012, that follows a snowflake design and will be used in the examples for this chapter. Figure 9-1 shows a diagram with some of the fact and dimension tables of AdventureWorksDW2012.

Fact tables are usually large and can store millions or billions of rows, compared to dimension tables, which are significantly smaller. The size of data warehouse databases tends to range from hundreds of gigabytes to terabytes. Facts are stored as columns in a fact table whereas related dimensions are stored as columns in dimension tables. Fact tables usually have foreign keys to link them to the primary keys of the

	Operational System	Analytic System
Purpose	Execution of a business process	Measurement of a business process
Primary Interaction Style	Insert, update, delete, query	Query
Scope of Interaction	Individual transaction	Aggregated transactions
Query Patterns	Predictable and stable	Unpredictable and changing
Temporal Focus	Current	Current and historic
Design Optimization	Update concurrency	High-performance query
Design Principle	Entity-relationship (ER) design in third normal form (3NF)	Dimensional design (star schema or cube)
Also Known As	Transactional system, online transaction processing (OLTP) system	Data warehouse system, data mart

Table 9-1 *Operational and Analytic Systems Compared*

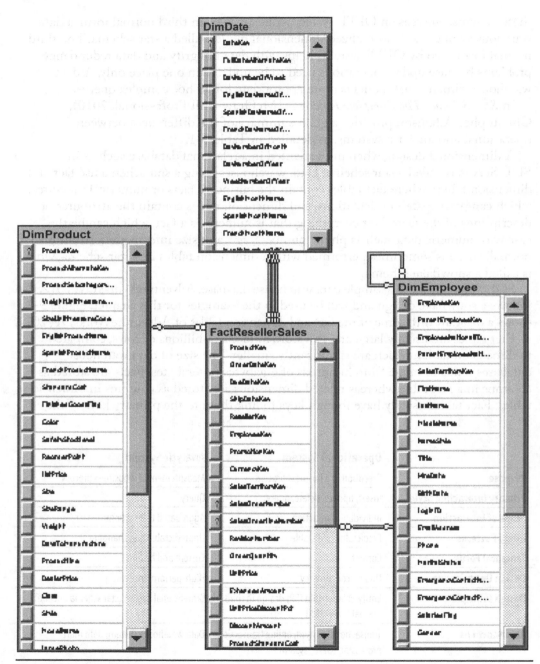

Figure 9-1 *Fact and dimension tables in AdventureWorksDW2012*

dimension tables. When used in queries, facts are usually aggregated or summarized whereas dimensions are used as filters or query predicates. A dimension table also has a surrogate key, usually an integer, which is also the primary key of the table. For example, in AdventureWorksDW2012, the table DimCustomer has CustomerKey, which is also its primary key, and it is defined as an identity.

NOTE

More details about data warehousing and dimensional design can be found in The Data Warehouse Toolkit (Wiley, 2013), *by Ralph Kimball and Margy Ross, and* Star Schema: The Complete Reference, *by Christopher Adamson.*

However, the world of data is rapidly evolving, and new trends such as increasing data volumes and new sources and types of data, along with the new requirement of support for near real-time processing, are changing the traditional data warehouse. In some cases, new approaches are being proposed in response to these trends.

Although SQL Server Enterprise Edition allows you to handle large data warehouses and contains the star join query optimizations and the xVelocity memory-optimized columnstore indexes covered in this chapter, SQL Server is also available as an appliance that can allow companies to handle databases of up to 6PB (petabytes) of data storage. Built on a Multiple Parallel Processing (MPP) architecture with preinstalled software, SQL Server Parallel Data Warehouse provides a highly scalable architecture to help with these large data warehouses.

As the amount of data increases in volume, velocity, and variety, with a wider range of data types and sources, the term *Big Data* has been used to define collections of data sets so large and complex that they cannot be easily managed by traditional data warehouse technologies. Because the traditional data warehouse didn't anticipate Big Data, side-by-side solutions are now being implemented, with one of the solutions being Apache Hadoop. For example, this could be a Hadoop data warehouse next to the relational data warehouse. Microsoft also introduced PolyBase to address the unification of the traditional relational data warehouse with Hadoop, thus giving you the ability to query relational and nonrelational data in Hadoop. PolyBase is integrated within SQL Server Parallel Data Warehouse.

In April 2014, Microsoft announced the Analytics Platform System (APS), which is an appliance solution with hardware and software components that include SQL Server Parallel Data Warehouse and Microsoft's Hadoop distribution, HDInsight, which is based on the Hortonworks Data Platform. For more details about this appliance solution, see http://blogs.technet.com/b/dataplatforminsider/archive/2014/05/20/architecture-of-the-microsoft-analytics-platform-system.aspx.

Star Join Query Optimization

Queries that join a fact table to dimension tables are called star join queries, and SQL Server includes special optimizations for this kind of query. A typical star join query joins a fact table with one or more dimension tables, groups by some columns of the dimension tables, and aggregates on one or more columns of the fact table. In addition to the filters applied when the tables are joined, other filters can be applied on the fact and dimension tables. Here is an example of a typical star join query in AdventureWorksDW2012 showing all the characteristics just mentioned:

```
SELECT TOP 10 p.ModelName, p.EnglishDescription,
    SUM(f.SalesAmount) AS SalesAmount
FROM FactResellerSales f JOIN DimProduct p
    ON f.ProductKey = p.ProductKey
JOIN DimEmployee e
    ON f.EmployeeKey = e.EmployeeKey
WHERE f.OrderDateKey >= 20030601
AND e.SalesTerritoryKey = 1
GROUP BY p.ModelName, p.EnglishDescription
ORDER BY SUM(f.SalesAmount) DESC
```

Because sometimes data warehouse implementations do not completely specify the relationships between fact and dimension tables and do not explicitly define foreign key constraints in order to avoid the overhead of constraint enforcement during updates, SQL Server uses heuristics to automatically detect star join queries and can reliably identify fact and dimension tables. One such heuristic is to consider the largest table of the star join query as the fact table, which in addition must have a specified minimum size. In addition, to qualify for a star join query, the join conditions must be inner joins and all the join predicates must be single-column equality predicates. It is worth noting that even in cases where these heuristics do not work correctly and one dimension table is incorrectly chosen as a fact table, a valid plan returning correct data is still selected, although it may not be an efficient one.

Based on the selectivity of a fact table, SQL Server can define three different approaches to optimize star join queries. For highly selective queries, which may return up to 10 percent of the rows of the table, SQL Server may produce a plan with Nested Loops Joins, Index Seeks, and bookmark lookups. For medium selectivity queries, processing anywhere from 10 to 75 percent of the rows in a table, the query optimizer may recommend Hash Joins with bitmap filters, in combination with fact table scans or fact table range scans. Finally, for the least selective of the queries, returning more than 75 percent of the rows of the table, SQL Server may recommend regular Hash Joins with fact table scans. The choice of these operators and plans is not surprising for the most and least selective queries because this is their standard behavior, as explained in

Chapter 4. However, what is new is the choice of Hash Joins and bitmap filtering for medium selectivity queries; therefore, we will be looking at those optimizations next. But first, an introduction to bitmap filters.

Although bitmap filters are used on the star join optimization covered in this section, they have been used in SQL Server since version 7.0. Also, they may appear on other plans, an example of which was shown at the end of the "Parallelism" section in Chapter 4. Bitmap filters are based on Bloom filters, a space-efficient probabilistic data structure originally conceived by Burton Bloom in 1970. Bitmap filters are used in parallel plans, and they greatly improve the performance of these plans by performing a semi-join reduction early in the query before rows are passed through the parallelism operator. Although it is more common to see bitmap filters with Hash Joins, they could be used by Merge Joins as well.

Also explained in Chapter 4, a hash join operation has two phases: build and probe. In the build phase, all the join keys of the build or outer table are hashed into a hash table. A bitmap is created as a byproduct of this operation, and bits in the array are set to correspond with hash values that contain at least one row. The bitmap is later examined when the probe or inner table is being read. If the bit is not set, the row cannot have a match in the outer table and is discarded.

Bitmap filters are used in star join queries to filter out rows from the fact table very early during query processing. This optimization was introduced in SQL Server 2008, and your existing queries can automatically benefit from it without any changes. This optimization is referred to as "optimized bitmap filtering" in order to differentiate it from the standard bitmap filtering available in previous versions of SQL Server. Although standard bitmap filtering can be used in plans with hash and Merge Joins, as indicated earlier, optimized bitmap filtering is only allowed on plans with Hash Joins. The prefix "Opt_" in the name of a bitmap operator indicates an optimized bitmap filter is being used.

To filter out rows from the fact table, SQL Server builds the hash tables on the "build input" side of the hash join (which in our case is a dimension table), constructing a bitmap filter that is an array of bits, which is later used to filter out rows from the fact table that do not qualify for the Hash Joins. There may be some false positives, meaning that some of the rows may not participate in the join, but there are no false negatives. SQL Server then passes the bitmaps to the appropriate operators to help remove nonqualifying rows from the fact table early in the query plan.

Multiple filters can be applied to a single operator, and optimized bitmap filters can be applied to exchange operators, such as Distribute Streams and Repartition Streams operators, and filter operators. An additional optimization while using bitmap filters is the in-row optimization, which allows for eliminating rows even earlier during query processing. When the bitmap filter is based on not-nullable big or bigint columns, the bitmap filter may be applied directly to the table operation, an example of which is shown next.

For this example, let's run the following query:

```
SELECT TOP 10 p.ModelName, p.EnglishDescription,
    SUM(f.SalesAmount) AS SalesAmount
FROM FactResellerSales f JOIN DimProduct p
    ON f.ProductKey = p.ProductKey
JOIN DimEmployee e
    ON f.EmployeeKey = e.EmployeeKey
WHERE f.OrderDateKey >= 20030601
AND e.SalesTerritoryKey = 1
GROUP BY p.ModelName, p.EnglishDescription
ORDER BY SUM(f.SalesAmount) DESC
```

With the current size of AdventureWorksDW2012, this query is not even expensive enough to generate a parallel plan because its cost is only 3.24627. Although we can do a little trick to simulate more records on this database, I encourage you to test this or similar queries in your data warehouse development or test environment.

To simulate a larger table with 100,000 rows and 10,000 pages, run the following statement:

```
UPDATE STATISTICS dbo.FactResellerSales WITH ROWCOUNT = 100000, PAGECOUNT = 10000
```

NOTE

The undocumented ROWCOUNT and PAGECOUNT choices of the UPDATE STATISTICS statement were introduced in Chapter 6. As such, they should not be used in a production environment. They will be used in this exercise only to simulate a larger table.

Clean the plan cache by running a statement such as

```
DBCC FREEPROCCACHE
```

and then run the previous star join query again. This time, we get a more expensive query and a different plan, as shown in Figure 9-2.

Figure 9-2   *Plan with an optimized bitmap filter*

As explained earlier, you can see that a bitmap filter was created on the build input of the hash join, which in this case reads data from the DimEmployee dimension table. Looking at Defined Values in the bitmap operator's Properties window, you can see that the name of the bitmap filter in this case shows the value Opt_Bitmap1006. Now look at the properties of the Clustered Index Scan operator, which are shown in Figure 9-3. Here, you can see that the previously created bitmap filter, Opt_Bitmap1006, is used in the Predicate section to filter out rows from the fact table FactResellerSales. Also notice the IN ROW parameter, which shows that in-row optimization was also used, thus filtering out rows from the plan as early as possible (in this case, from the Clustered Index Scan operation).

Finally, run the following statement to correct the page and row count we just changed on the FactResellerSales table:

```
DBCC UPDATEUSAGE (AdventureWorksDW2012, 'dbo.FactResellerSales') WITH COUNT_ROWS
```

Clustered Index Scan (Clustered)	
Scanning a clustered index, entirely or only a range.	
Physical Operation	Clustered Index Scan
Logical Operation	Clustered Index Scan
Actual Execution Mode	Row
Estimated Execution Mode	Row
Storage	RowStore
Actual Number of Rows	6208
Actual Number of Batches	0
Estimated I/O Cost	7.40979
Estimated Operator Cost	7.46487 (91%)
Estimated Subtree Cost	7.46487
Estimated CPU Cost	0.0550785
Estimated Number of Executions	1
Number of Executions	4
Estimated Number of Rows	10739.1
Estimated Row Size	27 B
Actual Rebinds	0
Actual Rewinds	0
Ordered	False
Node ID	17

Predicate
[AdventureWorksDW2012].[dbo].[FactResellerSales].
[OrderDateKey] as [F].[OrderDateKey]>=(20030601) AND
PROBE([Opt_Bitmap1006],[AdventureWorksDW2012].[dbo].
[FactResellerSales].[EmployeeKey] as [F].[EmployeeKey],N'[IN
ROW]')
Object
[AdventureWorksDW2012].[dbo].[FactResellerSales].
[PK_FactResellerSales_SalesOrderNumber_SalesOrderLineNum
ber] [F]
Output List
[AdventureWorksDW2012].[dbo].
[FactResellerSales].ProductKey, [AdventureWorksDW2012].
[dbo].[FactResellerSales].EmployeeKey,
[AdventureWorksDW2012].[dbo].
[FactResellerSales].SalesAmount

Figure 9-3 *Clustered Index Scan operator properties*

Columnstore Indexes

One of the main new features when SQL Server 2012 was originally released was columnstore indexes. By using a new column-based storage approach and new query-processing algorithms, memory-optimized columnstore indexes were designed to improve the performance of data warehouse queries by several orders of magnitude. Although the inability to update data was the biggest drawback when this feature was originally released back in 2012, the current release, SQL Server 2014, has addressed this limitation and now has the ability to directly update its data and even create a columnstore clustered index on it. The fact that columnstore indexes were originally limited to only nonclustered indexes was also considered a limitation because it required duplicated data on an already very large object such as a fact table.

As mentioned at the beginning of this chapter, in an OLTP system, transactions usually access one or a few rows whereas typical data warehouse star join queries access a large number of rows. In addition, an OLTP transaction usually accesses all the columns in the row, which is opposite to a star join query, where usually only a few columns are required. This data access pattern showed that a columnar approach could benefit data warehouse workloads.

The traditional storage approach used by SQL Server is to store rows on data pages, which we call a "rowstore." Rowstores in SQL Server include heaps and B-tree structures such as standard clustered and nonclustered indexes. Column-oriented storage like that used by columnstore indexes dedicates entire database pages to store data from a single column. Rowstore and columnstore are compared in Figure 9-4, where a rowstore contains pages with rows, each row containing all its columns, and a columnstore contains pages with data for only one column, labeled C1, C2, and so on. Because the data is stored in columns, a question frequently asked is how a row is retrieved from this columnar storage. It is the position of the value in the column that indicates to which row this data belongs. For example, the first value on each page (C1, C2, and so on) shown on Figure 9-4 belongs to the first row, the second value on each page belongs to the second row, and so on.

Column-oriented storage is not new and has been used before by some other database vendors. Columnstore indexes are based on Microsoft xVelocity technology, formerly known as VertiPaq, which is also used in SQL Server Analysis Services (SSAS), PowerPivot for Excel, and SharePoint. As with Hekaton, covered in Chapter 7, columnstore indexes are an in-memory technology.

As mentioned, columnstore indexes dedicate entire database pages to store data from a single column. Columnstore indexes are also divided into segments, which consist of multiple pages, and each segment is stored in SQL Server as a separate BLOB. As indicated earlier, in SQL Server 2014, it is now possible to define a columnstore index as a clustered index, which is a great benefit because there is no need for duplicated data.

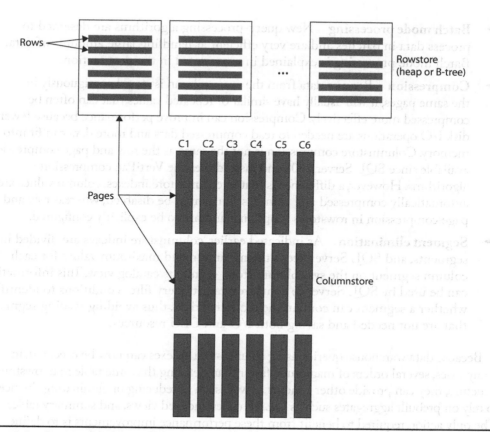

Figure 9-4 *Rowstore and columnstore data layout comparison*

For example, in SQL Server 2012, a nonclustered columnstore index had to be created on a heap or regular clustered index, thus duplicating the data of an already large fact table.

Performance Benefits

Columnstore indexes provide increased performance benefits based on the following:

▶ **Reduced I/O** Because in a rowstore pages contain all the columns in a row, in a data warehouse without columnstore indexes, SQL Server has to read all the columns, including the columns that are not required by the query. Typical star join queries use only 10 percent to 15 percent of the columns in a fact table. Based on this, using a columnstore to read only those columns can represent savings of 85 percent to 90 percent in disk I/O, compared to a rowstore.

▶ **Batch mode processing** New query-processing algorithms are designed to process data in batches and are very efficient at handling large amounts of data. Batch mode processing is explained in more detail in the next section.

▶ **Compression** Because data from the same column is stored contiguously in the same pages, it will usually have similar or repeated values that can often be compressed more effectively. Compression can improve performance because fewer disk I/O operations are needed to read compressed data and more data can fit into memory. Columnstore compression is not the same as the row and page compression available since SQL Server 2008 and instead uses the VertiPaq compression algorithms. However, a difference is that in columnstore indexes, column values are automatically compressed and compression cannot be disabled, whereas row and page compression in rowstores is optional and has to be explicitly configured.

▶ **Segment elimination** As indicated earlier, columnstore indexes are divided into segments, and SQL Server keeps the minimum and maximum values for each column segment on the sys.column_store_segments catalog view. This information can be used by SQL Server to compare against query filter conditions to identify whether a segment can contain the requested data, thus avoiding reading segments that are not needed and saving both I/O and CPU resources.

Because data warehouse queries using columnstore indexes can now be executed, in many cases, several orders of magnitude faster than defining the same table in a rowstore structure, they can provide other benefits as well, such as reducing or eliminating the need to rely on prebuilt aggregates such as OLAP cubes, indexed views, and summary tables. The only action required to benefit from these performance improvements is to define the columnstore indexes in your fact tables. There is no need to change your queries or use any specific syntax; the query optimizer will automatically consider the columnstore index—although, as always, whether or not it is used in a plan will be a cost-based decision. Columnstore indexes also provide more flexibility to changes than building these prebuilt aggregates. If a query changes, the columnstore index will still be useful, and the query optimizer will automatically react to those query changes, whereas the prebuilt aggregate may no longer be able to support the new query or may require changes to accommodate it.

Batch Mode Processing

As covered in Chapter 1 when we talked about the traditional query-processing mode in SQL Server, you saw that operators request rows from other operators one row at a time—for example, using the GetRow() method. This row processing mode works fine for transactional OLTP workloads where queries are expected to produce only a few rows. However, for data warehouse queries, which process large amounts of rows to aggregate data, this row-at-a-time processing mode may be very expensive.

With columnstore indexes, SQL Server is not only providing columnar-based storage, but is also introducing a query-processing mode that processes a large number of records, a batch at a time. A batch is stored as a vector in a separate area of memory and typically represents about 1,000 rows of data. This also means that operators now can run in either row or batch mode. As of SQL Server 2012, only a few operators can run in either batch or row mode, and those operators include Columnstore Index Scan, Hash Aggregate, Hash Join, Project, and Filter. Another operator, Batch Hash Table Build, works only in batch mode; it is used to build a batch hash table for the memory-optimized columnstore index in a hash join. In SQL Server 2014, the number of batch mode operators has been expanded and existing operators, especially the Hash Join operator, have been improved.

A plan with both row- and batch-processing operators may result in some performance degradation, as communication between row mode and batch mode operators is more expensive than the communication between operators running in the same mode. As a result, each transition has an associated cost which the query optimizer uses to minimize the number of these transitions in a plan. In addition, when both row- and batch-processing operators are present in the same plan, you should verify that most of the plan, or at least the most expensive part of the plan, is executed in batch mode.

Plans will show both the estimated and the actual execution mode, which you can see in the examples later in this chapter. Usually, the estimated and the actual execution mode should have the same value for the same operation. You can use this information to troubleshoot your plans and to make sure that, in fact, batch processing is used. However, a plan showing an estimated execution mode of "batch" and an actual execution mode of "row" may be evidence of a performance problem.

In SQL Server 2012, limitations on available memory or threads can cause one operation to dynamically switch from batch mode to row mode, thus degrading the performance of query execution. If the estimated plan showed a parallel plan and the actual plan switched to "serial," you could infer that not enough threads were available for the query. If the plan actually ran in parallel, you could tell that not having enough memory was the problem. In this version of SQL Server, some of the new batch operators might use hash tables, which are required to fit entirely in memory. When not enough memory is available at execution time, SQL Server might dynamically switch the operation back to row mode, where standard hash tables can be used and could spill to disk if not enough memory is available. Switching to row execution due to memory limitations can be caused by bad cardinality estimations, so you might consider verifying and updating your table statistics as well.

This memory requirement has been eliminated in SQL Server 2014; the build hash table of the Hash Join does not have to entirely fit in memory and can instead use spilling functionality. Although spilling to disk is not the perfect solution, it allows the operation to continue in batch mode instead of switching to row mode as in SQL Server 2012.

Finally, as of SQL Server 2012, the Hash Join operator supported only inner joins. This functionality has been expanded in SQL Server 2014 to include the full spectrum of join types, such as inner, outer, semi, and anti-semi joins. UNION ALL and scalar aggregation now support batch processing as well.

Creating Columnstore Indexes

Creating a nonclustered columnstore index requires defining the list of columns to be included in the index, which is not needed if you are creating a clustered columnstore index. A clustered columnstore index includes all the columns in the table and stores the entire table. You can create a clustered columnstore index from a heap or from a regular clustered index. However, although you can create clustered or nonclustered columnstore indexes on a table, different than with rowstores, only one columnstore index can exist at a time. For example, suppose you create the following clustered columnstore index using a small version of FactInternetSales2:

```
CREATE TABLE dbo.FactInternetSales2 (
    ProductKey int NOT NULL,
    OrderDateKey int NOT NULL,
    DueDateKey int NOT NULL,
    ShipDateKey int NOT NULL)
GO
CREATE CLUSTERED COLUMNSTORE INDEX csi_FactInternetSales2
ON dbo.FactInternetSales2
```

When you try to create the nonclustered columnstore index

```
CREATE NONCLUSTERED COLUMNSTORE INDEX ncsi_FactInternetSales2
ON dbo.FactInternetSales2
(ProductKey, OrderDateKey)
```

in the same table, this would return the following error message:

```
Msg 35303, Level 16, State 1, Line 1
CREATE INDEX statement failed because a nonclustered index cannot be created
on a table that has a clustered columnstore index. Consider replacing the
clustered columnstore index with a nonclustered columnstore index.
```

In the same way, if you already have a nonclustered columnstore index and try to create a clustered columnstore index, you get the following message:

```
Msg 35304, Level 16, State 1, Line 1
CREATE INDEX statement failed because a clustered columnstore index cannot
be created on a table that has a nonclustered index. Consider dropping all
nonclustered indexes and trying again.
```

Drop the existing table before running the next exercise, like so:

```
DROP TABLE FactInternetSales2
```

Let's now look at the plans created by columnstore indexes. Run the following code to create the FactInternetSales2 table on the AdventureWorksDW2012 database:

```
USE AdventureWorksDW2012
GO
CREATE TABLE dbo.FactInternetSales2 (
      ProductKey int NOT NULL,
      OrderDateKey int NOT NULL,
      DueDateKey int NOT NULL,
      ShipDateKey int NOT NULL,
      CustomerKey int NOT NULL,
      PromotionKey int NOT NULL,
      CurrencyKey int NOT NULL,
      SalesTerritoryKey int NOT NULL,
      SalesOrderNumber nvarchar(20) NOT NULL,
      SalesOrderLineNumber tinyint NOT NULL,
      RevisionNumber tinyint NOT NULL,
      OrderQuantity smallint NOT NULL,
      UnitPrice money NOT NULL,
      ExtendedAmount money NOT NULL,
      UnitPriceDiscountPct float NOT NULL,
      DiscountAmount float NOT NULL,
      ProductStandardCost money NOT NULL,
      TotalProductCost money NOT NULL,
      SalesAmount money NOT NULL,
      TaxAmt money NOT NULL,
      Freight money NOT NULL,
      CarrierTrackingNumber nvarchar(25) NULL,
      CustomerPONumber nvarchar(25) NULL,
      OrderDate datetime NULL,
      DueDate datetime NULL,
      ShipDate datetime NULL
)
```

We can now insert some records by copying data from an existing fact table:

```
INSERT INTO dbo.FactInternetSales2
SELECT * FROM AdventureWorksDW2012.dbo.FactInternetSales
WHERE SalesOrderNumber < 'SO6'
```

Run the following statement to create a clustered columnstore index:

```
CREATE CLUSTERED COLUMNSTORE INDEX csi_FactInternetSales2
ON dbo.FactInternetSales2
```

The following statement will show that, as of SQL Server 2014, columnstore indexes are now updatable and support the INSERT, DELETE, UPDATE, and MERGE statements, as well as other standard methods such as the bcp bulk loading tool and SQL Server Integration Services:

```
INSERT INTO dbo.FactInternetSales2
SELECT * FROM AdventureWorksDW2012.dbo.FactInternetSales
WHERE SalesOrderNumber > 'SO6'
```

Trying to run the previous statement against a columnstore index on a SQL Server 2012 instance would return the following error message, which also describes one of the workarounds to insert data in a columnstore index in that version of SQL Server:

```
Msg 35330, Level 15, State 1, Line 1
INSERT statement failed because data cannot be updated in a table with a
columnstore index. Consider disabling the columnstore index before issuing
the INSERT statement, then rebuilding the columnstore index after INSERT is
complete.
```

At this moment, running a star join query may not have enough records to produce batch processing. Test it by running the following query:

```
SELECT d.CalendarYear,
SUM(SalesAmount) AS SalesTotal
FROM dbo.FactInternetSales2 AS f
JOIN dbo.DimDate AS d
ON f.OrderDateKey = d.DateKey
GROUP BY d.CalendarYear
ORDER BY d.CalendarYear
```

Although the produced plan includes a Columnstore Index Scan operator, as shown in Figure 9-5, looking at the properties of this operator will actually show that Actual Execution Mode is, in fact, Row, meaning that row processing is being used.

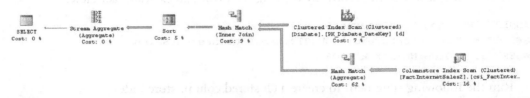

Figure 9-5   *Plan using a Columnstore Index Scan in row mode*

Let's add more records by running the following INSERT statement 20 times:

```
INSERT INTO dbo.FactInternetSales2
SELECT * FROM AdventureWorksDW2012.dbo.FactInternetSales
GO 20
```

Although copying the same data 20 times does not make it a perfect test, at least you can use it if you don't have access to a larger data warehouse. This time we get a more expensive parallel plan, using batch processing, part of which is shown in Figure 9-6.

The properties of the Columnstore Index Scan operator now show Actual Execution Mode as Batch (see Figure 9-7). The Storage property shows ColumnStore. Notice that the operator also shows an optimized bitmap, Opt_Bitmap1006, used in the predicate section. This is created in the top hash join using the DimDate dimension table as the build input, but it is not shown in the plan.

Similar to a rowstore, you can use the ALTER INDEX REBUILD statement to remove fragmentation of a columnstore index, as shown next:

```
ALTER INDEX csi_FactInternetSales2 on FactInternetSales2 REBUILD
```

Because a fact table is a very large table and an index rebuild operation in a columnstore index is an offline operation, you can partition it and follow the same recommendations you would for a large table in a rowstore. Here is a basic summary of the process:

▶ Rebuild the most recently used partition only. Fragmentation is more likely to occur only in partitions that have been modified recently.

▶ Rebuild only the partitions updated after loading data or heavy DML operations.

Similar to dropping a regular clustered index, dropping a clustered columnstore index will convert the table back into a rowstore heap. To verify this, run the following query:

```
SELECT * FROM sys.indexes
WHERE object_id = OBJECT_ID('FactInternetSales2')
```

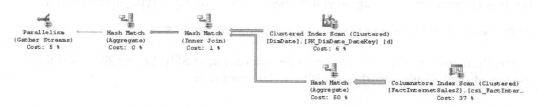

Figure 9-6   *Plan using a Columnstore Index Scan in batch mode*

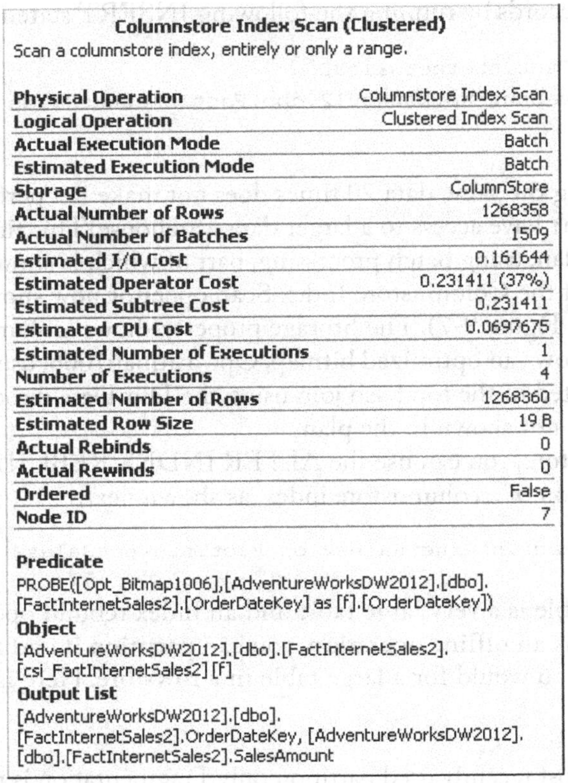

```
┌─────────────────────────────────────────────────────────────────────┐
│              Columnstore Index Scan (Clustered)                       │
│      Scan a columnstore index, entirely or only a range.              │
│                                                                        │
│   Physical Operation                          Columnstore Index Scan   │
│   Logical Operation                             Clustered Index Scan   │
│   Actual Execution Mode                                       Batch    │
│   Estimated Execution Mode                                    Batch    │
│   Storage                                               ColumnStore    │
│   Actual Number of Rows                                    1268358     │
│   Actual Number of Batches                                   1509      │
│   Estimated I/O Cost                                       0.161644    │
│   Estimated Operator Cost                           0.231411 (37%)     │
│   Estimated Subtree Cost                                   0.231411    │
│   Estimated CPU Cost                                      0.0697675    │
│   Estimated Number of Executions                                 1     │
│   Number of Executions                                           4     │
│   Estimated Number of Rows                                1268360     │
│   Estimated Row Size                                          19 B     │
│   Actual Rebinds                                                 0     │
│   Actual Rewinds                                                 0     │
│   Ordered                                                   False     │
│   Node ID                                                       7     │
│                                                                        │
│   Predicate                                                            │
│   PROBE([Opt_Bitmap1006],[AdventureWorksDW2012].[dbo].                 │
│   [FactInternetSales2].[OrderDateKey] as [f].[OrderDateKey])           │
│   Object                                                               │
│   [AdventureWorksDW2012].[dbo].[FactInternetSales2].                   │
│   [csi_FactInternetSales2] [f]                                         │
│   Output List                                                          │
│   [AdventureWorksDW2012].[dbo].                                        │
│   [FactInternetSales2].OrderDateKey, [AdventureWorksDW2012].           │
│   [dbo].[FactInternetSales2].SalesAmount                               │
└─────────────────────────────────────────────────────────────────────┘
```

Figure 9-7 *Columnstore Index Scan properties*

An output similar to the following will be shown:

object_id	name	index_id	type	type_desc
1762105318	csi_FactInternetSales2	1	5	CLUSTERED COLUMNSTORE

Dropping the index running by using the next DROP INDEX statement and then running the previous query again will change index_id to 0 and type_desc to HEAP:

```
DROP INDEX FactInternetSales2.csi_FactInternetSales2
```

Finally, if you are still using columnstore indexes under SQL Server 2012, you may use any of the following workarounds to update your data:

▶ **Use partition switching** This choice uses partitioning and requires you to use an updatable staging table to load new data into a fact table. Once the data has been loaded, you can create the columnstore index on the staging table and then switch the staging table into an empty partition in the main table. A similar procedure could be followed to update existing data, but you first need to switch the fact table partition into a staging table and drop or disable the columnstore index for the staging table so it can be updated. Once the data has been updated, you can create the columnstore index on the staging table and then switch the staging table into an empty partition in the main table, as mentioned in the first case.

▶ **Use UNION ALL** This choice requires a fact table using a columnstore index and a regular updatable table using the same schema, which will contain the most current data. Then you will be able to query both tables at the same time using UNION ALL. Care should be taken when following this procedure to make sure that, in fact, batch processing is being used by the heaviest operations.

▶ **Re-create the columnstore index** This choice involves dropping or disabling the columnstore index, updating or loading the required data, and then creating or building the columnstore index again. This is basically the recommendation given by the error message 35330, shown earlier.

Hints

Finally, a couple of hints could be useful in cases where the query optimizer is not giving you a good plan when working with nonclustered columnstore indexes. One case is when the query optimizer ignores this index. You can use the INDEX hint in this case to ask SQL Server to use the existing nonclustered columnstore index. To test it, create the following index on the existing FactInternetSales table:

```
CREATE NONCLUSTERED COLUMNSTORE INDEX csi_FactInternetSales
ON dbo.FactInternetSales (
        ProductKey,
        OrderDateKey,
        DueDateKey,
        ShipDateKey,
        CustomerKey,
        PromotionKey,
        CurrencyKey,
        SalesTerritoryKey,
        SalesOrderNumber,
        SalesOrderLineNumber,
```

```
        RevisionNumber,
        OrderQuantity,
        UnitPrice,
        ExtendedAmount,
        UnitPriceDiscountPct,
        DiscountAmount,
        ProductStandardCost,
        TotalProductCost,
        SalesAmount,
        TaxAmt,
        Freight,
        CarrierTrackingNumber,
        CustomerPONumber,
        OrderDate,
        DueDate,
        ShipDate
)
```

The following query shows how the INDEX hint can be used:

```
SELECT d.CalendarYear,
SUM(SalesAmount) AS SalesTotal
FROM dbo.FactInternetSales AS f
    WITH (INDEX(csi_FactInternetSales))
    JOIN dbo.DimDate AS d
    ON f.OrderDateKey = d.DateKey
GROUP BY d.CalendarYear
ORDER BY d.CalendarYear
```

Another case is when for some reason you don't want to use an existing nonclustered columnstore index. The new hint IGNORE_NONCLUSTERED_COLUMNSTORE_INDEX could be used in this case, as shown in the following query:

```
SELECT d.CalendarYear,
SUM(SalesAmount) AS SalesTotal
FROM dbo.FactInternetSales AS f
    JOIN dbo.DimDate AS d
    ON f.OrderDateKey = d.DateKey
GROUP BY d.CalendarYear
ORDER BY d.CalendarYear
OPTION (IGNORE_NONCLUSTERED_COLUMNSTORE_INDEX)
```

Finally, drop the created columnstore index by running the following statement:

```
DROP INDEX FactInternetSales.csi_FactInternetSales
```

Summary

This chapter covered data warehouses and explained how operational and analytic systems serve very different purposes—one helping with the execution of a business process and the other helping with the measurement of such a business process. The fact that a data warehouse system is also used in a different way than an OLTP system created opportunities for a new database engine design, which was implemented with the columnstore indexes feature when SQL Server 2012 was originally released.

Because a typical star join query uses only 10 percent to 15 percent of the columns in a fact table, a columnar-based approach was implemented, which seemed to be more appropriate than the traditional rowstore. Because processing a row at a time also didn't seem to be efficient for the large number of rows processed by star join queries, a new batch-processing mode was implemented as well. Finally, following new hardware trends, columnstore indexes, as with Hekaton, were implemented as in-memory technologies.

The SQL Server query optimizer is also able to automatically detect and optimize data warehouse queries. One of the explained optimizations, using bitmap filtering, is based on a concept originally defined in 1970. Bitmap filtering can be used to filter out rows from a fact table very early during query processing, thus improving the performance of star join queries.

Chapter 10

Query Processor Limitations and Hints

In This Chapter

Query optimization is an inherently complex problem, not only for SQL Server, but also for any other relational database system. Despite the fact that query optimization research dates back to the early 1970s, challenges in some fundamental areas are still being addressed today. The first major impediment to a query optimizer finding an optimal plan is the fact that, for many queries, it is just not possible to explore the entire search space. An effect known as *combinatorial explosion* makes this exhaustive enumeration impossible because the number of possible plans grows very rapidly, depending on the number of tables joined in the query. To make the search a manageable process, heuristics are used to limit the search space (that is, the number of possible plans to be considered), as covered in Chapter 3. However, if a query optimizer is not able to explore the entire search space, there is no way to prove that you can get an absolutely optimal plan, or even that the best plan is among the candidates being considered, whether it is selected or not. As a result, it is clearly extremely important that the set of plans a query optimizer considers contains plans with low costs.

This leads us to another major technical challenge for the query optimizer: accurate cost and cardinality estimation. Because a cost-based optimizer selects the execution plan with the lowest estimated cost, the quality of the plan selection is only as good as the accuracy of the optimizer's cost and cardinality estimations. Even supposing that time is not a concern, and that the query optimizer can analyze the entire search space without a problem, cardinality and cost estimation errors can still make a query optimizer select a nonoptimal plan. Cost estimation models are inherently inexact because they do not consider all the hardware conditions, and must necessarily make certain assumptions about the environment. For example, the costing model assumes that every query starts with a cold cache (that is, that its data is read from disk and not from memory), and this assumption could lead to costing estimation errors in some cases. In addition, cost estimation relies on cardinality estimation, which is also inexact and has some known limitations, especially when it comes to the estimation of the intermediate results in a plan. Errors in intermediate results in effect get magnified as more tables are joined and more estimation errors are included within the calculations. On top of all that, some operations are not covered by the mathematical model of the cardinality estimation component, which means the query optimizer has to resort to guess logic or heuristics to deal with these situations.

NOTE

As covered earlier in this book, SQL Server 2014 has introduced a new cardinality estimator to help improve the accuracy and supportability of the cardinality estimation process. For more details, refer to Chapter 6.

Query Optimization Research

As mentioned earlier, query optimization research dates back to the early 1970s. One of the earliest works describing a cost-based query optimizer was "Access Path Selection in a Relational Database Management System," published in 1979 by Pat Selinger et al., to describe the query optimizer for an experimental database management system developed in 1975 at what is now the IBM Almaden Research Center. This database management system, called "System R," advanced the field of query optimization by introducing the use of cost-based query optimization, the use of statistics, an efficient method of determining join orders, and the addition of CPU cost to the optimizer's cost estimation formulae.

Yet, despite being an enormous influence in the field of query optimization research, it suffered a major drawback: its framework could not be easily extended to include additional transformations. This led to the development of more extensible optimization architectures, which facilitated the gradual addition of new functionality to query optimizers. The trailblazers in this field were the Exodus Optimizer Generator, defined by Goetz Graefe and David DeWitt and, later, the Volcano Optimizer Generator, defined by Goetz Graefe and William McKenna. Goetz Graefe then went on to define the Cascades Framework, resolving errors that were present in his previous two endeavors.

What is most relevant for us about this previous research is that SQL Server implemented a new cost-based query optimizer, based on the Cascades Framework, in 1999, when its database engine was re-architected for the release of SQL Server 7.0. The extensible architecture of the Cascades Framework has made it much easier for new functionality, such as new transformation rules or physical operators, to be implemented in the query optimizer.

Join Orders

Join ordering is one of the most complex problems in query optimization and one that has been the subject of extensive research since the 1970s. It refers to the process of calculating the optimal join order (that is, the order in which the necessary tables are joined) when executing a query. Because the order of joins is a key factor in controlling the amount of data flowing between each operator in an execution plan, it's a factor to which the query optimizer needs to pay close attention. As suggested earlier, join ordering is directly related to the size of the search space because the number of possible plans for a query grows very rapidly, depending on the number of tables joined.

A join operation combines records from two tables based on some common information, and the predicate that defines which columns are used to join the tables is called a *join predicate*. A join works with only two tables at a time, so a query requesting data from n tables must be executed as a sequence of $n - 1$ joins, although it should be noted that a join does not have to be completed (that is, joined all the required data from both tables) before the next join can be started.

The query optimizer needs to make two important decisions regarding joins: the selection of a join order and the choice of a join algorithm. The selection of join algorithms was covered in Chapter 4, so in this section I'll talk about join orders. As mentioned, the order in which the tables are joined can greatly impact the cost and performance of a query. Although the results of the query are the same, regardless of the join order, the cost of each different join order can vary dramatically.

As a result of the commutative and associative properties of joins, even simple queries offer many different possible join orders, and this number increases exponentially with the number of tables that need to be joined. The task of the query optimizer is to find the optimal sequence of joins between the tables used in the query.

The commutative property of a join between tables A and B states that A JOIN B is logically equivalent to B JOIN A. This defines which table will be accessed first or, said in a different way, which role each table will play in the join. In a Nested Loops Join, for example, the first accessed table is called the outer table and the second one the inner table. In a Hash Join, the first accessed table is the build input and the second one the probe input. As you saw in Chapter 4, correctly defining which table will be the inner table and which will be the outer table in a Nested Loops Join, or the build input or probe input in a Hash Join, has significant performance and cost implications, and it is a choice made by the query optimizer.

The associative property of a join between tables A, B, and C states that (A JOIN B) JOIN C is logically equivalent to A JOIN (B JOIN C). This defines the order in which the tables are joined. For example, (A JOIN B) JOIN C specifies that table A must be joined to table B first, and then the result must be joined to table C. A JOIN (B JOIN C) means that table B must be joined to table C first and then the result must be joined to table A. Each possible permutation may have different cost and performance results depending, for example, on the size of their temporary results.

As noted earlier, the number of possible join orders in a query increases exponentially with the number of tables joined. In fact, with just a handful of tables, the number of possible join orders could be in the thousands or even millions, although the exact number of possible join orders depends on the overall shape of the query tree. Obviously, it is impossible for the query optimizer to look at all those combinations: it would take far too long. Instead, the SQL Server query optimizer uses heuristics to help narrow down the search space.

As mentioned before, queries are represented as trees in the query processor, and the shape of the query tree, as dictated by the nature of the join ordering, is so important in query optimization that some of these trees have names, such as left-deep, right-deep, and bushy trees. Figure 10-1 shows left-deep and bushy trees for a join of four tables. For example, the left-deep tree could be JOIN(JOIN(JOIN(A, B), C), D), and the bushy tree could be JOIN(JOIN(A, B), JOIN(C, D)).

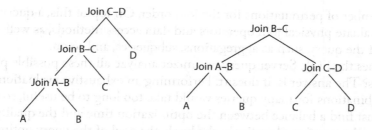

Figure 10-1   *Left-deep and bushy trees*

Left-deep trees are also called linear trees or linear processing trees, and you can see how their shapes lead to that description. Bushy trees, on the other hand, can take any arbitrary shape, and so the set of bushy trees actually includes the sets of both left-deep and right-deep trees.

The number of left-deep trees is calculated as $n!$ (or n factorial), where n is the number of tables in the relation. A *factorial* is the product of all positive integers less than or equal to n. For example, for a five-table join, the number of possible join orders is $5! = 5 \times 4 \times 3 \times 2 \times 1 = 120$. The number of possible join orders for a bushy tree is more complicated and can be calculated as $(2n - 2)!/(n - 1)!$.

The important point to remember here is that the number of possible join orders grows very quickly as the number of tables increase, as highlighted by Table 10-1. For example, in theory, if we had a six-table join, a query optimizer would potentially need to evaluate 30,240 possible join orders. Of course, we should also bear in mind that this

Tables	Left-Deep Trees	Bushy Trees
2	2	2
3	6	12
4	24	120
5	120	1,680
6	720	30,240
7	5,040	665,280
8	40,320	17,297,280
9	362,880	518,918,400
10	3,628,800	17,643,225,600
11	39,916,800	670,442,572,800
12	479,001,600	28,158,588,057,600

Table 10-1   *Possible Join Orders for Left-Deep and Bushy Trees*

is just the number of permutations for the join order. On top of this, a query optimizer also has to evaluate physical join operators and data access methods, as well as optimize other parts of the query, such as aggregations, subqueries, and so on.

So how does the SQL Server query optimizer analyze all these possible plan combinations? The answer is, it doesn't. Performing an exhaustive evaluation of all possible combinations for many queries would take too long to be useful, so the query optimizer must find a balance between the optimization time and the quality of the resulting plan. As mentioned earlier in the book, the goal of the query optimizer is to find a good enough plan as quickly as possible. Rather than exhaustively evaluate every single combination, the query optimizer tries to narrow the possibilities down to the most likely candidates, using heuristics (some of which we've already touched upon) to guide the process. This is explained in Chapter 3.

Break Down Complex Queries

As you saw in the previous section, in some cases, the SQL Server query optimizer may not be able to produce a good plan for a query with a large number of joins. The same is true for complex queries with both joins and aggregations. However, because it is rarely necessary to request all the data in a single query, a good solution for those cases could be to just break down a large and complex query into two or more simpler queries while storing the intermediate results in temporary tables. Breaking down complex queries this way offers several advantages:

▶ **Better plans**   Query performance is improved because the query optimizer is able to create efficient plans for simpler queries.

▶ **Better statistics**   Because one of the problems of some complex plans is the degradation of intermediate statistics, breaking down these queries and storing the aggregated or intermediate results in temporary tables allows SQL Server to create new statistics, greatly improving the cardinality estimation of the remaining queries. It is worth noticing that temporary tables should be used and not table variables, as the latter do not have statistics support.

It should be noted that a new trace flag has been just introduced with SQL Server 2012 Service Pack 2 which provides better cardinality estimation while using table variables. This trace flag is also expected to be implemented in SQL Server 2014. For more details, see http://support.microsoft.com/kb/2952444.

▶ **No hints required**   Because using hints is a common practice to fix problems with complex plans, breaking down the query allows the query optimizer to create an efficient plan without requiring hints. This has the additional benefit that the query optimizer can automatically react to future data or schema changes. On the other hand, a query using hints would require future maintenance because the hint used may no longer be helpful, or may even impact its performance in a negative way after such changes. Hints, which should be used only as a last resort when no other solution is available, are covered later in this chapter.

In the paper "When to Break Down Complex Queries," the author describes several problematic query patterns that the SQL Server query optimizer is not able to create good plans for. Although the paper was published in October 2011 and indicates that it applies to versions from SQL Server 2005 to SQL Server code-named "Denali," I was still able to see the same behavior in SQL Server 2014. Here are some of these query patterns, which I'll cover briefly:

- ▶ OR logic in the WHERE clause
- ▶ Joins on aggregated data sets
- ▶ Queries with a large number of very complex joins

OR Logic in the WHERE Clause

The SQL Server query optimizer is able to identify and create efficient plans when using OR logic in the WHERE clause for the following cases:

- ▶ WHERE a.col1 = @val1 OR a.col1 = @val2, which is the same as WHERE a.col1 IN (@val1, @val2)
- ▶ WHERE a.col1 = @val1 OR a.col2 = @val2
- ▶ WHERE a.col1 = @val1 OR a.col2 IN (SELECT col2 FROM tab2)

As you'll notice, all the listed cases use the same or different columns but in the same table. Here is an example of a query showing the first case:

```
SELECT * FROM Sales.SalesOrderHeader
WHERE CustomerID = 11020 OR SalesPersonID = 285
```

In this query, SQL Server is able to use index seek operations on two indexes, IX_SalesOrderHeader_CustomerID and IX_SalesOrderHeader_SalesPersonID, and use an index union to solve both predicates, showing the efficient plan in Figure 10-2.

However, poor plans may be created when filters on the OR operator evaluate different tables, basically following the pattern WHERE a.col1 = @val1 OR b.col2 = @val2.

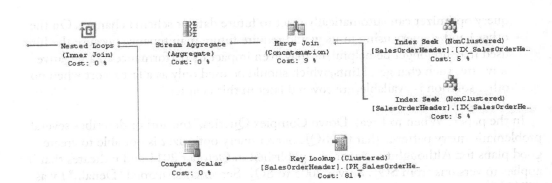

Figure 10-2 *Plan using WHERE a.col1 = @val1 OR a.col2 = @val2*

Running the following two queries using a very selective predicate will create two plans using efficient Index Seek operators on the IX_SalesOrderDetail_ProductID and IX_SalesOrderHeader_CustomerID indexes, returning two and three records, respectively:

```
SELECT SalesOrderID FROM Sales.SalesOrderDetail
WHERE ProductID = 897
SELECT SalesOrderID FROM Sales.SalesOrderHeader
WHERE CustomerID = 11020
```

However, if we join both tables using the same selective predicates (and just for demonstration purposes), SQL Server will now return a very expensive plan scanning the mentioned indexes, as shown in Figure 10-3, instead of using the more efficient seek operations shown previously:

```
SELECT sod.SalesOrderID FROM Sales.SalesOrderHeader soh
    JOIN Sales.SalesOrderDetail sod
      ON soh.SalesOrderID = sod.SalesOrderID
WHERE sod.ProductID = 897 OR soh.CustomerID = 11020
```

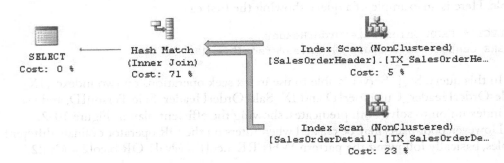

Figure 10-3 *Plan using WHERE a.col1 = @val1 OR b.col2 = @val2*

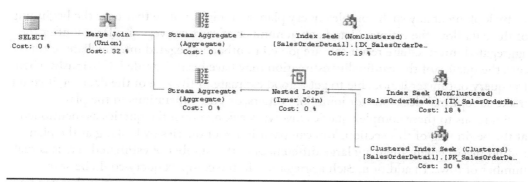

Figure 10-4 *Plan using UNION*

This kind of query pattern can be fixed using the UNION clause instead of an OR condition, as shown next, which produces the same results and now allows for performing seeks on all indexes, resulting in a more efficient plan:

```
SELECT sod.SalesOrderID FROM Sales.SalesOrderHeader soh
    JOIN Sales.SalesOrderDetail sod
    ON soh.SalesOrderID = sod.SalesOrderID
WHERE sod.ProductID = 897
UNION
SELECT sod.SalesOrderID FROM Sales.SalesOrderHeader soh
    JOIN Sales.SalesOrderDetail sod
    ON soh.SalesOrderID = sod.SalesOrderID
WHERE soh.CustomerID = 11020
```

Although the query looks more complicated and redundant, it produces the very effective plan shown in Figure 10-4.

Joins on Aggregated Data Sets

The second query pattern happens when the results of aggregations are joined in large and complex queries. As covered in Chapter 6, statistics can provide a good cardinality estimation for operations performed on the table owning the statistics (for example, estimating the number of records returned by a filter operation). However, the query optimizer has to use this estimate in an operation earlier in the plan, apply it to the next operation to get a new estimation, and so on. In some complex plans, these estimates can quickly degrade in accuracy.

By looking at any such complex query plan, you might notice that near the beginning of the data flow, the estimated and actual number of rows are very similar, but after the aggregated intermediate result sets are joined to other aggregated intermediate result sets, the quality of the cardinality estimation may have been degraded. Obviously, when the query optimizer is not able to get a good estimate of the size of the data set, it could make suboptimal decisions for joins, join orders, or other operations in the plan.

Solutions to these complex queries involve breaking down the queries as mentioned at the beginning of this section. You can partition your queries by looking at the plan to find places where there are large differences in the number of estimated versus actual number of rows. In addition, each aggregation in the complex query could be saved into a temporary table, which again would create better quality of statistics that can be used for the remaining parts of the query. Finally, a query with a large number of very complex joins is another query pattern that can benefit from being broken down into two or more simpler queries, with the intermediate results being stored in temporary tables. The problem of queries with a large number of joins was explained in more detail in the "Join Orders" section earlier in this chapter.

Hints

SQL is a declarative language; it only defines what data to retrieve from the database. It doesn't describe the manner in which the data should be fetched. That, as we know, is the job of the query optimizer, which analyzes a number of candidate execution plans for a given query, estimates the cost of each of these plans, and selects an efficient plan by choosing the cheapest of the choices considered.

But there may be cases when the execution plan selected is not performing as you have expected and, as part of your query troubleshooting process, you may try to find a better plan yourself. Before doing this, keep in mind that just because your query does not perform as you expected, this does not mean a better plan is always possible. Your plan may be an efficient one, but the query may be an expensive one to perform, or your system may be experiencing performance bottlenecks that are impacting the query execution.

However, although the query optimizer does an excellent job most of the time, it does occasionally fail to produce an efficient plan, as you've seen throughout this book. That being said, even in cases when you're not getting an efficient plan, you should still try to distinguish between the times when the problems arise because you're not providing the query optimizer with all the information it needs to do a good job, and those when the problems are a result of a query optimizer limitation. Part of the focus of this book so far has been to help you to provide the query optimizer with the information it needs to produce an efficient execution plan, such as the right indexes and good quality statistics, and also how to troubleshoot the cases when you are not getting a good plan. This chapter covers what to do if you hit a query optimizer limitation.

Having said that, there might be cases when the query optimizer just gets it wrong, and because of that we may be forced to resort to hints. Hints are essentially optimizer directives that allow us to take explicit control over the execution plan for a given query, with the goal of improving its performance. In reaching for a hint, however, we are going against the declarative property of the SQL language and, instead, giving direct instructions to the query optimizer. Overriding the query optimizer is risky business; hints need to be used with caution, and only as a last resort when no other option is available to produce a viable plan.

With this warning in mind, we will review some of the hints SQL Server provides, should the need arise, as well as how and when they might be used. We'll focus only on those hints I've most often seen provide positive performance benefits in certain circumstances. Some other query hints, such as OPTIMIZE FOR, OPTIMIZE FOR UNKNOWN, and RECOMPILE, have already been covered in Chapter 8, and will not be touched on again in this chapter.

When to Use Hints

Hints are a powerful means by which we can cause our decisions to overrule those of the query optimizer. However, you should only do so with extreme caution, because hints restrict the choices available to the query optimizer. They also make your code less flexible and will require additional maintenance. A hint should only be employed once you're certain you have no alternative options. At a minimum, before you reach for a hint, you should explore these potential issues:

▶ **System problems** You need to make sure your performance problem is not linked to other system-related issues, such as blocking or bottlenecks in server resources such as I/O, memory, and CPU.

▶ **Cardinality estimation errors** The query optimizer often misses the correct plan because of cardinality estimation errors. Cardinality estimation errors can sometimes be fixed via solutions such as updating statistics, using a bigger sample for your statistics (or scanning the entire table), using computed columns, multicolumn statistics, or filtered statistics, and so on. There might be cases where the cardinality estimation errors are caused by the use of features in which statistics are not supported at all, such as table variables and multistatement table-valued user-defined functions. In these particular instances, you may consider using standard or temporary tables if you are not getting an efficient plan. Statistics and cardinality estimation errors were covered in detail in Chapter 6.

▶ **Additional troubleshooting** You may need to perform additional troubleshooting before considering the use of hints. One of the obvious choices for improving the performance of your queries is providing the query optimizer with the right indexes. How to make sure that your indexes are selected by the query optimizer is covered in Chapter 5. You might also consider some other, less obvious troubleshooting procedures, such as breaking your query down into steps or smaller pieces and storing any intermediate results in temporary tables, as shown earlier in this chapter. You can use this method just as a troubleshooting procedure—for example, to find out which part of the original query is expensive so you can focus on it. Alternatively, you can keep it as the final version of your query if these changes alone give you better performance.

As discussed earlier in this chapter, query optimizers have improved radically after more than 30 years of research, but still face some technical challenges. The SQL Server query optimizer will give you an efficient execution plan for most of your queries, but will be increasingly challenged as the complexity of the query grows with more tables joined, plus the use of aggregations and other SQL features. If, after investigating the troubleshooting options and recommendations described previously and throughout this book, you still find that the query optimizer is not finding a good execution plan for your query, you may need to consider using hints to direct the query optimizer toward what you feel is the optimal execution path.

Always remember that, by applying a hint, you effectively disable some of the available transformation rules to which the query optimizer usually has access and thus restrict the available search space. Only transformation rules that help to achieve the requested plan will be executed. For example, if you use hints to force a particular join order, the query optimizer will disable rules that reorder joins. Always try to use the least restrictive hint because this will retain as much flexibility as possible in your query and make maintenance somewhat easier. In addition, hints cannot be used to generate an invalid plan or a plan that the query optimizer normally would not consider during query optimization.

Furthermore, a hint that initially does a great job might actively hinder performance at a later point in time when some conditions change—for example, as a result of schema updates, service packs, new versions of SQL Server, or even enough data changes. The hints may prevent the query optimizer from modifying the execution plan accordingly, and thus result in degraded performance. It is your responsibility to monitor and maintain your hinted queries to make sure they continue to perform well after such system changes or to remove those hints if they are no longer needed.

Also, remember that if you decide to use a hint to change a single section or physical operator of a plan, then after you apply the hint, the query optimizer will perform a completely new optimization. The query optimizer will obey your hint during the optimization process, but it still has the flexibility to change everything else in the plan, so the end result of your tweaking may be unintended changes to other sections of the plan. Finally, note that the fact that your query is not performing as you hoped does not always mean that the query optimizer is not giving you a good enough execution plan. If the operation you are performing is simply expensive and resource intensive, then it's possible that no amount of tuning or hinting will help you achieve the performance you'd like.

NOTE

As of SQL Server 2005 SP1, Microsoft also published trace flag 2301, which you can use to enable advanced optimizations specific to decision support queries with large data sets. For more details and a list of the scenarios where this trace flag can help, see http://blogs.msdn.com/b/ianjo/archive/2006/04/24/582219.aspx.

Types of Hints

SQL Server provides a wide range of hints, which can be classified as follows:

▶ Query hints tell the optimizer to apply the hint throughout the entire query. They are specified using the OPTION clause, which is included at the end of the query.

▶ Join hints apply to a specific join in a query and can be specified by using ANSI-style join hints.

▶ Table hints apply to a single table and are usually included using the WITH keyword in the FROM clause.

Another useful classification is dividing hints into physical operator and goal-oriented hints:

▶ Physical operator hints, as the name suggests, request the use of a specific physical operator, join order, or aggregation placement. Most of the hints covered in this chapter are physical hints.

▶ A goal-oriented hint does not specify how to build the plan, but instead specifies a goal to achieve, leaving the query optimizer to find the best physical operators to achieve that goal. Goal-oriented hints are usually safer and require less knowledge about the internal workings of the query optimizer. Examples of goal-oriented hints include the OPTIMIZER FOR and FAST N hints.

Locking hints do not affect plan selection, so they will not be covered here. Plan guides, which allow you to apply a hint to a query without changing the code in your application, and the USE PLAN query hint, which allows you to force the query optimizer to use a specified execution plan for a query, are covered later in the chapter.

In the next few sections, I discuss hints affecting joins, join order, aggregations, index scans or seeks, views, and so on.

> **NOTE**
> _Note that with a very simple and small database like AdventureWorks2012, SQL Server most likely will give you an optimal plan for the examples in this chapter without requiring any hint. However, we will be exploring alternative plans using hints for demonstration purposes only, some of which could be potentially more expensive than the unhinted version._

Joins

We can explicitly ask the query optimizer to use any of the available join algorithms: Nested Loops Join, Merge Join, and Hash Join. We could do this at the query level, in which case all the existing joins in the query will be affected, or we can request it at the join level, impacting only that specific join (although as you will see later, this last choice will also impact the join order on the plan).

Let's focus on join hints at the query level first, in which case, the join algorithm is specified using the OPTION clause. You can also specify two of the three available joins, which basically asks the query optimizer to exclude the third physical join operator from consideration. The decision between which of the remaining two joins to use will be cost based. For example, the following unhinted query will produce the plan in Figure 10-5, which uses a Hash Join:

```
SELECT *
FROM Production.Product AS p
JOIN Sales.SalesOrderDetail AS sod
ON p.ProductID = sod.ProductID
```

On the other hand, the following query will ask SQL Server to exclude a Hash Join by requesting either a Nested Loops Join or Merge Join. In this case, SQL Server

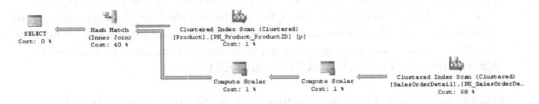

Figure 10-5 _Execution plan using a Hash Join_

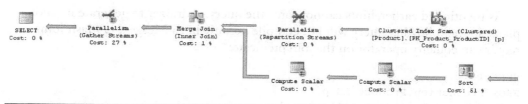

Figure 10-6 *Execution plan excluding a Hash Join*

chooses a more expensive plan with a Merge Join operator, also showing that the query optimizer was making the right decision in the first place. This plan is shown partially in Figure 10-6.

```
SELECT *
FROM Production.Product AS p
JOIN Sales.SalesOrderDetail AS sod
ON p.ProductID = sod.ProductID
OPTION (LOOP JOIN, MERGE JOIN)
```

Join hints not only can force the joins we explicitly specify in our query text, but can also impact most of the joins introduced by the query optimizer, such as foreign key validation and cascading actions. Other joins, such as the Nested Loops used in a bookmark lookup, cannot be changed because it would defeat the purpose of using the bookmark lookup in the first place. For example, in the following query, the hint to use a Merge Join will be ignored, as shown in the plan in Figure 10-7:

```
SELECT AddressID, City, StateProvinceID, ModifiedDate
FROM Person.Address
WHERE City = 'Santa Fe'
OPTION (MERGE JOIN)
```

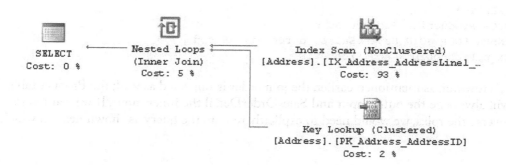

Figure 10-7 *Hint ignored in a bookmark lookup example*

As mentioned earlier, hints cannot force the query optimizer to generate invalid plans, so the following query will not compile because both Merge and Hash Joins require an equality operator on the join predicate:

```
SELECT *
FROM Production.Product AS p
JOIN Sales.SalesOrderDetail AS sod
ON sod.ProductID > p.ProductID
WHERE p.ProductID > 900
OPTION (HASH JOIN)
```

Trying to execute the previous query will return the following error message:

```
Msg 8622, Level 16, State 1, Line 1
Query processor could not produce a query plan because of the hints defined
in this query. Resubmit the query without specifying any hints and without
using SET FORCEPLAN.
```

However, as mentioned before, keep in mind that using a query-level hint will impact the entire query. If you need explicit control over each join in a query, you can use ANSI-style join hints, the benefit of which is that a join type can be individually selected for every join in the plan. However, be warned that using ANSI join hints will also add the behavior of the FORCE ORDER hint, which asks to preserve the join order and aggregation placement, as indicated by the query syntax. This behavior will be explained in the "FORCE ORDER" section, later in this chapter.

In the meantime, let me show you an example. The first query used in this section employs a Hash Join accessing the Product table first when used with no hints, which means that Product will be the build input and the SalesOrderDetail the probe input. This plan was shown in Figure 10-5. The following query will use a hint to request a Nested Loops Join instead. Notice that the INNER keyword is required this time.

```
SELECT *
FROM Production.Product AS p
INNER LOOP JOIN Sales.SalesOrderDetail AS sod
ON p.ProductID = sod.ProductID
```

However, as mentioned earlier, the join order is impacted as well; the Product table will always be the outer input and SalesOrderDetail the inner input. If we wanted to reverse the roles, we would need to explicitly rewrite the query as shown next, in which

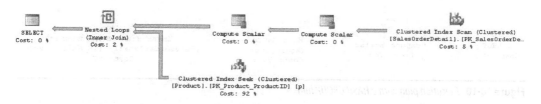

Figure 10-8 *Execution plan with ANSI-style join hints*

case SalesOrderDetail will be the outer input and Product the inner input, as shown in the plan in Figure 10-8.

```
SELECT *
FROM Sales.SalesOrderDetail AS sod
INNER LOOP JOIN Production.Product AS p
ON p.ProductID = sod.ProductID
```

In addition, the following warning is shown in the Messages tab when the code is executed using Management Studio, which indicates that not only was the join algorithm forced, but the join order was forced as well (that is, the tables were joined using exactly the order specified in the query text):

```
Warning: The join order has been enforced because a local join hint is used.
```

Aggregations

Just like join algorithms, aggregation algorithms can also be forced by using the GROUP hints. Specifically, the ORDER GROUP hint requests that the query optimizer use a Stream Aggregate algorithm, and the HASH GROUP hint requests a Hash Aggregate algorithm. These hints can be specified only at the query level, so they will impact all the aggregation operations in the query. To see the effects of this, take a look at the following unhinted query, which produces the plan in Figure 10-9 using a Stream Aggregate operator:

```
SELECT SalesOrderID, COUNT(*)
FROM Sales.SalesOrderDetail
GROUP BY SalesOrderID
```

Figure 10-9 *Query using a Stream Aggregate*

Figure 10-10 *Execution plan with a HASH GROUP hint*

Because the SalesOrderDetail table has a clustered index on the SalesOrderID column, and therefore the data is already sorted on the GROUP BY column, using a Stream Aggregate operator is the obvious choice. However, if we add a HASH GROUP hint to the previous query, as shown next, it will force a Hash Aggregate operator and will produce the plan shown in Figure 10-10, which, not surprisingly, makes the query more expensive than necessary:

```
SELECT SalesOrderID, COUNT(*)
FROM Sales.SalesOrderDetail
GROUP BY SalesOrderID
OPTION (HASH GROUP)
```

On the other hand, a scalar aggregation will always use a Stream Aggregate operator. A hint to force a Hash Aggregate on a scalar aggregation, as in the following query, will simply be ignored in SQL Server 2014 and SQL Server 2012. SQL Server 2008 R2 and earlier versions, however, will trigger the compilation error 8622, shown earlier, complaining about the hints defined in the query.

```
SELECT COUNT(*) FROM Sales.SalesOrderDetail
OPTION (HASH GROUP)
```

FORCE ORDER

The FORCE ORDER hint can give the user full control over the join and aggregation placement in an execution plan. Specifically, the FORCE ORDER hint asks the query optimizer to preserve the join order and aggregation placement as indicated by the query syntax. Notice, also, that the ANSI-style join hints explained before can give you control of the join order, in addition to control over the choice of the join algorithm. Both the FORCE ORDER and ANSI-style join hints are very powerful, and because of that they need to be used with extreme caution. As explained earlier in this chapter, finding an optimum join order is a critical and challenging part of the query optimization process because the sheer number of possible join orders can be huge, even with queries involving only a few tables. What this boils down to is that, by using the FORCE ORDER hint, you are attempting to optimize the join order yourself.

You can use the FORCE ORDER hint to obtain any form of query, such as left-deep tree, bushy tree, or right-deep tree, which were all explained earlier in this chapter.

The SQL Server query optimizer will usually produce a left-deep tree plan, but you can force bushy trees or right-deep trees by changing the location of the ON clause in the join predicate, using subqueries, using parentheses, and so on. Be aware that forcing join order does not affect the simplification phase of query optimization, and some joins may still be removed if needed, as explained in Chapter 3.

If you do need to change the join order of a query for some reason, you can try starting with the join order recommended by the query optimizer, and change only the part you think is suffering from a problem, such as cardinality estimation errors. You can also follow the practices that the query optimizer itself would follow, as explained in Chapter 4. For example, if you are forcing a Hash Join, select the smallest table as the build input; if you're forcing a Nested Loops Join, use small tables in the outer input and the tables with indexes as the inner input. You could also start by joining small tables first, or tables that can help to filter out the most possible number of rows.

Let me show you an example. The following query, without hints, will show you the plan in Figure 10-11:

```
SELECT LastName, FirstName, soh.SalesOrderID
FROM Person.Person p JOIN HumanResources.Employee e
    ON e.BusinessEntityID = p.BusinessEntityID
JOIN Sales.SalesOrderHeader soh
    ON p.BusinessEntityID = soh.SalesPersonID
WHERE ShipDate > '2008-01-01'
```

As you can see, the query optimizer does not exactly follow the join order specified in the query syntax (for example, the Person table is not accessed first). Instead, the query optimizer found a more efficient join order based on cost decisions. Now let's see

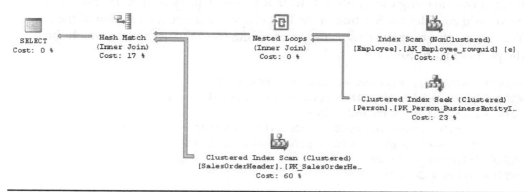

Figure 10-11 *Execution plan without hints*

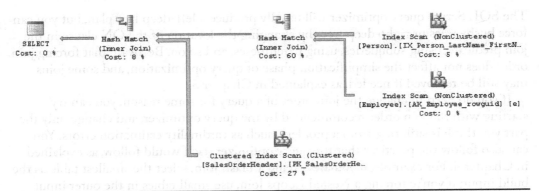

Figure 10-12 *Execution plan with FORCE ORDER hint*

what happens if we add a FORCE ORDER hint to the query. It will produce the plan in Figure 10-12.

```
SELECT LastName, FirstName, soh.SalesOrderID
FROM Person.Person p JOIN HumanResources.Employee e
      ON e.BusinessEntityID = p.BusinessEntityID
JOIN Sales.SalesOrderHeader soh
      ON p.BusinessEntityID = soh.SalesPersonID
WHERE ShipDate > '2008-01-01'
OPTION (FORCE ORDER)
```

In this query using the FORCE ORDER hint, the tables will be joined in the order specified in the query, and by default, a left-deep tree will be created. On the other hand, if you are using the FORCE ORDER hint in a query with ANSI joins, SQL Server will consider the location of the ON clauses to define the location of the joins. You can use this to create a right-deep tree, as shown in the next query, which shows the plan in Figure 10-13:

```
SELECT LastName, FirstName, soh.SalesOrderID
FROM Person.Person p JOIN HumanResources.Employee e
JOIN Sales.SalesOrderHeader soh
      ON e.BusinessEntityID = soh.SalesPersonID
      ON e.BusinessEntityID = p.BusinessEntityID
WHERE ShipDate > '2008-01-01'
OPTION (FORCE ORDER)
```

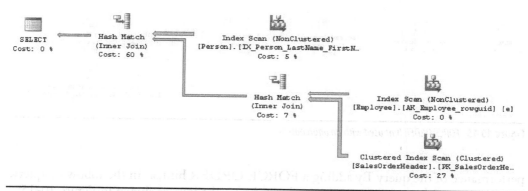

Figure 10-13 *Plan forcing a right-deep tree*

Although the order in which the tables are joined is specified as Person, Employee, and SalesOrderHeader, the placement of the ON clauses defines that Employee and SalesOrderHeader are to be joined first, thus creating a right-deep tree.

In addition to taking control of join orders, as mentioned in the introduction of this section, FORCE ORDER can be used to force the order of aggregations. Consider this unhinted example, which produces the plan shown in Figure 10-14:

```
SELECT c.CustomerID, COUNT(*)
FROM Sales.Customer c
JOIN Sales.SalesOrderHeader o
ON c.CustomerID = o.CustomerID
GROUP BY c.CustomerID
```

As you can see, in this case, the query optimizer decided to perform the aggregation before the join. Remember that, as mentioned in Chapters 3 and 4, the query optimizer may decide to perform aggregations before or after a join if this can improve the

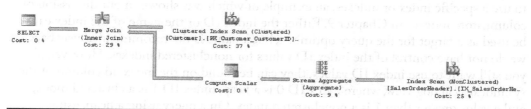

Figure 10-14 *Plan with aggregation before the join*

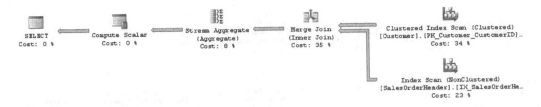

Figure 10-15 *FORCE ORDER hint used with an aggregation*

performance of the query. By adding a FORCE ORDER hint, as in the following query, you can cause the aggregation to be performed after the join, as shown in Figure 10-15:

```
SELECT c.CustomerID, COUNT(*)
FROM Sales.Customer c
JOIN Sales.SalesOrderHeader o
ON c.CustomerID = o.CustomerID
GROUP BY c.CustomerID
OPTION (FORCE ORDER)
```

Finally, a related statement, SET FORCEPLAN, can also be used to preserve the join order, as indicated in the FROM clause of a query. However, it will request only Nested Loops Joins, unless other types of joins are required to construct a plan for the query, or the query includes any query hint or join hint. A difference between this statement and the hints shown so far is that SET FORCEPLAN needs to be turned on, and will stay in effect until turned off. For more information regarding the SET FORCEPLAN statement, refer to Books Online.

INDEX, FORCESCAN, and FORCESEEK Hints

The INDEX, FORCESCAN, and FORCESEEK hints are table hints, and we'll consider each in turn. The INDEX hint can be used to request the query optimizer to use a specific index or indexes, an example of which was shown in our discussion of columnstore indexes in Chapter 9. Either the index ID or the name of the index can be used as a target for the query optimizer, but a name is the recommended way because we do not have control of the index ID values for nonclustered indexes. However, if you still want to use index ID values, they can be found on the index_id column of the sys.indexes catalog view, where index ID 0 is a heap, index ID 1 is a clustered index, and a value greater than 1 is a nonclustered index. On a query using a heap, using the INDEX(0) hint results in a Table Scan operator being used, whereas INDEX(1) returns an error message indicating that no such index exists. A query with a clustered index, however, can use both values: INDEX(0) will force a Clustered Index Scan, and INDEX(1) can use either a Clustered Index Scan or a Clustered Index Seek.

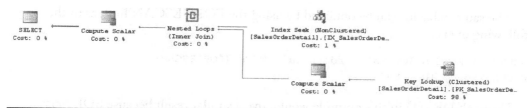

Figure 10-16 *Plan with a Nested Loops Join*

The FORCESCAN hint requests the query optimizer to use only an index scan operation as the access path to the referenced table or view and can be specified with or without an INDEX hint. On the other hand, the FORCESEEK hint can be used to force the query optimizer to use an Index Seek operation, and can work on both clustered and nonclustered indexes. It can also work in combination with the INDEX hint, as you'll see later.

In addition to helping to improve the performance of your queries, in some cases, you may want to consider using an index hint to minimize lock contention or deadlocks. Notice that when you use an INDEX hint, your query becomes dependent on the existence of the specified index and will stop working if that index is removed. Using FORCESEEK without an available index will also result in an error, as shown later in this section.

You can also use the INDEX hint to avoid a bookmark lookup operation, as in the example shown next. Because the query optimizer estimates that only a few records will be returned by the next query, it decides to use an Index Seek and Key Lookup combination, as shown in Figure 10-16.

```
SELECT * FROM Sales.SalesOrderDetail
WHERE ProductID = 897
```

However, suppose that you want to avoid a bookmark lookup operation; you can use the INDEX table hint to force a table scan instead, which could be the scan of either a heap or a clustered index. The following query will force the use of a Clustered Index Scan operator, as shown in the plan in Figure 10-17:

```
SELECT * FROM Sales.SalesOrderDetail WITH (INDEX(0))
WHERE ProductID = 897
```

Figure 10-17 *Plan with an INDEX hint*

The same behavior can be obtained by using the FORCESCAN hint, as in the following query:

```
SELECT * FROM Sales.SalesOrderDetail WITH (FORCESCAN)
WHERE ProductID = 897
```

Using INDEX(1) in this example would give a similar result because SQL Server cannot use the clustered index to perform an Index Seek operation; the clustered key is on SalesOrderID and SalesOrderDetailID, so the only viable choice is to scan the clustered index. Of course, you can also force the opposite operation. In the following example, the query optimizer estimates that a high number of records will be returned, so it decides to use a plan with a Clustered Index Scan:

```
SELECT * FROM Sales.SalesOrderDetail
WHERE ProductID = 870
```

Because we have an index on ProductID (IX_SalesOrderDetail_ProductID), we can force the plan to use such an index, as shown in the following query. The produced plan will in fact use an Index Seek on the IX_SalesOrderDetail_ProductID index and a Key Lookup operation on the base table, which in this case is the clustered index.

```
SELECT * FROM Sales.SalesOrderDetail WITH (INDEX(IX_SalesOrderDetail_ProductID))
WHERE ProductID = 870
```

You can also achieve a similar result by forcing a seek using the FORCESEEK table hint, which was introduced in SQL Server 2008. The following query will create the same plan, similar to the previous query:

```
SELECT * FROM Sales.SalesOrderDetail WITH (FORCESEEK)
WHERE ProductID = 870
```

You can even combine both hints to obtain the same plan, as in the following query. Keep in mind that using the INDEX hint does not necessarily mean that an Index Seek operation will be performed, so the FORCESEEK hint could help to achieve that.

```
SELECT * FROM Sales.SalesOrderDetail
WITH (INDEX(IX_SalesOrderDetail_ProductID), FORCESEEK)
WHERE ProductID = 870
```

Using FORCESEEK when SQL Server cannot perform an Index Seek operation will cause the query to not compile, as shown next, and will instead return the error message 8622, shown earlier, complaining about the hints defined in the query:

```
SELECT * FROM Sales.SalesOrderDetail WITH (FORCESEEK)
WHERE OrderQty = 1
```

FAST N

FAST N is one of the so-called "goal-oriented hints." It does not indicate what physical operators to use, but instead just specifies what goal the plan is trying to achieve. This hint is used to optimize a query to retrieve the first *n* rows of results as quickly as possible. It can help in situations where only the first few rows returned by a query are relevant, and perhaps you won't be using the remaining records of the query at all. The price to pay for achieving this speed is that retrieving those remaining records may take longer than if you had used a plan without this hint. In other words, because the query is optimized to retrieve the first *n* records as soon as possible, retrieving all the records returned by the query may be very expensive.

The query optimizer usually accomplishes this FAST N goal by avoiding any blocking operators, such as Sort, Hash Join, and Hash Aggregation, so the client submitting the query does not have to wait before the first records are produced. Let's look at an example. Run the following query, which returns the plan shown in Figure 10-18:

```
SELECT * FROM Sales.SalesOrderDetail
ORDER BY ProductID
```

In this case, the Sort operator is the most effective way to get the records sorted by ProductID if you want to see the entire query output. However, because Sort is a blocking operator, SQL Server will not be able to produce any row until the entire sort operation has completed. Now, supposing that your application wants to see a page with 20 records at a time, you can use the FAST hint to get these 20 records as quickly as possible, as seen in the next query:

```
SELECT * FROM Sales.SalesOrderDetail
ORDER BY ProductID
OPTION (FAST 20)
```

This time, the new plan, shown in Figure 10-19, scans an available nonclustered index while performing Key Lookups on the clustered table. Because this plan uses random I/O, it would be very expensive for the entire query, but it will achieve the goal of returning the first 20 records very quickly.

Figure 10-18 *Plan using a Sort operation*

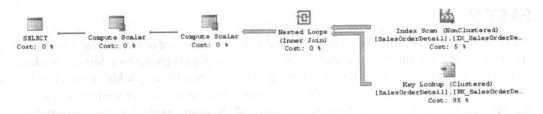

Figure 10-19 *Plan using a FAST N hint*

There is also a FASTFIRSTROW hint, but it is not as flexible as FAST N because you can specify any number for N. Essentially, FASTFIRSTROW would be the same as specifying the FAST 1 hint.

NOEXPAND and EXPAND VIEWS Hints

Before talking about the NOEXPAND and EXPAND VIEWS hints, let's discuss the default behavior of queries when using indexed views so that you can see how these hints can change this behavior. As explained in Chapter 3, SQL Server expands views in the early steps of query optimization during binding, when a view reference is expanded to include the view definition (for example, to directly include the tables used in the view). This behavior is the same for every edition of SQL Server. Later on in the optimization process, but only in the Enterprise edition, SQL Server may match the query to an existing indexed view. So, basically, the view was expanded at the beginning but was later matched to an existing indexed view. The EXPAND VIEWS hint removes the matching step, thus making sure the views are expanded but not matched at the end of the optimization process. Therefore, this hint only has an effect in SQL Server Enterprise edition.

On the other hand, the NOEXPAND hint asks SQL Server not to expand any views at all and to use the specified indexed view instead. This hint works in every SQL Server edition, and it is the only way (when using a SQL Server edition other than Enterprise) to ask SQL Server to match an existing indexed view. Here's an example. Create an indexed view on AdventureWorks2012 by running the following code:

```
CREATE VIEW v_test
WITH SCHEMABINDING AS
SELECT SalesOrderID, COUNT_BIG(*) as cnt
FROM Sales.SalesOrderDetail
GROUP BY SalesOrderID
GO
CREATE UNIQUE CLUSTERED INDEX ix_test ON v_test(SalesOrderID)
```

Figure 10-20 *Plan using an existing indexed view*

Next, run the following query:

```
SELECT SalesOrderID, COUNT(*)
FROM Sales.SalesOrderDetail
GROUP BY SalesOrderID
```

If you are using SQL Server Enterprise edition (or the Enterprise Evaluation or Developer edition, which share the same database engine edition), you will get the plan in Figure 10-20, which actually matches the existing indexed view.

Alternatively, you can use the EXPAND VIEWS hint, as in the following query, to avoid matching the index view. You will get the plan shown in Figure 10-21.

```
SELECT SalesOrderID, COUNT(*)
FROM Sales.SalesOrderDetail
GROUP BY SalesOrderID
OPTION (EXPAND VIEWS)
```

Different from EXPAND VIEWS, which is a query hint, NOEXPAND is a table hint, and the following query shows how to use it to get the same results as our previous query. Note that the name of the indexed view is directly mentioned.

```
SELECT * FROM v_test WITH (NOEXPAND)
```

Not surprisingly, the plan selected will scan the v_test indexed view in a similar way to the plan in Figure 10-20.

Finally, drop the indexed view you just created:

```
DROP VIEW v_test
```

Figure 10-21 *Plan using the EXPAND VIEWS hint*

Plan Guides

There might be situations when you need to apply a hint to a query but you are unable or unwilling to change your query code or your application. A common case where this occurs is if you are working with third-party code or applications that you cannot change.

Plan guides, a feature introduced with SQL Server 2005, can help you in these cases. Plan guides essentially work by keeping a list of queries on the server, along with the hints you want to apply to them, basically separating the hint specification from the query itself. To use a plan guide, you need to provide SQL Server with the query you want to optimize and either a query hint using the OPTION clause or an XML plan using the USE PLAN hint, which will be explained in the next section. When the query is optimized, SQL Server will apply the hint requested in the plan guide definition. You can also specify NULL as a hint in your plan guide to remove an existing hint in your application. Plan guides can also match queries in different contexts—for example, a stored procedure, a user-defined scalar function, or a standalone statement that is not part of any database object.

You can use the sp_create_plan_guide stored procedure to create a plan guide, and the sp_control_plan_guide to drop, enable, or disable plan guides. You can also see which plan guides are defined in your database by looking at the sys.plan_guides catalog view.

To make sure the query in the plan guide definition matches the query being executed, especially for stand-alone statements, you can use the Profiler's Plan Guide Successful event class, which will show whether an execution plan was successfully created using a plan guide. On the other hand, the Plan Guide Unsuccessful event will show if SQL Server was unable to create an execution plan using a plan guide, meaning that the query was instead optimized without it. You could see the Plan Guide Unsuccessful event, for example, if you try to use a plan guide to force a Merge or Hash Join with a nonequality operator in the join condition, as shown earlier in this chapter.

Let's look at an example of these events. Suppose we want to use plan guides to avoid a Merge or Hash Join in our previous query in order to avoid high memory usage. Before running this code, open a SQL Server Profiler session, connect it to your instance of SQL Server, select the blank template to start a new trace definition, select both Plan Guide Successful and Plan Guide Unsuccessful on the Performance section of the Events tab, and then start the trace.

Next, create the following stored procedure:

```
CREATE PROCEDURE test
AS
SELECT *
FROM Production.Product AS p
JOIN Sales.SalesOrderDetail AS sod
ON p.ProductID = sod.ProductID
```

Before creating a plan guide, execute the stored procedure and display its execution plan to verify that it is using a Hash Join operator. Next, create a plan guide to force the query to use a Nested Loops Join.

```
EXEC sp_create_plan_guide
@name = N'plan_guide_test',
@stmt = N'SELECT *
FROM Production.Product AS p
JOIN Sales.SalesOrderDetail AS sod
ON p.ProductID = sod.ProductID',
@type = N'OBJECT',
@module_or_batch = N'test',
@params = NULL,
@hints = N'OPTION (LOOP JOIN)'
```

Now, if you execute the stored procedure again, you can verify that it is indeed using a Nested Loops Join operator, as shown in the plan in Figure 10-22. However, notice that this is a more expensive plan because the query optimizer was originally choosing the right join type before using a hint.

In addition, during this execution, SQL Server Profiler should capture a Plan Guide Successful event, showing that SQL Server was able to use the defined plan guide. The TextData column in Profiler will show the name of the plan guide, which in this case is plan_guide_test. You could also see if an execution plan is using a plan guide by looking at the PlanGuideName property, which in this case will also show plan_guide_test.

When you create a plan guide, it is automatically enabled, but you can disable it or enable it back at any time. For example, the following statement will disable the previous plan guide, and the stored procedure will again use a Hash Join when executed:

```
EXEC sp_control_plan_guide N'DISABLE', N'plan_guide_test'
```

To enable the plan guide again, use this:

```
EXEC sp_control_plan_guide N'ENABLE', N'plan_guide_test'
```

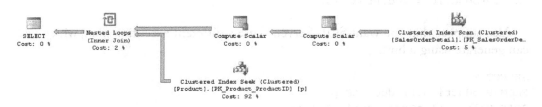

Figure 10-22 *Query using a plan guide*

Finally, to clean up, drop both the plan guide and the stored procedure. Note that you need to drop the plan guide first because you cannot drop a stored procedure that is currently referenced by a plan guide.

```
EXEC sp_control_plan_guide N'DROP', N'plan_guide_test'
DROP PROCEDURE test
```

USE PLAN

Finally, let's take a look at the USE PLAN query hint, which also was introduced with SQL Server 2005. The USE PLAN hint takes the use of hints to the extreme by allowing the user to specify an entire execution plan as a target to be used to optimize a query. This hint is useful when you know that a better plan than the query optimizer's suggestion exists. This can be the case, for example, when a better-performing plan was produced in the past, or in a different system, or even in a previous version of SQL Server. The plan should be specified in XML format, and you will generally use SQL Server itself to generate the XML text for the desired plan because it can be extremely difficult to write an XML plan manually.

The USE PLAN hint can force most of the specified plan properties—including the tree structure, join order, join algorithms, aggregations, sorting and unions, and index operations such as scans, seeks, and intersections—so that only the transformation rules that can be useful in finding the desired plan are executed. In addition, starting with SQL Server 2008, USE PLAN supports UPDATE statements (INSERT, UPDATE, DELETE, and MERGE), which was not the case when the hint was first introduced in SQL Server 2005. Some statements still not supported include full-text and distributed queries as well as queries with dynamic, keyset-driven, and forward-only cursors.

Suppose we have the same query we saw in the "Plan Guides" section, which produces a Hash Join:

```
SELECT *
FROM Production.Product AS p
JOIN Sales.SalesOrderDetail AS sod
ON p.ProductID = sod.ProductID
```

Also suppose that you want SQL Server to use a different execution plan, which we can generate using a hint:

```
SELECT *
FROM Production.Product AS p
JOIN Sales.SalesOrderDetail AS sod
ON p.ProductID = sod.ProductID
OPTION (LOOP JOIN)
```

You can force this new plan to use a Nested Loops Join instead of a Hash Join. In order to accomplish that, display the new XML plan (by right-clicking the graphical plan and selecting Show Execution Plan XML…), copy it to an editor, replace any existing single quotes with double quotes, and then copy the plan to the query as shown:

```
SELECT *
FROM Production.Product AS p
JOIN Sales.SalesOrderDetail AS sod
ON p.ProductID = sod.ProductID
OPTION (USE PLAN N'<?xml version="1.0" encoding="utf-16"?>
...
</ShowPlanXML>')
```

Of course, the XML plan is too long to display here, so I've just displayed the start and end. Make sure the query ends with `')` after the XML plan. Running this SELECT statement will request SQL Server to try to use the indicated plan, and the query will be executed with a Nested Loops Join, as requested in the provided XML execution plan.

You can combine both plan guides and the USE PLAN query hint to force a specific execution plan in a situation where you don't want to change the text of the original query. The following (and final) query will use the same test procedure included in the "Plan Guides" section, together with the XML plan generated (you may need to re-create the stored procedure if it was previously dropped). Note the use of two single quotes before the XML plan specification, meaning that, this time, the query text needs to end with `'')'`.

```
EXEC sp_create_plan_guide
@name = N'plan_guide_test',
@stmt = N'SELECT *
FROM Production.Product AS p
JOIN Sales.SalesOrderDetail AS sod
ON p.ProductID = sod.ProductID',
@type = N'OBJECT',
@module_or_batch = N'test',
@params = NULL,
@hints = N'OPTION (USE PLAN N''<?xml version="1.0" encoding="utf-16"?>
...
</ShowPlanXML>'')'
```

Finally, bear in mind that when the USE PLAN hint is used directly in a query, an invalid plan will make the query fail. However, when the USE PLAN hint is used in a plan guide, an invalid plan will simply compile the query without the requested hint, as mentioned in the previous section.

Summary

The SQL Server query processor typically selects a good execution plan for your queries, but there may still be cases when, even after extensive troubleshooting, you do not get good performance from a selected plan. Query optimization is an inherently complex problem, and despite several decades of query optimization research, challenges in some fundamental areas are still being addressed today.

This chapter provided recommendations on what to do when SQL Server is not giving you a good execution plan. One such methodology, which you can use in the cases when the SQL Server query optimizer is not able to produce a good plan for complex queries, is to break these queries down into two or more simpler queries while storing the intermediate results in temporary tables.

Although hints can be used to improve the performance of a query in these cases by directly taking control of the execution plan selection, they should always be used with caution, and only as a last resort. You should also be aware that code using hints will require additional maintenance, and is significantly less flexible to changes in your database or application or to changes due to software upgrades.

Finally, my hope is that this book has provided you with the knowledge needed to write better queries and to give the query processor the information it needs to produce efficient execution plans. At the same time, I hope you've learned more about how to get the information you need to diagnose and troubleshoot the cases when, despite your best efforts, you are not getting a good plan. In addition, having seen how the query processor works and some of the limitations this complex piece of software still faces today, you can be better prepared to decide when and how hints can be used to improve the performance of your queries.

Appendix

References

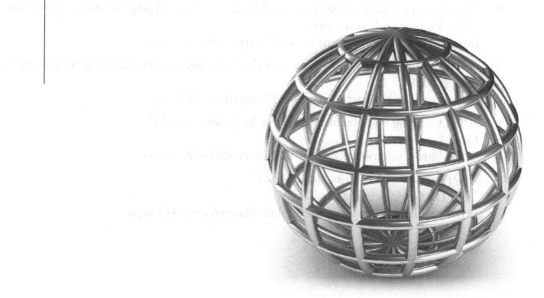

This appendix provides you with a list of white papers, articles, research papers, and books that you can use to learn more about query tuning and optimization in SQL Server or to explore some specific topics at a deeper level. Although most of us are very familiar with the content provided by SQL Server white papers, articles, and books, research papers may be new to some. Reading research and academic papers generally requires a stronger computer science background compared to the SQL Server documentation, books, and blogs we read every day. They usually focus on a specific area or research problem and always reference other papers, which you can find at the end of each article. By following these references, which will also have their own references, you can find an almost unlimited source of information.

Most of the documents listed here are freely available, and current links are provided where you can download them.

White Papers

- ▶ "Clustered Indexes and Heaps"
  Burzin Patel and Sanjay Mishra
  http://technet.microsoft.com/en-us/library/cc917672.aspx

- ▶ "Columnstore Indexes for Fast Data Warehouse Query Processing in
  SQL Server 11.0"
  Eric N. Hanson
  http://download.microsoft.com/download/8/C/1/8C1CE06B-DE2F-40D1-
  9C5C-3EE521C25CE9/Columnstore%20Indexes%20for%20Fast%20DW%20
  QP%20SQL%20Server%2011.pdf

- ▶ "In-Memory OLTP–Common Workload Patterns and Migration Considerations"
  Mike Weiner and Ami Levin
  http://msdn.microsoft.com/en-us/library/dn673538.aspx

- ▶ "Optimizing Your Query Plans with the SQL Server 2014 Cardinality Estimator"
  Joseph Sack
  http://msdn.microsoft.com/en-us/library/dn673537.aspx

- ▶ "Plan Caching and Recompilation in SQL Server 2012"
  Greg Low
  http://msdn.microsoft.com/en-us/library/dn148262.aspx

- ▶ "SQL Server 2005 Waits and Queues"
  Tom Davidson and Danny Tambs
  http://technet.microsoft.com/en-US/library/cc966413.aspx

▶ "SQL Server In-Memory OLTP Internals Overview"
Kalen Delaney
http://msdn.microsoft.com/en-us/library/dn720242.aspx

▶ "Statistics Used by the Query Optimizer in Microsoft SQL Server 2008"
Eric N. Hanson and Yavor Angelov
http://msdn.microsoft.com/en-us/library/dd535534(v=sql.100).aspx

▶ "Troubleshooting Performance Problems in SQL Server 2008"
Sunil Agarwal, Boris Baryshnikov, Keith Elmore, Juergen Thomas, Kun Cheng, and Burzin Patel
http://technet.microsoft.com/en-us/library/dd672789(v=sql.100).aspx

▶ "Using Star Join and Few-Outer-Row Optimizations to Improve Data Warehousing Queries"
Dayong Gu, Ashit Gosalia, Wei Liu, and Vinay Kulkarni
http://technet.microsoft.com/en-us/library/gg567299.aspx

Articles

▶ "Ascending Keys and Auto Quick Corrected Statistics"
Ian Jose
http://blogs.msdn.com/b/ianjo/archive/2006/04/24/582227.aspx

▶ "Changes to automatic update statistics in SQL Server – traceflag 2371"
Juergen Thomas
http://blogs.msdn.com/b/saponsqlserver/archive/2011/09/07/changes-to-automatic-update-statistics-in-sql-server-traceflag-2371.aspx

▶ "Controlling Autostat (AUTO_UPDATE_STATISTICS) behavior in SQL Server"
http://support.microsoft.com/kb/2754171

▶ "Enable plan-affecting SQL Server query optimizer behavior that can be controlled by different trace flags on a specific-query level"
http://support.microsoft.com/kb/2801413/en-us

▶ "FIX: Poor performance when you run a query that contains correlated AND predicates in SQL Server 2008 or in SQL Server 2008 R2 or in SQL Server 2012"
http://support.microsoft.com/kb/2658214

▶ "FIX: Poor performance when you use table variables in SQL Server 2012"
http://support.microsoft.com/kb/2952444

▶ "Intro to Query Execution Bitmap Filters"
http://blogs.msdn.com/b/sqlqueryprocessing/archive/2006/10/27/query-execution-bitmaps.aspx

▶ "Query Fingerprints and Plan Fingerprints (The Best SQL 2008 Feature That You've Never Heard Of)"
Bart Duncan
http://blogs.msdn.com/b/bartd/archive/2008/09/03/query-fingerprints-and-plan-fingerprints_3a00_-the-best-new-sql-2008-feature-you_2700_ve-never-heard-of.aspx

▶ "Query Processor Modelling Extensions in SQL Server 2005 SP1"
Ian Jose
http://blogs.msdn.com/b/ianjo/archive/2006/04/24/582219.aspx

▶ "Sql_Handle and Plan_Handle Explained"
http://blogs.msdn.com/b/sqlprogrammability/archive/2007/01/09/2-0-sql-handle-and-plan-handle-explained.aspx

▶ "Statistical maintenance functionality (autostats) in SQL Server"
http://support.microsoft.com/kb/195565

▶ "The coming in-memory database tipping point"
Dave Campbell
http://blogs.technet.com/b/dataplatforminsider/archive/2012/04/09/the-coming-in-memory-database-tipping-point.aspx

▶ "When to Break Down Complex Queries"
Steve Howard
http://blogs.msdn.com/b/sqlcat/archive/2013/09/09/when-to-break-down-complex-queries.aspx

Research Papers

▶ "Access Path Selection in a Relational Database Management System"
P. Griffiths Selinger, M. M. Astrahan, D. D. Chamberlin, R.A. Lorie, and T. G. Price
http://citeseerx.ist.psu.edu/viewdoc/summary?doi=10.1.1.129.5879

▶ "An Efficient, Cost-Driven Index Selection Tool for Microsoft SQL Server"
Surajit Chaudhuri and Vivek Narasayya
http://citeseerx.ist.psu.edu/viewdoc/summary?doi=10.1.1.114.771

▶ "An Overview of Cost-based Optimization of Queries with Aggregates"
Surajit Chaudhuri
http://citeseerx.ist.psu.edu/viewdoc/summary?doi=10.1.1.137.3356

▶ "An Overview of Data Warehousing and OLAP Technology"
Surajit Chaudhuri and Umeshwar Dayal
http://citeseerx.ist.psu.edu/viewdoc/summary?doi=10.1.1.133.6667

▶ "An Overview of Query Optimization in Relational Systems"
Surajit Chaudhuri
http://citeseerx.ist.psu.edu/viewdoc/summary?doi=10.1.1.137.3356

▶ "C-Store: A Column-oriented DBMS"
Mike Stonebraker, Daniel J. Abadi, Adam Batkin, Xuedong Chen, Mitch
Cherniack, Miguel Ferreira, Edmond Lau, Amerson Lin, Sam Madden, Elizabeth
O'Neil, Pat O'Neil, Alex Rasin, Nga Tran, and Stan Zdonik
http://citeseerx.ist.psu.edu/viewdoc/summary?doi=10.1.1.60.4717

▶ "Counting, Enumerating, and Sampling of Execution Plans in a Cost-Based
Query Optimizer"
Florian Waas and Cesar Galindo-Legaria
http://citeseerx.ist.psu.edu/viewdoc/summary?doi=10.1.1.28.2115

▶ "Do Query Optimizers Need to be SSD-aware?"
Steven Pelley, Thomas F. Wenisch, and Kristen Lefevre
http://citeseerx.ist.psu.edu/viewdoc/summary?doi=10.1.1.363.7595

▶ "Optimizing Join Orders"
Michael Steinbrunn, Guido Moerkotte, and Alfons Kemper
http://citeseerx.ist.psu.edu/viewdoc/summary?doi=10.1.1.17.8155

▶ "Optimizing Star Join Queries for Data Warehousing in Microsoft SQL Server"
Cesar A. Galindo-Legaria, Torsten Grabs, Sreenivas Gukal, Steve Herbert,
Aleksandras Surna, Shirley Wang, Wei Yu, Peter Zabback, and Shin Zhang
http://dl.acm.org/citation.cfm?id=1546682.1547293

▶ "Query Evaluation Techniques for Large Databases"
Goetz Graefe
http://citeseerx.ist.psu.edu/viewdoc/summary?doi=10.1.1.108.3178

▶ "Query Optimization"
Yannis E. Ioannidis
http://citeseerx.ist.psu.edu/viewdoc/summary?doi=10.1.1.24.4154

▶ "Query Optimization in Microsoft SQL Server PDW"
Srinath Shankar, Rimma Nehme, Josep Aguilar-Saborit, Andrew Chung, Mostafa
Elhemali, Alan Halverson, Eric Robinson, Mahadevan Sankara Subramanian,
David DeWitt, and Cesar Galindo-Legaria
http://dl.acm.org/citation.cfm?id=2213953

▶ "Query Processing Techniques for Solid State Drives"
Dimitris Tsirogiannis, Janet L. Wiener, Stavros Harizopoulos, Goetz Graefe, and
Mehul A. Shah
http://citeseerx.ist.psu.edu/viewdoc/summary?doi=10.1.1.187.7568

▶ "Self-Tuning Database Systems: A Decade of Progress"
Surajit Chaudhuri and Vivek Narasayya
http://citeseerx.ist.psu.edu/viewdoc/summary?doi=10.1.1.107.8842

▶ "Testing Cardinality Estimation Models in SQL Server"
Campbell Fraser, Leo Giakoumakis, Vikas Hamine, and Katherine F. Moore-Smith
http://dl.acm.org/citation.cfm?id=2304526

▶ "Testing SQL Server's Query Optimizer: Challenges, Techniques and Experiences"
Leo Giakoumakis and Cesar Galindo-Legaria
http://citeseerx.ist.psu.edu/viewdoc/summary?doi=10.1.1.143.3767

▶ "The Cascades Framework for Query Optimization"
Goetz Graefe
http://citeseerx.ist.psu.edu/viewdoc/summary?doi=10.1.1.98.9460

▶ "The History of Histograms"
Yannis Ioannidis
http://citeseerx.ist.psu.edu/viewdoc/summary?doi=10.1.1.10.4839

Books

▶ *Database System Concepts*
Abraham Silberschatz, Henry F. Korth, and S. Sudarshan
McGraw-Hill, 2010

▶ *Inside the SQL Server Query Optimizer*
Benjamin Nevarez
Red Gate Books, 2011

▶ *Microsoft SQL Server 2012 Internals*
Kalen Delaney, Bob Beauchemin, Conor Cunningham, Jonathan Kehayias,
Benjamin Nevarez, and Paul S. Randal
Microsoft Press, 2013

► *SQL Server 2005 Practical Troubleshooting: The Database Engine*
Ken Henderson
Addison-Wesley Professional, 2006

► *Star Schema: The Complete Reference*
Christopher Adamson
McGraw-Hill Professional, 2010

► *The Data Warehouse Toolkit: The Complete Guide to Dimensional Modeling*
Ralph Kimball and Margy Ross
Wiley, 2002

Index